STUDIES IN
IMPERIALISM

general editor John M. MacKenzie

Established in the belief that imperialism as a cultural
phenomenon had as significant an effect on the dominant
as on the subordinate societies, Studies in Imperialism
seeks to develop the new socio-cultural approach which
has emerged through cross-disciplinary work on popular
culture, media studies, art history, the study of education
and religion, sports history and children's literature.
The cultural emphasis embraces studies of migration and
race, while the older political and constitutional,
economic and military concerns will never be far away.
It incorporates comparative work on European and
American empire-building, with the chronological focus
primarily, though not exclusively, on the nineteenth and
twentieth centuries, when these cultural exchanges were
most powerfully at work.

Emigrant homecomings

MANCHESTER

ress

AVAILABLE IN THE SERIES

Emigrant homecomings

THE RETURN MOVEMENT OF EMIGRANTS, 1600–2000

edited by
Marjory Harper

MANCHESTER
UNIVERSITY PRESS
Manchester and New York

distributed exclusively in the USA by
PALGRAVE

Published by Manchester University Press
Oxford Road, Manchester M13 9NR, UK
and Room 400, 175 Fifth Avenue, New York, NY 10010, USA
www.manchesteruniversitypress.co.uk

Distributed exclusively in the USA by
Palgrave, 175 Fifth Avenue, New York NY 10010, USA

Distributed exclusively in Canada by
UBC Press, University of British Columbia, 2029 West Mall,
Vancouver, BC, Canada V6T 1Z2

British Library Cataloguing-in-Publication Data
A catalogue record for this book is available from the British Library

Library of Congress Cataloging-in-Publication Data
A catalog record for this book is available from the Library of Congress

ISBN 13: 978 0 7190 7071 6

First published by Manchester University Press 2005

First digital paperback edition published 2011

Printed by Lightning Source

CONTENTS

CONTENTS

ILLUSTRATIONS

TABLES

CONTRIBUTORS

Marilyn J. Barber is Professor of History, Carleton University, Ottawa.

Paul Basu is Lecturer in Anthropology, University of Sussex.

Kathleen Burke is Professor of History, University of New Brunswick.

Bruce S. Elliott is Professor of History and Director of the Carleton Centre for the History of Migration, Carleton University, Ottawa.

Patrick Fitzgerald is Lecturer and Development Officer at the Centre for Migration Studies, Ulster-American Folk Park, Omagh, Northern Ireland.

Alexia Grosjean is Research Fellow, Scottish Parliament Project, St Andrews University.

Marjory Harper is Reader in History, University of Aberdeen.

Andrew Mackillop is Lecturer in History, University of Aberdeen.

Steve Murdoch is Lecturer in Scottish History, St Andrews University.

Eric Richards is Professor of History, Flinders University, South Australia.

Alistair Thomson is Director of the Centre for Continuing Education, University of Sussex.

Mark Wyman is Distinguished Professor of History, Illinois State University, Normal.

GENERAL EDITOR'S INTRODUCTION

In a BBC television programme on *Scotland's Empire* in January 2004, it was suggested that three million Australians claim Scottish ancestry. Many meet at Caledonian Society events, since, as one interviewee with an Australian accent put it, 'Scottish culture and the Gaelic language are very important in Australia because we are so far from home.' Another remarked, 'We went to Scotland and it was like coming home.' This repeated use of the word 'home', in some cases by residents of Australia – or wherever it might be – of several generations standing, constitutes a remarkable testimony to the power of ethnic identity and cultural forms to offer a sense of multiple domicile. This kind of modern sentimental attraction is, perhaps, only tangential to the principal theme of this book, but migration tourism is one form of 'emigrant homecoming'. As Paul Basu in this volume demonstrates, it can be bound up with slanted visions of the past, with a sense of victimhood, for example, emerging from the Highland Clearances, even among those whose pasts were in no way connected with any form of clearance. Among those of Irish descent, the great famine would have a similar resonance.

Emigration studies have been a major historiographical concern for many years. We can add to that a considerable interest in the manner in which multiple identities from different parts of the British Isles, or indeed from elsewhere in Europe, have been dissected in an effort to constitute the complex make-up of being a Canadian, an Australian, a New Zealander or even a white South African, an Argentinian or whatever. Yet there have been scarcely any studies of return migrants. This chapters in this book offer some of the first studies of the phenomenon of returns. They deal with the former British 'dominions', with Europe, India and the United States.

Return migration took many different forms. Some homecoming emigrants consciously came back as failures to try to restore their fortunes with the support of kinsfolk, amid familiar surroundings. Many were simply homesick, had failed to 'settle' adequately, having decided that the 'promised' land held less promise than the prospects of return. They sought consolation from disillusionment with what they found in the colonies or elsewhere. Many returned to study, to pursue scholarly or artistic careers at what they judged to be the centre of their chosen interests. Others again returned as major successes, anxious to recover the status and fortunes of families which had gone down in the world, or perhaps eager to rise up the social scale. A few, like Andrew Carnegie at Skibo Castle in Sutherland, wanted to parade their wealth and success in a baronial setting symbolizing the transformation wrought in their social standing. Many of these were born in Scotland, Ireland, England or Wales and took satisfaction from a sort of circular odyssey. Others again were born overseas of families settled in 'foreign parts' for some time. Those in Europe had either not fully integrated or had discovered that the skills they had customarily offered were no longer required. This is by no means an exhaustive list.

At any event, all such practitioners of 'remigration' inevitably had an effect upon the home communities to which they returned. Some brought back plenty of money, reinvested or indulged in conspicuous consumption. Others were moderately successful and were proud to demonstrate how well they had done. (In my Perthshire village there is a house called 'Natal', built by a return migrant in the early twentieth century who had done well in that province of South Africa.) Others came back in poverty, looking to community for support, or alternatively trying to obscure their apparent failure in a new location. They may well have had a negative influence upon some who contemplated emigration. My Perthshire example reveals the manner in which these effects can be studied on a local basis (there is just such a study of Aberdeenshire in this volume). As we move from the local to the regional to the national, these studies become, perhaps, more complex. As with all migration, the statistics are highly problematic. Nevertheless, there are some attempts to quantify the phenomenon of return migration in this book.

One reason for the problems in identifying so much of the character of emigrant homecomings is that here was a migration which was very little noticed. There are any number of press and literary references, paintings and later photographs, as well as documentary sources, relating to conventional outward migration. But returning migrants seldom received such publicity. There are, apparently, no illustrations of an eager, or apprehensive, family looking out at 'home' from an arriving ship, preparing for a new phase in life.

Nevertheless, the chapters here cover an extraordinary range of aspects of return migration. They reveal the sophistication that can be brought to the statistical, economic, cultural and social consequences of movements that have so far received almost no attention from historians. All those interested in migration, in ethnic identity, in the interaction of migratory destination and visions of home, in the significance of inward investment and of migration tourism should find much to enlighten them here.

John M. MacKenzie

CHAPTER ONE

Introduction

Marjory Harper

Recent years have seen an upsurge of interest in the study of migration, emigration and immigration, at both scholarly and popular levels. Throughout Europe, North America and the Antipodes, the enduring popularity of diaspora studies is reflected in numerous research projects and publications, as well as teaching, media and museum coverage, cultural tourism and the promotional and co-ordinating work of bodies such as the Association of European Migration Institutions.[1] But despite all this activity one crucial theme has been largely neglected in terms of serious attention, that of return movement. Emigrants returned home for a variety of reasons. Although some came back with their pockets empty, their health ruined or their illusions shattered, by no means all were bankrupt, ailing or disaffected. Some who had left home with no thought of returning revised their initial decision. A significant number, however, went overseas with no intention of settling permanently in the new land, but with the goal of repatriating the profits they hoped to make in a range of enterprises, from fur trading in the Arctic to coffee planting in Ceylon or sheep farming in Patagonia. Others sojourned abroad out of curiosity, duty, pleasure or religious zeal. Successful sojourners were also potent recruitment agents, spreading a knowledge of overseas conditions and incentives in the local communities to which they returned. They are worthy of serious investigation as an integral part of the global diaspora.

There is a solid but narrow foundation of scholarly research on which to build, not least in a continental European context, where the phenomenon has attracted some attention.[2] Return migration has been incorporated into quantitative investigations, which chart the ebb and flow of movement on an intercontinental scale, and sometimes into studies whose main focus has been on the outward movement from specific countries. Dudley Baines in particular has demonstrated the statistical impact of returners in the nineteenth century, when between a quarter and a third of all emigrants from Europe returned to their countries of origin.[3] England and Wales probably experienced a return movement of approximately 40 per cent between 1870 and 1914, while Scotland, the country which, along with Ireland and Norway, sustained the highest European emigration rates in the nineteenth century, saw more than a third of its emigrants returning.[4] The American perspective has also been addressed, sometimes by those who have considered return movement anecdotally or tangentially, through the study of individual or group case histories, or the discussion of emigrant employment that involved temporary or seasonal movement.[5] Highlighting the negative reasons for the backward flow, W.S. Shepperson, in *Six who Returned*, drew attention to the long-standing tradition of transatlantic return, before focusing on the experiences of six returners to Britain who found the United States in the nineteenth century to be 'politically confused, economically unrewarding, or culturally immature'.[6] In the last decade the subject has been opened up fruitfully, from an American and antipodean perspective respectively, by Mark Wyman's wide-ranging study of approximately 4 million American immigrants who returned to Europe between 1880 and 1930 and Eric Richards' explorations of similar trends among those who went to colonial Australia.[7]

While such studies have demonstrated the contribution of returners to the fabric of emigration history, they have also illuminated the need for further investigation of a complex and multifaceted subject which was – and is – of global relevance. Little attempt has yet been made to consider the movement thematically or comparatively, in terms of the motives of returners, the mechanisms by which they maintained links with the various places where they had alighted, or put down roots, or the economic, social and cultural impact they made on the adopted countries they left and the homelands to which they returned. The international conference which gave rise to this study aimed both to identify continuities and changes in the return movement of emigrants from the British Isles and Europe over four centuries and to suggest avenues of future exploration. Sponsored by the AHRB Research Centre for Irish and Scottish Studies,[8] the conference brought together scholars from different disciplines, reflecting a wide geographical and chronological range, and using a variety of methodologies. The richness and diversity of the material presented generated a lively debate, identified some knotty problems and highlighted a cluster of significant themes.

Chronological patterns

The chronological spread of papers raised issues of continuity and change over the 400 years covered. Demographic historians often stress similarities and recurring patterns in the mobility that has for centuries been an integral part of European history, regarding emigration as an extrapolation of internal migration. Even in the seventeenth century, as David Cressy's work on New England has shown, people moved backwards and forwards across the Atlantic for reasons of business, nostalgia or family duty.[9] Steve Murdoch's chapter, dealing with the same era, notes how many second- and third-generation Scots in northern Europe felt the pull of their parents' homeland and sojourned or settled in Scotland, expressing concerns about alienation, assimilation and identity that were echoed by their successors in the eighteenth, nineteenth and twentieth centuries.[10] Whatever their origins and destinations, emigrants in all generations tended to construct and freeze their own chosen image of the homeland as they left, an image which became more indelible and unalterable as time went on. Such distorted memories sometimes impeded successful assimilation by those who returned to a country or community that, to their consternation, they found was unrecognizable and alien. In every era there were also those who, infected temporarily with emigration fever, made hasty, unwise and – if they were lucky – reversible decisions simply because they were following the dictates of fashion and the example of their compatriots. Although return migration in the Age of Sail was more difficult than after 1850 and remains largely unquantifiable, it was by no means impossible or unknown. Bruce Elliott's chapter demonstrates how in the early nineteenth century letters to and from emigrants reflected notable levels of return from seacoast ports in North America, particularly among the young, single people who dominated movement to such places.[11] The clear significance of return migration before the 1850s is echoed in several other chapters, perhaps most surprisingly in the chapter by Eric Richards. He highlights a return rate of 10 per cent among convicts, a group that would seem especially unlikely to return, given the great distances and costs involved and the convicts' predictable lack of resources.[12]

But if the participants' sentiments and reactions remained the same throughout the centuries, the onward march of time and technology brought about significant changes in patterns of emigration and return, notably in the sheer scale of the movement. Until the nineteenth century emigration fluctuated in a fairly straightforward response to war, peace, harvests, domestic growth and mobility. In Scotland the extensive outflow of the first half of the seventeenth century was exemplified in the probable loss of about 2,000 people a year out of an estimated total population of 1.2 million, and the presence of 100,000 Scots in Scandinavia. That trend was reversed in the eighteenth century, which saw lower rates of emigration – both absolutely and relatively – from England as well as Scotland, while Irish patterns were similar in both centuries.[13] But in the 'long' nineteenth century up to 1914, over 50 million Europeans emigrated, primarily from Britain and Ireland in the first half of the century, from parts of Scandinavia and several German states in mid-century, and from southern and eastern Europe in the decades before the First World War. This explosion in the scale of movement was provoked primarily by a multifaceted revolution in communications and information. Best known and probably most dramatic was the coming of steamships, which from the 1860s rapidly replaced sailing vessels, cutting journey times dramatically and bringing the option of seasonal, episodic and return migration within the reach of a much larger number of emigrants. For the first time skilled craftsmen could compare wage rates on either side of the Atlantic with the knowledge that they could easily, and quickly, return home if opportunities in the labour market so dictated. It was also easier for the Norwegian farmer who had been smitten by 'America fever' in the 1860s to reverse a hasty and ill founded decision than for the Scottish Highlander who had been sucked into 'the dance called America' in the 1770s to return from an unsuccessful overseas sojourn.[14]

The option of return was also facilitated from the mid-nineteenth century by other crucial improvements in communications, such as the expanding railway network at home and abroad, the transatlantic telegraph and a fast and reliable postal service, as well as a vast expansion in the information field, represented by newspapers, pamphlets, guidebooks and the recruitment activities of professional emigration agents. While emigrants themselves were able to write or return home more easily in order to encourage family and friends to emigrate as well, others were sent back to stimulate emigration in a professional capacity, as agents and representatives of overseas governments and railway companies. James Adam, whom the Otago provincial government sent to Britain as a recruitment agent in 1857, had himself emigrated from Aberdeen in the pioneer party a decade earlier. During 1858 he encouraged 4,000 new colonists to go to Otago, and returned to Britain in the same capacity fifteen years later. Henry Jordan, who represented the new colony of Queensland in Britain from 1860 to 1865, with considerable success, had emigrated from Derby to Sydney as a dentist and missionary in the 1850s.[15] When the Canadian government began appointing federal emigration agents to strategic locations in the British Isles from the late 1860s, these men were carefully chosen with reference to local needs and connections: W.L. Griffith, who was sent to Bangor in North Wales in 1897, was a Welsh-speaking native of that town, with a useful connection in that his cousin controlled a syndicate of Welsh newspapers; John MacLennan, appointed in 1907 to cover the north of Scotland, was a Gaelic-speaking Canadian of Highland descent; and his assistant, Hugh McKerracher, had Scottish connections through his Aberdeenshire-born wife and Perthshire-born parents.[16]

A century after the Victorian communications revolution, expectations and experiences of emigration were again redefined, both practically and psychologically, by two further technological developments, the advent of mass intercontinental air travel and the widespread use of the telephone. Not only did these inventions shrink the world, dilute even further the finality of the emigrants' leave-taking and allow them to maintain regular and rapid contact with home; they also gave rise to mass tourism and to the marketing of selected parts of the homeland as a mecca for returning emigrants. Ironically, however, a greater awareness of home, or the promotion of a particular image of home, could also impede the return of emigrants who realized or feared that they could not simply slot back into a world that had remained static. As Donald Akenson has remarked, it is harder for the Irish than for the non-Irish to return to Ireland.[17] Another important twentieth-century change with clear implications for return migration, at least from the 1920s, was increasing state involvement in the decision-making and selection process, particularly the imposition of entry restrictions by a range of destinations, as well as the presence on the statute book, for fifty years, of the Empire and Commonwealth Settlement Acts.[18]

Geographical perspectives

State regulation may have had a part to play in the second major theme to emerge from the conference, that of spatial diversity, and the significance of continuities and changes according to geographical perspectives. For instance, were the bounty emigrants of the 1840s and the '£10 tourists' of the 1960s who had signed up for government schemes more likely to return from Australia than those who had committed their own savings to a new life overseas? Did public and political hostility in the United States precipitate an increasing tendency to return among southern and eastern European immigrants during and after the 1880s? Different European countries, and different regions within these countries, certainly experienced significantly different rates of return. By 1900 Balkan, Italian and other southern European emigrants showed the highest rates of return, along with Russians, while emigrants from

Scandinavia were least likely to return. Ireland, which topped the European 'league table' of emigrant-sending countries in the nineteenth century, experienced only a 10 per cent return rate, while the British Isles as a whole, which saw 40 per cent of emigrants return between 1870 and 1914, experienced, says Baines, a rate of return 'probably consistently higher than to anywhere else in Europe.[19]

Differences in rates of return are hardly surprising, in view of the disparities in initial emigration. Within the British Isles, the county of Cornwall recorded by far the highest out-migration rate of any county in England and Wales between 1861 and 1900, while some of the south-eastern and east midland counties recorded the lowest rates.[20] Areas such as Ireland and the Scottish Hebrides, where the expulsive influences were strongest and those leaving had fewest resources, might well be expected to register the lowest rates of return, since the poorest emigrants were usually most handicapped in their efforts to establish themselves successfully enough to fund their return. But an examination of distinct regional patterns in the Irish experience indicates that low return rates cannot be equated simply with emigrant poverty. As Patrick Fitzgerald points out, there was a much higher return rate to the impoverished west of Ireland than to the more prosperous east, a disparity that was closely related to opportunities for land acquisition, manifested particularly through the practice of partible inheritance in the west.[21] In many areas of Scotland and England, however, where land was generally leased and allocated exclusively on the basis of single tenancy, and where consolidation was eroding the ambitions of an army of existing and aspiring tenant farmers, from Dorset to Dundee, emigration to vast expanses of freehold land in North America and the Antipodes was more likely to be a permanent move.

Conditions and opportunities in the countries of origin and destination therefore influenced geographical patterns of return movement. In this context regional and local variations may well have been of greater significance than national boundaries, a claim exemplified by the Irish experience in North America, where the disparities were between urban and rural regions on either side of the border rather than between Canada and the United States. If emigrants were sometimes reluctant to commit themselves to an urban environment, they were also less likely to settle in areas where mechanisms of chain migration were less developed, and where it was therefore more difficult to put down roots, than in locations where many of their compatriots had settled and might well offer a helping hand to new arrivals. For example, although only around 25,000 Irish, mainly male, emigrants went to South Africa in the nineteenth century, it was the country from which they were most prone to return, and in 1904 the country had a first-generation

Irish population of only 18,000.[22] This was partly because South Africa lacked a tradition of chain migration but also probably because of the nature of employment and the changing skills base, particularly in the mining industry, which required an élite with technical, professional and commercial skills. By the end of the century, however, as that élite was increasingly displaced by white Afrikaners, the Irish technocrats and businessmen took their skills elsewhere, either back to Ireland or on to Britain, the Americas or the Antipodes. A changing skills base, coupled with the communications revolution and the internationalization of the labour market, was also of crucial importance in the geographical mobility of other types of industrial workers, including Welsh colliers in Pennsylvania, Aberdeen granite masons who participated in seasonal emigration to the United States and the worldwide wanderings of Cornish 'cousin Jacks', who took their tin and copper-mining skills to Australia, North and South America and South Africa.[23]

Perceptions of identity

Complexities in return migration are not confined to issues of chronological and spatial continuity and change. Perceptions of identity among temporary and permanent emigrants alike pose some challenging conundrums, particularly in relation to the tendency of successful emigrants and their descendants to nurture a culture of victimhood. As Paul Basu demonstrates, this trait was developed perhaps most clearly, yet most paradoxically, among Scots.[24] Despite enjoying a long-standing reputation overseas as materially successful sojourners and settlers, despite participating fully – even disproportionately – in the running of the British Empire, and despite the voluntary mobility and urban origins of the vast majority of emigrants from the 1860s, the prevailing picture of Scottish emigration remains that of the enforced exile of cleared Highlanders, harried aboard overcrowded, leaky tubs to the doleful strains of 'Lochaber No More'. Images of impoverished, unwilling emigrants were even more firmly embedded in the Irish psyche, and little attention has been paid to the significant number of middling farmers who left Ireland in the 1840s in order to avoid paying Poor Rates. But those who stayed and those who returned often perceived the emigrant experience in very different ways. Some of those who settled successfully overseas portrayed themselves as victims, perhaps from fear that their very success was eroding the distinctiveness of their ethnic identity, perhaps from a subconscious guilt that their own appropriation of colonial land tarred them with the same avaricious brush as those who had caused them to emigrate, perhaps from a Presbyterian ethic that, frowning on success, covered it with a cloak of victimhood. Conversely, some of those who returned, even if they had been unsuccessful, presented their adventures in a positive way, claiming that by travelling and seeing the world they had enjoyed a more enriching experience than their neighbours who had stayed at home, or even those who had emigrated but lacked the vision and resources to return.

Exploring emigrant homecomings: problems and approaches

Our debates identified challenges and lacunae, as well as recurring themes. Particularly challenging is the need to navigate through what Eric Richards describes as the 'statistical soup' that surrounds return migration, as well as addressing the related problem of defining both migration and return movement, especially in the highly mobile world of the twentieth century. There is clearly a need for much more quantitative research where the records permit, as well as further comparative investigation of the timing of return migration, the motives of the returners, their impact on the societies to which they returned and the extent and nature of their reintegration into those societies. Scandinavia, with its superb demographic and literacy records, but an area featuring only briefly at the conference,[25] might spearhead further developments, perhaps by establishing an international forum for return migration studies, based largely on regional research programmes. Irish return migration also needs to be further investigated, particularly to incorporate the vital movement from Britain back across the Irish Sea. Other themes to explore could include a comparison of the rites of passage practised by emigrants and returners. While the Irish living wake is a well known phenomenon, little attempt has been made to explore rituals of disengagement in other countries, or among return migrants. The heavy emphasis on élites that characterizes chapters covering the early period might be counteracted by the investigations of labour historians into tramping artisans and mobile farm workers, as well as by the use of oral history techniques. More research is also needed into the relationship between land-holding structures and return migration, into missionary migration and return, into the dynamics of military migration and return, and, in a spatial context, into the unexplored but crucial areas of South America and the whole continent of Africa.

Much therefore remains to be done. This book aims to open the debate by addressing some of the major issues in four thematic sections. The construction of a coherent running order for eleven very diverse chapters posed a major editorial problem. A chronological approach was inappropriate, since some contributions spanned huge periods, while others were highly focused, and a geographical division threatened to impede the recognition of global issues by creating a disjointed and perhaps imbalanced emphasis on a few selected locations. It was therefore decided to base the running order on the major – if sometimes overlapping – themes suggested by the contributions themselves, even though this meant a degree of chronological and geographical incoherence. Long-term overviews of the process of return migration are presented in the first two chapters. The four chapters that comprise Part II address the motives of those who returned from a wide variety of locations over a period ranging from the seventeenth century to the present day. Part III consists of three chapters which look at mechanisms of return, while the final part considers the crucial question of the impact on the homeland of those who returned. Yet these divisions should be regarded as seamless rather than rigid, since several chapters clearly encompass more than one of the four general themes, and there are many parallels between, as well as within, the parts.

The analytical model of return migration offered by Mark Wyman, which embraces the motives, characteristics and impact of the migrants, is exemplified repeatedly throughout the book. Success and failure overseas are examined by Patrick Fitzgerald, Eric Richards and Andrew Mackillop, while the powerful theme of homesickness is at the centre of Alistair Thomson's interviews with migrants who returned from Australia in the late twentieth century. But the experience of emigration and return defies straightforward categorization. While every chapter challenges the simplistic and unqualified correlation of success with settlement and failure with return, there are, not surprisingly, contradictions, as well as similarities, between the narratives, and difficulties in undertaking meaningful statistical analysis of a phenomenon with such fluid parameters and definitions. Eric Richards' suggestion that poor people had less incentive to come home challenges the relationship between failure and return mentioned by both Wyman and Fitzgerald, although Richards also cites correspondence which demonstrates that the desire to return diminished with the passage of time and the acquisition of a stake in the new land. The link between growing material success and diminishing enthusiasm for return is confirmed by Fitzgerald, but partially contradicted both by Thomson's evidence of the emergence of homesickness years after the emigrant had left home, and the way in which the acquisition of funds could facilitate return, as Bruce Elliott demonstrates in the example of the Woodside family from north Antrim. For sojourners in climatically hostile regions such as the East and West Indies, the goal was to make money and return as quickly as possible, often with scant regard for morality. In Sir Walter Scott's memorable words, temporary migrants to India 'laid down their consciences at the Cape of Good Hope' on the outward journey and 'forgot to take them up again when they returned'.[26]

Curiosity and pilgrimage as motives for return feature prominently in the chapters by Steve Murdoch and Paul Basu, most of whose subjects 'returned' to a Scotland they had never left, and with which they sometimes had only tenuous links. The selective or even spurious ethnicity demonstrated by those who wished to invoke the exilic heritage of the Highland Clearances is a reflection of the current status of genealogical victimhood as a desirable cultural attribute, a phenomenon which Stephen Constantine has examined in the context of the settlement of British 'home children' in Canada.[27] With a less charged agenda, even some of Thomson's interviewees, weary of the arid heat of Australia, became homesick for a green and pleasant rural England they had never known except in books, songs and poetry. For Bruce Elliott's north Antrim emigrants, however, the decision to stay or return was clearly linked with rites of passage, particularly marriage, so that those who had acquired no exogamous family ties in North America were more likely to come back to Ireland than their countrymen who had married outside the Irish diaspora.

Personal correspondence and connections were crucial mechanisms in the orchestration of return. Their importance is reflected not only in Elliott's focused analysis of a set of emigrant letters as a vehicle for understanding transnational networks, but in other contributors' references to the way in which information, advice and instructions were transmitted in such correspondence, if not always acted upon.[28] That return migration could also take place under the auspices of institutions is demonstrated in the chapters by Kathleen Burke and Marilyn Barber. The Canada Club and the Fellowship of the Maple Leaf had both practical and cultural functions, providing a formal channel through which returned migrants could not only assuage homesickness and maintain Canadian contacts, but could also act as 'living links of empire' by informing a largely ignorant British public about needs and opportunities in the senior dominion.[29] Although the FML's first two directors from 1917 until the 1960s were both male, as well as being themselves return migrants, virtually all the recruits were women, many of whom welcomed the opportunity to travel, at the same time as pursuing a career in teaching, medicine or church work.[30] They were generally open-minded about their future intentions. Some reflected Wyman's template of return migration by coming home to fulfil family responsibilities, while others, in a manner reminiscent of Robert McLeese from north Antrim, came home only briefly as part of the rite of passage that led to permanent emigration.

The difficulty in repatriating their overseas investments that was experienced by some members of the Canada Club was not unlike the problems encountered by sojourners in both the West and East Indies in translating their wealth into landed property back home. Although the Scottish sojourners who flocked to the Caribbean frequently earned enough money to purchase large estates and numerous slaves, these assets could not easily be translated into the acquisition of Scottish land, and, paradoxically, the more successful they became, the greater the difficulty they encountered in extracting their fortunes. Many therefore became reluctant permanent settlers, repeatedly post-poning their homecoming in pursuit of ever-expanding ambitions.[31] Even greater problems were experienced in the East Indies, where British investors were legally obliged to remit money home through the East India Company. Not only did that mean a low rate of exchange; it could also take up to twenty years to repatriate invest-ments, creating a strange contradiction between the mobility of the sojourners themselves and the immobility of their wealth, the pursuit of which had lured them overseas.[32]

Repatriation of overseas investments is integrally linked with the book's final theme, the impact of migrants on the communities to which they returned. Andrew Mackillop demonstrates the consum-mate skill with which Sir Hector Munro of Novar avoided the criti-cism often heaped on returning nabobs by 'de-orientalizing' the fortune and status he had acquired as a result of his sojourn in India. By invest-ing heavily in estate improvement and cultivating the image of a responsible local patriarch in both a political and military context, he celebrated these Indian links in a way that was acceptable to domestic sensitivities. Ironically, however, his very return – and the patronage to which he had access – expedited an ongoing movement of local landed gentry and their sons to India, while his estate development policies provoked discontent and permanent transatlantic emigration on the part of many of his tenants.

Although Munro avoided the opprobrium often heaped on return migrants, friction within the home community was a common con-comitant of return. Wyman notes how the negative comments of Polish priests in 1913 about the loss of faith of short-term migrants among their flocks still finds ready echoes in the concern of Mexican priests about the apostasy, immorality and drug addiction manifested by those returning from a twenty-first-century sojourn in the United States. But, as Fitzgerald suggests, even if the returner imported no bla-tantly bad habits, friction could still arise, particularly as younger sons or brothers attempted to reintegrate – perhaps with enhanced status – into the families and communities they had earlier left behind.

The size of Sir Hector Munro's fortune, and the impact he made on his home county of Ross-shire, were considerable. In a more modest way, Belhelvie's returned migrants – many of whom had also made their money in the service of the East India Company – acquired Scottish estates, though families like the Lumsdens invested in charitable ventures as well. Perhaps the most visible impact of the successful returner was the big house and surrounding estate. The Woodsides from north Antrim, having made their money as merchants in Philadelphia, used it to buy not only land, but the accompanying gentry status back in Ballycastle, where they could be big fish in a small pond in a way that was impossible in America. At the same time, pastoralists, merchants and manufacturers who had made fortunes in Australia marked their wealth by building country houses in Britain rather than the Antipodes, though Eric Richards raises the conundrum of whether such fortunes were British or Australian. Perhaps the answer is that these individuals, like so many returners who feature in this book, were keen to advertise and exploit their dual identity and make the best of the credentials they had earned in both worlds.

Notes

1 The Association of European Migration Institutions was formed in 1992, starting with seven countries. It currently has over thirty member institutions in eighteen countries and meets annually.

2 See, for instance, R.F. Foerster, *The Italian Emigration of our Times* (Cambridge MA: Harvard University Press, 1919); T. Saloutos, *They Remember America: The Story of the Repatriated Greek-Americans* (Berkeley CA: University of California Press, 1956); K. Virtanen, *Settlement and Return: Finnish Emigrants in the International Overseas Migration Movement* (Turku: Migration Institute, 1979). See also Anthony H. Richmond, 'Return Migration from Canada to Britain', *Population Studies*, 22 (1968), 271; Russell King, *Return Migration: A Review of the Literature* (Oxford: Oxford Polytechnic, 1983).

3 Dudley Baines, *Migration in a Mature Economy: Emigration and Internal Migration in England and Wales, 1861–1900* (Cambridge: Cambridge University Press, 1985), 28, 126. See also J.D. Gould, 'European Inter-continental Emigration: The Road Home. Return Emigration from the USA', *Journal of European Economic History*, 9:1 (1980), 41–112.

4 Baines, *Migration in a Mature Economy*, 128–40; T.M. Devine, *The Scottish Nation* (London: Allen Lane, 1999), 475–6.

5 See, for example, Marjory Harper, 'Emigrant Strike-Breakers: Scottish Granite Tradesmen and the Austin Capitol Boycott' in *The Texas State Capitol: Selected Essays from the* South-Western Historical Quarterly (Austin TX: Texas State Historical Association, 1995), 63–85.

6 Wilbur S. Shepperson, *Six who Returned: America viewed by British Repatriates* (Reno NV: University of Nevada Press, 1961). See also Shepperson, *Emigration and Disenchantment: Portraits of Englishmen repatriated from the United States* (Norman OK: University of Oklahoma Press, 1965).

7 Mark Wyman, *Round Trip to America: The Immigrants Return to Europe, 1880–1930* (Ithaca NY and London: Cornell University Press, 1993); Eric Richards, 'Return Migration and Migrant Strategies in Colonial Australia' in David Fitzpatrick

INTRODUCTION

(ed.), *Home or Away? Immigrants in Colonial Australia: Visible Immigrants* III (Canberra: Division of Historical Studies and Centre for Immigration and Multicultural Studies, Research School of Social Sciences, Australian National University, 1992), 64–104. In an Australian context see also R.T. Appleyard, 'The Return Movement of United Kingdom Migrants to Australia', *Population Studies* 15 (1962), 214, 225; J. Zubrzycki, *Enquiry into the Departure of Settlers from Australia* (Canberra: Government Printer of Australia, 1973).

8 Based at the University of Aberdeen, but operating in partnership with the Queen's University of Belfast and Trinity College, Dublin.
9 David Cressy, *Coming Over: Migration and Communication between England and New England in the Seventeenth Century* (Cambridge: Cambridge University Press, 1987), 191–212.
10 See below, Steve Murdoch, Chapter Four.
11 See below, Bruce Elliott, Chapter Eight.
12 See below, Eric Richards, Chapter Five.
13 Nicholas Canny (ed.), *Europeans on the Move: Studies on European Migration, 1500–1800* (Oxford: Clarendon Press, 1994), 50, 59, 90–1, 94, 101, 111–12, 127.
14 James Boswell, *The Journal of a Tour to the Hebrides, with Samuel Johnson*, ed. R.W. Chapman (Harmondsworth: Penguin, 1984), 345–6.
15 Marjory Harper, *Adventurers and Exiles: The Great Scottish Exodus* (London: Profile, 2003), 136–7.
16 Gwyn Jenkins, 'W.L. Griffith and the Welsh Emigration to Canada, 1897–1906' in Muriel Chamberlain (ed.), *The Welsh in Canada* (Swansea: Canadian Studies in Wales Group, 1986), 81–93; Marjory Harper, *Emigration from Scotland Between the Wars: Opportunity or Exile?* (Manchester: Manchester University Press, 1998), 56.
17 Akenson's comment was made in 'Dreams of Home', the fifth programme in a five-part documentary series, *The Irish Empire*, co-produced by Little Bird, Cafe Productions and Hilton Cordell Associates for RTE, BBC Northern Ireland and SBS Independent in Australia, and broadcast in 1999–2000. Thanks to Dr Patrick Fitzgerald for the reference.
18 Stephen Constantine, 'Waving Goodbye? Australia, Assisted Passages and the Empire and Commonwealth Settlement Acts, 1945–72', *Journal of Imperial and Commonwealth History* 26:2 (1998), 176–95.
19 Baines, *Migration in a Mature Economy*, 282. See also J.D. Gould, 'European Intercontinental Emigration: The Road Home', 51; Dudley Baines, *Emigration from Europe, 1815–1930* (Basingstoke: Macmillan, 1991), 39–42.
20 Baines, *Migration in a Mature Economy*, 153, 157, 282.
21 See below, Patrick Fitzgerald, Chapter Three.
22 Andy Bielenberg, 'Irish Emigration to the British Empire, 1700–1914' in Bielenberg (ed.), *The Irish Diaspora* (Harlow: Longman, 2000), 222. See also D.H. Akenson, *The Irish Diaspora: A Primer* (Belfast: Institute of Irish Studies, Queen's University of Belfast, 1996), 123–40.
23 See, for instance, William D. Jones, *Wales in America: Scranton and the Welsh 1860–1920* (Scranton PA: University of Scranton Press, 1993); Marjory Harper, 'Transient Tradesmen: Scottish Granite Workers in New England', *Northern Scotland*, 9 (1989), 53–75; Philip Payton, *The Cornish Miner in Australia: Cousin Jack Down Under* (Redruth: Dyllansow Truran, 198); J. Rowe, *The Hard-rock Men: Cornish Immigrants and the North American Mining Frontier* (Liverpool: Liverpool University Press, 1974).
24 See below, Paul Basu, Chapter Seven.
25 See below, Steve Murdoch, Chapter Four; Alexia Grosjean, Chapter Eleven.
26 Sir Walter Scott, *The Surgeon's Daughter* (Edinburgh: Cadell, 1833), 176.
27 Stephen Constantine, 'Children as Ancestors: Child Migration to Canada', *British Journal of Canadian Studies* 16:1 (2003) 150–9.
28 See particularly the chapters by Wyman, Fitzgerald and Richards.
29 See below, Marilyn Barber, Chapter 10.

[13]

30 George Exton Lloyd, the founder of the FML, returned to England twice before settling permanently in Canada in 1922. See below, Marilyn Barber, Chapter 10.
31 Allan L. Karras, *Sojourners in the Sun. Scottish Migrants in Jamaica and the Chesapeake, 1740–1800* (Ithaca, NY: Cornell University Press, 1992), 52–3, 170–88.
32 Peter J. Marshall, *East Indian Fortunes: The British in Bengal in the Eighteenth Century* (Oxford: Clarendon Press, 1976), 222–5. See also Glasgow City Archives, Campbell of Succoth Papers, TD219/10/51; National Archives of Scotland, Kinross House Papers, GD29/2056/6.

PART I

Overviews of return

This part of the book comprises two chapters which offer long-term overviews of the process of return migration, from a European and Irish perspective respectively. Mark Wyman's analysis is concerned with the best-known and most extensively documented place which return migrants left, the United States, and highlights the range of reasons for return, the characteristics of those who came back and the effect of their overseas sojourning on their homeland. Patrick Fitzgerald focuses on Ireland, one of the locations to which emigrants returned, and draws extensively on correspondence in the Irish American Database at the Ulster-American Folk Park's Centre for Migration Studies. Like Wyman, he discusses the reasons for return and the reception accorded to those who returned, as well as the significant part played by returners as agents of emigration among their fellow countrymen.

Both these introductory chapters touch on themes which are raised or elaborated in subsequent parts of the book. Wyman's comments on homesickness as a factor in return are elaborated in Alistair Thomson's account of post-war return migration from Australia, while the 'American house', a common manifestation of return migration in many parts of continental Europe, appears in Alexia Grosjean's detailed study of the Aberdeenshire parish of Belhelvie. Fitzgerald's focus on Irish military and mercantile migration and return is taken up by Steve Murdoch in the context of seventeenth-century Scotland, albeit many of Murdoch's 'returners' had not actually been born in Scotland. Fitzgerald's reference to the part played by bardic poets in stamping an enduring exilic motif on the Irish emigrant experience is also relevant to Paul Basu's exploration of the semantics of the Scottish diaspora in relation to modern 'roots tourism', while his suggestion that some return migrants may have engendered friction in their home communities is also mentioned, as we have seen, by both Wyman and Andrew Mackillop.

CHAPTER TWO

Emigrants returning:
the evolution of a tradition

Mark Wyman

Until recently the idea of emigrants returning has rarely been broached by historians of emigration, either in the major receiving countries of North America or in Europe. This seems surprising, for the totals are so enormous: at least one-third of the 52 million Europeans who left Europe between 1824 and 1924 returned permanently to their homelands. Both academics and non-academics are surprised to learn this. In 1911, a magazine noted how surprised American officials were after the publication of steamship statistics showing that, from 1897 to 1907, almost one-third of those emigrating from Europe had gone back. In certain years the return rates were even higher, especially during the sharp economic downturns that characterized the US economy: in 1931, for example, only 43,000 immigrants arrived in the United States, but 89,000 left.[1]

These totals are inviting to anyone who wants to probe change among traditional groups in Europe. Ingrid Semmingsen looked at Norway's Vest-Agder county on the south coast and found that the 25 per cent return rate there meant that in 1920 every fourth man over the age of 15 had lived at least two years in America. Dino Cinel's study of Italy found that as America went into a depression in 1908, 131,000 Italians had nevertheless gone to the United States – but 240,000 Italians had returned, the majority of them to the most economically backward regions of the Mezzogiorno.[2] What did such massive returns mean for the homelands?

If such percentages and statistics seem rather general, this is because return estimates vary widely, by national groups, by years – and by collecting agency. An American historian has come up with return rates for 1899–1924, going back to Europe from the United States, of 9 per cent for the Irish, 14 per cent for Germans, 15 per cent for Scandinavians, 33 per cent for Poles, 45 per cent for Italians, 53 per cent for Greeks and 87 per cent for Russians. He put the British return rate at

[16]

just under 20 per cent.[3] However, according to another scholar, 'An estimated 40 per cent of the English and Welsh who emigrated between the 1870s and the First World War returned, likely the highest percentage of all nationalities.' Another historian of British emigration writes that in 1889 the return rate was one in three.[4]

The Finnish scholar Keijo Virtanen has done some of the most careful work in taking apart return migration – finding, for example, that within Finland's 20 per cent return rate, the urban return movement was tiny, often around 8 per cent; while in one rural district almost 58 per cent of the emigrating farmers came back but only 11 per cent of non-landowning workers. And Virtanen notes the problems with these statistics: sometimes the government did not even count those returning; or a group would travel on a single passport; or some used a false passport. Investigators elsewhere have found that for some countries on the Continent, only those coming back through a port of that nation were counted; those who landed at – say – Bremen, and then went home to Italy by train, were never included in return migration totals. And as late as 1981, the editor of the published papers from a conference on modern European return migration conceded that 'returns are quite difficult to assess with any statistical accuracy'.[5]

This chapter will avoid any examination of the statistical issues, but will instead focus briefly on the early record of return migration; then on how return was affected by new modes of transport; the relation to seasonal migration; American industry's use of return migration; some of the major issues revolving around those returning, and a look at today's return migration.

The origins of return migration

Snippets of information from the earliest settlement of the Americas indicate that from the beginning, persons emigrating were returning to their homelands. From all areas of settlement overseas, emigrants chose to head back. The Golden Age of Spanish literature frequently touches on the theme; such as Cervantes' story of 1613, 'The Jealous Estramaduran', about a Spaniard who emigrated to Peru and returned twenty years later, carrying his gold with him. He found his friends at home all deceased, but then he married a pretty teenager and had to fight off other men who wanted her.[6]

In the same general era, the outflow from colonial New England was so great that a later governor claimed more persons went back to England than arrived in Massachusetts during the 125 years after 1640. His claim was overblown, but it is recorded that young Puritans in those early years were not only asking, 'How shall we go to Heaven?', but also 'How shall we go to England?' In 1642 seven of Harvard's first nine graduates decided to return to England. The Harvard classes of 1647 through 1650 graduated twenty young men, twelve of whom went to England. Near the close of the colonial era the ebb tide still attracted attention, and Benjamin Franklin worried that the extensive exodus to England was counterbalancing the immigration from there, a development he felt might lead to a German Pennsylvania.[7]

The movement out of Europe rested on a lengthy tradition of temporary migration within the Continent. In Scandinavia, evidence has been compiled showing a mobile population at least since the Middle Ages. Similarly, Hungary's tradition of people travelling near by to seek work runs back several centuries; historians have almost identical findings for France, Italy, and the Balkans. By 1800 the commercial region centring on the Netherlands had a seasonal in-migration of some 30,000 workers annually, for mowing and haymaking, building and tending dikes, digging canals, making bricks, and similar jobs; in Amsterdam at that time, almost half of the unskilled jobs were filled by the foreign-born. And of course, into England came labour migrants from Scotland, Wales, and Ireland, and sometimes from across the Channel.[8] There were also Italians heading north to Switzerland and France, Galician peasants to Prussia and Ukraine, and Balkan peoples travelling throughout southern Europe for jobs.

These may have been overwhelmingly farm people, peasants, but they were quickly drawn into the new industrial centres. Lódź – now in Poland, then in Russia – grew from 31,000 in 1860 to 314,000 in 1897 as its factories boomed and it became 'the Manchester of Russia'. A majority of its labour force came in the form of seasonal peasant-migrants. Other Poles were pouring into the German Ruhr, while Italians moved into French textile mills and Irish workers were drawn to Manchester.[9]

The switch from farm to factory began to attract attention. Church officials, especially, worried about this short-term migration. It came to a head in Galicia – today's southern Poland – with a survey of parishes in 1907. One parish reported: people leaving to Saxony-Prussia, 400 in the past year; to America, 400; to Budapest, 10. Another: to Saxony, Silesia, and girls who went to sugar beet factories in Denmark, 1,500; to Budapest, 50; to America, 20. A third: to Saxony, 220; to Prussia, 483; to Budapest, 140; and to America, 290.

Priests' comments appended to a later survey in 1913 indicated that mainly men, youths, and some young girls went to work elsewhere, usually travelling in groups, returning by wintertime. Those going to Prussia were singled out as returning with weaker faith and belief. One priest wrote that 'The worst are those working in Moravia and

Silesia.' Another: 'Whoever comes back from Budapest, is indifferent toward the faith.' 'Prussian hooligans' were coming back. On another occasion a Galician priest said 'Emigration should be stopped, particularly the seasonal' migration. 'People from one parish should stay together', the priests advised during a meeting in Kraków. 'The older should go with the younger; women should go with girls. They should protect and control the younger. Before they leave they should go to confession; there should be a Mass. Good Catholic newspapers should be mailed to them . . . In summer, priests should visit them.'[10] Short-term migration, then, was not without its perils.

Returning from America

By the middle of the nineteenth century the phenomenon of temporary emigration had become established in America, as well as Europe. The industrial transformation entered its American take-off phase after the Civil War, bringing a sudden need for large numbers of workers, often in remote areas without resident labouring populations. And so immigrants poured into western mining, for example, and soon also into the post-war wave of railway construction exemplified by the first transcontinental line, completed in 1869. Industry's needs were easily stated: a young male work force that could be brought in easily for low wages, trained in the new ways, willing to work amid the dangers of untested technology, and then let go when the project was completed. Such a labour force promptly appeared in the west. It was the Chinese, crossing the Pacific with expectations of earning up to $30 a month, almost ten times the earnings at home. Labour circulars distributed around Chinese ports advertised high wages in California, but one Chinese immigrant later recalled that at the age of 16 he saw something else: a returning emigrant who came back to his village and then proceeded to purchase vast areas – as spacious as 'four city blocks' – on which he built a palace and laid on a grand feast for relatives and friends to encourage them to follow suit.[11] This was a recruitment method that would appear in Europe as well.

And so the Chinese began disembarking in San Francisco Bay by the thousand as the Gold Rush spread from the Mother Lode in the Sierras to other areas of the west, and they soon branched into railway work. The year that the transcontinental railway was completed, in 1869 Chinese immigration to the United States totalled almost 15,000, almost all single men or married men without families; by 1870 there were only 4,500 Chinese women out of a Chinese population in the United States of 64,000.[12] Many did not stay in America. Chinese departures were never under 25 per cent of the incoming total in any single year, and sometimes the outflow exceeded the inflow, as in 1866 when almost 2,700 entered while over 3,900 were leaving. By 1930 the total arrivals of Chinese over the years reached 400,000, but only half of them stayed. The rest went back to China, carrying enormous savings kept from their meagre wages.[13]

Soon employers in other parts of the country began to look upon the Chinese as potential labourers in their areas, too. A strike-bound Massachusetts shoe factory transported Chinese all the way from California to replace striking white workers, a move which brought dismay to the Knights of Labor but excited others, such as a writer for *Scribner's Monthly*. To the reporter, the 'heathen Chinee' could be the 'final solution' to America's growing industrial labour needs.[14] But the Chinese did not become America's industrial labour force. Rising opposition from white workmen, climaxing with riots in San Francisco in 1874 and the passage in 1882 of the federal Chinese Exclusion Act, soon ended the possibility of Chinese providing the muscle for expanding American capitalism.

The steamship then came to the rescue of US industrialists. Steam power applied to water transport meant that steamships could cross the Atlantic in two weeks, in contrast with the journeys by sailing vessel that not infrequently lasted more than a month and were known to reach two months. By 1870 immigrant arrivals by sail in American ports were down to 3 per cent of the total. Steam had triumphed. It was the catalyst that soon was bringing thousands of Europeans – increasingly from peasant villages in the south and east of Europe – crossing on vigorously competing shipping lines whose fare wars sometimes cut the cost of travel to as little as $10 to cross the Atlantic.[15] This opened up North and South America to a new type of immigrant. Political and religious refugees continued to cross the ocean, as did those seeking farmland in the west. But the spread of the railway network across the European continent, linked to steamship lines, brought the western hemisphere closer than ever before envisioned in emigrant dreams. And so the old patterns of seasonal migration, and of short-term migration to earn some money for home expenses, were juxtaposed on Atlantic emigration to the New World.

With the steamship, emigration no longer had to be seen as a lifetime move. A recently arrived Italian told American congressional investigators that the steamship agent in his village 'used to talk to them about coming to America; he said, "You will find good wages there, and if you can't find anything there you can always come back."'[16] And a Galician Jew would later recall that his uncle had once travelled to the United States and returned, a migration he described as 'an ancient custom. A lot of Jews left Eastern Europe, they went to

America, they worked for a couple of years and then they would come back and bring some money.' It is significant that he called this 'an ancient custom' by the time he was born, around 1900.[17] As traditional seasonal migration patterns were imposed ever more regularly on transatlantic routes, an Italian observer noted in 1911 that his nation's emigration to the Americas 'was becoming more and more like traditional Italian emigration to Europe' as trips by single persons, and by married men without families, became dominant.[18]

Reasons for return

There were many, many explanations for making emigration into a round trip. Most can be condensed to five major reasons: success in the new home; failure; homesickness; a call to return to take over the family farm or other property; rejection of life overseas.

The goal of the successful emigrant was to work until he had saved $800. This he accomplished in, say, two and a half years. He went home with the money to buy a plot of land. Or a single young woman saved up enough for a substantial dowry. One Polish emigrant from Zaborów in Galicia inherited two and a half morgas, a morga being 1.38 acres, so that two morgas are slightly larger than one hectare. His bride brought an equal amount to their marriage: two and a half morgas, giving them five morgas. The husband then went to the United States and Canada, to work, spending most of his five years employed by a Chicago laundry. During that time he sent home enough money to purchase five more morgas. Upon his return to Galicia he carried enough money for another four morgas, bringing the total to fourteen morgas (more than 19 acres), and buying machinery and improving buildings.[19] It was a common story.

Also common, however, was failure. The emigrant had planned to save $800, but he did not do so. In fact, just as he arrived the American economy went into one of its periodic crises – 1873, 1877, 1894, 1907, 1919–20, to say nothing of 1929. Or he was injured or became ill: Italy began to study return migrants, and found the health of those coming back was much worse than those heading westward across the Atlantic – in 1909, for example, tuberculosis occurred in only 0.07 cases per thousand travellers westbound, but eastbound, coming back, there was an average of 9.71 cases.[20] If saving money was a goal, missing that goal or falling on hard times could be a strong reason to head home again. An East European Jewish woman who emigrated in the early 1920s told of earlier being warned by a man who came back: 'Don't go! . . . You'll have to sit at the machine for nine hours and you wouldn't be able to get up even. You wouldn't be able to do it. You'll get consumption. You'll get sick.'[21] There were plenty of reasons, it seems, to go back.

Homesickness is a sentiment that emerges in many interviews. A 1982 thesis written at the University of Oslo was based on interviews with returned Norwegians. Of those coming home before 1930, more than half listed 'homesickness' as their major reason. Even among those who stayed abroad, of course, the longing for home often remained, but submerged. Years after her return to Ireland, a woman admitted she had never been happy in America: 'I never got up a morning in it but I thought how nice it would have been to be rising in Ballighan and seeing the sun on top of the Cruach.'[22]

If emigration was often part of a family plan to acquire more land or buy a shop, anything at home that would upset those plans could bring the emigrant back quickly. A death in the family was such an event. Any question as to disposition of family property might bring a pleading letter for a son or father to come back immediately. In many areas the land question was becoming ever more crucial by the end of the nineteenth century: in some Polish areas partible inheritance meant the number of individual land holdings increased enormously, while the average size decreased – leading to the Central European folk saying: if a dog lies down on your property, his tail is on your neighbour's property. And, in fact, there were strips of land reported as only 1.5m wide. A farmer might own fifty or more plots of this size.[23]

There was also much in America that could repel an emigrant; very much that could discourage a sensitive person expecting fairness in a democratic society. The Yiddish *Daily Forward* in New York ran a 'Bintel Brief' letters column that frequently revealed the underside of this other America. An unemployed man who had fled from the Russian army wrote that he was surviving on 5c a day: 'One goes about with strong hands, one wants to sell them for a bit of bread, and no one wants to buy', he wrote. 'They tell you cold-bloodedly: "We don't need you."' And he added, 'If I had known it would be so bitter for me here, I wouldn't have come. I didn't come here for a fortune, but where is bread?'[24]

Reporters quizzing the vast numbers returning to Europe in the early 1920s were given an earful about what was wrong with America. It was, after all, the era of Prohibition and a re-energized Ku Klux Klan. Lingering on from the super-patriotism of the First World War years, some local laws forbade the use of foreign languages. A Catalan told of being threatened by whites just for helping a black woman find a street address. A Norwegian concluded, 'It isn't the old America any more', as he headed home after seventeen years in the north-west. 'That was a fine country, a real freedom's land, but not any more.' A Scandinavian dressmaker told an interviewer that the United States was all right – 'if you think the way they want you to think'.[25]

Characteristics of return migrants

American industry adapted rapidly to the new influx of Europeans seeking immediate work and regular wages rather than a life of struggle on a farm. The new industrial machine was soon subdividing tasks so minutely that the bulk of workers from non-mechanical backgrounds could learn them quickly. The workers did not even need to know English; the primary requirement was muscle. A lengthy apprenticeship was certainly unnecessary: the head of Carnegie Steel argued in 1901 that he could now take a 'green hand' and turn him into a skilled melter in as little as six weeks. Henry Ford's foundry had 95 per cent unskilled labourers by 1914, each one doing just one task – which Ford said 'the most stupid man can learn in two days'.[26]

The organizing principle of this new economy was best illustrated in a tale told by a returned Irishman who had been hired soon after arrival by a sand quarry near Boston. A friend recalled his description of how the owner

> used to meet the boats coming into Boston and engage the immigrants. A lot of Irishmen were engaged by him and he used to tell them this was the way to work – here informant made the motion of shoveling very rapidly with a spade he held in his hands – if they wished to get on well in America. Very few were able to endure the work for very long, but he was always able to obtain fresh relays from the incoming boats. In this way he managed to keep the sand pits going at full pressure.[27]

Soon, immigrants outnumbered the native-born in blast furnace work, rolling mills, public works construction, railway labour and ready-made clothing manufacture. Carnegie Steel at one point had 14,000 common labourers in one plant, and over 11,000 of them were East Europeans. It was similar throughout American industry.[28]

Once, canal-digging had been an 'immigrant job', and if a well was to be dug an immigrant was hired. But the new industry soon had other 'immigrant jobs', and newly arrived European peasants were eager to take them as long as wages were good and there were regular paydays – something they had never known before. A visitor to an oil refinery observed workers in one such immigrant job:

> Wearing iron shoes, and wrapped in layers and layers of sacking, they enter the still in turns to break out the red-hot 'cokes' left by the oil. In a temperature of over two hundred degrees they work furiously – a man can only stand it for three or four minutes at a time – from three to four hours a day. Almost every day someone collapses in the still and has to

be rescued, sometimes with his clothing on fire. When they come out after their spell, they strip and throw themselves down in the snow, if it be winter, or dash buckets of water over each other. One man said they looked like 'boiled meat'.[29]

Newly-arrived immigrants lined up eagerly for such work. The Chicago stockyards were accurately described as a jungle – but each morning outside the gates there were up to 5,000 men trying to gain employment. Usually less than 10 per cent were hired. It was a common scene throughout American industry.

These immigrant workers, though, saved vast sums. Banking and postal records provide ample documentation of just how much they sent home. A job was good not because it was easy, not because the surroundings were pleasant, not because it promised future promotions. It was good if it paid well now, so the immigrant could save: Pittsburgh common labourers were reported to be saving up to $15 a month at the turn of the century; $100 to $200 a year was common, although Italian railroad workers did better, saving $25 monthly. A Serbian banker in Pittsburgh reported in 1908 that he was sending home as much as $25,000 daily for immigrant workers. One scholar who has scrutinized the Slovak banking records estimates that from 1870 to 1914 Slovak immigrants sent back $200 million. Their goal was not to become American, not to learn English, not to join a labour union, not to assimilate. The goal was back in Europe. America was merely the means to reach that goal.[30]

But it should not be assumed that those in 'immigrant jobs' were ignorant. True, they took these difficult jobs upon arrival, because they needed money immediately and were not aware of other possibilities. But when they learned of other employment, not so dangerous or strenuous, paying as well or better, they quit. As a result, American industry had extremely high turnover rates – usually 100 per cent and more throughout this era. Henry Ford had 416 per cent turnover at one plant in 1913; this meant hiring 54,000 men during one year to keep a work crew of 13,000. It became a major problem: in 1914, a study of twenty metal manufacturing plants in the Middle West found that to maintain an average of 44,000 employees, they had been forced to hire 69,000 men during the year.[31]

The impact of return migration

Many of these workers returned home. Carlo Levi had a view of one of the results of this return migration in a little southern Italian town, where he had been forced into internal exile by Mussolini in the mid-1930s. In his book *Christ Stopped at Eboli*, Levi explained how he spent his initial days wandering around the poverty-scarred community where the only light entering most homes came through an open door, while chickens fluttered in and out, competing for space on the dirt floor with pigs and dogs and humans. But here and there were other sorts of houses – painted, with a second floor and balcony, the doorknobs bearing fancy varnish. 'Such houses belonged to the "Americans",'Levi wrote.[32] In fact, the American house became the most visible result across much of Europe of the return migration that swept progressively in waves over the Continent. Such houses were built by the emigrants coming back with their savings from America, or Canada, or even Argentina, where many southern Italians went.

There were many other results, of course. Some of those returning introduced new crops – tobacco was planted in Norway, tomatoes in Finland, improved grape varieties in the Italian Mezzogiorno. It was Finnish returnees who began the practice of feeding turnips to cattle and who introduced mink farming. But most of those returning had never set foot on American farms, as an Italian government agent discovered when he quizzed a returned farmer. In America, the returned emigrant told him, the corn grows in 'perfect rows'. The government man realized that that was what one would see from a passing train.[33] In fact relatively few of those heading home again had ever worked on an American farm. Their America was a country of heavy industry.

Historian Dino Cinel refers to those coming back to southern Italy as 'conservative adventurers' – adventurous in daring to cross the ocean, but conservative in that when they came home they fell back into traditional ways. They used their savings to improve their social standing, with more land, a bigger house, not in revolutionizing local agricultural practices.[34] This was very often the case; return migrants were not always innovators.

Some of those who went back did end up in industrial jobs, however, and in some cases they were able to use their overseas work experiences. Studies in Sweden by Per-Olof Grönberg and Hans Lindblad document the extent to which Swedish industry benefited from return migrants who had gained American know-how. Lindblad quotes an earlier historian as summarizing the major changes carried back to Sweden as 'Bessemer and prayer meetings'. That is, the steel industry drew heavily on ideas from abroad, while Sweden's state religion was now faced with competition from Baptists, Mormons, and other denominations. Grönberg found that there was an extremely high return rate among Swedish engineers, who went to the United States and worked for General Electric, Westinghouse, and other companies.[35]

Others stress the political impact when emigrants returned from democratic counties such as the United States and Canada back to homelands which were often under authoritarian rule. Records of many localities across Europe show the returned emigrants being elected to local governing boards and committees, as well as to national Parliaments. Three Prime Ministers eventually emerged among those coming back before 1930, having learned their organizing and political skills in the United States. When Finland gained its independence in 1917 its first Prime Minister was Oskari Tokoi, who had been a miner in America; the following year independent Latvia was reborn, and its Parliament chose returned emigrant Kārlis Ulmanis as its first Prime Minister. Johann Nygaardsvold, once a construction worker in the United States, became Norway's Prime Minister during the 1930s and the Second World War.

Conclusion: the modern return migrant

Can studying the history of return migration shed light on the modern maze of immigration controversies? The public seems oblivious to any nuances, other than that there has always been immigration. The *New York Times* noted in 1998 that the story of the earlier return migration experience of the 1880–1930 period 'was largely erased from popular consciousness by the mid-century immigrants, most of whom, fleeing war, never looked back.' But today, the *Times* reporter noted, 'few modern immigrants abandon their motherlands forever . . . Instead, they straddle two worlds, in varying degrees', a lifestyle made possible by, again, another revolution in transportation and communications, aeroplanes and the Internet.[36]

US census data show that from 1980 to 1990 an average of 195,000 of the foreign-born left the United States each year. These included 20,000 going back to Mexico, almost 12,000 to Germany, 11,000 to Canada and to the Philippines, 10,000 to China/Taiwan, and over 9,000 to the United Kingdom.[37] These are the official data; illegal border crossers, of course, were not included.

Some return to their homelands today because of political and economic improvements there, as with the new influx back into prosperous Ireland.[38] A Soviet Jewish 'refusenik' who came to the United States in 1979 and has now made a few visits to the new Russia reports that some who go back there to live are from that group that was told by Soviet authorities some decades ago go 'go either west or east' – that is, 'Emigrate or we'll send you to camps.' Others originally arrived in the United States as children. Some now move back as representatives of Western firms.[39]

A Russian immigrant newspaper published in Brooklyn interviewed three who were going back after a few years in America. Like many earlier return migrants, these individuals bemoaned America's obsession with materialism and its ugliness; they also criticized the lack of trees in their district of Brooklyn, and the inelegance of 'the American uniform, jeans and sneakers'.[40]

Europe's post-war industrial boom has been closely bound up with return migration. The Turkish and Yugoslav labour migration northward began in the 1950s, and soon German cars and German goods began appearing in remote Yugoslav and Turkish towns. This in turn created a labour shortage for the Yugoslav tourist industry, which soon brought in workers from communist Czechoslovakia and Poland, who could travel more easily to another communist country,[41] and many of the episodes harked back to similar movements of workers in the late nineteenth century.

Other reports tell of the Moroccans flooding into southern Spain, carefully saving their money to buy more land at home. In Portuguese towns there is the *casa francesa*, built with earnings from France, just as in another part of the world there are 'sterling' houses in parts of China, built by earnings brought home from British areas such as Hong Kong. Dirk Hoerder sums up German and Yugoslav scholarship on these trends in return migration by noting that upward mobility is often the goal, seeking to rise out of the lower ranks of the middle class.[42]

This should all be familiar to students of the earlier return migration – the desire to buy more land along with the goal of improving one's social status. But different historical conditions have perhaps brought forth some new issues as well, as in the reports of Second World War refugees heading back to live in homelands freed from Soviet control. Known in the late 1940s as Displaced Persons, or DPs, most were placed initially in camps in West Germany, but eventually resettled in Britain, Sweden, Belgium, Australia, Canada and the United States, among other nations.

A Latvian friend of the author who has returned on visits to the homeland he fled in 1944 recalled three Latvian DPs who returned there permanently. All three were fairly prosperous in the United States, and were able to regain family properties that had been seized by the communists after the war. They all return to the United States once a year for visits with their adult offspring. They have invested in Latvian business ventures, and are generally received without problems – although one of them encountered some jealousy over the fact that she wore elegant clothes and could hire a maid; in a store a woman began criticizing her and spat in her face.[43] Some DPs who return hear criticisms that 'We suffered while you led the good life in the West.'

Even in this new version of return migration there are echoes from a century ago. Exposure to democratic processes and elections has helped several returning emigrants move up the political ladder in their homelands. One of these is Valdus Adamkus, a Lithuanian who first came to the United States with his family around 1950; he eventually rose to occupy prominent positions in the federal Environmental Protection Agency. Adamkus returned to his homeland in 1998 and won election as Lithuania's president. A DP was also elected as Slovenia's leader.[44]

The return migrant's advantage can perhaps be appreciated by looking at an unsuccessful election campaign. It was run by an Estonian, Rein Taagepera. He fled his country after the war, eventually reaching the United States, where he followed an academic career and ultimately became a professor at the University of California, Irvine. After the Soviets left Estonia a decade ago, Taagepera returned there to open a Western-style school of social sciences, and soon was invited to run for president of now-independent Estonia. 'I was the only candidate with practical experience in democracy,' he recalled. So he campaigned Western-style: shaking hands. 'This was new to Estonia and was well received'. The press both attacked him and ignored him, but he had learned from watching American politics that he could not let such things bother him. He avoided emotional reactions, never losing his temper during meetings. He lost the election, but received almost 25 per cent of the vote.[45]

Return migration's impact can also be seen in today's reverse flow to poorer communities in Mexico. In 1997 National Public Radio in the United States sent a reporter to Cheran, in the state of Michoacan in south-western Mexico. There he found that 60 per cent of the town's adults migrated seasonally to work in the United States. This is comparable to the situation in many southern European and North African villages, which send their young people north into the European Union. In the case of the temporary migrants from Cheran – many but not all of whom enter the United States illegally – the American jobs are mainly as taxi drivers, harvest hands, and restaurant workers.

The results back home are easily noticed. Now, as the NPR reporter told it, the 'rows of primitive, dilapidated brick homes are interrupted by the odd façade of a house built or remodelled with dollars. It's a stunning sight – a hovel, another hovel, then an attached stucco duplex with a new Chevy in front, and then another hovel.'[46] American houses in Mexico, too. But there were also less visible changes, changes within the people who travelled north to work and then came home. A Mexican anthropologist who studied Cheran found 'a different value attached to work' – 'they value much more work that is strenuous, but that pays well'. The village priest, however, was not so happy with some of these inner changes and what they meant: drug use, cases of

AIDs, abandonment of spouse, rejection of Catholicism. The Polish priests almost a century earlier would have recognized the problems.

As one US historian has written, 'Expatriation and repatriation represent nothing new in the history of [the United States]; it is new only to those who are unfamiliar with its history.'[47] The same can be said of Europe's emigration history: there is nothing new in today's stories. To listen to the foreigners who today wash cars, serve food and work in factories, brings echoes of another time, when an earlier revolution in transport also led to major shifts in emigration. The goals remained in the homeland, not in the country of destination. Perhaps the scholars' emphasis on assimilation and acculturation has impeded an awareness that love of one's homeland must always be taken into account when we study emigration: after all, many of the DPs waited fifty years to again touch their native soil. All the wonders of the West, the wealth, the technology, the democratic traditions, could not stop them from becoming return migrants. Perhaps those heading back today to North Africa and Mexico will also prove to be agents of change, as has occurred so often in the past. Their examples should serve as a further reminder that understanding return migration can help us understand the contemporary world.

Notes

1 Wilbur Shepperson, *Emigration and Disenchantment: Portraits of Englishmen Repatriated from the United States* (Norman OK: University of Oklahoma Press, 1965), 5–6; Herbert F. Sherwood, 'The Ebb and Flow of the Immigration Tide', *American Review of Reviews* 44 (December 1911), 698.
2 Ingrid Semmingsen, *Norway to America: A History of the Emigration* (Minneapolis MN: University of Minnesota Press, 1978), 120; Dino Cinel, 'Land Tenure Systems, Return Migration and Militancy in Italy', *Journal of Ethnic Studies* 12 (fall 1984), 56–7.
3 Thomas J. Archdeacon, *Becoming American: An Ethnic History* (New York: Free Press, 1983), 138–40. For my own estimates and discussion of sources on return migration statistics see Mark Wyman, *Round-Trip to America: The Immigrants Return to Europe, 1880–1930* (Ithaca NY: Cornell University Press, 1993, 1996), chapter I.
4 Shepperson, *Emigration and Disenchantment*, 5; William E. Van Vugt, *Britain to America: Mid-Nineteenth-Century Immigration to the United States* (Urbana IL: University of Illinois Press, 1999), 155.
5 Keijo Virtanen, *Settlement or Return: Finnish Emigrants (1860–1930) in the International Overseas Return Migration Movement* (Helsinki: Suomen historiallinen seura, 1979), 21, 65–7, 200–1; Daniel Kubat (ed.), *The Politics of Return: International Return Migration in Europe* (Rome: Centro studi emigrazione, 1984), 4.
6 Miguel de Cervantes Saavedra, 'The Jealous Estramaduran' in *The Exemplary Novels* (1613; repr. New York, 1960), 105–37.
7 Shepperson, *Emigration and Disenchantment*, 3–4.
8 See discussion in Wyman, *Round-Trip to America*, chapter II. Ewa Morawska, *For Bread with Butter: The Life-Worlds of East Central Europeans in Johnstown, Pennsylvania, 1890–1940* (Cambridge: Cambridge University Press, 1985), 66–7; Dirk Hoerder, 'Migration in the Atlantic Economies: Regional European Origins and

Worldwide Expansion' in Dirk Hoerder and Leslie Page Moch, *European Migrants: Global and Local Perspectives* (Boston MA: Northeastern University Press, 1996), 34–5.

9 Klaus J. Bade, 'German Emigration to the United States and Continental Immigration to Germany in the Late Nineteenth and Early Twentieth Centuries' in Dirk Hoerder (ed.), *Labour Migration in the Atlantic Economies: The European and North American Working Classes during the Period of Industrialization* (Westport CT and London: Greenwood Press, 1985), 132. Christoph Klessman, 'Polish Miners in the Ruhr District: their Social Situation and Trade Union Activity' in Hoerder, *Labour Migration*, 253–4; Morawska, *For Bread with Butter*, 36–7.

10 Polish church survey and priests' convention reports are taken from materials in the Archive of the Metropolitan Curia in Kraków, Poland: Convention of Priests, 28 November 1907, Part IV; 1907 survey in folder 'Wizyty aziekanskie 1901–10'; and 1913 survey in *Wychodźstwo* volume.

11 Ronald Takaki, *A Different Mirror: A History of Multicultural America* (Boston MA: Little Brown, 1993), 192–4.

12 Ronald Takaki, *Iron Cages: Race and Culture in Nineteenth-Century America* (New York: Knopf, 1979, 2000), 236–8.

13 Takaki, *A Different Mirror*, 194–5.

14 Takaki, *Iron Cages*, 239–40.

15 See Wyman, *Round-Trip to America*, 22–32, for discussion of fares.

16 US Fiftieth Congress, First Session, HMD 572, *Testimony Taken . . . into the Alleged Violation of the Laws prohibiting the Importation of Contract Labourers . . .* ; Serial Set 2579 (Washington DC, 1888), 100–1, 121.

17 Morris B., interviewed in David Leviatin, *Followers of the Trail: Jewish Working-Class Radicals in America* (New Haven CT: Yale University Press, 1989), 76.

18 Francesco Coletti, *dell'Emigrazione Italiana* (Milan: Ulrico Hoepli, 1912), quoted in J.D. Gould, 'European Inter-continental Emigration: the Road Home. Return Migration from the USA', *Journal of European Economic History* 9:1(1980), 51.

19 Kazimiera Zawistowicz-Adamska, *Społeczność wiejska* (Łódź, n.p., 1948), 19–20.

20 Wyman, *Round-Trip to America*, 85–6, discusses the Italian and other studies.

21 Bella S., interviewed in David Leviatin, *Followers of the Trail*, 53.

22 Irish Folklore Commission (University College Dublin, Ireland) Questionnaires (1951), MS 1411, 93.

23 Benjamin P. Murdzek, *Emigration in Polish Social-Political Thought, 1870–1914* (Boulder CO: East European Quarterly, 1977), 141–2.

24 Isaac Metzker (ed.), *A Bintel Brief* (New York: Ballantine, 1971), 70–1.

25 These and other 1920s return comments are discussed in Wyman, *Round-Trip to America*, 122–4.

26 See discussion of immigrants in different US industries in Wyman, *Round-Trip to America*, chapter III.

27 Irish Folklore Commission Questionnaires, MS 1409, 57.

28 Paul Douglas, 'The Problem of Labour Turnover', *American Economic Review* 8:2 (1918), 308–9.

29 John Reed, 'Industrial Frightfulness in Bayonne', *Metropolitan Magazine*, January 1917, quoted in John J. Bukowczyk, 'The Transformation of Working-Class Ethnicity: Corporate Control, Americanization, and the Polish Immigrant Middle Class in Bayonne, New Jersey, 1915–1925', *Labor History* 25 (winter 1984), 56.

30 See discussion of savings in Wyman, *Round-Trip to America*, 60–1.

31 Douglas, 'Problem of Labour Turnover', 308–9.

32 Carlo Levi, *Christ Stopped at Eboli* (New York: Noonday Press, 1947), 43.

33 George R. Gilkey, 'The Effects of Emigration on Italy, 1900 to 1923', dissertation (Northwestern University, 1950), 150.

34 Dino Cinel, 'Conservative Adventurers: Italian Migrants in Italy and San Francisco' dissertation (Stanford University, 1979).

35 Hans Lindblad and Ingvar Henricson, *Tur och retur Amerika: Utvandrare som förändrade Sverige* (Stockholm: Fischer, 1995), with English summary by John E. Norton:

'America and Home Again. A Summary', 9–23: Per-Olof Grönberg, 'Returned Engineers in Sweden, 1890–1930', paper presented to 'People on the Move' conference, Stavanger, Norway, 3–6 May 2000.

36 'The New Immigrant Tide: A Shuttle between Worlds', *New York Times*, 19 July 1998.

37 Bashir Ahmed and J. Gregory Robinson, 'Estimates of Emigration of the Foreign-born Population, 1980–1990', US Bureau of the Census Population Division Working Paper No. 9 (1994), accessed at www.census.gov/population/www/documentation/twps0009/tws0009.html.

38 *Wall Steet Journal*, 15 March 1991.

39 Adele Nikolsky, New York, 9 November 2000, letter to author.

40 Alison Smale, 'Their Hearts belong to Mother Russia', *New York Times*, 22 August 2000.

41 Ivo Baučič, *The Effects of Emigration from Yugoslavia and the Problems of Returning Emigrant Workers* (The Hague: Nijhoff, 1972), 1, 4, 6, 8, 14–16; Dirk Hoerder, 'Immigration and the Working Class: The Remigration Factor', *International Labour and Working Class History* 21 (spring 1982), 36; Jon C. Swanson, 'The Consequences of Emigration for Economic Development: A Review of the Literature' in Robert E. Rhoades (ed.), *The Anthropology of Return Migration: Papers in Anthropology* 20 (spring 1979), 48.

42 Dirk Hoerder, 'Immigration and the Working Class: The Remigration Factor', 37.

43 John Osits, Bullfrog AZ, telephone interview, 16 June 2001.

44 Evan Osnos, 'On the Record', *Chicago Tribune*, 17 September 2000.

45 Dr Rein Taagepera, University of California – Irvine, telephone interview, 20 September 1997.

46 Robert Siegel, 'All Things Considered' broadcast, National Public Radio, 5 May 1997.

47 Theodore Saloutos, *Expatriates and Repatriates: A Neglected Chapter in United States History* (Rock Island IL: Augustana College Library, 1972), 18–19.

CHAPTER THREE

'Come back, Paddy Reilly': aspects of Irish return migration, 1600–1845

Patrick Fitzgerald

By 1914, when the popular song 'Come back, Paddy Reilly, to Bally-jamesduff' was written and composed by Percy French, return migration had long been a significant theme within the Irish diaspora. French, born in Cloonyquin, County Roscommon, in 1854, had served, during the early 1880s, as Inspector of Loans to Tenants with the County Cavan Board of Works before turning his attention on a full-time basis to the world of song, poetry and painting. Travelling around the Cavan countryside, he not only met many of the characters who later featured in his popular music hall verses, but also became acutely aware of the heavy emigration taking place from that predominantly rural western county. Recognizing that the motif of leaving and returning to one's home place had a resonance with a popular audience, he incorporated images of departure and return into his writings. Two songs were entitled 'The Emigrant Ship' and 'The Emigrant's Letter', while his poems, 'In Exile' and 'An Irish Mother' dealt explicitly with emigrant themes.[1] The Paddy Reilly whom French exhorted to return to Ballyjamesduff had acted as chauffeur in the jaunting car that carried him around Cavan in the 1880s and the song was composed when he returned years later to find that his old friend had emigrated. It was thus a lyrical call to a real former aqcuaintance to return to his real native place.

This chapter casts a backward eye over almost 300 years preceding the era of Percy French in order to evaluate the under-explored phenomenon of return migration to Ireland. The lengthy timeframe serves as a reminder that significant outward migration from Ireland, like that from Scotland, began in the early seventeenth century and remained a fairly constant feature of Irish society until relatively recently. The seventeenth century also saw the evolution of modes of thinking about emigration and the notion of return that had at least some bearing upon later experience, while the inclusion of the pre-Famine period highlights the relevance of return migration in a period that is generally overlooked in favour of an almost exclusive – albeit still limited – focus on the later nineteenth and twentieth centuries.[2]

The seventeenth century

Seventeenth-century Ireland is generally perceived as a society characterized by mass immigration, or plantation, as it is more popularly framed. However, while approximately 280,000 British settlers entered Ireland during the century this influx was paralleled by the outward movement of something like 130,000 people.[3] Irish society in the seventeenth century thus demonstrated considerable fluidity, with relatively high rates of population turnover. As the 'forgotten' century of Irish emigration it is worthy of note that relative to population levels the outward flow from Ireland in the seventeenth century was marginally greater in volume than that of the eighteenth century. Since this outward movement from Ireland has been under-explored it is not altogether surprising that we know little about the volume or character of return to Ireland in the seventeenth century. The broad outline and character of emigration in such a formative phase of modern Irish history would perhaps lead us to anticipate low levels of return. The central dynamic behind movement out of Ireland during this period was defeat in warfare, and many emigrants could be properly labelled military migrants.[4]

Defeats in the Nine Years' War, the wars of the 1640s and the Williamite war paved the way for large-scale movements of Irish military personnel. The Crown was generally happy to see the removal of those they dubbed 'idle swordsmen' even if its forces should later confront them on some European battlefield. For the rank-and-file soldiers who sought to join Irish regiments in the Spanish or French armies there was little incentive to attempt a return to Ireland and the consistently high attrition rates in the European armies ensured that most died on the Continent. The officer class gained access to patronage denied them at home and appeared to make the trip back to Ireland only when the fleeting prospect of military success enticed them or the financial inducement of undertaking further recruitment for Continental paymasters beckoned.[5]

A second major stream of migration from Ireland to Europe in the seventeenth century was driven by the establishment throughout Europe of Irish Colleges which provided theological and lay education for Irish Catholics. The main purpose behind the training of Irish priests abroad, in particular, was the reinforcement of the counter-Reformation effort in Ireland. However, there is clear evidence that large number of Irish students who completed their training in European seminaries preferred to remain in Europe and pursue a career in the Continental Church rather than return to the hostile and impoverished environment of Ireland.[6]

A third identifiable emigrant stream comprised Irish merchants who established footholds in many of the Continental ports with which they traded. For these emigrants there is more evidence of return or certainly of coming and going. Catholic merchants had greater incentive to return to Ireland, where they could engage in trade, than members of the Catholic gentry abroad, whose ability to retain land in Ireland was increasingly circumscribed. Within this migrant mercantile group one can perhaps most easily distinguish patterns of behaviour similar to transatlantic migrants of the following centuries. The chain migration pattern is evident, as is the emphasis upon keeping in touch with home through emigrant correspondence. In 1696, for example, an Irish mariner named Luke Quirke wrote from Saint-Malo, in Brittany, France to his cousin John Kearney, also on the Continent, to ask 'how all our poor friends in Clonmel do?'[7] Quirke's concern was to become a familiar refrain in Irish-American emigrant letters in the following centuries.

The seventeenth century also saw an important development in relation to the way in which Catholic Ireland perceived and represented emigration. With the establishment of a sizable Irish community overseas, the long-held notion of the Catholic nation's deliverance from English Protestant oppression was increasingly framed by native bardic poets, writing in Irish, as a deliverance which would come from abroad. In the years after the Treaty of Limerick in 1691, which brought the Williamite war in Ireland to a close, the poets looked forward to the return of Patrick Sarsfield with an army of deliverance, and later the Jacobite Pretender, as well as Catholic France itself, fitted into this messianic prophecy. For the next half-century at least such a threat was perceived to be quite real by the Protestant interest in Ireland, which grew decidedly uneasy in the wake of English military reverses on the Continent.[8] It was in addition the bardic poets of this era who did so much to stamp the exilic motif upon the Irish emigrant experience. Kerby Miller's classic study, *Emigrants and Exiles*, emphasizes the significance of this early modern conditioning to later representations of transatlantic Irish migrations.[9]

Return migration – or 'coming and going' – in the seventeenth century was perhaps most likely among those who constituted the most numerically significant migration flow into Ireland, that is, British migrants who crossed the Irish Sea. This backwash effect could reach spectacular proportions in crisis years such as 1641 or in periods such as the late 1680s, but there is clear evidence of a more consistent movement of migrants, across the social range, crossing the Irish Sea in an eastward direction throughout the century.[10] Arguably one of the perceived advantages of Ireland over colonial America in the seventeenth century was the recognition that geographical proximity afforded the migrant from Britain an easier return in the event of disappointed expectations. Nonetheless, it may be necessary to take fuller account of those whose migrant journeys embraced Britain, Ireland and America and encompassed emigration and return. They included men such as John Tuttle, Samuel Shepard and George Cooke, who went to New England in the mid-1630s but were found in Ireland during the following decade.[11]

The eighteenth century

It was actually the last quarter of the seventeenth century that witnessed the beginnings of the emigration from the northern province of Ulster to colonial America that would prove to be the dominant outward migration flow of the eighteenth century. The scale and character of this phenomenon remain an area of contention but the most recent estimates suggest the movement of somewhere between 70,000 and 100,000 individuals across the Atlantic in the period between the Glorious Revolution and the American War of Independence.[12] Probably something like two-thirds of those departing from Ulster ports were Presbyterians, predominantly of Scottish stock, a migrant group that would later come to be referred to in America as the Scotch-Irish. The emphasis within the historiography relating to this emigration has been upon the individualistic and opportunistic impetus behind the movement and settlement process. The whiteness, Protestantism and literacy of the immigrant group undoubtedly eased this. As Leyburn, in his standard text on the 'Scotch-Irish' concluded, these immigrants were 'full Americans almost from the moment they took up their farms in the backcountry'.[13]

There has been virtually no focused exploration of the issue of return migration as it relates to this movement and those works which have dealt with emigration from eighteenth-century Ireland are notable for the consistent absence of index references to return or reverse migration. An important source base for attempting to address the void is the Irish Emigration Database, housed at the Centre for Migration Studies at the Ulster-American Folk Park, Omagh, Northern Ireland. This keyword-access computer database is focused on the collection of archive material relating to emigration from Ireland to North America between 1700 and 1950. It houses some 32,000 documents, and particularly useful in relation to discussion of actual or considered return are 4,000 letters, 364 of which pre-date 1800.[14]

A number of factors could be advanced to support the anticipation of relatively low rates of return from colonial America. Many of those who left Ireland in this period crossed the Atlantic as indentured servants, prepared to give up three to five years of their labour in order to realize the dream of eventually attaining a foothold on the land and securing economic independence. Indentured servitude represented a significant investment in the New World and a passage home constituted both an admission of failure and something which would have to be paid for. Many Ulster emigrants went as paying passengers, probably on the back of capital compensation allowed them for improvements made to their holdings upon the termination of their leases – the so called 'Ulster custom'. Investing this sum in emigration and settlement across the Atlantic was very much a statement of commitment and in a sense a negative inducement to remain in America.[15] Evidence also suggests a significant female and family presence among the emigrant stream, perhaps further easing acculturation and reducing the inclination to consider relocation to Ireland.[16] Nor should the challenge represented by an Atlantic crossing in the colonial period be underestimated. Few who had spent eight or more weeks crossing the ocean in the hold of what was essentially a mercantile vessel would lightly undertake a return voyage.

Insight into the mind of one Ulster emigrant, weighing up the possibility of return, is provided by a 1767 letter by Job Johnson, from Oxford township, Pennsylvania, to his brother Robert, at home in County Londonderry. After telling his brother that 'I was fully determined to have gone home this fall, but I could not get ready in time,'[17] he passed on news of another brother, William, also in Pennsylvania, noting that 'he likes this country so well that he does not know whether he shall ever return home or not'.[18] That Job himself found it difficult to leave for home became clear further on in his letter. Drawing his thoughts together, he informed his brother that America was:

> as good a country as any man needs to dwell in; and it is much better than I expected it to be in every way I assure you, and I really likes it so well and it is so pleasant to me that it would be a good estate in Ireland that would make me stay there, and indeed many times when I have been by myself and think of the Lord's good dealings unto me, I cannot but admire him for his mercies that ever he turned my face hitherward.[19]

Such expressions of general contentment with America are not untypical of letters sent back from America to Ulster in the eighteenth century.

While there were thus influential factors serving to anchor these migrants in the American colonies there is evidence that certain types of migrant displayed a stronger propensity to undertake the eastward passage back to the Old World. As might be anticipated, the mercantile community was liable to higher rates of oceanic mobility. Here, at the level of both merchant and seaman, one arguably encounters a perception of the Atlantic as a highway or bridge rather than an impediment. The major American ports of Philadelphia, New York, Baltimore and even Charleston had by the eve of the revolution identifiable clusters of Irish-American merchants, who not only ran trading houses and had economic interests on both sides of the Atlantic, but could also travel between America and Ireland.[20] One notable example of such an individual was Waddell Cunningham, who left Ballymacilhoyle, County Antrim, in the late 1740s for New York City. By the spring of 1756 he had entered into partnership with Thomas Greg, a rising star of the Belfast merchant community, and had established the company of Greg, Cunningham & Co., which rapidly became one of the most important trading houses in the city. In July 1763, however, Cunningham fought a duel on Broadway with a rival merchant who was severely wounded and initiated legal proceedings against his opponent. In early 1764 Cunningham beat a retreat to Belfast, leaving the company's New York office in the hands of two junior partners.

That was not quite the end of the story, however, because during the disturbances associated with the secret society known as the Hearts of Steel in 1770, Cunningham was identified as a particular target. It would appear that Cunningham's acquisive appetite, no doubt honed on the banks of the Hudson, subsequently clashed with the value system associated with a moral economy as expressed by smallholding tenants in Ulster. It was Cunningham's speculation in land which had been blamed for the eviction of tenants who could not afford to meet rising rents, and the anger of the mob expressed itself in the burning down of Cunningham's splendid house in Hercules Lane, Belfast. The tension between Old World and New World values, so evident by the mid-nineteenth century, would appear to have been already evident in the 1770s.[21]

Other merchants, land promoters and speculators who had been born in Ireland, men like James Patton, Henry McCulloch, William Johnson and Alexander McNutt, similarly moved back and forth across the Atlantic in pursuit of profit.[22] The Quaker community, in particular, seems to have exhibited a high rate of transoceanic mobility. In December 1771 the prominent Irish-Philadelphian and Quaker merchant, Israel Pemberton, wrote to a trading contact, Thomas Greer, in County Tyrone. In the course of his letter, Pemberton made mention of two friends from Ireland who had come to America but were now considering the prospect of return. One, Samuel Neal, was planning to head homeward in the spring but another, Joseph Oxley, was so eager to get back across the Atlantic that he could not be dissuaded from undertaking a winter passage.[23] Another example of an Irish Quaker returning from America to Ireland is that of John Grubb, of Rathronan, south Tipperary. During the famine conditions that prevailed in Ireland during the later 1720s, Grubb was forced to leave his wife and children behind and head for America. In 1730, however, he returned, in poor health and without having made his fortune, and died the following year.[24]

Return migration to Ireland, however, does not appear to have been the preserve only of those from mercantile or landed élites. One significant group, who ended up crossing the Atlantic, if not by free will, were the convicts and vagrants transported from Ireland between 1707 and 1790, with perhaps as many as 18,000 Irish finding their way to America through penal transportation.[25] Sentenced to seven or fourteen years' hard labour in the colonies, often in Maryland or Virginia, it seems that more than a few of these reluctant migrants were able to find their way back across the ocean. One, admittedly spectacular, example is that of Mary Young, who, having been born and raised near Ballymena, County Antrim, made her way at the tender age of ten to London, where she became involved in a pickpocketing ring. When eventually arrested and tried, she was convicted and sentenced to transportation to the American colonies for a seven-year term. Only a few years later, however, she was rearrested for the same offence in London and sentenced to transportation for a further fourteen years. Not lacking in spirit, Mary again managed to make the passage back to London, where she ultimately, and somewhat predictably, met her ultimate fate at Tyburn, on the day after St. Patrick's Day 1741.[26] It was likely to be those associated with the more organized urban criminal underworld who had the best chance of making such returns and it seems that Dublin, as the second city in the British Isles, contained malefactors with experience of penal transportation. For example, a Dublin newspaper, the *Hibernian Journal*, reported that Christopher Thompson, who in January 1791 robbed a Dublin women at pistol-point, had only three years previously been transported to America.[27] The same newspaper noted in April 1789 that one Eleanor Scarf, who had turned a house in Plunkett Street in the city into a fence for stolen goods, was found under examination to have returned from transportation before her sentence had run its course.[28]

One significant function performed by those who returned to Europe more generally was to promote the idea of emigration among their fellow countrymen. As Mark Wyman has suggested, in relation to the later nineteenth century, the 'American houses' constructed upon return and the stories which circulated thereafter probably promoted emigration to America as effectively as any commercial propaganda issued by agents or shippers.[29] Two specific types of migrants who may be identified as at least potentially playing such a role in eighteenth-century Ireland were seasonal migrants and recruits into the British army and navy. Seasonal migration, long established across the Irish Sea, also operated across the Atlantic. The movement was highly regionally specific, with those from the south and east of Ireland boarding fishing vessels in ports such as Waterford every spring in order to sail west to exploit the rich fishing grounds off the Newfoundland Banks.[30] This seasonal employment inevitably brought fishermen into contact with the ports and peoples of maritime Canada and many settled permanently, while others almost certainly came back to Ireland with stories of the New World and practical information about the migration and settlement process. Newfoundland itself today remains one of the most explicitly Irish corners of the diaspora, with the bulk of settlers drawn to the island tracing their origins to counties such as Waterford, Cork and Kilkenny which fuelled this seasonal migration flow.[31] As was the case in the following century in relation to seasonal agricultural labour migration to Britain, this pattern of movement could act as a preparatory stage towards further permanent migration and as a catalyst to spurring others within a locality to uproot.[32]

Eighteenth-century military migrants are often neglected in accounts of the Irish diaspora. From the time of the Seven Years' War (1756–63) increasing numbers of Irish Catholics were being recruited into the British military, and while many died in service abroad others settled where they had served. Equally neglected are the thousands of troops and sailors who returned to Ireland after completing their tour of duty, often on the far side of the Atlantic. The demobilization of these military migrants in Ireland was clearly a form of return migration, and there are grounds for suggesting that such individuals, and often their partners too, may have played some role in mediating the experience of North America to other Irish Catholics who in the last quarter of the eighteenth century showed less entrenched opposition to the concept of transatlantic emigration. With the legislative relaxation of restrictions on the recruitment of Catholics into the forces in 1774, the stream of Irish rank and file serving in British regiments expanded during the course of the American War of Independence (1776–82).[33] Demobilization after the Treaty of Paris could be measured in Dublin in the rise in crime statistics and the increased demand for poor relief but it should also be noted that 1783 and 1784 were the busiest seasons in the eighteenth century for emigration to America through Dublin.[34] After the outbreak of the war with revolutionary France in 1793 the flow of recruitment from Ireland turned into a virtual flood. Nothing could reflect the demand for such recruitment more graphically than the printing and circulation by the government in Dublin Castle in 1806 of a recruitment poster in the Irish language.[35] Irish soldiers returning after the war with America (1812–14), in even greater numbers, equally filtered back into the Irish countryside with news of the world that awaited the emigrant on the far side of the Atlantic.

That the figure of the sojourner, within eighteenth-century Irish society in general, may not have been as rare as might be supposed is suggested by a passing reference in the estate papers of the Abercorn estate in County Tyrone. In 1769 the Earl of Abercorn received a letter from his agent at Baronscourt, informing him, among other estate business, that Thomas Mackay of Tullywhisker was going to America on a visit. The matter-of-fact manner in which this information was communicated might be taken as an indication that it was not as exceptional as might be anticipated in the 1760s.[36]

1782–1845

The American War of Independence clearly had a significant impact upon all those who had come to the New World in the preceding decades. Much of the earlier writing about the Scotch-Irish, tending towards the bombastic, depicted all Ulster settlers as instant and committed patriots in 1775.[37] The reality, as with most wars, was a good deal more complex. Many from the north of Ireland who had set-tled in the Appalachian backcountry understandably wished to remain neutral, while there were many examples of Ulster immi-grants who positively sided with the Crown. As the war ran its course and it became clear that the patriots would win out, large numbers of those with roots in the British Isles who had identified themselves with the Tory cause made their way back across the Atlantic, rather than face the difficult and uncomfortable transition to a new Ameri-can Republic. This phenomenon has been relatively under-explored. In 1974 a book was published by Mary Beth Norton which dealt with loyalist exiles in England during this period but the work had a strong metropolitan focus and merely confirmed that individuals also returned to Ireland and Scotland.[38] Genealogical research at the Centre for Migration Studies has brought to light the interesting case of one James McCullough, who returned to his birthplace in County Armagh following the fall of Charleston to the revolutionary army in December 1782. Having immigrated to that city in 1761, McCul-lough prevaricated about his loyalties until 1779, when he opted to support the British. Yet, having returned to Armagh, he did not settle there for good. In 1796, amid heated sectarian strife following the battle of the Diamond, he sailed with his family to Canada,[39] giving rise to speculation that he had retained contacts with some of the estimated 40,000 loyalists who left the United States for Lower Canada following the Treaty of Paris.

Emigrant correspondence of this era often contained expressions of resolve to return to familiar surroundings and old acquaintances and relatives at home. Hamilton Young, a Belfast merchant who had gone to New York for business reasons in the wake of the war with America, exemplified such a voice of contrition. Learning of his mother's deteriorating health in a letter from his brother in September 1786 and of 'the anxiety of his sisters for his return', Young clearly found himself under a certain emotional pressure.[40] The competing draw of commercial enterprise in the New World and familial obligation in the Old weighed heavily on his mind. In a letter home to his brother a full year later, Young exclaimed, 'I am heartily Disposed to return as soon as I possibly can' but almost by way of compensation went on to promise to send home some fine apples during the coming winter.[41] On New Year's Eve, a date no doubt evocative of home, he again wrote back to Belfast, telling family and friends that he had just dispatched 'a barrell of very fine Newtown Peppers' and a box of seeds. Again he assured those in Ireland that 'I am using every means in my power to settle affairs here, so as to return to my native Country, & hope that wont be long.'[42] It is evident, however, from a later letter that Young was still resident in New York in January 1793.[43]

Other collections of correspondence chart the gradually diminishing likelihood of an emigrant's return. James Horner, a young emigrant from the townland of Bovevagh, County Derry, arrived in Philadelphia in 1801. Writing to his parents in Ireland the following year, he sought to offer reassurance by promising 'if I live I will make a return.'[44] In a letter of December 1803 he reported sending home a little flaxseed shirt and talked of the prospect of his brother, Jacob, coming out to join him in America. More specifically he noted, 'if ever it be my lot to return to see you and my Native Country I will not promise how soon as there is nothing but one thing certain'.[45] By September 1804, when James once more wrote to his parents, his impression of the New World and its contrast with Ireland appeared clearer in his mind. By then doing well as a teacher, he reported that 'we generally are busy, no time to idle but everyone for themselves'. More pointedly he confirmed that 'it requires a man to be industrious to accumulate wealth' and pronounced his judgement upon the two societies by reporting that 'if I balance Ireland and this together I should give this country the preference by 100 per cent'.[46] Further on in the same letter he speculated about his return. 'I cannot at present say the time when it shall please the Governor of the Universe to convey me to my native land once more. Alas! There are many there that I never shall behold again in this world who have gone to the land of forgetfulness.' Towards the end of the letter he distanced himself further from the prospect of reuniting with his father and mother in Ireland when he wrote, 'Dear mother you will have a house prepared for me if ever I return to see you once more; I should wish that time to arrive and to see you all collected together as you were at my departure.'[47] The image of his departure, as well as the recognition of its finality, seemed almost seared in his memory, as he resignedly concluded, 'time soon runs past and cannot be brought back, a moment lost is lost for ever'.[48] Finally, by November 1810 James Horner had clearly become an established settler with a stake in the New World and the beacon for further chain migration rather than a prospective returnee. He now reported home that

> I have been keeping store this year past and doing well. My Brother wished me to return but at present it is out of my power as I am engaged in business but should any of my brothers think it prudent and come over here I might be the means of getting them into business.[49]

Political factors could also impinge upon the migrant's decision-making process. This was particularly the case in the wake of the failed rising of 1798. A significant number of those radicals who had been to the forefront of the revolutionary United Irish cause in the 1790s ended up in the United States.[50] One such individual was John Chambers, who, following incarceration at Fort George, near Inverness, eventually made his way to New York City. There, in 1805, despite having cast a cold eye on American greed and materialism, he opened his own bookstore at 129 Water Street.[51] Writing in June 1807 to an old radical friend, Robert Simms, of Belfast, he informed him that 'Our friend Jackson has sold his farm in Pennsylvania and will return home I suppose in the fall or spring.'[52] Speculating about the future intentions of others in this circle, Chambers revealed how the course of politics afar could shape decisions in America, observing that 'the change of administration which has lately taken place in England has cooled the wishes for many for seeing once more their native soil'.[53]

The political climate in the destination country could also shape decisions about return migration. In 1814, with Britain and the United States at war, Adam Duffin went from Ireland to Halifax, Nova Scotia, but remained discontented with life on the far side of the Atlantic. Writing his first letter home to family in Broughshane, County Antrim,

Duffin reported, 'If the prospect of public affairs don't assume soon a more conciliating and peaceable appearance, my intention,' he determined, 'is to return home'.[54]

Mark Wyman has referred to those individuals who reversed their migration as a consequence of failure and pointed out how individual failure could often be linked with the periodic crises that afflicted the American economy.[55] This relationship was nothing new, although the rapid replacement of sailing ships by steamships on the Atlantic in the 1860s clearly accentuated the effect. Evidence of sensitivity to trading conditions and economic downturn can be detected in the correspondence of Irish emigrants in the period following the financial panic of 1819 in the United States. In November that year, for example, Robert McClorge wrote home from Philadelphia to his father, in Templemoyle, County Derry. Rather than considering return himself McClorge observed the phenomenon amongst his fellow countrymen. Informing his father about the recession, he noted that for 'strangers coming into this country, business here is very dull'.[56] With a letter of recommendation and a circle of friends in the city, McClorge stood a better chance of finding a niche but told those at home that 'emigrants here are so numerous that many seeing the depression of the Times go back to Ireland'.[57] While the rhythm of Old and New World economic cycles was already helping to shape patterns of transatlantic migration, there were those for whom the recollection of want in Ireland seemed to prevent even the briefest consideration of return. On New Year's Day 1827 a Tyrone emigrant, David Bailey, sat down to write a letter to his brother John, back in Ireland. David, declaring himself 'well suited with this place', stated emphatically, 'hard times was so plenty when I was there that I will not go back to Ireland'.[58]

In 1837 another serious financial panic seriously dented economic confidence in America, leading the country into recession and generating, in the period that followed, a feeling that life for the newly arrived emigrant was harder than it had ever been. Even as late as January 1840 the chill winds of a struggling economy could be detected in the correspondence of Irish emigrants. In that month Robert Smith wrote home from Philadelphia to his brother in County Antrim to caution against any enthusiasm at home for emigration and to signpost his own possible return to Ireland. Signalling a metaphorical red light, Robert warned, 'I advise you from coming to this country at this present season as times is very bad here' and amplified the message with the opinion that 'I never saw the man that is happier in this country than in Ireland'.[59] Furthermore he held out the prospect of his own return and the benefits which might accrue. 'Stay at home till I return,' he urged James, 'and then I will start my brother John at his trade and assist you in getting a larger farm'.[60] Conscious of his brother's ardour for emigration, Robert adopted a different strategy in a letter penned three months later, pleading for James and John to put off any departure until he came home so that he could at least advise them as to 'what would be of use in this country'.[61] By the summer of 1840, and no doubt aware of his brothers watching the emigration season slipping away, Robert offered a more specific promise of his arrival back in Ireland. In this letter he told them that 'when you are drinking each others health on Mosside May fair evening 1841 expect me to be sailing out of the sandy banks of the river Delaware'.[62] It seems that Robert Smith never realized his promised rendezvous, for he wrote home again in 1844 telling of his lucrative position as a custom house officer.[63]

Further evidence of an increasing reverse flow during the early 1840s can be drawn from a letter of September 1842, from John Anderson to his family at home in the townland of Lisnamuck, near Maghera, County Derry. Like many Irish emigrant letter writers, Anderson reported a conversation with a friend from the old country. In recounting his dialogue with a Mr Cathcart he repeated the latter's opinion that there had been a great change in America, and the fact that he had witnessed 'hundreds of passengers returned back to Ireland this summer and hundreds in New York and Philadelphia that cannot find employ'.[64]

Sometimes those left behind in Ireland offered encouragement to emigrants finding the going tough in the New World. A letter of January 1843 from Charles Hagan to his children in New York throws further light on the difficulties to be encountered by those immigrants of the early 1840s. Hagan reassured his offspring by telling them that 'we understand that that country you are in is not as good as it was some time past and if you are not in a prosperous way of doing we advise you to return, and we shall receive you with open arms and you will all three be more welcome than if you never had left us'.[65]

Just as the network of personal contacts played a crucial role in easing an emigrant into his or her new life in America, so the process could be applied in reverse to ease the path of a prospective returnee. In August 1844, James Heather of New York wrote to his old friend, Thomas Greeves, of Dungannon, County Tyrone, to request, among other things, that he should post him a copy of the local newspaper. In addition, he informed Greeves that his son, George, who was by then a young man, wished to know if he should go back to Dungannon and asked, 'would there be any chance of him making out a living as he would like to spend the remainder of his days where he was born'.[66] Whether George Greeves ever came back to his native town is not known but in light of the imminent calamity in Ireland, it might have been better if he had been discouraged from returning to his roots.

Evidence relating to the actual reception offered to returnees in this period is limited but at least one emigrant homecoming is documented in the contemporary press. The subject was a man called Hugh Campbell who had emigrated to Philadelphia in 1818. Campbell's home, Aughalane House, near Plumbridge in County Tyrone, has been relocated to the Ulster-American Folk Park and the journal that he kept on his outward journey to America represents one of the most informative and vivid accounts of a pre-Famine emigrant passage. As younger sons, Hugh and Robert Campbell had gone to America and left their elder and somewhat wayward brother Andrew to manage the family's lands. In early December 1835 Hugh came back to Aughalane in order to sort out estate affairs. The *Londonderry Journal* of 22 December 1835 contains a report of his procession to the home farm and his reception in his home locality.

> On the evening of Friday, the 11th inst., arrived at Aughalane, near the Plum Bridge, the residence of his ancestors, Hugh Campbell, Esq., after an absence of seventeen years in the United States of America: and, although at a late hour, the banks and braes of Glenelly, below and above the Plum bridge for miles, were in immediate illumination by bonfires, with firing of huzzas &c., each side, without party distinctions, of a warm hearted cead miellia faultagh [welcome]. Such have been highly gratifying to this deserving young gentleman, (an encouraging liberal landlord), and most pleasing to the feelings of of an aged widow mother and relatives.[67]

The warm welcome accorded to Hugh may have been attributable to the expectation that, in terms of running the estate, he offered a perceived improvement on his brother Andrew. Moreover, since this was only a visit rather than a final return, it posed less of a risk than the return of younger sons or brothers who came back permanently and whose resettlement was undoubtedly more likely to cause discontent and spark friction.

While there are few surviving descriptions of the emigrant's return there are other references in emigrant correspondence to visits being made across the Atlantic in the decades before the Great Famine. A letter of 1827 mentions the possibility of a Robert Campbell, from Savannah, Georgia, tagging on a visit to Ireland to a business trip to London.[68] Another reference in a letter of 1838 discussed the possibility of a James Montgomery being able to return to his family in County Antrim at the close of his European tour.[69] Visits like this were clearly no casual undertaking in the Age of Sail and may well have been additions to other business, but they were clearly not unknown.

A final area that should not be neglected in analysing migration patterns is the more personal world of romance, partnership and marriage. Emigrant letters, more than any other source, offer a striking reminder of the importance of factors particular to the individual in shaping migration behaviour. His old friend, John Campbell of Baltimore, Maryland, reported just one example of this to Robert Simms of Belfast in a letter of 1814. Alerting Simms to expect the return of Mr Thompson, a mutual acquantance who had also been in America, he reported that Thompson 'returns poor fellow, in part, to alleviate the distress he suffered for the loss of Mrs. Thompson'.[70] Marital friction, as much as bereavement, may also have contributed to a spouse heading back across the ocean. In 1833 a Tyrone emigrant in New York, George Anderson, informed his brother in Ireland that an old friend, referred to merely as James, had been 'in this city on his return to Ireland' but that Anderson had not been able to meet with him as 'he went off very suddenly when his wife came up'.[71]

That migration was an easier option for someone who was unmarried was a widely held opinion. James Horner, the emigrant who dismissed the prospect of return owing to business commitments in 1810, nonetheless left some hope for those at home by declaring that 'as long as I am a bachelor some hope may remain of my return'.[72] The other reluctant returnee, Robert Smith, suggested in a letter of 1844 that romance might yet draw him back to Ireland. He told his family 'if I receive an encouraging letter from my girl . . . I will pay Ireland a visit, I wish her to write immediately to encourage me in well doing but I have too high a spirit to be fooled'.[73] Confirmation of Ireland as a perceived 'hunting ground' for a suitable match emerges from the correspondence of one particular cluster of Ulster families who settled in the American south from the 1790s. In 1822 John Campbell, one of these emigrants, noted that 'Thomas Adams returns to Ireland to marry' while his own nephew, Harper Bryson, after working in his uncle's business, returned to Randalstown, County Antrim, in order to marry Ellinor Henry, daughter of the local Presbyterian minister.[74] From the same circle, John Bones, after the death of his first wife in 1833, returned to Ireland in order to marry his cousin, Mary Brown.[75] That such matches were not altogether unusual is suggested by the fact that more than a dozen pre-1845 newspaper notices of marriages in Ireland involving one partner from the New World can be located in the Irish Emigration Database at the Centre for Migration Studies.[76]

The most passionate and romantic correspondent, who had emigrated from Ulster to South Carolina and was also acquainted with John Campbell, was the young Joseph Carswell. While thriving materially in his new surroundings, Carswell had clearly left his one true love behind in Ireland. In January 1822 he wrote back pleadingly to Margaret Sinclair, resident somewhere in County Down.

> I should have prepared to have went home immediately after receiving this letter from you had it been more explicit, but I will not go on an uncertainty as no other inducement could be held out to make me go but you – if you will write to me immediately on receiving this and tell me in plain words you will give me your hand and heart . . . that will induce me to visit Ireland and nothing else.[77]

A somewhat 'cat and mouse' correspondence continued into the following year. The eventual outcome of the romance is unknown, but the manifest of the ship *Hannibal* sailing from Liverpool to New York in September 1827 includes the name of a 26-year-old Joseph Carswell, prompting speculation that, having returned to Ireland to pursue his love, he was spurned and turned his face westward once again.[78]

Conclusion

This chapter has explored a neglected area of Irish migration studies, namely the phenomenon of return migration to Ireland in the two and a half centuries prior to the Great Famine. It has not been possible to offer any statistical estimation of the rate of return but this is not surprising given the imprecision of estimated figures for Irish emigration for much of the period. What is clear, however, from reviewing the evidence is that from an early stage in the formation of the Irish diaspora the reversal of emigration and the consideration of the option of more or less permanent return were established features of migrant mentality and behaviour.

Professor Wyman has highlighted the sporadic evidence which suggests that return migration was a feature of European settlement in the New World from at least the seventeenth century. Meaningful comparison between patterns of return migration by emigrants from Ireland and other European ethnic groups during the Age of Sail must await further research in relation to the latter phenomenon. In comparing patterns of migration from pre-Famine and post-Famine Ireland, the emphasis seems to be on continuity rather than contrast. While technological changes such as the advent of the railway and the switch to steamships on the Atlantic route undoubtedly had some impact upon migrant psychology and practice, it is difficult to detect dramatic change in relation to the movement from Ireland to America. A relatively small, if growing, proportion of emigrants continued, after the 1860s, to return to Ireland. This raises a broad, but central, question. Were post-Famine emigrants less different from those who had gone before, in important respects, than has traditionally been assumed?

It is therefore vital that studies of return movement should be more fully incorporated into work on the history of Irish emigration. Analysis of those who came back to Ireland and those who recognized and weighed up that option opens another window upon emigration, settlement, assimilation and Irish society itself. The behaviour of any individual emigrant or emigrant stream can best be understood through the consideration of the entire migration profile. The exploration of previous internal migration, later onward migration and return migration can provide an enriching and revealing context through which to understand and interpret the whole emigrant experience.

Notes

1 B. O'Dowda, *The World of Percy French* (Dundonald: Blackstaff, 1981); *The Best of Percy French* (EMI, 1980).
2 M. Wyman, *Round-Trip to America: The Immigrants Return to Europe, 1880–1930* (Ithaca NY: Cornell University Press, 1993); M. Hart, 'Heading for Paddy's Green Shamrock Shore: The Return Emigrants in Nineteenth Century Ireland', unpublished MA thesis (University of Groningen, 1981); J. Eccles Wight, 'It is a Lonesome Thing to be away from Ireland always', *Irish Roots* (1998), 1, 12–13; D. Fitzpatrick, 'Emigration, 1801–1870' in W.E. Vaughan (ed.), *A New History of Ireland* (Oxford: Clarendon Press, 1989), 566–7; D. Fitzpatrick, 'Emigration, 1871–1921' in W.E. Vaughan (ed.), *A New History of Ireland* (Oxford: Clarendon Press, 1996), 633–7; K.A. Miller, *Emigrants and Exiles: Ireland and the Irish Exodus to North America* (Oxford: Oxford University Press, 1985), 426–8.
3 L.M. Cullen, 'The Irish Diaspora of the Seventeenth and Eighteenth Centuries' in N. Canny (ed.) *Europeans on the Move: Studies on European Migration, 1500–1800* (Oxford: Clarendon Press, 1994), 139; N. Canny, 'English Migration into and across the Atlantic during the Seventeenth and Eighteenth Centuries' in Canny, *Europeans on the Move*, 62–3; R.A. Houston, *The Population History of Britain and Ireland, 1500–1750* (Basingstoke: Macmillan, 1992), 62.
4 L.M. Cullen, 'The Irish Diaspora of the Seventeenth and Eighteenth Centuries', 139.
5 On aspects of seventeenth century military migration see G. Henry, *The Irish Military Community in Spanish Flanders, 1586–1621* (Blackrock: Irish Academic Press, 1992); R.A. Stradling, *The Spanish Monarchy and Irish Mercenaries: The Wild Geese in Spain, 1618–68* (Blackrock: Irish Academic Press, 1994); J. McGurk, 'Wild Geese: The Irish in European Armies' in P. O'Sullivan (ed.), *The Irish World Wide: History, Heritage, Identity I, Patterns of Migration* (Leicester: Leicester University Press, 1992), 36–62; H. Murtagh, 'Irish Soldiers Abroad, 1600–1800' in T. Bartlett and K. Jeffery (eds), *A Military History of Ireland* (Cambridge: Cambridge University Press, 1996), 294–315.
6 T. O'Connor (ed.), *The Irish in Europe, 1580–1815* (Dublin: Four Courts Press, 2001).
7 Luke Quirke to John Kearney, 29 August 1696, reproduced as No. 418 in B. Jennings (ed.), *The Louvain Papers, 1606–1827* (Dublin: Stationery Office, for the Irish Manuscripts Commission, 1968).
8 Interview with Professor Tom Bartlett, BBC Television programme 'Study Ireland: The Battle of the Boyne', broadcast BBC NI, 18 February 1992.
9 K.A. Miller, *Emigrants and Exiles*.
10 K. Lindley, 'The Impact of the 1641 Rebellion upon England and Wales, 1641–1645', *Irish Historical Studies* 70 (1972), 143–76; J. Young, 'The Scottish Response to the Siege of Londonderry, 1689–1690' in W. Kelly (ed.), *The Sieges of Derry* (Dublin: Four Courts Press, 2001), 53–74; P. Fitzgerald, 'Like Crickets to the Crevice of a Brew-house: Poor Irish Migrants in England, 1560–1640' in O'Sullivan, *Patterns of Migration*, 13–35.

11 A. Games, *Migration and the Origins of the English Atlantic World* (Cambridge MA: Harvard University Press, 1999), 203–4; D. Cressy, *Coming Over: Migration and Communication between England and New England in the Seventeenth Century* (Cambridge: Cambridge University Press, 1987).

12 J. Horn, 'British Diaspora: Emigration from Britain, 1680–1815' in P.J. Marshall (ed.), *The Oxford History of The British Empire: The Eighteenth Century* (Oxford: Oxford University Press, 1998), 28–52; P. Griffin, *The People with no Name: Ireland's Ulster Scots, America's Scots Irish, and the Creation of a British Atlantic World, 1689–1764* (Princeton NJ: Princeton University Press, 2001), 1.

13 J.G. Leyburn, *The Scotch-Irish: A Social History* (Chapel Hill NC: University of North Carolina Press, 1962), 272.

14 The vast majority of these letters have been transcribed from originals held in the major collection of emigrant correspondence archived at the Public Record Office of Northern Ireland (PRONI). Keyword access allows these letters to be searched on the basis of terms likely to be associated with return migration.

15 On the patterns of servant and paying passenger migration see M.S. Wokeck, *Trade in Strangers: The Beginnings of Mass Migration to North America* (University Park PA: Pennsylvania State University Press, 1999). On the evolution and implications of the 'Ulster custom' see M.W. Dowling, *Tenant Right and Agrarian Society in Ulster, 1600–1870* (Dublin: Irish Academic Press, 1999).

16 D.N. Doyle, 'Scots Irish or Scotch Irish' in M. Glazier (ed.), *The Encyclopedia of the Irish in America* (Notre Dame IN: University of Notre Dame Press, 1999), 842–51.

17 This source has been consulted on the Irish Emigration Database at the Centre for Migration Studies, Ulster-American Folk Park, Omagh, hereafter cited as IED and followed in brackets by the original source; IED 1200267 (PRONI T3700/1A).

18 *Ibid.*

19 *Ibid.*

20 T.M. Truxes, *Irish-American Trade, 1660–1783* (Cambridge: Cambridge University Press, 1988), 106–26.

21 Truxes, *Irish-American Trade*, passim; J. Bardon, *Belfast: An Illustrated History* (Dundonald: Blackstaff Press, 1982), 34–5, 54–5; W.A. Maguire, *Up in Arms: The 1798 Rebellion in Ireland* (Belfast: Ulster Museum, 1998), 54–5. Truxes has also produced an edited volume of the letter book of Greg & Cunningham: T.M. Truxes (ed.), *Letterbook of Greg & Cunningham, 1756–1757* (Oxford: Oxford University Press, 2001).

22 P.G. Johnson, *James Patton and the Appalachian Colonists* (Verona VT: McClure Press, 1973); R.J. Dickson, *Ulster Emigration to Colonial America, 1718–1785* (Belfast: Routledge, 1966), 54, 128, 134–52, 163–7.

23 IED 9612193 (PRONI D1044/313).

24 G.W. Grubb, *The Grubbs of Tipperary* (Cork: Mercier, 1972), 41–9.

25 P. Fitzgerald, 'A Sentence to Sail: The Transportation of Irish Convicts and Vagrants to Colonial America in the Eighteenth Century' in P. Fitzgerald and S. Ickringill (eds), *Atlantic Crossroads: Historical Connections between Scotland, Ulster and North America* (Newtownards: Colourpoint, 2001), 114–32.

26 P.W. Coldham, *Emigrants in Chains: A Social History of Forced Emigration to the Americas, 1607–1776* (Stroud: Sutton, 1992), 140–1.

27 *Hibernian Journal*, 26 October 1789 10, 14 January 1791.

28 *Ibid.*, 20 April 1789.

29 Wyman, *Round-Trip to America*, 206.

30 J. Mannion, 'Vessels, Masters and Seafaring: Patterns of Voyages in Waterford Commerce, 1766–1771' in W. Nolan and T.P. Power (eds), *Waterford: History and Society* (Dublin: Geography Publications, 1992), 373–402.

31 T.P. Power (ed.), *The Irish in Atlantic Canada, 1780–1900* (Fredericton NB: New Ireland Press, 1991); J. Mannion, *Irish Settlements in Eastern Canada: A Study of Cultural Transfer and Adaption* (Toronto: University of Toronto Press, 1974); M. McCarthy, *The Irish in Newfoundland, 1600–1900* (St John's, Nfld: Creative Publishers, 1999).

[49]

32 C. O'Gráda, *Ireland: A New Economic History, 1780–1939* (Oxford: Oxford University Press, 1994), 233–5.
33 S. Conway, *The British Isles and the War of American Independence* (Oxford: Oxford University Press, 2000), 189.
34 J. Kelly, 'The Resumption of Emigration from Ireland after the American War of Independence, 1783–1787', *Studia Hibernica*, 26 (1992), 61–88.
35 N. Kissane (ed.), *Treasures from the National Library of Ireland* (Drogheda: Boyne Valley Honey Co., 1994), 44–5.
36 Quoted in M. Rogers, *Prospect of Tyrone* (Enniskillen: Watergate Press, 1988), 106; PRONI D/623/A/38/159.
37 C.A. Hanna, *The Scotch-Irish, or The Scot in North Britain, North Ireland, and North America* (2 vols, New York and London: Putnam, 1902); M. Glasgow, *The Scotch-Irish in Northern Ireland and in the American Colonies* (New York: Putnam, 1936); H.J. Ford, *The Scotch-Irish in America* (Princeton NJ: Princeton University Press, 1915).
38 M.B. Norton, *The British-Americans: The Loyalist Exiles in England, 1774–1789* (London: Constable, 1974).
39 Information supplied by Bill and Jean McCullough, Gettysburg PA, at CMS UAFP on 20 March 2001.
40 IED 9601197 (PRONI D 729/20); IED 9605183 (PRONI D 729/22).
41 IED 960425 (PRONI D 729/22).
42 IED 9604082 (PRONI D 729/22).
43 IED 9601203 (PRONI D 729/19).
44 IED 8810079 (PRONI T 1592/8).
45 IED 9006140 (PRONI T 1592/14).
46 IED 9006137 (PRONI T 1592/15).
47 *Ibid.*
48 *Ibid.*
49 IED 9006135 (PRONI T 1592/18).
50 D.A. Wilson, *United Irishmen, United States: Immigrant Radicals in the Early Republic* (Dublin: Four Courts Press, 1998).
51 *Ibid.*, 58–60.
52 IED 8609107 (PRONI T 1815/8).
53 *Ibid.* Chambers' reference would seem to relate to the replacement of Lord Grenville's Whig-Dominated coalition, the so-called 'Ministry of all the Talents', by the Duke of Portland's Tory administration in March 1807.
54 IED 8905060 (PRONI T710/6).
55 Wyman, *Round-Trip to America*, 9.
56 IED 9406161 (PRONI T 2125/7/2).
57 *Ibid.* Fuller discussion of return migration at this time can be found in E. Godfrey, 'Some Aspects of Irish Emigration to North America, 1815–1820', MSSc, dissertation (Centre for Migration Studies, Queen's University of Belfast, 1999).
58 IED 8903169 (PRONI T 2332/1).
59 IED 9409344 (PRONI D 1828/14).
60 *Ibid.*
61 IED 9501016 (PRONI D 1828/15).
62 IED 9504032 (PRONI D 1828/18).
63 IED 9503130 (PRONI D 1828/25).
64 IED 9403029 (PRONI D 1859/5).
65 IED 9309119 (PRONI T 3682).
66 IED 9601082 (PRONI D 593/46).
67 *Londonderry Journal*, 22 December 1835. For a fuller discussion of this episode see B.K. Lambkin, 'The Return of Hugh Campbell in 1635 from the United States to Ulster and the Issue of Linguistic Diversity', *Journal of Scotch-Irish Studies* 1:1, (2000), 61–71.
68 IED 9310447 (PRONI T 3597/11).
69 IED 9501031 (PRONI D 1828/8).

70 IED 8809112 (PRONI T 1815/13).
71 IED 9409340 (PRONI T 1664/1/2).
72 IED 9006135 (PRONI T 1592/18).
73 IED 9503130 (PRONI D 1828/25).
74 IED 9310021 (PRONI T 3597/6).
75 IED 9904149 (PRONI D 1558/1/1/6).
76 Irish Emigration Database, Centre for Migration Studies, Ulster-American Folk Par, Omagh. Based on a search of Chapter BDM, Births, Deaths and Marriages.
77 IED 9805355 (PRONI D 3305/4/1).
78 IED 8815109 (PRONI Mic. 333/4/2).

PART II

Motives of return migrants

The following part of the book, which explores the motives of returners, ranges from the seventeenth century to the present day, and incorporates the British Isles, Scandinavia and Australia. The individuals who 'returned' from Scandinavia to Scotland in the seventeenth century were, Steve Murdoch points out, not Scottish-born, but were drawn to their parents' homeland out of curiosity, duty or the pursuit of gain. Two centuries later, those who came home from colonial Australia, at least until the gold discoveries of the 1850s, had to overcome the psychological as well as the physical barrier of distance to a much greater extent than transatlantic sojourners. Eric Richards traces the wide variety of strategies adopted by these largely invisible and unquantifiable people to justify their real or imaginary returns, but notes that the haemorrhage was not sufficiently large to cause serious consternation in Australian government circles. Although 40 per cent of immigrants to Australia returned between 1870 and 1914, migration histories continue to ignore their experiences in favour of a focus on the stayers and survivors, both in that period and later. Of more than a million British people who emigrated to Australia after the Second World War, over a quarter later returned home. The stories of some of those who came back between 1947 and 1972 are evaluated by Alistair Thomson, through a series of written life stories and recorded oral histories that echo the sentiments of Richards' nineteenth-century returners, and also challenge the accepted stereotypes of settlement, assimilation and multiculturalism. Paul Basu's analysis of the implications of the Scottish diaspora for roots tourism, particularly in the Highlands, revisits in a modern context some of the issues discussed in Murdoch's seventeenth-century study. He explores how the burgeoning interest in genealogical research has led to a steady influx into Scotland of North American, antipodean and other visitors in search of their roots, and he investigates the perception of Scotland as 'homeland' by people who – no matter how distant the connection – often consider themselves to be exiles on pilgrimage, rather than tourists on holiday.

The discussion of returners' motives demonstrates, as do many of the other contributions, that personal needs and family obligations often loomed large in the migrants' decisions to return. In all eras and locations, migrants came home to assuage homesickness, find a spouse, recover their health, care for aging parents, or take over a family business. The Scottish land speculator and author Adam Fergusson recalled a meeting with a homesick emigrant during his travels in Canada in 1831.

> We met this forenoon one of those soft ones who raise an outcry against Canada, as they would do against any other country rather than their CALF one. Having enquired the distance to Martin's Tavern, the man's answer betrayed his native land to be our own. I asked him how he liked Canada? He replied 'Middling, Sir: no sae weel as hame.' 'Have you kept your health?' – 'Never a day's sick since I came out'. – 'Have you a farm of your own, or good employment?' – 'I have two brothers in farms of their own and I have constant work, and good wages.' 'What is your objections, then, to the country?' 'Deed, I dinna ken' but I just like hame better.'[1]

Note

1 Adam Fergusson, *Practical Notes made during a Tour of Canada and a Portion of the United States in MDCCCXXXI* (2nd edn, Edinburgh: Blackwood, 1834), 419. Thanks to Dr Terry McDonald for this reference.

CHAPTER FOUR

Children of the diaspora:
the 'homecoming' of the second-generation
Scot in the seventeenth century

Steve Murdoch

Defining the ethnicity of foreign-born Scots

At the start of the seventeenth century, the population of Scotland
was estimated to be 1.2 million.[1] By its close, it is possible to make a
conservative estimate that some 150,000 Scots had left the country
either as merchants, artisans, soldiers, political or religious refugees
or had been exiled for some other reason. Between 10,000 and 20,000
had gone to Ireland by 1652, with another, larger wave in the 1690s,
perhaps as many as 40,000.[2] While populations seeking land opportunities were attracted to Ireland, Scottish trade centred on Denmark–
Norway, Sweden, and the Polish–Lithuanian Commonwealth. Where
Scottish trade flourished, Scottish communities soon emerged and
Norway in particular sustained numerous Scottish communities
around Stavanger and Bergen.[3] The Scots also emigrated and spread
into the Baltic towns at a phenomenal rate, and their presence in
Poland–Lithuania in the seventeenth century has been shown to have
been both large and influential.[4] Indeed, by 1620 there are several contemporary estimates indicating the presence of around 30,000 Scots
within the Polish–Lithuanian Commonwealth.[5] Many of these individuals formed themselves into brotherhoods and societies designed to
ensure that the Scottish community upheld a solidarity with members
of their own nation.[6] They also frequently concealed numbers of illegal
Scottish migrants who traded in the towns. This bolstered the size of
the Scottish communities and enlarged the population of the cities to
an estimated number of around 40,000 by 1650.[7] Added to the numbers
of Scottish civilians in Scandinavia were up to 50,000 Scottish soldiers
who participated in the anti-Habsburg armies, especially those of
Sweden and Denmark–Norway, during the Thirty Years' War
(1618–48).[8] Many of these men took their families and servants with
them, considerably increasing the numbers of Scots in the region –

albeit many of them went straight to Germany rather than Scandinavia directly.[9] The Scots were indeed a mobile nation and even in the seventeenth century were as likely to be found operating in China as they were in Europe, if not yet in the numbers of their Baltic-bound countrymen. By way of two examples, William Cunningham of Veere worked for the Dutch East India Company (VOC) in Cambodia, Java and Malaysia in the 1620s.[10] A man of the same surname, Dr James Cunningham, FRS (d. 1709), served as a surgeon to the Honourable East India Company from 1698 to 1709 in various locations from China to Borneo.[11]

Many of the Scots who took part in these migrations eventually returned to Scotland, and indeed some of them are described elsewhere in this volume.[1] In a volume dedicated to the theme of 'return migration', the place of the foreign-born Scot coming to Scotland is actually something of an anomaly. This is because, strictly speaking, such individuals were not actually 'returning' from anywhere, as they had never left Scotland in the first place. However, it is clear from the evidence they have left us that many of them saw their travel to the British Isles as a return to either their spiritual or their ancestral home. Even many of those who never set foot in the country viewed Scotland in this way. Mattias Forbes, for instance, was the son of Ernald Forbes of Mecklenburg and no member of his family had been born in Scotland since his great-grandfather Jacob Forbes of Corsindale in the early sixteenth century. Nonetheless, Mattias served in Scottish regiments in Swedish service such as that of Samuel Cockburn in 1618.[13] More important, when Forbes was ennobled in Sweden along with his brother Arvid in 1638, he obtained a genealogy from Aberdeen dated 12 June 1634 which was signed by twenty-five members of the Forbes family.[14] If nothing else this highlights the degree to which the members of Scottish families remained in contact during this period. Another member of the same family and equally far removed was Johannes Alexander Forbes. He was a fifth-generation Scot who studied in Uppsala in 1644 and thereafter joined the army with the rank of ensign in Hugh Hamilton's infantry regiment. He thereafter became a lieutenant with the Lifeguard and reached the rank of lieutenant-colonel in Johnstoun's Viborg regiment.[15] Despite being so many generations removed from Scotland, he petitioned Charles II regarding his service in the Swedish army, probably seeking a commission within the exiled Stuart's forces.[16]

It is unlikely that either Mattias or Johannes Forbes considered himself a Scot, but they clearly retained a strong Scottish connection – enough indeed for one of them to write unsolicited to a Scottish king. However, the whole issue of who was and who was not a Scot is a highly subjective point, and one on which there is no consensus among historians. The Russian historian, Dr Dimitri Fedosov, includes Ivan Famiston in his book of Scots in Russia because he moved to Russia in 1681 and was the great-grandson of one Tobias Thomson, a Scot in Poland.[17] Does this one great-grandparent make Famiston a Scot? After all, he may have had seven great-grandparents who were not Scots. In trying to determine the identity of those we study, we must also ask if there is really much difference between an individual, born of Scottish parents in Scotland, but who left Scotland at the age of one, and another individual born abroad but whose parents migrated only six months or a year before he was born? It is probably safest to conclude that no strict criteria can be applied when trying to determine an individual's nationality. Take, for instance, the example of two young men, Brett and Connor Strachan. Both individuals were born in Iserlohn in Germany. Their father, Bruce Strachan, served as a noncommissioned officer in a British regiment and was himself born in Bückeberg in Germany, the son of another Scottish soldier, Sergeant Lindsay Strachan and his wife Elaine. So what nationality should we ascribe to these men – Scottish or German? The answer in this case is Scottish. We know that for a fact because Bruce was the best man at my wedding and Brett and Connor are my godsons. Bruce may have been born and lived most of his life outwith Scotland but, as he points out, he was raised in the very Scottish community of the Black Watch regiment. Research into the Scottish military community in the seventeenth century appears to show that the retention of Scottish identity displayed within the Strachan family replicates similar patterns found in the early modern period.[18]

Perhaps issues relating to our understanding of seventeenth-century Scottish identity abroad do not matter, since often the Scots, even those born abroad, were often distinguished as foreigners by the indigenous population of the countries in which they lived.[19] Indeed, historians of many countries continue the practice to this day owing to the different ways each nation has of classifying national identity. For example, Dimitri Fedosov talks about the Scot, James Daniel Bruce, as the highest-ranking foreigner in Russian service, despite the fact that Bruce was born and bred in Russia.[20] Fedosov, among others, has been careful to highlight that an individual could not become naturalized in Russia without embracing Orthodoxy, which led to differing rates of integration, depending on the individual or strength of belief among family members. Bruce's family were Lutheran and he could therefore not fully integrate into Russian society despite being born there. Alexander Leslie of Auchintoul, on the other hand, simply converted, which made the assimilation process both quicker and easier.[21] It was not just in Russia that Scots remained outwith their host community.

Hence in Poland in 1651 we find Scots and Englishmen being forced to pay a tax for Charles II of Great Britain despite one Alexander Dickson complaining that 'I was born here: I have lived in Cracow for fifty-seven years, and continue to live here'.[22]

In some parts of the Scottish diaspora, the Scots retained such a strong sense of their own community that contemporary observers viewed people of Scottish stock simply as Scots regardless of where they were born, or how many generations out of Scotland they may have been. In a description of the Danish island of Laaland in November 1627, Robert Monro mentioned that the island 'is plentiful of wood for building of ships, where his majesty every yeare hath some built by his owne master builder, a worthy gentleman begotten of Scots ancestors, called Mr. Sinclaire, who speaks the Scottish tongue, and is very courteous to all his countrymen which come thither'.[23] Clearly Sinclair's Norwegian birth did not form a barrier in Monro's mind to his being part of the Scottish nation. Similar forms of identification occurred elsewhere. In Swedish church records we find reference to Anna Hansdotter, probably Swedish born and wife of the Scottish merchant Blasius Dundie, as 'en gammal skottzk Hustru' (an old Scottish wife) after her funeral.[24] This retention of identity in the foreign-born Scottish community led to comments from men like Colonel James Turner about one 'Johnstone a Scot, but born in Ireland'.[25] Johnstone's place of birth was an interesting aside to Turner, but in terms of nationality his foreign birth did not detract from his identification as a Scot. Similarly, when Patrick Ruthven wrote an account of the war in Germany in 1633 he noted the actions of Jacob Macdougall 'ane Scottis man bot borne heir'.[26] Jacob (ennobled posthumously as Baron Duwall in Sweden) had been born in Altmark in 1589, the son of Albert Macdougall of Mackerston, and was clearly regarded as a Scot by Ruthven and other contemporaries.[27] Other foreign-born Scots went out of their way to reaffirm their Scottish nationality by registering themselves as native Scots under the Great Seal of Scotland, a route taken in 1634 by the Dutch born Scots, Thomas Cunningham of Veere (a brother or half-brother of William Cunningham noted above) and James Weir.[28] Even when the formality of registering as native Scots had not taken place, some of the foreign-born generations identified themselves in other ways with kith and kin in Scotland. In September 1681 the Earl of Mar received a letter from one Alexander Erskine, eldest son of a Scot who had settled in Sweden and served in the German and Polish wars.[29] The soldier in question was in fact the German-born Scot, Alexander von Erskine, one of the Swedish signatories to the Treaty of Westphalia in 1648, and later made a Swedish baron.[30] The purpose of his son's letter was to send respects to the Earl of Mar and to reiterate that the Swedish

Erskines claimed the earl as the head of their family despite their own noble status!

Reasons for return

This chapter discusses a number of case studies of individuals born out-with Scotland but who, for various reasons, returned to the British Isles either temporarily or on a permanent basis. These fall into a few general classes, each of which will be dealt with in turn. Return migration has a number of push and pull factors discussed in detail in all the chapters of this book. Without some general appreciation of the way these factors affected native-born Scots during the seventeenth century, any attempt to interpret the arrival in Britain of the foreign-born Scot would be harder to understand. In many cases the migrant simply could not settle in a foreign environment, or felt that to remain there any longer would be detrimental either to himself or to his family. In May 1634 the main Stuart ambassador for Scandinavia and Germany, Sir Robert Anstruther, wrote to Sir Henry Vane requesting permission to return home after thirty years and more abroad during which time he had been kept apart from several families, his wife and his children.[31] He further complained that owing to his extended time in Europe his estate had become 'weak' and he was personally in debt both at home and abroad.[32] In Anstruther's case, homesickness combined with other pressing personal issues to make him push for his return to Britain. Charles I had other ideas and kept him on the Continent until 1638, when Anstruther resigned his position in order to go home.[33]

The devastating rates of attrition in seventeenth-century warfare often made the trip to the Continent a one-way voyage. The permanent nature of their migration did not go unnoticed by the soldiering class and many took steps to secure the interests before departure. One soldier wrote in his will:

> Be it kend till all men herefter that me Colonell Harrie Lindsay foras-meikle as I am . . . willing to depart firth of this realm of Scotland to Germanie or else farther afield abroad thair to attend my charge upon the wares and . . . considering that thair is nothing more certaine than death given the dissposition of this fraill and mortale bodie and that there is nothing more uncertaine than the hour and tyme thairoff I have thoucht it expedient [to write this] for disposing of my bodie and dispertion of my goods for peace and tranquilitie amongst my friends . . . [34]

However, many of those who survived a specific period of the Thirty Years' War were decommissioned from the combatant armies, leading to their return to Scotland. Hence in 1629, Christian IV of Denmark–Norway released the Scottish regiments to return to Scotland in a combination of Danish and Scottish merchant vessels.[35] Several thousand Scots were forced to return from the wars abroad as invalids and some of their able-bodied counterparts took leave to return to Scotland temporarily so that they could establish hospitals for their well-being, albeit recruiting replacements for them was also a motive.[36] After completing both missions, Monro returned to the war in Germany, where he remained until 1639, when he once more returned to Scotland, that time as a regimental commander in the Army of the National Covenant of Scotland.

Monro's return in 1639 was symptomatic of a much larger return migration. Indeed, many hundreds, if not more Scottish troops came home from Swedish service between 1639 and 1641 in order to create the Army of the National Covenant.[37] Many of these Scots viewed Sweden as their home and, indeed, agreed to return to Scotland only to sort out the 'problems' between the Covenanting leadership and Charles I before going home to Sweden to continue their service there.[38] Their return to Scotland, for many after absences of up to thirty years, was supposed to be only an interlude to their Swedish service, although events in Britain and Ireland made certain that many never saw Sweden again. What this return migration did show was that despite having settled in a new country, many were prepared to risk their new-found status and security to risk all in what they believed was the defence of their native land. As discussed in more detail below, even their children were prepared to risk all in the defence of one or other of the contesting parties in the numerous British and Irish wars of the seventeenth century.

Many more migrants returned home because their native land could offer them something quite specific that they just could not get in their new country. One return migrant who had always longed to visit his homeland was Charles I. When James VI was about to make a return visit to Scotland in 1617, Prince Charles begged to go with him, stating 'let me see the country where I was born and the customs of it'.[39] As an exile since the age of 4, he clearly had a longing to get to know his native country better. When he did return, in 1633, it was to be crowned King of Scots. He simply could not do that in England and had to go home to Scotland to be crowned. When he again returned in 1641 it was as part of the peace arrangements at the end of the Bishops' Wars and again he had little choice in the matter. Charles I, of course, was a Scot by birth and strictly falls outwith the scope of this chapter. His nephew, however, Prince Elector Palatine Charles Louis – son of Frederik V of the Palatinate and Elizabeth Stuart, Queen of Bohemia – provides a good example of a return migrant of the second-generation Scot.

On 14 August 1641, Charles I and Charles Louis sat together in the Scottish Parliament.[40] While Charles was there to cement his peace agreement with the Scottish Covenanters, Charles Louis also had an agenda that stretched beyond a casual interest in his mother's native country. What he wanted was the support of the Scottish Parliament and army in the restoration of his royal dignity in the German Reich. Indeed his visit to Scotland brought him the promise of 10,000 soldiers to be levied by the Scots, albeit that events in Britain and Ireland prevented them from actually leaving.[41] Had Charles Louis not needed military and financial assistance, it is doubtful if he would have visited Scotland. Indeed, his visit is symptomatic of a whole slew of second-generation Scots who arrived in Britain with an agenda seeking to gain something either for themselves personally or for the country of their birth. Like Charles Louis, the commodity so often sought by the foreign-born Scot was Scottish military expertise.

In search of something?

James Spens Jr was the first son of the Fife-born man James Spens of 'Wormeston and Orreholmen' and his wife Agnes Durie.[42] It is not known when or where he was born, but he certainly served in the Swedish army. He had two brothers, David and William, and three sisters, Cecillia, Isabella and one other. He also had two half-brothers, Axel and Jacob, both of whom similarly served in the Swedish army. James travelled to Britain with his brother William in 1623 and received authorization throughout 1623–24 from the Scottish Privy Council to recruit and arm 1,200 Scottish soldiers for Swedish service.[43] William Spens and his comrade, Captain James Ramsay (a native-born Scot), focused on England where they received permission to recruit as many volunteers as would go with them to Sweden.[44] William thereafter returned to Sweden, where he became a lieutenant-colonel and member of the Swedish Parliament.[45] James Spens, however, remained in Britain for some time, and indeed it is not certain that he ever went back to Sweden. It was probably he, referred to only as 'the young Spens', who the Swedish Privy Council noted was covertly recruiting a regiment of Scots for Swedish service in October 1634.[46] The Spens brothers both came to Scotland, but while the official mission to recruit soldiers appears to have satisfied William's curiosity, James proved keener to remain in his parents' native country, albeit still apparently in the employ of his country of birth.

These men were not the only second-generation Scots to travel to Britain for military purposes. Bengt Belfrage was born in 1642, the son of John Belfrage, the mayor of Vannersborg, and a Swedish mother.[47]

After some study at Uppsala University in 1653, he entered military service in 1659 as an ensign in the Älvsborg regiment. Thereafter he studied the art of war abroad, and that is when he visited France, England and Scotland. He returned to Sweden in 1667 and rejoined his regiment, where he eventually became a lieutenant-colonel.[48] In this instance, all Belfrage wanted was military experience that he could not gain in Swedish service, as the country was at peace on all fronts after 1660. Undoubtedly he also used the opportunity to visit relations in Scotland. Indeed, his father John produced proof of his noble Scottish origins from the magistrates and Belfrage family of Culross in 1665, and was ennobled on 3 December 1666.[49] Knowing that his son visited Scotland at this time, it is tempting to suggest that Bengt secured the document for his father, although that is yet to be confirmed.

Baron Carl Magnus Stuart, the son of David Stuart of Farsta and Britta Nilsdotter Lillieram, was born in Sweden. After entering naval service in 1668 he travelled to Britain and became a musketeer in the king's guard.[50] It is not known if he came to Scotland, but the stint at the Stuart court was undoubtedly his way of forming a connection with his father's sovereign and distant kinsman. His enlistment was not exactly a selfless act however. He remained in London for two years, where he studied fortifications technology and planned the defence of the garrison town of Karlskrona before returning to Sweden to become a court gentleman, fortifications expert and lieutenant general in the Swedish army.[51] After serving against the Turks he was appointed tutor and gentleman of the chamber to the crown prince Charles XII in 1689 and eventually lieutenant-general of the infantry and director of fortifications.[52] Another soldier, this time from Russia, was James Daniel Bruce, the son of Colonel William Bruce of Clackmannan in Scotland.[53] He was born in Russia and served that country as a military general, statesman, diplomat and scholar. In 1686, Bruce became a cornett and went on the first of his military expeditions, eventually becoming a friend of Peter the Great. In 1698 Bruce studied in Britain owing to Russia's weakness in modern artillery. While in Britain, he visited the Greenwich Observatory, the Woolwich Arsenal and the mint at the Tower of London and indeed he became Russia's earliest Newtonian.[54] On his return from Britain, Bruce commanded and reformed the artillery in the Great Northern War as Master of Ordinance, eventually retiring with the rank of field-marshal in 1726. Bruce took pride in his Scottish ancestry and frequently corresponded with his kinsmen and countrymen. It is interesting to note that the Russian historian Fedosov talks of Bruce serving his 'adopted country' when referring to Russia, rather than his country of birth, indicating that Scotland must have been regarded as his mother country by Bruce throughout his life.[55]

If Stuart and Bruce were sent to Britain for a particular purpose, they were not the only ones. Johan, Jacob and Bengt Skytte were the sons of the Swede Johan Skytte and the Scot Mary Neaf, a daughter of Jacob Neaf – a soldier of Johan III of Sweden.[56] The Skytte brothers were born in Stockholm in 1612, 1613 and 1614 respectively. At the age of 10 Bengt matriculated at Uppsala University and five years later in 1629 he and the young Swedish nobleman Schering Rosenhane accompanied the Swedish ambassador, James Spens, to the Stuart court in London.[57] The practice of sending young noblemen on embassies was a common practice by the Swedes, and was designed to educate young men in a kind of diplomatic apprenticeship. During this visit, Bengt Skytte was knighted by Charles I and after returning to Sweden he became a gentleman of the bedchamber to Queen Christina.[58] Johan junior, now a colonel in the Swedish army, and Jacob made the journey to Britain with their father in 1635, and Jacob was knighted by Charles I.[59] More important, Johan junior also became a 'naturalised person of the said Kingdome of Scotland in respect that his decent on his mother's side is from there [. . . and . . .] naturalised as a native subject borne within the said kingdome'.[60] While all three men fared well from the journeys by being knighted and naturalized, they did have another, very specific reason for being in Britain. In September 1615, Johan Skytte corresponded with James Spens regarding the inheritance of land in Scotland in which his wife's father had had an interest.[61] Skytte accepted the fact that his father-in-law was not the nearest heir to the lands of Methie, but that Scottish claims that he was entitled to nothing were contradicted in a letter Skytte had from King Johan III. This shows that the inheritance wrangle had been ongoing since at least 1592 when Johan III died. Skytte also noted in the letter that:

> I am still consumed with the greatest desire to know who in fact were my said father-in-law's ancestors both on the paternal and maternal side in direct line of ancestry and where they lived, who and what they were, what rank they held, what coats of arms they had, see to it I pray you that you show all the more the readiness of your disposition in enquiring into these matters and thereafter in communicating them to me . . .[62]

Clearly Skytte had a vested interest in pursuing these associations as he obviously felt there might be something to gain from them. We know that when Johan sent his boys to London the hope of some kind of compensation for the lost inheritance had a role to play. Indeed, this hope was clearly expressed in Johan Skytte junior's naturalization document which stated that he could pursue all such claims, purchase any land and goods which he liked in Scotland, and on his death the rights would pass on to his successors.[63] With his death the following year, all these rights had indeed been transferred.

Despite the warm welcome from Charles I, neither surviving Skytte brother settled in Britain. Jacob returned within the year, became assessor and later regional governor in Linköping from 1645 till his death in 1654. Bengt went on to become regional governor in Uppsala in 1646 and later joined the Riksdag in 1648.[64] He also received promotion to become Governor of Estonia in 1655. Despite his high profile in Swedish public life, Bengt Skytte maintained his Scottish and British connections. In 1643 he was proposed as the new Swedish consul to reside in Edinburgh.[65] Undoubtedly his parentage and previous experience of Britain played an important part in his selection although it was another Scot, Hugh Mowatt, who eventually took the post.[66] Nonetheless, Bengt returned to London, where he resided as a private person in 1659.[67] His correspondence shows that he also gathered information on the rapidly changing politics of republican England and persuaded a few individuals to enlist in Swedish service.[68] He did not, however, remain in Britain long and left to pursue a career as a Swedish legate in Germany.[69]

The Skytte brothers were not alone in having problems claiming their inheritance in Britain. Thomas Livingstone was the son of George Livingstone and Margaret Bursie. Thomas was born in 1634 in Elbing while his father was on campaign with the Swedish army.[70] In adulthood, Thomas served in the Jönkoping regiment and was eventually ennobled in Sweden in 1668.[71] His career and promotions continued, and he became lieutenant-colonel of his regiment in 1678, a position he held until at least 1682, two years before his death. Livingstone married into the Swedish nobility when he wed Maria Stierna (1638–1719) and took the name of Hubbestad. Despite never having seen Scotland, Livingstone maintained an interest in the country. In 1667 his mother, Margaret Bursie, wrote a letter in Swedish to the Krigskollegium – War College – referring to her husband Captain George Livingstone and adding in a Scots hand 'god bles zour lordship may zour lordship pitey me'.[72] She also noted that Thomas Livingstone served in his father's company in Fleetwood's 'Engelske' regiment in Livland. A separate note attached to this letter recorded that in the year 1657 Thomas Livingston received a commission to transport parts of his regiment from England to Livland, suggesting he may have travelled to Britain by that date. The purpose of Margaret's correspondence appears to have been to get the War College to contemplate releasing Thomas from service temporarily to allow him to travel to Scotland to deal with some family business. Certainly at around the same time Thomas approached the regimental secretary, Maarten Jonsson, to establish if his position would be secure if he took leave.[73] Permission for eight months' leave of absence to travel to England and Scotland was granted on 24 May 1669. Although his military commitments prevented him from travelling that year, he reapplied in 1670 and made his journey to the land 'hvar mina föräldrar födda ähre' – where my parents were born.[74] In the same letter, Livingstone was explicit that his reason for making the journey was to sort out some private business and establish his rights in Scotland. On his return to Sweden it appears that Secretary Jonsson had reneged on his earlier pledge and Livingstone found himself in correspondence with the War College trying to get reinstated at his former rank in the regiment.[75] Details of the success of his British trip, unfortunately, remain elusive.

The Swedish ambassador in London, Christoffer Leijoncrona, received a request in 1694 from the British resident in Stockholm, Dr John Robinson, regarding the case of one Captain Beaton, a grandson of a Scottish emigrant, Hercules Beaton.[76] For over a year Captain Beaton had been trying to pursue the possibility of coming to Scotland to chase up an inheritance he believed he had there, as well as to establish his 'pedigree'. However, on being told that trying to recover his inheritance would be almost impossible, Beaton resolved to go to Scotland anyway in order to pursue his family connections. Rather than gain from his trip, Beaton knew it would cost him, but was also prepared to spend 100 crowns on the project anyway and hoped the ambassador could help him with introductions in Edinburgh.

We know for sure that some of the foreign-born Scots were successful in their claims. Robert Forbes was the son of Alexander, eleventh Lord Forbes, and his wife Elizabeth Forbes of Rires. Robert was born in Rotterdam while his father was on a diplomatic mission. On returning to Britain, Alexander Forbes found himself imprisoned for debt. He was released in 1649 and allowed to leave for Sweden with his family, where he remained for the duration of his life. In his will, made in 1672 only a few weeks before his death, Alexander left the barony of Tollies (Towie) in Aberdeenshire to his son Robert.[77] Having returned to Scotland to claim it, Robert died in Castle Forbes on 6 May 1678.[78]

'Scots' even more generations removed than Livingstone, Beaton and Forbes came to Scotland and were very explicit in their requests for financial aid, based on links of nationality. In 1731 a delegation arrived from the Lithuanian town of Kedainiai composed of a 'Scot', Reverend Jacub Gordon, and an 'Englishman', Jakub Grey. They presented a pamphlet entitled 'A Representation of the Distressed Case of the British Protestants of Kieydan in Lithania'.[79] The three-page pamphlet introduced the town as 'almost wholly consisting of English and Scotch, or Descendants of such who formerly settled there, and who still retain the same principles with Great Britain in Matters of Religion'.[80] Their mission was apparently successful, funding was made available to them and the Scottish and English community in Kedainiai was temporarily relieved of the burdens inflicted on them in the Great Northern War.

For the 'mother country'

Some of the foreign-born Scots who came to Britain intended to do some service for their parents' country. James Sinclair of Sinklarsholm was the eldest son of Andrew Sinclair of Ravenscraig and hailed from Denmark. James followed his father in serving both the House of Stuart and the House of Oldenburg. From an early age, James Sinclair was in the service of James VI and I in Britain.[81] During his absence from Denmark, Hendrik Gyldenstjerne was ordered by Christian IV of Denmark–Norway to look after Sinclair's affairs and ensure that he did not lose anything 'by being abroad'. However, despite having made Britain his home, Sinclair returned to Denmark to serve in the *hoffane*, or Royal Horse, in 1629 during the end of the Danish phase of the Thirty Years' War (1625–29). After Christian IV made peace with the emperor, Sinclair returned to Britain some time around 1630 on Christian IV's behalf, but also to collect his remaining wages due to him from the Stuart court. His purpose in returning was therefore both professional and private. Sinclair's wages were not paid promptly and he found himself retained for debt in London. In 1639 he petitioned the Privy Council of England about a slander made against the kings of Denmark, Sweden, France and Spain by one George Bland.[82] In particular he argued that, as a Danish subject, he was forced to take action against Bland's accusations. For his troubles Sinclair was locked up for a week, during which time he 'endured very much extremity far unworthy [of] a gentleman of his rank'.[83] He was eventually released from jail and from his debts about 1640 when Charles I, after repeated interventions by Christian IV, agreed to pay them. On his return to Scandinavia, Sinclair became a naval and military officer.[84] However, in 1649 he asked for a recommendation for a commission to serve in Charles II's army in Scotland, which Frederik III gave him on 10 September 1651, a week after the battle of Worcester.[85] After the defeat of Charles II's forces, service with the Stuarts was not feasible and so Sinclair travelled to Norway in 1652 where he joined the Trondheim regiment.[86] There he received a farm at Kurøn in Nordland from Frederik III.[87] Three times James Sinclair had returned to Britain (or tried to) and indeed, he had offered service for three different British monarchs despite enduring a significant amount of personal hardship to do so.

Other Scandinavian Scots also returned to serve in various armies that contested control of the British Isles during the seventeenth century. Lieutenant-colonel Jacob David Montgomery, a Swedish-born son of Lieutenant-colonel James Montgomery, already had fifteen years' experience in Swedish service when he ventured to Scotland to join the remnants of Charles I's royalist army. He evaded capture and eventually received a pass from the Marquess of Montrose to return to Swedish service in 1649.[88] Another royalist volunteer, Colonel James Maclean, came from Gothenburg and was the son of the merchant there, John Maclean, first Baronet Duart. His father had variously supported the Covenanters in Scotland in 1638–40 and also the 1649–50 Montrosian landing in Scotland.[89] James enlisted into the small army of Charles II based in the Spanish Netherlands in 1652 and remained in Stuart service until after the Restoration in 1660, although always in contact with the Swedish authorities.[90] By then, and with the rank of colonel, he made it to the British Isles where he eventually died in Ireland in 1663.[91] In the case of these two men, service for the Stuart monarchy of their parents' native country provided the motive for the return to Britain. However, such allegiance to the Stuarts was not automatic. We simply do not know where Captain William Scott was born, only that he entered the Danish–Norwegian army as an ensign in the Bergenhus regiment on 18 May 1659 and served until his death on 25 April 1706 after forty-seven years in Norwegian service.[92] There had been at least one break in that service however. On 2 June 1690 Scott sought leave to travel to Scotland, perhaps to sort out some private business or to enlist in the *hjælptropper* sent from Denmark–Norway to assist William of Orange in his British and Irish campaigns. He received leave to travel on 14 June, but returned the following year to receive promotion to captain which he claimed he was due after twenty-eight years of service. Once again, the exact motive for the return is unclear, but the timing suggests some relation to the arrival of the Orange regime in Britain. Not all foreign-born individuals served voluntarily in British forces. Michael Gabrielsson Spalding ended up in the Royal Navy after being press-ganged while visiting Britain. The future admiral of the Swedish navy was released only after intervention by the Swedish agents John Oriot and Christoffer Leijoncrona.[93]

There were many ways to help one's country in times of trouble, and not all of them were directly martial. The Dutch-born Scots Thomas Cunningham and James Weir were respectively elder and deacon in the Scottish Staple Kirk at Veere in the Dutch Republic in 1634. That year the session entrusted these men with the duty of returning to Scotland with a sum of money to help towards the release of some Kirkcaldy men held captive by the Turks.[94] Before handing over any money, they were instructed to determine if the ransom had already been raised, as the Veere Kirk did not want the money given over only to find it had been wasted. Clearly Scottish frugality continued down through the foreign-born generations. Thomas Cunningham also helped his country by supplying large quantities of arms for the armies of the Covenant and Solemn League and Covenant in the 1640s. He received a summons to return to Edinburgh in 1644, after which he was made Conservator of the Scottish Staple by an Act of the Scottish Parliament as well as Commissioner and Ordinary Scottish Agent for the Solemn League and Covenant.[95] However, lack of payment for his goods and services led to financial hardship for Cunningham and resulted in yet another return visit to Scotland.[96] During that visit, in July 1647, Cunningham was admitted burgess and gildbrother of Edinburgh and feted by the Covenanting military leadership.[97] The debt however remained unpaid and Cunningham travelled to London to try to prove to Oliver Cromwell that the debts of the Solemn League were wholly English and thus remove the burden of debt from Scotland. His sons, Thomas and Arnold, likewise became Conservators of the Scottish staple at Veere. Arnold, a third-generation Scot, certainly travelled to Britain on several occasions, and always to 'carry through to a settlement here all transactions with the Scotch nation'.[98]

The curious

Some individuals are born curious, others restless and some both. Christian Sinclair of Sinklarsholm (1607–45), was another son of Andrew Sinclair of Ravenscraig who was also born in Denmark like his brother James. After study at the Danish academy of Sorø in 1618, he left Denmark between 1622 and 1624 to study in Germany, after which he spent a year in the Netherlands. From 1626 to 1629 he studied in both Britain and France.[99] Sinclair's arrival in Britain then seems to have been more part of a general scheme designed to broaden his education than anything to do with an urge to visit Scotland. Indeed, given his future career as a secretary in the foreign chancery, it looks as though he was sent out to acquire language skills which, given Britain's alliance with Denmark–Norway at the time, would have necessitated a period of time in Britain.[100] Likewise, James Hunter (a.k.a. Jacob Petri Hunterus) came to Britain to study. He had been born in Uppland in Sweden at the end of the 1500s and was the son of the Scot, Peter Thomson Hunter (Honther) and Christina Johansdotter. After studying at Uppsala, Hunter travelled to Britain for further study at Oxford and Cambridge throughout 1620–21.[101] Hunter later studied in both the Netherlands and France where he understudied the Dutchmen Hugo Grotius and Lucas Holstenius. In 1627 he worked in Vienna and became the secretary in the Furstiga Hus or Imperial Electoral College. Ferdinand II dismissed him in 1630 owing to his Swedish birth –

a reaction to Gustav II Adolf's entry into the Thirty Years' War.[102] Hunter's career was facilitated by his education and grasp of languages, and his return to Britain was part of the general learning process of this particular scholar. It is a very similar path to that of Henry Hamilton from Copenhagen who variously studied in Germany, France, Spain, Italy and Britain before he eventually died in Egypt some time after 1623.[103] Johan Robert Stuart, a brother of Carl Magnus Stuart mentioned above, also chose to receive part of his education in Britain.[104]

Those who settled 'at home'

In addition to those who visited Britain with the intention of leaving again, some wished to settle in their ancestral lands. Colonel Gustavus Hamilton was the son of Ludovick Hamilton, Baron of Dalserf and Baron and Lord of Nabben and Anna Catherina Grubbe-Stjernfelt (1631–89). His father received his final dismissal permit from Swedish service in 1662 along with a travel pass to England, though he was either killed on his homeward journey or died before leaving Gothenburg. His mother made it to Ireland where she was styled Anna Catherine, Lady Hamilton of Tullykeltyre, County Fermanagh.[105] Gustavus Hamilton must have been back in Ireland by 1686, as his son Ludovick was born in Enniskillen that year. The colonel was also forfeited in 1689 and in response raised six regiments for William of Orange, two of which were Enniskilliners.[106] His brother Malcolm had also served in the Swedish army as a cornett, and joined his brother Gustavus's Enniskillen Regiment. Gustavus also served as governor of the city, but died by December of 1691.[107] Baron James Hamilton (1664–1726) was the son of Baron Malcolm Hamilton of Hageby and Christina Maclean, daughter of Baron John Maclean of Gothenburg. In 1683 he served as sergeant with the Älvsborg regiment and by 1691 he had been commissioned as an ensign and was still listed on Swedish muster rolls until 1696. However, perhaps owing to the familial links with Gustavus Hamilton, James chose to retire to Ireland where he settled until the end of his life.[108]

While the Hamiltons provide examples of the foreign-born community who came 'home' to settle by choice, there were other individuals who were forced to return. Perhaps the most numerous of these were the thousands of Scottish settlers driven from their homes during and after the 1641 uprising in Ireland. However, individuals from elsewhere were also forced to return. Karen Mowatt was the daughter of the Shetlander Andrew Mowatt of Hoveland. Karen's father ensured she received her education from a Scottish governess and she could apparently write better Scots than Norwegian. She married Eric Ottesen

Orning, who later became an admiral in the Danish–Norwegian navy, about 1616. The marriage was considered illegal in Norway as the couple were first cousins once removed. They spent eighteen years in Scotland before they were allowed back to Norway in 1627.[109] Their protracted stay in Scotland ultimately benefited the Mowatts' connections with Scotland. Christoffer Orning, Karen's son, frequently traded with Scottish merchants, and though he never settled, he visited the country often. During his several voyages there in the 1650s, Christoffer always carried with him greetings to and from Axel Mowatt's good friends in Scotland, associations that were undoubtedly strengthened through Karen's enforced stay in the country.[110]

Conclusion

This chapter has presented a number of case studies relating to the arrival in Britain of foreign-born Scots. Their reasons for returning are usually quite different from those of Scottish-born return migrants for a variety of reasons. It is unlikely that any of these people ever longed for their homeland in the same way as Robert Anstruther did. It is clear that, to many of them, their parents' homeland was a curious place that they felt they should probably see once in their lives. Hence the Swedish-born secretary to the Dutch Republic, Johan Porteous, appears to have used his official visit to England in 1689 to make contact with members of the Porteous family in Edinburgh, probably seeking confirmation of his origins.[111] The examples examined also show that the 'homeland' could also take on a wider geographic significance than simply Scotland, and could include trips to the British Stuart court in London and Scottish-held lands in Ireland, as well as visits to Scotland itself. They also reveal a highly mobile population which could see Scottish brothers, like the Cunninghams of Veere, working in Cambodia, Java, Scotland, England and the Netherlands, and yet their sojourns would not appear anomalous to the larger Scottish community.

The confines of source material might appear to place an emphasis on élite migration out of, and back to, Scotland. Seventeenth-century written records being what they are, there has been little chance to scrutinize the movements of children of the numerous 'ordinary' peddlers, artisans and others who poured out of Scotland in their thousands. However, the return of apparently high-status foreign-born Scots belies the fact that many of them were actually the children of non-élite emigrants. Many of their parents were of humble background and were ennobled, or raised in social status only owing thanks to their own endeavours abroad. For example, in Sweden it was usual for anyone who served in the army for twenty years and reached the rank of major to become ennobled or at least receive grants of land and many officers began their careers as enlisted men. Ennoblement was a feat achieved by over 100 Scots in the seventeenth century, resulting in many more 'noble' Scottish offspring. Even one cobbler, George Wright, a refugee from Cromwell's Scotland, became ennobled in Sweden.[112] It appears that some Scots, perhaps owing to a higher degree of education that many of their contemporaries at the time, were able to achieve high status in foreign service through their higher standards of literacy.[113] Indeed, some families used their talent to mislead others into thinking they were of noble family and clearly made up their genealogies and supplied forged documents to secure their noble status abroad.[114] The city and regal authorities in Scotland seem to have been quite aware of this practice and supplied documentation of noble birth where it was quite without foundation, and even to enemies of the Scottish Crown like Admiral Simon Stewart, once declared both rebel and pirate and later supplied with proof of his noble birth by Charles I.[115]

Whether of high status or not, for many foreign-born Scots a journey to Britain coincided with an aspiration to gain some advantage, for themselves, their family or their host country. In fact their return to Scotland often repeated the very aspirations that had led their parents away in the first place. For some, the object of the return to Scotland was security of status or wealth. This is exemplified by Thomas Cunningham and James Weir, who claimed Scottish citizenship in 1634 to protect their goods from marauding Flemish pirates, although both men did later demonstrate their loyalty to Scotland during the early Covenanting period. For many others, an education was the goal, either emulating James Hunter in his pursuit of academic knowledge, or of the same ilk as James Daniel Bruce and Carl Magnus Stuart in their pursuit of specific military abilities unobtainable in their respective countries of birth. Not a few were out to claim their inheritance and there were undoubtedly many more cases like those of the Skytte brothers and Thomas Livingstone. However, not all the second-generation migrants to Scotland possessed a selfish motive. Quite a few sought to settle back in their parents' homeland despite the advantages they gave up in their county of birth by doing so, men like the younger James Spens of Wormiston. Peaceful resettlement also led to the retirement to Ireland of Gustavus and James Hamilton, while there are probably hundreds of examples of Scandinavian or Baltic Scots, like Blasius Dundie junior, of whom we know little other than a fleeting reference in a journal saying 'probably left Sweden to live in Scotland'.[116] However, to some individuals there was something more than passive settlement. The examples of Jacob David Montgomery, James Maclean and William Scott highlight willingness to become involved in some cause or other pertaining to the British Isles. There were doubtless many more like them who, like James Sinclair of Sinklarsholm, returned to their ancestral homeland frequently, and for protracted periods of time – no matter how much it seemed to cost them to do so.

Notes

1 *Calendars of State Papers and Manuscripts relating to English Affairs, existing in the Archives and Collections of Venice and in other Libraries of Northern Italy* (38 vols, London: HMSO, 1864–1947), XV, 1617–19, 393; Antonio Foscarini's 'Relation of England', 19 December 1618. Foscarini put the population of England at about 3 million and that of Ireland at 500,000.

2 R. Mitchison, 'Ireland and Scotland: The Seventeenth-Century Legacies Compared' in T.M. Devine and D. Dickson (eds), *Ireland and Scotland, 1600–1850* (Edinburgh: John Donald, 1983), 7.

3 See A. Espelland, *Skottene i Hordaland og Rogaland fra aar 1500–1800* (Norheimsund: Hordaland Folkeblads trykkeri, 1921), 31; A.M. Wiesener, 'Axel Movat og hans slegt' in *Bergens Historiske Forening Skrifter* 36 (Bergen: Beyer, 1930), 98; F. Tennfjord, *Stamhuset Rosendal* (Oslo: Jacob Dybwads Forlag, 1944), 7–8; E. Vaage, *Kvinnherad* (Bergen: n.p., 1972), 206–13; A. Lillehammer, 'The Scottish–Norwegian Timber Trade in the Stavanger Area in the Sixteenth and Seventeenth Centuries' in T.C. Smout (ed.), *Scotland and Europe, 1200–1850* (Edinburgh: John Donald, 1986), 97–111.

4 A. F. Steuart (ed.), *Papers relating to the Scots in Poland, 1576–1793* (Edinburgh: Scottish History Society, 1915); Stanislaw Seliga and Leon Kocz, *Scotland and Poland: A Chapter of Forgotten History* (Glasgow: Sikorski Historical Institute, 1969); A. Biegańska, 'Scottish Merchants and Traders in Seventeenth and Eighteenth Century Warsaw', *Scottish Slavonic Review* 5 (autumn 1985), 19–34; A. Biegańska, 'A Note on the Scots in Poland, 1550–1800' in Smout, *Scotland and Europe*; A. Biegańska 'In Search of Tolerance: Scottish Catholics and Presbyterians in Poland', *Scottish Slavonic Review*, 17 (autumn 1991), 37–58.

5 There are at least two contemporary sources for this piece of information. See *Calendars of State Papers, Domestic* (hereafter *CSPD*), First Series, 1547–1625 (13 vols, London: HMSO, 1856–1992), 1619–23, 237, Chamberlain to Carleton, 24 March 1621; William Lithgow, *The Totall Discourse of the Rare Adventures and Painefull Peregrinations of long Nineteene Yeares Travayles from Scotland to the most famous Kingdomes in Europe, Asia and Affrica* (Glasgow: Maclehose, 1906), 368.

6 Seliga and Koczy, *Scotland and Poland*, 6.

7 Frost, 'Scottish Soldiers, Poland–Lithuania and the Thirty Years' War' in S. Murdoch (ed.), *Scotland and the Thirty Years' War, 1618–1648* (Leiden: Brill, 2001), 192; Anna Biegańska, 'A Note on the Scots in Poland, 1550–1800' in Smout, *Scotland and Europe*, 159.

8 For numbers of Scots in various armies see Murdoch, *Scotland and the Thirty Years' War*, introduction, 9–14.

9 A. Grosjean, *An Unofficial Alliance: Scotland and Sweden, 1569–1654* (Leiden: Brill, 2003), 74–111; M. Glozier 'Scots in the French and Dutch Armies during the Thirty Years' War' in Murdoch, *Scotland and the Thirty Years' War*, 131–7.

10 Arsip Nasional Indonesia. Microfilm 'Fiches Collecyie' Reel No. 29, [ANI MF 29C] Group C. William Cunningham.

11 *Dictionary of National Biography* (Oxford: Oxford University Press) V, 312–13; W.Ph. Coolhaas (ed.), *Generale missiven van gouverneurs-generaal en raden aan Heren XVII der Verenigde Oostindische Compagnie* (11 vols, 's-Gravenhage, 1960–97), VI, 1698–1713, 474, 528, 530, 569.

12 See in particular Chapter Eleven by Alexia Grosjean, below.

13 G. Elgenstierna, *Den Introducerade Svenska Adelns Ättartavlor, med tillägg och rättelser* [hereafter *SAÄ*] (9 vols, Stockholm, 1925–36), II, 788; Swedish Krigsarkiv

CHILDREN OF THE DIASPORA

(hereafter SKRA), Muster Roll, 1624/5; 1625/4; 1630/1, 21; 1631/9–11; 1632/8, 9; 1635/1; 1637/15.

14 A. and H. Tayler (eds), *The House of Forbes* (Bruceton Mills WV: Scotpress, 1987), 469–71.

15 SKRA, Muster Roll, 1642/9; 1645/1; 1646/1; 1648/25; 1649/16–18; 1655/6, 7.

16 *SAÄ*, II, 788.

17 D. Fedosov, *The Caledonian Connection* (Aberdeen: Centre for Scottish Studies, University of Aberdeen, 1996), 37.

18 Grosjean, *An Unofficial Alliance*, 138–62; Murdoch, *Scotland and the Thirty Years' War*, passim, but particularly M. Glozier, 'Scots in the French and Dutch armies during the Thirty Years' War', 131–7; see also M. Ailes, 'From British Mercenaries to Swedish Nobles: The Immigration of British soldiers to Sweden during the Seventeenth Century', unpublished PhD thesis (University of Minnesota, 1997).

19 See the numerous examples in the following: J.H. Burton, *The Scot Abroad* (2 vols, Edinburgh and London: Blackwood, 1864); Th.A. Fischer, *The Scots in Germany* (Edinburgh: Schulze, 1902); Th.A. Fischer, *The Scots in Eastern and Western Prussia* (Edinburgh: Schulze, 1903); Th.A. Fischer, *The Scots in Sweden* (Edinburgh: Schulze, 1907); A.F. Steuart, *Scottish Influences in Russian History, from the End of the Sixteenth to the beginning of the Nineteenth century* (Glasgow: Maclehose, 1913); T. Riis, *Should Auld Acquaintance be Forgot ... Scottish–Danish Relations c. 1450–1707* (2 vols, Odense: Odense University Press, 1988); Grosjean *An Unofficial Alliance*; S. Murdoch, *Britain, Denmark–Norway and the House of Stuart 1603–1660* (East Linton: Tuckwell Press, 2003).

20 D. Fedosov, 'The First Russian Bruces' in G.G. Simpson (ed.), *The Scottish Soldier Abroad* (Edinburgh: John Donald, 1992), 63.

21 S. Murdoch, 'The Database in Early Modern Scottish History: Scandinavia and Northern Europe, 1580–1707', *Northern Studies* 32 (1997), 85.

22 A.B. Pernal and R. Gasse, 'The 1651 Polish Subsidy to the Exiled Charles II', *Oxford Slavonic Papers*, 32 (1999), 15.

23 R. Monro, *Monro his Expedition with a worthy Scots Regiment (called Mac-Keyes Regiment)* (London: Jones, 1637) I, 42.

24 F.U.W., 'Blasius Dundie. Några anteckningar om en skotsk köpman i Stockholm under 15- och 1600 talen', *Personhistorisk Tidskrift* 3 (1901), 52.

25 Sir James Turner, *Memoirs of his own Life and Times* (Edinburgh: Bannatyne Club, 1829), 111.

26 National Archives of Scotland (hereafter NAS), GD 246/26/5 f. 21. Account of the German Warres, July 1633.

27 *SAÄ*, II, 356.

28 J.M. Thomson (ed.), *Register of the Great Seal of Scotland, AD 1634–1651*, IX (Edinburgh: HM General Register House, 1984), 95, Nos. 232 and 233; E.J. Courthope (ed.), *The Journal of Thomas Cuningham of Campvere, 1640–1654* (Edinburgh: Scottish History Society, 1928), xiii.

29 NAS, GD 124/15 f. 171. Erskine to Mar, 19 September 1681.

30 B. Schlegel and C.A. Klingspor, *Den med sköldebref förlänade men ej å riddarhuset introducerade svenska adelns ättartaflor* (Stockholm: Norstedt, 1875), 69.

31 Public Record Office (hereafter PRO), SP75/13, f. 198. Anstruther to Vane, 31 May 1634.

32 *Ibid.*

33 Murdoch, *Britain, Denmark–Norway and the House of Stuart*, 85.

34 National Library of Scotland (hereafter NLS), Saltoun papers Mss 17606, ff. 4–4a c. 1638–40.

35 *Kancelliets Brevbøger-vedrørende Danmarks indre forhold i uddrag* (13 vols, Copenhagen: I kommission hos C. A. Reitzel, 1925–69), 727; Missives to Neils Krag, 28 June 1629; R. Monro, *His Expedition with a worthy Scots Regiment* I, 85.

36 *Register of the Privy Council of Scotland* (hereafter RPCS), second series, V, 333–6. Robert Monro's information to the Privy Council 1634, and 352–6, Warrant under the Great Seal to Colonel Robert Monro to erect a hospital for soldiers disabled in

foreign wars, 2 August 1634; see also W. Brockington (ed.), *Monro, His Expedition with a worthy Scots Regiment called Mac-keys* (Westport CT: Praeger, 1999), xvi–xvii.

37 A. Grosjean, 'General Alexander Leslie, the Scottish Covenanters and the Riksråd debates, 1638–1640' in A. Macinnes, T. Riis and F. Pedersen (eds), *Ships, Guns and Bibles in the North Sea and Baltic States, c. 1350–c. 1700* (East Linton: Tuckwell Press, 2000), 115–38.

38 See for example the case of Field Marshal Alexander Leslie recorded in N.A. Kullberg et. al. (eds), *Svenska Riksrådets Protokoll, 1621–1658* (18 vols, Stockholm: n.p., 1878–1959) VII, 9 August 1638; Grosjean, 'General Alexander Leslie', 117.

39 Quoted in C. Carlton, *Charles I: The Personal Monarch* (London: Routledge, 1983), 17.

40 J.R. Young, 'The Scottish Parliament and European Diplomacy, 1641–1647: The Palatine, the Dutch Republic and Sweden' in Murdoch, *Scotland and the Thirty Years' War*, 78.

41 PRO, SP 81/52, f. 221. Extract of a Statement from the Scottish Parliament, 12 November 1641; *The Acts of the Parliaments of Scotland* (12 vols, London: HMSO, 1814–75) V, 650; J.R. Young, 'The Scottish Parliament and European Diplomacy 1641–1647: The Palatinate, the Dutch Republic and Sweden', in Murdoch, *Scotland and the Thirty Years' War*. 79–81.

42 *SAÄ*, VII, 429.

43 *RPCS*, XII, 1622–25, 478. 30 March 1624.

44 *Acts of the Privy Council of England, 1623–1625* (London: HMSO, 1933), 204.

45 SKRA, Muster Roll, 1625/3, 5, 6; 1626/3–9; 1629/22; 1631/22–7; *SAÄ*, VII, 429.

46 *Svenska Riksrådets Protokoll*, IV, 229. 7 October 1634.

47 *SAÄ*, I, 265–6.

48 SKRA, E. 50. 1. MR 1660, vol. 3, f. 301 Vastgöta Cavalry Regiment: MR 1667–96.

49 *SAÄ*, I, 265–6.

50 Fischer, *The Scots in Sweden*, supplement, 215–67.

51 H. Marryat, *One Year in Sweden, including a Visit to the Isle of Gotland* (London: John Murray, 1862), 481.

52 L. von Munthe, *Kungl. Fortifikationens Historia, 6: I, Biografiska anteckningar* (Stockholm: Norstedt, 1919), 515.

53 Fedosov, *The Caledonian Connection*, 13–14.

54 Fedosov, 'The First Russian Bruces', 55–66.

55 *Ibid.*, 63.

56 J. Berg and B. Lagercrantz, *Scots in Sweden* (Stockholm: Nordiska museet, 1962), 18. Mary is also known in some sources as Margaret.

57 Å. Davidsson, 'Ett memorial för en adlig ynglings englandresa på 1630 talet', *Personhistorisk Tidskrift* 51 (1953), 106; *SAÄ*, VII, 319–20.

58 *SAÄ*, VII, 319–20.

59 *Ibid.*

60 Swedish Riksarkiv (hereafter SRA), Deposito Skytteana A:5, E5412. Johan Skytte d.y. arkiv, vol. Ix. True copy of Charles I's naturalization document for Johan Skytte, signed by James Philip, 9 May 1635.

61 SRA, Anglica V, Skytte to Spens, 29 September 1615.

62 *Ibid.* Spens must have concluded his part of the bargain, for in 1634 Johan Skytte placed a stone on Jacob Neaf's grave that included eight Scottish coats of arms, although the right of Neaf to have used them is questionable. Berg and Lagercrantz, *Scots in Sweden*, 18. The shields are thought to be those of Neff Baron of Methie/Lord de Gray/Leslie Earl of Tothes/Lindsay Earl of Crawford/Wishart Baron of Pitarro/D. Lindsay/Lord Ogilvie/Ramsay, Lord of Auchterhouse.

63 SRA, Deposito Skytteana A:5, E5412. Johan Skytte d.y. arkiv, vol. Ix. True copy of Charles I's naturalization document for Johan Skytte, signed by James Philip, 9 May 1635.

64 Johan Kleberg (ed.), *Svenska ambetsverk 6, Kammarkollegium I, 1634–1718* (Norrköping and Stockholm: 1957), 51–2.

65 S. Tunberg *et al.* (eds), *Den Svenska utrikes förvaltningens historia* (Uppsala: Uppsala University Press, 1935), 77.
66 For more on Mowatt's mission see Grosjean, *An Unofficial Alliance*, 202–12; Young, 'The Scottish Parliament and European Diplomacy, 93–9.
67 *SAÄ*, VII, 319–20.
68 See various letters in SRA, Anglica II, Riksrådet Bengt Skyttes bref till Kongl. Majt. 1659.
69 SRA, Svenska Sändebuds till Utländske Hof och Deras Sändebud till Sverige, 1841, 78.
70 *SAÄ*, V, 53.
71 SKRA, MR Jönköping Regiment, 1662–82.
72 SKRA, Krigskollegium kansli inkommna handlingar brevböcker 1666, del 1, 1667:2 No. 1181. Margaret Bursie to Krigsråd, 5 May 1667. The 'yogh' in particular denotes a Scottish hand wrote this letter.
73 SKRA, Krigskollegium inkommna handlingar breefbok för åhr 1670 andre delen, No 4015. Livingstone to Krigskollegium, 9 December 1670.
74 *Ibid.*, No. 4013. Livingstone to Krigsråd, 31 March 1670.
75 *Ibid.*, No. 4015. Livingstone to Krigskollegium, 9 December 1670.
76 SRA, Anglica, vol. 191, section R. J. Robinson to C. Leijonrona, 11 December 1694.
77 NAS GD 52/1159, 'Testament of Alexander Lord Forbes', dated Stockholm, 6 April 1672.
78 Tayler and Tayler, *The House of Forbes*, 190.
79 S. Nishigawa, 'Across the Continent: The Protestant network between the Society for Promoting Christian Knowledge and Kedainiai' in *Kulturu Sankirtos* (Vilnius, 2000), 296–308. Thanks to Rimantas Zirgulis for providing me with a copy of this article.
80 Quoted in L. Eriksonas, 'The Lost Colony of Scots: Unravelling Overseas Connections in a Lithuanian Town' in Macinnes *et al.*, *Ships, Guns and Bibles*, 181–2.
81 Riis, *Should Auld Acquaintance* II, 75.
82 *CSPD*, 1639, 130. 7 May 1639.
83 *Ibid.*
84 Y. Nielsen and E.A. Thomle (eds), *Norske Rigsregistranter* (Christiania, 1887) X, 362, and 599–600; J.C.W. Hirsch and K. Hirsch (eds), 'Fortegnelse over Dansk og Norske officerer med flere fra 1648 til 1814' (12 vols, Copenhagen, unpublished Ms compiled 1888–1907) X, 399.
85 Riis, *Should Auld Acquaintance* II, 76.
86 O. Ovenstad, *Militærbiografier. Den Norske Hærs Officerer* (Oslo: Norsk slektshistorisk forening, 1948), 411.
87 Y. Nielsen and E.A. Thomle (eds), *Norske Rigsregistranter* (Christiania, 1890) XI, 90, 274.
88 *SAÄ*, V, 278.
89 *SAÄ*, V, 142.
90 SRA, Oxenstierna samlingen (1), skrivelser till Axel Oxenstierna, March 1652; SRA, Brev till Brahe (8), 1658.
91 J.N.M. Maclean, *The Macleans of Sweden* (Edinburgh: Ampersand, 1971), 27.
92 Hirsch and Hirsch, 'Fortegnelse over Dansk og Norske officerer' X, II, 175; Ovenstad, *Militærbiografier* II, 390–1.
93 SRA, Anglica, vol. 191, section O: J. Oriot to C. Leijoncrona, 5 December 1704.
94 Courthope, *The Journal of Thomas Cuningham of Campvere*, xviii.
95 Young, 'The Scottish Parliament and European Diplomacy', 88.
96 Courthope, *The Journal of Thomas Cuningham of Campvere*, xii.
97 *Ibid.*, xii.
98 *Ibid.*, xxiii.
99 Riis, *Should Auld Acquaintance* II, 75.
100 For more on the alliance see Murdoch, *Britain, Denmark–Norway and the House of Stuart*, passim.
101 *Svenska Män och Kvinnor* (8 vols, 1942–55) III, 559–60; see C. V. Jacobowsky, 'Svenska studenter i Oxford, c. 1620–1740', *Personhistorisk Tidskrift* 28 (1927), 108, 112;

SRA, Oxenstierna Samlingen (4), Skrivelser till Axel Oxenstierna July 1619–September 1620.

102 SRA, Brev till Ture Nilsson Bielke (7) 1626–28.
103 C.F. Bricka et al., Dansk biografisk leksikon (16 vols, 3rd edn, 1979–1984) V, 511; Riis, Should Auld Aquaintance II, 194–5.
104 Jacobowsky, 'Svenska studenter i Oxford, c. 1620–1740', 115.
105 Lieutenant Colonel George Hamilton, A History of the House of Hamilton (Edinburgh: n.p., 1933), 1014–15.
106 This man has previously been confused with Gustavus Hamilton, Viscount Boyne, who fought in the Williamite army at the same time. See J.S. Crone, A Concise Dictionary of Irish Biography (Dublin: Talbot Press, 1937), 87.
107 Hamilton, A History of the House of Hamilton, 1014–15
108 SKRA, Muster Roll, 1683/8, 17, 19; 1685/13; 1697/7; 1691/6; 1696/8, 9; Hamilton, A History of the House of Hamilton, 1104–5, 1083.
109 A.M. Wiensener, 'Axel Movat og Hans Slegt' in Bergens Historiske Forening Skrifter 36 (Bergen, 1930), 93; A. Espelland, Skottene. Hordaland og Rogaland fra aar 1500–1800 (Norheimsund: Hordaland Folkablads trykkeri, 1921), 31–2.
110 A. Næss, 'Skottehandelen på Sunnhordland', Sunnhordland Tidsskrift, VII (1920), 43; Wiesener, 'Axel Movat og Hans Slegt', 103.
111 His trip to 'England' is noted in J. Kleberg, Svenska ambetsverk 6, Kammarkollegium I, 1634–1718, 70. For his contact with George Porteous in Edinburgh see SRA, Anglica, vol. 191, section P: G. Porteous to C.Leijoncrona, Edinburgh, 31 April 1690. George Porteous sent some package to Johan Porteous, care of Leijoncrona, and rejoices doing all he can for the business involving one of the same name.
112 SAÄ, IX, 69.
113 This point remains speculative at the moment, but is a subject currently under investigation as part of the Migration and Mobility diaspora project at RIISS, University of Aberdeen.
114 This practice has led to quite vitriolic exchanges in Sweden between descendants of various noble families trying to expose the 'flaws' in the arguments of some of their fellow noblemen. For some examples see SRA, Riksarkivarien Ingvar Anderssons arkiv, del I, kartong 12. Robert Douglas's folder of evidence and articles compiled and collected by G.B. Montgomerie. See also Möller, 'Colquhon – Cahun – Gahn – Canonheilm: en boskillnad', Personhistorisk Tidskrift 64 (1966), 85–119. Despite Möller's devastating refutation of the Canonheilm geneology, the updated edition of SAÄ sticks to the corrupt version.
115 SAÄ, VII, 607. Charles I sent a letter regarding Stewart to Sweden, dated 27 September 1633, which included 'bevis om sitt skotska adelskap' – proof of his Scottish nobility. Charles I was well aware of Simon Stewart's banishment by his father, and also the fact that he was far from noble. However, it appears that in the interests of advancing one of his subjects, and perhaps ensuring that he never returned, Charles was prepared to bend the truth slightly.
116 F.U.W., 'Blasius Dundie', 52.

CHAPTER FIVE

Running home from Australia: intercontinental mobility and migrant expectations in the nineteenth century

Eric Richards

British and Australian traffic

In the summer of 1886 about 5 million people visited the Colonial and Indian Exhibition in London and 12,000 attended the official opening at the Albert Hall, graced by the Prince of Wales. Among them were large numbers of Australians who made their presence felt all around the metropolis. When they finally left to return to Australia, Melbourne *Punch* depicted Queen Victoria anxiously counting her spoons, and missing four. This Australian jest registered the much-increased familiarity of colonial Australia with the mother country and its cutlery.[1]

The traffic between the British Isles and Australia began in earnest with convict colonization in 1788, mainly in one direction but never exclusively so. Such is the fragmentary and bamboozling nature of the shipping records that the trends are rarely clear, even now. But we do know that in recent decades British migration has performed a somersault – not only has a substantial two-way migration emerged but the net flow has now been reversed. Now there is the spectacle of the 'British diaspora' in reverse gear.

There has been another remarkable turnabout. Since the mid-1980s the number of British people arriving in Australia far exceeds the Australians travelling to Britain, and the numbers are now much larger than any found in the classic Age of Migration. In 1999, for instance, and before the Sydney Olympics, 569,000 UK residents came to Australia, and 337,000 Australians arrived in the UK. Mostly they were visitors and tourists.[2] They are difficult to categorize but are part of the long history of two-way movement between these very distant places. This chapter concentrates on the nineteenth-century segment of the story, the time when the return movement became significant.

Emigration to colonial Australia

On the last day of 1879, Ettie Thurston was in mid-voyage, emigrating from England to Tasmania. She wrote to her family in Kent asking them to 'tell mother to keep herself as well as she can for four or five years and I will run over and see her'. She reported that she had met more than a dozen passengers on board who were 'returning to N.Z. or Australia. They think no more of it than London.'[3] In these words she captured three elements in emigrant history. One, of course, was the shrinkage of distance on this longest of all migrant routes. Another was the actual experience of going home but not staying. The third was the statistical tangle that such movements make in the measurement of emigrant flows.

Even if such passengers as the Thurstons had been recorded we would not know if they were first time emigrants, re-emigrants, holidaymakers, 'retro-migrants', 'repatriants', 'category jumpers', 'transients', 'transilients', 'double migrants', 'sojourners', 'pensionados', 'back-emigrants' or 'quasi-migrants'. They were part of the statistical awkward squad. Under whatever name, they constitute part of the 'dark figure' in international migration, accounting for much of the difference between gross and net migration. This is a problem by no means exclusive to the Australian story.

The history of Australian immigration has a number of distinctive features which bear upon the question of returning home – much of it to do with the tyranny said to have been exercised by its distance from the homelands in the British Isles. The people coming home were the least visible of migrants and, in the Australian context, the least probable. Australia was simply too far away; it was expensive to get there and, even more so to return home. When an emigrant left the British Isles for Sydney or Melbourne or Adelaide or Hobart, he or she was usually saying goodbye for good, embarking on a one-way journey. Most regarded the outward voyage in this way; it was part of their expectations. Moreover, the colonies wanted the emigrants on a permanent basis.[4]

In a nutshell[5] we can say that Australian immigration began in 1788 and was almost exclusively convict-supplied until the 1830s. At that point assisted immigration, paid for from colonial land revenues, began and continued through until the mid-twentieth century – countering the heavy expense of passage compared with the alternative destinations in the Atlantic and South Africa. Assistance rose and fell with each cycle of economic activity in Australia, high in the early 1840s and mid-1850s, the 1870s and before the First World War. Assisted immigration was highly selective and enabled the Australian colonies to plan a relatively well balanced and well educated population in the decades after 1840. A parallel flow of unassisted immigrants also arrived in Australia – people able to pay their own passages and often keen to buy assets, especially land. The breakthrough in attracting private emigrants was the expansion of pastoralism in the 1830s (many of whose practitioners were Scots) and most explosively in the Gold Rushes of the 1850s. Almost half the private emigrants of the entire nineteenth century arrived in the single decade of the 1850s.

The composition and proportions of these inflows are significant for the question of return migration. About 1.6 million people arrived in Australia, almost but not quite exclusively from the British Isles. One-tenth of them were convicts, most of these before 1841. Of the uncoerced, 46 per cent were assisted and mainly relatively low-income people; and just over half were self-financed. There were some interesting non-British components – a substantial number of Germans in mid-century; about 100,000 Chinese to the goldfields and 60,000 Pacific Islanders to the Queensland sugar industry after 1860.[6] But Australian immigration was an essentially homogeneous intake of people, overwhelmingly from the British Isles. Within this uniformity the Irish were very significantly overrepresented. Australia was a very Irish place, and a third of these people came from Ireland both as convicts and especially as the assisted, and were mainly Catholic in background.

We have a generic figure for English and Welsh return rates of migration from the calculations of Dudley Baines. He estimates that up to 40 per cent of all emigrants in the fifty years before the First World War returned home.[7] It is not clear what proportion of this number were returnees from Australia, though we know that Australia was taking about a fifth of all British emigrants during the pre-war decades.[8] If Australians returned at less than the average rate then this must inflate the proportions from other destinations.[9]

Several other factors made coming home from Australia less likely. The real and psychic distances between Europe and Australia were much greater than those between Europe and America, and it seems unlikely that many migrants before the First World War (with the possible exception of those involved in the Gold Rushes) would have regarded emigration to Australia as a temporary move.

Many of Australia's immigrants were modest folk recruited specifically as domestic servants and agricultural labourers; large numbers were from poor parts of Ireland and Scotland. They required heavy subsidies to get them to Australia in the first place and it seems unlikely that they would have prospered so quickly that they could afford a double passage. Poor people generally have least incentive to return home in terms of the differentials of income between home and colony. Australian living standards were as high as any in the world in the second half of the nineteenth century.

Emigrant prosperity probably worked in two contradictory ways on the strategies of the immigrants. Higher living standards diminished the desire to return, while simultaneously increasing the means of doing so. Wages and incomes were generally very high in Australia and the ships did not return empty. This may have been expressed in the increasingly frequent reports of Australian visitors returning to England for holidays in the years after 1860. Indeed, the rise of the passenger trade, and the floating hotels, as they were called,[10] suggests that at least some part of Australian affluence was expressed in the passage home, though it was likely to be for pleasure rather than permanent return.

Of all propositions in the history of return migration the most confidently held is that the Irish were the least likely of all migrants to go home. The fact that Australia had a very high rate of Irish immigration therefore also suggests a low rate of Australian return though this has never been tested against any evidence. We also know that the Australian colonies (and their successors) invested very heavily in their immigration programmes and would have been extremely sensitive to the idea of large-scale haemorrhaging by way of return migration. Had assisted immigrants leaked away in significant numbers the political repercussions should have been noisy, and return migration would have made an impact on the public mind. The only serious anxieties about the loss of migrants in the nineteenth century were related to intercolonial movements of recently arrived migrants within Australia, and during periods of remigration to New Zealand. There seems to have been little apprehension about the return home of immigrants from the British Isles. Return migration became a matter of serious political consternation only in the mid-twentieth century.[11]

How much homecoming from Australia?

In the early days of Australian immigration there were complaints that the vessels carrying emigrants experienced difficulty obtaining return cargoes in Australia. Thus in 1846–47 some of the ships sailed homewards in ballast; others had to travel to Asian ports to find paying cargo. But at other times there was a chronic shortage of cargo space on return voyages and much vocal complaint.[12]

W.A. Brodribb was a middlingly successful mid-century squatter in New South Wales and also a colonial MP. In March 1862 he made a return trip to England aboard the *Dover Castle* with his family, six children, a governess, her sister and a servant maid. Aboard ship Brodribb wrote a pamphlet about his experiences as a squatter and he also made some remarks about his fellow passengers, who numbered 250: 'The whole of these had done well in the colony; and, on inquiry, I found the second-class passengers were all well-off; and were going home, for the purpose of visiting their relatives and friends for a few months, and then returning to the colony.'[13] The general presumption is that returning home from Australia at that time was quite rare. Unhappily the actual record of movement was poorly recorded in the shipping lists of the nineteenth century and even during the twentieth century the trends remained indistinct. For nineteenth-century Australian migration, the return figure is not only 'dark' but also probably small. Yet the idea of returning home, either for or against, was rarely far from the mind of the emigrant, from the moment of expatriation to the time of death.

The most obvious place to look for evidence of return migration is in the official shipping statistics, in data relating to outward passenger movements. These data were indeed collected but, unfortunately, so far, they have proved scarcely usable. There was gross under-recording, as well as confusion and unclarity about the categories of travel which they encompass. People were leaving Australia for all manner of purposes: on business, for schooling,[14] for holidays, to visit relatives, to play cricket (Frederick Spofforth, the 'Demon Bowler', made seven trips to England in eight years and eventually settled in England),[15] to represent governments and institutions. Permanent return migration was contained within, and essentially obscured by, these other forms of intercontinental travel.

Rising colonial incomes and the improvement in transport facilities between Australia and Britain were elements in this increasing mobility. For instance, in April 1851 Dr George Witt (who had emigrated from Bedfordshire for the sake of his wife's health) wrote home from Sydney that 'People here think nothing of what they call running home; one man, it is said, went home to hear Jenny Lind, stayed in London a fortnight, and then returned to Sydney.'[16] In 1862 Archibald Stuart reported back to his native Scotland from Victoria that 'there is a great maney [sic] went home from hear [sic] to see the exhibition this year'.[17] David Atkinson had also hoped to return with his wife to see the International Exhibition, but his employer fell bankrupt -'so now I must stop a little longer', he explained to his mother in Yorkshire.[18]

There are, therefore, two great difficulties in the identification of Australian return migration in the nineteenth century. The first is the paucity of shipping lists; the second is the entanglement of return migration with every other class of outward passenger movement from Australia.

The official data are so dubious that colonial statisticians rejected the information altogether or made arbitrary corrections to the figures. Yet, amid this statistician's soup, there are some evident signs of increasing movement and of rising mobility. The most renowned colonial statistician, T.A. Coghlan, thought that about 1,000 people a year were leaving New South Wales to return to the United Kingdom in the mid-1860s, in a period of recession in the local economy. Informal passenger lists relating to Melbourne show larger movements into and out of the port in the years during and after the Gold Rushes. For example, there seems to have been a sudden rise in the number of people leaving Victoria after 1853. The newspaper data show that, in 1854, 3,043 people left Melbourne for foreign destinations, including 1,123 in steerage and a further 732 in intermediate or steerage. In the first half of 1855 no less than 3,443 passengers departed. The obvious swelling of numbers in 1854–55 may well represent a reaction after the Gold Rushes – perhaps the planned return home of some of the adventurers who came to the gold fields with little intention of settling.[19] A substantial proportion of the outward passengers travelled steerage – suggesting return by ordinary migrants unable or unwilling to pay for a better class of passage. This evidence does not show whether they were returning with gold or with empty pockets: there are plenty of cases of both in the literary records of the time.

The official returns for 'emigration' from the Australian colonies are riddled with problems and though the departures refer to the passengers as 'emigrants' there are no distinctions drawn between Australian-born and British, between permanent and temporary departures, nor between business and leisure categories. But the total numbers are extraordinary. Thus, for instance, a sampling of the Victorian data shows that in the 1860s so-called 'emigration' to the United Kingdom was running at an average of 4,568 per annum, falling in the 1870s and rising to about 6,850 per annum in the following two decades. Between 1901 and 1910 the number of arrivals in Victoria from the United Kingdom was only slightly greater than the departures.

Perhaps the most striking feature of the Victorian data is the sheer scale of the aggregate movements recorded in the official account. Thus, between 1852 and 1915, Victoria received about 808,000 'immigrants' from the United Kingdom; over the same period about 320,000 departed from Victoria in the guise of 'emigrants' to the United Kingdom. The meaning of these data is highly debatable. For the shipping trade, the implication is relatively straightforward – there was evidently a large and little studied passenger trade to the British Isles. But, for return migration, there are no clear conclusions, since we do not know the composition of the departures. Nor are we able to assume a standard or constant relationship between total outward movements and the degree of return migration. The dimensions of these two-way movements mean that there were far more people in Britain with first-hand experience of Australia than we would tend to assume; it means that the intra-Imperial dialogue was more intimate than we would expect.[20]

We also know that the census of 1911 showed that 23,000 Australian-born people were living in England and Wales, of whom, surprisingly, almost 60 per cent were female.[21] By the late 1880s 10,000 passengers a year were arriving in British ports from Australia. Increasingly they travelled in ocean liners which completed the great voyage in a mere four weeks.

Categories of Australian returnees

In colonial history the best documented parts of the population were located at the two ends of the social spectrum, the rich and the poor; in between the majority of the people are mainly anonymous, especially in the statistical sense.

Convicts

Some former convicts, the least privileged section of colonial life, apparently achieved a 10 per cent return-rate, though the average was probably close to 5 per cent.[22] Atkinson suggests that up to a third of the earliest convicts returned.[23] These estimates (the provenance of which is elusive) are surprisingly high. During most of the convict period, the passage to England was more expensive than it later became. Moreover, a quarter of the convicts were not allowed to return under the terms of their original sentences. Many of them, it is often claimed, made a positive choice not to return: 'most of them did not want to go home'.[24] One possible corollary is that the costs of return were not prohibitive, even for the least favoured echelons of Australian society.[25]

Plutocrats

At the other end of the society were the affluent, successful immigrants: some of them corresponded to an antipodean version of the nabob or plutocratic model of British emigration.[26] They were the people on the make, arriving in Australia with the transparent intention of making their pile and then returning home to live on the proceeds. Inglis reports that the returned colonist was a familiar figure in certain parts of London society, and a handful of them sought to embellish their career through the House of Commons. One of them, Henniker Heaton, became known as 'the member for Australia'.[27]

There were certainly many pastoralists, as well as colonial merchants and manufacturers, in this category and their propensity to return home may account for the relative scarcity of great country houses in some parts of Australia.[28] On the other hand some of them stayed on despite their original intentions and despite the fact that they prospered in the colonies; Australia turned out better than they had expected. The category of the 'affluent immigrant' also accommodates the professional elements, especially a surprising number of doctors who emigrated to Australia, often in the grip of a rural myth, intending to set up as country gentlemen in a newer and better version of English landed society.

There are many examples of the double flows of capital in the careers of these returned migrants. For instance, John McIntyre had studied divinity and arts at Edinburgh University but had not graduated. He was an authentic pioneer in South Australia, beginning as an overseer and then emerging as manager to Robert and Edward Leake, founders of the Glencoe Station. McIntyre subsequently made money speculating in land and left the colony after only fifteen years in 1860. He took with him 'a pretty large fortune' of £20,000. Only by chance does his story survive: he never returned to South Australia and left no relatives in the colony. He settled at the spa village of Bridge of Allan in central Scotland and also bought several estates in Argyll where he started sheep farming. He died in 1882, unmarried and wealthy. Sometimes colonial visitors came upon former colonists in their British retirement. When Henry Hussey visited England in 1854, he discovered an old friend who had been prominent in the early business life of Adelaide and had retired to 'a pretty country place in Essex', Coggeshall. Another had 'had enough of colonial life and intended to spend the rest of her days in Old England' in Derby.[29]

A primitive indicator of return migration of this class can be derived from a comparison between immigrants' places of birth and their final resting-places: the prosopography of death holds considerable promise. In his two volumes of *The Pastoral Pioneers of South Australia*,[30] Rodney Cockburn examined the most successful and celebrated of the early monied immigrants to the new colony. Of the 250 or so pastoralists, it is clear that between 5 per cent and 10 per cent retired to Britain and died there. They lived off their colonial winnings and investments in their retirement in Britain.[31] Some returned to their original birthplace, like Malcolm Gillies, who died in North Uist; at least one spent most of his final years in London's 'club-land'; others seem to have returned to Britain on the death of a wife or a close relative. A few continued to return again to South Australia on visits. Some of these early returned pastoralists sent their children to Britain for schooling and university: one of them put three sons through Edinburgh University. As Kingston says, 'Education in a British university was still the making of Australian gentlemen.'[32]

A similar exercise on the volumes of the *Australian Dictionary of Biography* yields comparable (and equally tentative) results.[33] Thus, in the third volume (1851–90), there are 1,540 people listed as having been born in the British Isles, of whom 204 (13 per cent) also died in Britain; and at least forty-two of these died at, or close to, their place of birth. Many of them ended their days in well known and favoured places of retreat such as Tunbridge Wells, Bournemouth, Margate, Brighton, Bath, Eastbourne, Rothesay and the Isle of Wight – a pattern which fits the 'nabob model' with comfort.[34] The repatriation of this interesting segment of the 'anglo-colonial' population creates a number of accounting problems, as W.D. Rubinstein recognizes in his studies of wealth generation in the colonies.[35] Were these British or Australian fortunes?

Some of the return migration was more accurately 'retirement migration': some successful colonists returned home to splash their success about in the most conspicuous fashion. Scottish cases would include Alexander Matheson from the China trade and even Andrew Carnegie, buying up Hebridean islands and old castles or building new ones in remote romantic places. There were parallel antipodean versions, Australians buying fine mansions, or renting mansions, in London.[36] Others were more refined and modest – slipping into those comfortable niches for the successful Victorian retiree in Leamington or Torquay, or Bognor Regis, or Aberystwyth, or Strathpeffer, or Helensburgh, or Blackrock or Dunloaghre. They returned to the centre of empire as the final demonstration of the excellence of their imperial credentials and, of course, to die at home, as part of their own personal apotheoses of empire.

K.S. Inglis studied some of the 'going home mentality' among these returning Australians in the late nineteenth century. It was captured in the claim made in 1892 that 'All good Australians hope to go to England when they die. Not only does everybody, now-a-days, go "home" when able to do so, but many stay there.'[37]

Assisted and unassisted migrants

Assisted migrants to Australia, generally speaking, expected to emigrate for good: they had neither the funds, nor the anticipation of future income, to indulge the expectation of returning to the original homeland. But the low anticipation of return may be juxtaposed with the many cases quoted later in this chapter in which quite ordinarily successful immigrants (and not only those of the Gold Rushes[38]) could and did return to Britain.

The unassisted were more likely to possess the resources to return; they were also less likely to tolerate the rigours of colonial life. The self-financed were more likely to emigrate with their options open and were more likely to write home about their state of mind. Their general command of capital gave them a flying start in colonial life and they were able to gain high returns in various parts of the Australian economy. This offered some consolation for the discomforts of colonial conditions and would have been within the original expectations of the middling emigrant. But this was a broad category and included, for instance, 'scions' of good families who were sent out 'on spec', possibly to get them out of the hair of their long-suffering families or as a kind of familial investment, hoping that the son would make a fortune and return to be the pride of the family. Anthony Trollope sent out his son Fred to become a squatter. Dickens sent out two of his sons, one of whom fell into debt but was prevented by his father from returning home and who eventually succeeded in New South Wales. There were many other sons of famous families in Australia; some returned; others, like Fred Trollope, stayed despite the many difficulties he encountered in the colony.

Migrant strategies

Individual migrant mentalities are best captured in their letters and memoirs. Most of them at some point wrestled with the problem of 'home'; many of them declared their intentions as they departed the home country and some of them spent much of the rest of their lives reconsidering the prospect of 'home', weighing the pros and cons of return. Most immigrants contemplated their future in terms of staying or returning or, with the passage of time, moving on to somewhere else in Australia or abroad. They had adopted a mentality of mobility. Their interior dialogue required them to compare the past, the present and the future circumstances of their lives; and this also meant that they were endlessly conjuring with their thoughts of home. The particulars of these individual immigrants suggest broad trajectories in the wide variety of migrant experience. The remainder of this chapter is devoted to this exercise in categorization.

Failed emigrants

In the annals of immigration there appears a tragic category of which little was spoken. Immigrant failure must include those who neither stayed nor returned but, instead, took their own lives. It is evident that, though rarely referred to in contemporary material (being another 'dark figure' in colonial social history), a small minority of people were driven to suicide by the trauma of emigration, some of them *en route*, others on arrival.

Sarah Brunskill, for example, spoke of one such tragedy in South Australia in 1839. She reported that a labourer who came out 'with a Mr Taylor [had] on landing shot himself'.[39] The voyage of the *Hercules* from the West Highlands in 1852–53 was racked by storm and disease – a woman threw herself from the ship even before it left the Irish Sea. There was also evidence of suicide among other Highland immigrants when they arrived in Robe in South Australia to be greeted by extreme heat and unemployment, which sapped their morale and produced the greatest distress.[40] Suicide represented an alternative to staying or returning and we have little idea of the numbers in this category.

Another group may have felt suicidal but nevertheless lived on. There was a 'substantial minority of immigrants for whom the journey to Australia was a personal disaster'. Some returned, but others were trapped by their own failure, and 'remained unhappy exiles to the end of their lives'. Thomas Dobeson and his wife were in this category. Dobeson recorded their mental distress: 'My wife tells me plain out that she wishes we were back home again.'[41]

The Gold Rushes brought to Australia many single male immigrants in similar circumstances. Francis Whitgreave had been sponsored to the Gold Rushes by his parents in Walsall in Staffordshire. But he soon gave it up as hopeless: only one in 500 of the diggers, he claimed, was at all successful. He himself had been sick and had decided to return home:

> I quite gave it up as a bad job and thought it was best not to lose what little I had got ... I shall be able to bring home the same quantity of money almost as it cost you to send me out ... I detest the colony so much that I would rather be working at anything in England than remain here even as an independent man.

He was comprehensively negative about the colony, but his family speculation had at least broken even.[42]

Henry Parkes, the illustrious Premier of New South Wales, had arrived in 1839 and reported soon after that 'I have yet to see one single individual who came out with me in the *Strathfieldsaye* but most heartily wishes himself back home.' Yet within a few months they were mainly very well settled.[43]

Categories of 'exile' should also accommodate the stock literary/colonial figure, the 'remittance man': the ne'er-do-well son of a well-to-do family at home, sent to the colonies with a regular remittance from home, provided on the condition that the prodigal stayed away. Such a figure helped to give easy confirmation to colonial prejudices about the British and was useful to novelists such as Henry Kingsley and Rolf Boldrewood. Banjo Patterson was memorably rude about English jackeroos who always wanted to 'slip across to England'.[44]

Repatriated emigrants

Some immigrants pleaded to go home, and some were indeed sent back at their own request, others with no option.[45] There were surprising cases in which colonial governments were prepared not only to pay for the passage of migrants to Australia, but also to return them to Britain within a short time of their arrival. In August 1852, Thomas Kidd, a 28-year-old agricultural labourer from Forfarshire, arrived in Port Adelaide together with his wife and four children. Kidd took employment as a policeman but in December was suddenly struck down with apoplexy and died in the Royal Adelaide Hospital. Mrs Kidd and her family were assisted by the Destitute Asylum. Six months later the colony had decided to pay most of the cost of returning them to England, with an extra £5 to enable them to reach Scotland. This was a case of government-assisted return migration, prompted ostensibly by humanitarian motives.[46]

A special recruitment scheme which brought domestic servants to South Australia in the years just before the First World War also produced a small catalogue of human casualties which caused the government to pay return passages. The returnees included women who were discovered to be mentally disabled on arrival – though presumably they had been regarded as acceptable before they departed. They may have been damaged in transit. The return of domestic servants from South Australia was usually on grounds of illness or emotional disturbance. For instance, three of them were found to be suffering from epilepsy (possibly induced by the journey itself) and were returned to England; similarly, a married woman who had taken to drink was sent home to her husband.[47] Another was Mary Ethel Palmer, a 34-year-old domestic and needleworker from Forest Hill in London, who was described by the Immigration Agent as being 'simple-minded' and one who would 'never be able to earn her own living – we are fond of her'. She was sent back to England on the SS *Benalla* in December 1913 at the cost of £12 16s. Her subsequent fate is unknown.[48] Another immigrant, Hetty Watson, was sent back home on the same ship eighteen months later: she had got into bad company and was 'weak and easily led', having fallen into the habit of drinking and smoking. She was described as 'a menace to society whilst she remains here and there is a possibility of reforming her if sent to her own people in England'.[49] Alice Fraser arrived in December 1911 and was found to be epileptic.

She had wilfully misled the government on her medical form. She was sent back to England in May 1912 – it being known that she had no money and would require the rail fare to Carlisle from the Agent General when she arrived in London.[50]

There were also cases of women being returned at their own request and at least partially paid for by the government. The mental instability of some of the single women was one of the greatest anxieties of the immigration officials, who may have feared that they would become a permanent burden on the public purse. Nevertheless the paid repatriation of persons who had already been paid to emigrate to Australia indicates a stronger vein of humanity and sensitivity than is commonly associated with immigration authorities.

Circulating labour

At the turn of the century, immigration officers were surprised to discover that some of the domestic servants recruited for assisted passages were remarkably widely travelled, veritable globetrotters in their normally restricted trade. In March 1914 the 'Lady Assistant' in Adelaide complained of the unsettled behaviour of a recently arrived domestic helper, remarking that the woman had already emigrated to Canada, South Africa and another Australian state. She asked, 'Why do we get girls who have travelled all over the world?'[51] Janice Gothard (writing of the period 1860–1920) has remarked that 'a surprising number of those who returned to Britain made the journey out again at some other colony's expense'.[52] Some emigrants were evidently so familiar with the emigration systems that they could work the regulations and the subsidies to their particular advantage. Domestics, at the bottom of the labour market, were surprisingly mobile.

At a much higher level of the labour market was Stanley Jevons, a young chemistry student from London University who left difficult family circumstances in Liverpool as an emigrant in 1854. He was appointed an assayer in the Sydney Mint at the age of 18 on the remarkable salary of £500 per annum. He stayed for five years, during which time he also completed his education informally – in writing, climatology, statistics and social survey. He conducted a survey of social conditions in Sydney which has since attracted serious historical interest. He then returned to Liverpool, eventually to become the most influential economist of his generation. He was the technician as emigrant, and the return emigrant. Indeed, his stretch in New South Wales set him up for independence in England, eventually to become the prominent political economist. He was a carrier of what Michael Roe calls the 'moral enlightenment'. He returned to England in 1859.[53]

Double migrants

Until the Australian shipping lists have been fully computerized, it will be difficult to gauge the proportion of double migrants in the systems. Two cases may be cited which at least demonstrate the feasibility of proletarian return. One is William Clayton, who managed to extract two assisted passages for himself and his family from the South Australian immigration authorities. Clayton was born in Manchester in 1833 and began his long working career as an errand boy at the age of 7, graduating through various trades until he married a mill girl in 1855. They managed to secure an assisted passage to South Australia, during which Mrs Clayton gave birth to twins. In the colony Clayton continued his varied career, swinging between near destitution and modest comfort. In 1864 he and his family of five decided to return to England. A much anticipated family reunion in Selby was a monumental mistake and seems to have provoked the decision to seek a second passage to Australia, duly achieved in 1866. The immigration office, acceding to the application, warned that it could never be repeated. Clayton continued his restless itinerant ways in the colonies but never again returned to England and died in 1933.[54]

Return migration was taken to extremes in the case of Ewan Gillies, one of the extraordinary group of people who emigrated from the remote Hebridean island of St Kilda to Port Phillip in 1853. Gillies and his wife survived the voyage, though they lost their young child. After his first job in the brickfields at Brighton, Gillies was sacked for indolence, whereupon he set off for the goldfields. He there accumulated enough income to buy a farm on which he struggled and finally failed. Within two years he returned to Melbourne where he left his wife and two children while he went to New Zealand, again in pursuit of gold. He was away for eighteen months and during his absence his wife, assuming she had seen the last of him, remarried. When Gillies returned, he found himself rejected and consequently departed again, this time for California. He joined the Union army in the Civil War, but in 1861 deserted and joined the renewed Gold Rush to California. He now made a fortune and, according to the story, returned to Australia, where he reclaimed his children. Then he returned to St Kilda but, though he found a new wife, was not well received by the islanders. Within a few months Gillies and his family returned to Australia. The new bride did not take to Australia and they decided, after a stay of only eight months, to go back to St Kilda. Yet again Gillies found himself unable to get along with his island kinsfolk and in 1889 he finally departed, this time for Canada, where he finished his days.[55] Known in St Kilda as 'California Gillies', his was an extreme example of the post-migration mobility which seemed to infect so many immigrants to

Australia. His peripatetic career amounted to at least ten migrations and is the migration statistician's perfect nightmare.

Sometimes return migration was undoubtedly a mark of failure, a confession of colonial disappointment. But return migration was often ambiguous in its meanings and it could also manifest itself as an expression of the sheer triumph of mobility.

Psychological transitions

Any gallery of emigrant types should accommodate both the mobile and the immobile. The dialogue of these people with their relatives in the British Isles almost always conveyed implicit comparisons between the new world and the old, as well as a measure of the resolution to return or to stay.[56] Rosina and William Ferguson, from Annan in Dumfriesshire, clung to the notion of returning home year after year, but never left South Australia. They emigrated in the year after their marriage in 1836 and Rosina bore a child on the journey to Port Adelaide. In a letter written aboard the *Buffalo*, Rosina mainly envisaged seeing her parents in their next existence. She remarked that 'although we are parted we have all the promised blessing of Meeting at a throne of Grace where we never more will be parted'. At the end of her letter she said her husband hoped 'we will see each other before so many years expire please God to spare us'. But a spiritual reunion was more likely than one in life. Rosina wrote: 'I often fancy I am at home from home . . . Home I shall still call Mount Annan. I may see it and may not. This is all unknown to us. If God thinks proper it would be good for us if we could resign our minds to our fates although far distant from one another.' Death, she said, was only 'a temporary separation . . . until that season of reunion'. The Fergusons began as farmers and stock agents in the new colony but were bankrupted in the crisis of 1841, recovering by 1848 to become comfortable and respected farmers on the Adelaide plains. Four years later, Rosina Ferguson wrote home to her mother pointing out that 'this is the fifteenth since we parted. Many, many a change has taken place since then. At that time we did not expect to have been here till now, but it seems we must stay a little longer.' This suggests that they never thought of staying for more than a few years. In 1854 William was saying that in two more years they would return: 'I don't say remain, but we will see.' Their letters were full of nostalgia and good feeling, but they had now become too contented in South Australia to think of a permanent return:

> We are so happy in our own family, plenty of what the body requires and a good kind minister, kind friends, etc, etc, but the separation is just the sting. . . . We always say 'Home' when speaking of Scotland. Willy said one day to me, 'Mother, have you been to Scotland?' I said 'Yes.'

The Fergusons evidently found Australia better than they expected. They wrote homesick letters back to Scotland, for instance, relating how their younger daughter (born in the colony) 'wished she could get to Scotland to see you all'. But they never returned. Rosina died in Adelaide in 1893, a year after her husband.[57]

Another mid-century immigrant family, Sarah Brunskill and her husband, used their letters to England at least partly to reconcile themselves and their kin to the idea of not returning, gradually assimilating the reality of their circumstances despite their emotional yearnings. They had emigrated to South Australia in 1838–39, intent on setting up in farming and trade for 'a comfortable and independent livelihood and a very fair prospect of doing something for our children'. In fact, both their children died on the journey. Writing to her parents in Ely, Sarah Brunskill remarked, 'If you were all here I should not wish to return.' Like many other migrants she was reluctant to advise her relatives about emigrating:

> I have said nothing about coming out for on a matter of such vital impor-
> tance I shrank from the responsible office of adviser. Each ought to judge
> for themselves. Should however any of your friends or neighbours find
> the shoe pinch at home I have no doubt of their bettering their condition
> by coming here.

For the Brunskills, the meaning of home was in the loss of friends and their moral support:

> Remember we are alone – very happy and tolerably comfortable, but still
> alone; how often do we wish we had some one to share our joys and
> sorrows with us!

The Brunskills arrived with the equivalent of £300. Despite the effects of the depression of 1841–43 they were able to recommend Adelaide to their friends: 'There is plenty of land intrinsically better than any he ever tills, capable of growing as much (or more) of anything in the land.'

By 1848 they had three children and George Brunskill reported that 'things look more sunny with us . . . we have much to be thankful for. . . . Although I am on the verge of Fifty I am essentially a younger man than when I last saw you.' They were prosperous too. They wrote: 'There is now in England one of us who came out an emigrant without a shilling in his pocket and who at this moment is in the receipt of about £2000 in a mine of which he borrowed half the money.' In 1851 Brunskill reported: 'Be assured that although our lot is cast at the antipodes we do not forget those who in other days were dear to us.' They now referred to 'our adopted country'.[58] This marked their psychological transition – 'home' had receded decisively.

Sometimes the challenge from home was more pressing. Thus when Ellen Welch wrote from England to her brother in South Australia in December 1864, she reminded him of his promise: 'I wonder if we shall ever meet again in this world. You said when you went you would come back in ten years; that's passed now.' Boucher Welch was a trained chemist who emigrated from Lincolnshire in 1853. He paid his own passage, bought land on arrival, settled into farming and, despite his original undertakings, seems never to have returned to England.[59]

In the case of Patrick McAuliffe, the pressure from home came close to emotional blackmail. Living in Port Augusta in 1884, he received a letter from his father in Croughcroneen, Ireland. He was reminded of his promise to return home at the end of seven years – 'but you have not come home', said his father. The younger McAuliffe had sent money back to his family, but they wanted him to return: 'after many years we are bewailing your absence . . . and may the Lord spare you your health to make your wife and family some wealth'. His parents also explained their difficulties at home: their landlord was trying to lever them off their land and the whole country was being upset. Moreover the rest of the family had departed, save for one son. They:

> imagine they aught to see you coming every day. Write to us regular. Dont have it as an excuse to be waiting to send money. We have as much welcome for your empty letter as if it was loaded with gold and you had no right to leave your Mother so long in trouble. Her hart is broke from thinking of ye all and it is many a silent tear she had shed for the last seven years . . . Dear Patrick your home is still in Crough, waiting for you. I hope you wont fail in coming.[60]

The tension between home and the colony was more commonly expressed in the form of affection and longing. Thus one of the Tonkin family wrote home from Mount Barker in South Australia in 1849: 'Sometimes when I look on this country, and think of home and past circumstances, I cannot tell how thankful I feel to the Lord for directing us to this glorious place, a land with every blessing. Oh! how glad I should be if you were all here to enjoy some of the good things of this land.' The Tonkins also gave expression to their homesick effusions but ended with a common enough restraint: 'I do not persuade anyone to come; I should be glad to see you here, but you must follow your own mind. I have simply laid before you the state of the country; but I come very far short of pointing out its real beauty and excellence.' The final salutation was more sobering still: 'My family give their love to you all, and hope if we never meet more on earth, we shall meet in heaven.'[61]

Triumphal migrants

Some emigrants were absurdly triumphant about their new life in the colonies, scorning the idea of return. One was Aleck Gibson, who ended one letter saying, 'All that I can say is, we are in Australia Felix, you in miserable Scotland.' In reality, Gibson had little to crow about. He had emigrated with several hundred pounds in his pocket, some of which he had borrowed from his father. Writing back from Geelong in December 1853, in a more reflective mood, he conceded that he had not been successful and was unable to redeem any of his loan. He explained that he had been 'obliged to work as a day labourer'– clearly a come-down from his original expectations – and had been unemployed for much of the time. Gibson had intended to make money to help the family he had left behind in Scotland. In his note home in August 1854 he reported: 'I am afraid it has been and will be quite out of my power to send you any [money which] I had anticipated doing when I left home.' He was brought so low that he had had to ask his family to send him funds to start afresh. But he managed to remain minimally cheerful, comforting himself with the thought that 'we often talk and think of you all and often wish that the time may not be far distant when we shall have it in our power to pay you a visit'.

Better-off immigrants possessed a lower tolerance of the rigours of colonial life and were more likely to crave the forsaken comforts of the home country. Thus, Gibson wrote of the cruder aspects of life in Victoria:

> How often my dearest Helen do we wish we were partaking of a nice dinner at York Place and having a nice chat at your coal fire side; sincerely do we hope that pleasure is still in store for us. No one knows what they have to go through until they come to the sweet Colony of Victoria, the word comfort ought to be obliterated out of the Colonial dictionary. We are now as well housed as many who are well off but for all that I rise in the morning when I see day light appearing through the roof or through some of the crevices with which the room is surrounded, if it blows very hard I put my cap on for fear of my hair being blown off. If anyone comes out here, tell them when bidding Adieu to their friends and to their native country also to bid adieu to comfort. . . . [yet] with all our knocking about I must say that our health has been exceedingly good.[62]

Lower down the social scale were Lucy and John Hart, working immigrants who rejected the idea of return. From Winchester in Hampshire, they arrived in Adelaide in 1849, after a voyage during which Lucy was badly injured. Both suffered ill health and misfortunes on arrival which included treatment in hospital and the heavy burden of medical bills. Lucy Hart's letters to her relatives in England demonstrate an extraordinary level of fortitude and tolerance of discomfort.

Lucy Hart, indeed, was even able to recommend the journey as excellent and on arrival described Australia as 'perfect'. John Hart went to the gold diggings in October 1851 and achieved some success, which was further reflected in his wife's remarkably optimistic letters home: 'Should I have been so well off in England', she asks herself. 'NO', was her emphatic answer: for her, England meant 'work hard and be half starved'. She had thought of returning and dismissed the idea. 'I would not come back to England again unless I had enough to keep me without work [and] on no account neither would my husband.' She declared, 'I am speaking now the very sentiments of our hearts.' She also referred to people doing well and returning to England: 'There are many poor [working people] that I know have got three or four thousand pounds and gone back to England . . . this is a second California.' Her own response to success was not to return; instead she implored her kinsfolk to come to the colony: 'Mother there was many older women than you came out in our vessel and are now doing well if you wont come do let the boys come.'[63]

The imbalance in the emigration of the sexes had several consequences for colonial Australia. One was the disproportionate and successful recruitment of young single Irishwomen who intermarried with the non-Irish in high proportions. The other was the return of males to the British Isles specifically to find a wife. This was not return migration in the usual sense: rather it was an interesting variant on chain migration.

William Purling, for instance, was an agricultural labourer from East Anglia who emigrated to South Australia in 1853. A highly pragmatic and calculating emigrant, Purling was entirely clear in his attitude to returning to England: the only reason he would think of it would be to get a wife. Writing home to his relatives he indicated that there was plenty of employment in South Australia as well as good prospects in Victoria. He echoed the common refrain of working men in the colonies when he compared the conditions of employment: 'You are afraid to say anything to your master in England but that is quite the other way hear. They are afraid to say anything to you for they know you will go to the gold diggers and they cannot get men to do their work.' As he set off with two companions for the goldfields, his plan was clear. 'If we do well we shall all three of us come home fore a wife each and go back again[.] their is not so many women hear as in England.

Purling appears not to have returned to England, perhaps because he found a wife in the colonies. In 1859 he described his growing family and now harboured no thoughts of returning to England. Rather, he was full of regret that he could not show his children off to his own distant family –'i wish all of you could be hare to go with me to hare them [singing]'. In 1864 he was reporting that:

> it is not all plesher in australia but we are better ouf out hare than we should be in England. I have no wish to come back to live thare agin if it was not for our [?Dear Friends]. I must say that I should like to see you all. We have bin got this last 2 years rather hard up but not so as we must have bin had we bin in England.

In fact he did not have money enough to help his mother to emigrate, mainly because he had bought 200 acres of land and exhausted his funds. At this point he was adamant about not going home: 'I would not come back to work in England if thy wood give me the same wages as they gave hare for this is a free country you are not obliged to move your hat to your Masters for the man is as good as his Master and all set at one tabel.' In 1865 Purling wrote again to his parents, pointing out that he had now been in Australia for twelve years: 'It havent bine all sunshine. I thought when we first came we ware going to get rich all at once.' Instead they had produced half a dozen children, and other relatives had joined them. But the reality, for him and his parents, was that 'I do not think we shall ever see each other in this world.' The only consolation he could offer was that of spiritual reunion – when they had all 'travelled through this veal of tears' they would be reunited.[64] This is a common lament in the letters of ocean-divided migrants.

In her study of the *mores* of colonial life in late nineteenth-century Australia Beverley Kingston suggests that the imbalance of the sexes (and social aspirations) were not confined to working people. Looking at the higher echelons of colonial society, she finds that the richer families sent their sons to England, ostensibly for an education and cultured leisure: in reality the sons were sent 'home' in search of a suitable wife. As Kingston says: 'The shy, mysterious, financially attractive but no longer entirely youthful bachelor from the colonies in search of a wife was a favourite of romantic tales of the time. Likewise the beautiful debutante of uncertain colonial origins and perhaps even more uncertain parentage could be found.'[65]

Return illusions and the visiting option

In the unsentimental words of modern geographers, 'one never finds so much philosophising about returning as amongst migrants who will never in fact return'. This they bluntly term 'the return illusion'. It is an attitude which operates effectively as a mechanism against assimilation: 'No matter how unsettled, migrants keep open in their minds the possibility that one day they will return.'[66] Equally probable was the substitution of a short visit home in place of a permanent return, and there are many examples of this in the Australian account.

Peter Wilmot, from Malpas, in Cheshire, near the Welsh border, arrived in New South Wales in 1833. There he led a life of mobility as a storekeeper among many other jobs, and later spent time on the goldfields. For himself the migration enterprise was less than totally successful. As early as 1839 he made a rather bleak assessment of his colonial career. He had borrowed £100 which he was paying back in instalments after his arrival in the colony. His strategy had been a matter of inter-generational upward mobility – his children, he said, would reap the benefit. He wrote to his mother in Cheshire:

> God only knows if ever I shall [return home] and I am thankful to say I do not desire ever to return to remain. I am still satisfied that if ever I fight my way up in the world I have a better chance here than in the 'old country' and if I do not do it, perhaps my successors may, and I do not think they would have as good chance perhaps on the other side as I had. I have however still an affection for my friends at home which neither time nor distance will ever lessen and the pleasure to visit 'Home' again to be in the midst of old scenes and old associations is too great to think much about. My thoughts sometimes ramble on that point and I may sometimes realise it but God only knows what the future may bring.[67]

The modest success of many first-generation working migrants tended to strengthen their resolve to stay in Australia. The original commitment was replaced by a promise to visit home instead, though sometimes the possibility of staying was held open. Thus Thomas Hampton, from Ararat, wrote back to his brother in Richmond, Yorkshire, in 1859:

> I should very much like to take a trip home and see you all . . . If I should happen to leave here with the idea of returning I might alter my opinion when I got home, the fact is I should like a change not that I dislike the diggings but the diggings is a place where there was little society.

Hampton kept finding reasons to keep him in the colonies and he probably never saw Yorkshire again.[68]

James Little from Bolton had a similar attitude. He wrote to his mother from Melbourne in 1853: 'I only say I could have done well in England perhaps better . . . but I do not regret coming here. I should like to see old England again and a few friends I have left there but I think I could not settle there but I should return here to the colonies.' Little was not financially successful as an emigrant but he liked the colony too well even to accept the return passage money offered by his family in England. In 1866 he observed, 'I hope you will not deem me too proud if I say I would rather refuse any assistance except under imperative circumstances.'[69] There was frequently a great deal of pride and bravado mixed together in the minds of the emigrants, many of them very young, male and alone, away from home for the first time. Archibald and John Stuart in 1862 wrote home to say they would stay for about six or eight years and would then return home: essentially because there were not enough marriageable women in the colonies.[70]

The relative scarcity of single women in the colonies was undoubtedly a factor in the making of many emigrant strategies, both male and female. John Feazey was helped in his emigration to Port Phillip by money from his parents in Bedfordshire. He wrote home to his brother in 1844:

> I am getting money and doing very well indeed. Times are not so good here as they was two or three years back, but we can get a good living and some money now, Port Phillip is a splendid country and I like it much ... If the Lord spare me until my time is up with Mr Stroughton I intend to come home and get me a wife and then go back to Port Phillip a few more years until I get enough to keep me in England to live at my ease.[71]

The visiting option became much more realistic and prevalent in the last part of the century, and swelled the passenger lists, thereby helping to confuse the category of return migration.

Absolutely clear intentions were also to be seen in the account of Thomas Tourle, a well heeled speculative emigrant writing in 1839: 'I most assuredly intend returning as soon as I have made a fortune to come back with.' But, he went on, he would 'not stay to make a fortune, if I can get enough to live in England on a small Farm I shall return'. He was looking to make £5,000, 'but if I can keep myself here and cannot at home I must of course remain here until I can'. Tourle was a highly calculating immigrant continually debating with himself the costs and benefits of his migration. By 1843 he had made good progress and his thoughts of home were now reduced to merely visiting 'Old England' – 'I doubt not if I shall have a competency by the end of ten years to enable me to return to England.'[72] There may have been a common notion of what constituted 'success' for a migrant intending to return with assets accumulated in the colony. George Johnson (who eventually became an architect in Brisbane and Melbourne) had similar sums in mind when he wrote back to his native Derbyshire in 1861. He declared that 'when I have £5 or 6000 I will settle in England. I am getting all square now.' He, like so many others, had arrived with a goal in mind – success would be counted by the manner and opulence of his return to England. Johnson's colony was merely a means of fulfilling an English ambition.[73]

Melancholy and failed emigrants

Peter Matthews scanned his fellow immigrants on the goldfields with feelings of anxiety. He was a working man who had difficulty writing his own letters. He reported that he was saving £20 a month and sending home to England some of his earnings: 'On the whole I think there is a better chance here than at home for the labouring man especially.' But he was not fully persuaded: 'if I am spared to return to my native land again I intend to remain there'. He noted that 'some have been taken off in the bloom of youth and laid in a cold grave. Others have been very fortunate and returned to their native land.' Matthews seems to have stayed on until 1862, when he returned to London with six of his working acquaintances.[74]

Not many emigrants were as outspoken as George Underwood. In 1879 he complained acrimoniously about the negative response of his family in England to all his plans. Though thousands of miles from home, he was still caught in the web of family politics. Underwood's letters from Queensland, to his sister in the East Riding of Yorkshire, declared that his family at home had never given him the least support: 'Had they given me a few words of encouragement I might have been back in England now, not that I wish you to think that I should ever come back to England to stop but I should like to take a trip someday if I live.' He also pointed out that he would have to save the necessary few hundred pounds to do so; he had few friends still alive in England and, in any case, he would not want to return permanently. In an acid aside, he said that he particularly had no taste for that 'hand to mouth way of living into which our family has fallen'. Nevertheless, Underwood continued to describe his migration to Australia as 'my self-imposed banishment'. In his letters back to Yorkshire, from sentence to sentence, his feelings swung from guilt to recrimination and back again. He continued to live in the turmoil of separation.[75]

Among the comparative colonial failures was William White in Queensland who told his family back in England that, as soon as he made some money (in mining), 'I shall clear out of the country at once'. Meanwhile he was trapped by his own poverty.[76] Similarly Frank Bushby, a rolling stone in the colonies, certainly regarded his migration to Australia as a mistake and decided to move on to San Francisco in 1866.[77] Others intended to return but found that success had changed them: one was William Campbell, from Fort William, who arrived in Australia in 1838 with £100, expecting to return home in less than ten years, independent if not actually wealthy; instead he stayed on and on and became a colonial half-millionaire.[78]

The migrant mental cycle

When Albert and Annie Thurston arrived in Tasmania in 1879 they thought that they were already home: 'It seems impossible that we are away from England. Everything is just like England.'[79] But most immigrants were much less settled in their minds and it is in their shifting moods that we find the commonest theme in their letters home. Many of them passed through hope, disappointment and homesickness into acceptance and even assimilation, until they found a stable equilibrium of mind and place. Some of them were perfectly aware of the immigrant's mental cycle. William Leonard was the son of a Stockport weaver who emigrated himself from Scotland in 1863 to join his uncle in Woolloomooloo. Leonard declared that most immigrants, especially in their first year, were thoroughly miserable and felt trapped in an alien place. He wrote home to say that 'this country is not the Heaven some people imagine it to be . . . It is not uncommon for persons when first they come to this country to look upon it as the most unlucky thing they ever did, but his opinion generally alters when they have been some time here.' Leonard's own correspondence was a litany of various types and intensities of homesickness. Significantly, though he claimed to have earned enough to return home, he chose to stay – that is, until he proceeded further, this time to New Zealand.[80]

The idea or dream of 'home' was ubiquitous in the letters of Australia's colonial immigrants. But it is difficult to discern systematic differences in the behaviour or thinking of the various types of migrants, for instance between English and Scots immigrants. There is a better case for saying that family migrants were more committed to permanent migration than single men; there may be also a suggestion that middling migrants were more likely than labouring immigrants to be disappointed with colonial living conditions and social conventions; and it may be that during the Gold Rushes a comparatively high proportion of the immigrants arrived never expecting to stay for long – hoping to dig for a few years and return home with quick gains.

For the rest, the untested impression remains that relatively few emigrants to Australia were totally committed to return before they left the British Isles. Unlike emigrants from eastern and southern Europe to the United States at the end of the century, Australian immigrants seem not to have retained assets in the homeland. Few, for instance, appear to have held on to land at home as a sort of hostage to the old country, as an earnest of their return.[81]

There were endless modulations among the emigrant strategies, a great array of coexisting and shifting expectations of the colonies and of 'home'. And the image of home was itself a fabrication in the mind of every migrant. The aggregate consequence of these internal struggles with the idea of staying on, or going home, was the actual 'rate of return'. This, for Australia even more than elsewhere, remains as elusive as ever. The matter of returning was not simply a measurable and predictable outcome of an economic calculus. Nevertheless, economic success in the colonies was arguably the most important single influence on the rate of return. Australia probably sustained a relatively low rate of return migration. The high level of wages in Australia was a great dampener on thoughts of repatriation. During the many years of antipodean prosperity it is likely that the rate of exodus, and the level of immigrant angst, were much reduced. Nevertheless, even in the farthest theatre of the great age of British emigration, there was a remarkable and growing interchange of trade, commercial and leisure travel and two-way migration which stretched between the two sides of the globe. The traffic between Britain and Australia swelled decade by decade and contributed to the developing 'ambiguity of emigration' which continues to the present day.

Notes

1 Cited by K.S. Inglis, 'Going Home: Australians in England, 1870–1900' in David Fitzpatrick (ed.), *Home or Away? Immigrants in Colonial Australia*, Visible Immigrants III (Canberra: Division of Historical Studies and Centre for Immigration and Multicultural Studies, Australian National University, 1992), 117–18.
2 Australian Bureau of Statistics Records, *Overseas Arrivals and Departures, 1995–1999* (2000).
3 Thurston Correspondence, Kent Archives Office. I thank Dr James Jupp for access to copies of this material.
4 Parts of this chapter draw on a longer and earlier treatment in Eric Richards, 'Return Migration and Migrant Strategies in Colonial Australia' in Fitzpatrick (ed.), *Home or Away?*, 64–104.
5 See Eric Richards, 'Emigration to Colonial Australia: Paradigms and Disjunctions' in Jan and Leo Lucassen (eds), *Migration, Migration History, History: Old Paradigms and New Perspectives* (Berne and New York: Peter Lang, 1997), 251–80.
6 Both of these groups had high return rates either under the terms of their labour contracts or by government decree and compulsion.
7 D.E. Baines, *Emigration from Europe, 1815–1930* (Basingstoke: Macmillan, 1991), 39. See also C.J. Erickson, 'Who were the English and Scots Emigrants to the United States in the Late Nineteenth Century?' in D.V. Glass and R. Revelle (eds), *Population and Social Change* (London: Edward Arnold, 1972), 350 n. 8.
8 Throughout this chapter the terms 'British' and 'Britain' refer to the British Isles, including Ireland.
9 See Richards, 'Return Migration and Migrant Strategies', 65–7.
10 Inglis, 'Going Home', passim.
11 As Australia diversified its immigrant intakes after 1950 the catchment inevitably included many more people from countries which already had a history of very high return rates – especially those of the Balkan and south-east European countries. In the years 1959–65 more than 16 per cent returned, according to Jean Martin, *The Migrant Presence* (Sydney and London: Allen & Unwin, 1978), 39. In the twentieth century it was a serious problem for Australian assistance schemes, undermining the impact of heavy government expenditure on immigration programmes.
12 See John Bach, *A Maritime History of Australia* (West Melbourne, Victoria: Nelson, 1976), 59.
13 W.A. Brodribb, *Recollections of an Australian Squatter* (Sydney: Woods, 1883; repr. Sydney: John Ferguson, 1978), 127.

14 Beverley Kingston, *The Oxford History of Australia III, 1860–1900: Glad Confident Morning* (Melbourne: Oxford University Press, 1988, paperback edition, 1993), 204, 206.

15 See Inglis, 'Going Home', 109. This turnover was, of course, later matched by the lethal English bowler Harold Larwood, who emigrated to Sydney.

16 Letter of George Witt to Thomas Barnard, 6 April 1851, in Andrew Underwood, 'Some Letters from Bedfordshire Pioneers in Australia, 1842–86', *Bedfordshire Historical Record Society Publications* XL, 234. Lind (1820–87), known as 'the Swedish nightingale', was considered the greatest soprano of her day.

17 Archibald Stuart to John Stuart, 5 March 1862: National Library of Australia (hereafter NLA), MS 993.

18 David Atkinson to his mother, 18 June 1862: NLA, MS 670.

19 There was a report as late as 1889 of old diggers, having returned home, re-emigrating to Australia, 'to the land of their adoption after a spell at home'. Quoted in Inglis, 'Going Home', 128.

20 The status of the statistics is discussed in detail in Richards, 'Return Migration and Migrant Strategies', passim. On the idea of an imperial dialogue in an earlier emigrant context see James Horn, '"To Parts beyond the Seas": Free Emigration to the Chesapeake in the Seventeenth Century', in Ida Altman and James Horn (eds), *'To Make America': European Emigration in the Early Modern Period* (Berkeley CA: University of California Press, 1991), 116–17.

21 Inglis, 'Going Home', 105–6.

22 See A.G.L. Shaw, *Convicts and the Colonies* (London: Faber, 1966), 65, 103, 142–3; S. Nicholas, *Convict Workers: Reinterpreting Australia's Past* (Cambridge: Cambridge University Press, 1988), 9, 58.

23 Alan Atkinson, 'The Pioneers who left early', *Push from the Bush* 29 (1991), 110–16.

24 Clive James, reviewing *The Fatal Shore* by Robert Hughes in *Snake-Charmers in Texas* (London: Picador, 1988), 7.

25 See also the comments of Inglis, 'Going Home', 105.

26 There is a most suggestive account in K.S. Inglis, *The Australian Colonists* (Melbourne: Melbourne University Press, 1974), 28–9. See also Nicole McLennan, '"From home and kindred": English Emigration to Australia, 1860–1900', unpublished PhD thesis (Research School of Social Sciences, Australian National University, 1998), 105–7.

27 Inglis, 'Going Home', 110, 115.

28 This point is made by my colleague, Peter Howell. Some account also should be taken of the flow of 'Anglo-Indians' into Australia during the nineteenth century, some of them for reasons of health and often bringing considerable capital.

29 Henry Hussey, *More than Half a Century of Colonial Life and Christian Experience* (Adelaide: Hussey & Gillingham, 1897), 238, 243.

30 Rodney Cockburn, *Pastoral Pioneers of South Australia* (2 vols, Adelaide: Published Limited, 1925–27); cf. S.M. Macklin, 'Pastoral Pioneers of South Australia: A Quantitative Analysis', BA thesis (Flinders University, 1975).

31 This represents a leakage of capital out of the colonial economy, though some of the returned pastoralists maintained their properties in the colony even though they had retired to Britain. The actual rate of return on original capital is not known, nor is the alternative cost to Britain of the loss of human capital that the colonies received free and which they paid for only in the form of assisted passages.

32 Kingston, *The Oxford History of Australia*, 204.

33 *Australian Dictionary of Biography* (Melbourne: Melbourne University Press, 1966–)

34 Affluent Irish and Scottish colonists may have had a tendency to return not to their homelands but to England – see, for instance, Inglis, 'Going Home', 111.

35 See W.D. Rubinstein, *Wealth and the Very Wealthy in the Modern World* (London: Croom Helm, 1980), 18 f., 'The Top Wealth-holders of New South Wales, 1817–1939', *Australian Economic History Review* 20 (1980), 138. The return of very successful emigrants to Britain from colonial Australia, as measured in probate returns, would tend to inflate the British component and deflate the Australian.

36 Inglis, 'Going Home', 112.
37 *Ibid.*, 107.
38 See the sad case of the unsuccessful immigrant Frank Bushby, who, instead of return-
    ing home, sailed to San Francisco but went down with his ship *en route*. McLennan,
    'From home and kindred', 119.
39 Sarah Brunskill to her siblings, 11 August 1839: Brunskill Letters, Mortlock Library
    of South Australia (hereafter MLSA). D 5203/63 (L). Cf. case reported by William
    Pratt in a letter reproduced in *Adelaide Chronicle*, 4 April 1840, and further corre-
    spondence in *ibid.*, 23 July 1840.
40 See Eric Richards, 'The Highland Scots of South Australia', *Journal of the Historical
    Society of South Australia* 4 (1978), 49–58.
41 Graeme Davison and Shirley Constantine (eds), *Out of Work Again: The Autobio-
    graphical Narrative of Thomas Dobeson, 1885–1891* (Clayton, Victoria: Department
    of History, Monash University, 1990), 2, 22.
42 William Whitgreave to his parents, 1 January 1853: NLA, MS 1087.
43 Inglis, 'Going Home', 108.
44 G.C. Bolton, 'The Idea of a Colonial Gentry', *Historical Studies ANZ* 13 (1968), 307,
    citing Henry Kingsley, *The Recollections of Geoffrey Hamlyn*, and Rolf Boldrewood,
    A Sydney-side Saxon.
45 See J.M. Macdonald and Eric Richards, 'Workers for Australia: A Profile of British
    and Irish Migrants assisted to New South Wales in 1841', *Journal of the Australian
    Population Association* 15 (1998), 1–35, which documents some of the early assisted
    immigrants who were rejected as unsatisfactory on arrival in Sydney and returned
    home at the expense of the shippers.
46 South Australian Archives (hereafter SAA), GRG 35/48A, 52/12, GRG 35/43. The
    South Australian Register, 16 December 1852, reported that Kidd 'died by a visita-
    tion of God'.
47 SAA,GRG, 7/23/85/1814.
48 *Ibid.*, 7/23/165/1913.
49 *Ibid.*, 7/23/8/1915.
50 *Ibid.*, 7/54/2/5/1912.
51 *Ibid.*, 7/23/48/1914.
52 Janice Gothard, in J. Jupp (ed.), *The Australian People* (North Ryde, NSW: Angus &
    Robertson, 1988), 89.
53 Graeme Davison, 'The Unsociable Sociologist: W.S. Jevons, and his Survey of
    Sydney, 1856–1858' in D. Walker and M.J. Bennett (eds), *Intellect and Emotion*
    (Geelong, Victoria: Faculty of Arts, Deakin University, 1998), 127–50.
54 For a fuller account see Eric Richards, 'Voices of British and Irish Migrants in Nine-
    teenth-Century Australia' in Colin G. Pooley and Ian D. Whyte (eds), *Migrants, Emi-
    grants and Immigrants* (London: Routledge, 1991), 28–30.
55 Most of this information is drawn from Charles Maclean, *Island on the Edge of the
    World* (London: Tom Stacey, 1972), 125–7, and Eric Richards, 'St Kilda and Australia:
    Emigrants at Peril, 1852–1853', *Scottish Historical Review* 71 (1992), 129–55.
56 There is probably a bias in emigrant letters. Those who wrote home were likely to
    have a higher than average propensity to return. Emigrant letters may have masked
    the true depths of feelings. See the important but disconcerting comparison of an
    emigrant letter with a memoir by the same hand in Davison and Constantine, *Out
    of Work Again*, 7, 97–8.
57 Letters of Rosina Ferguson: MLSA, D 2685 1–6 (L); cf. George C. Morphett (ed.),
    William and Rosina Ferguson (Adelaide: Pioneers' Association of South Australia,
    1943) located in MLSA, SAA 1384/14.
58 George Brunskill to his brother, 31 March 1838; 29 May 1848; and to George Stevens,
    24 March 1851: MLSA, D 5203 (L).
59 Pat Roberts, *Emily's Journal: The Welch Letters* (Richmond, South Australia:
    Roberts, 1986), 63. I thank Mrs Roberts for bringing this to my notice.
60 Letter dated 25 January 1884: by courtesy of Mrs Pat Tedmanson of Adelaide.
61 W. and E. Tonkin to their siblings, 11 October 1849, in *Emigrants' Penny Magazine.*

Though described as 'Extracts from Original Emigrant Letters', the exact provenance of the letters reproduced in this journal is in doubt.

62 Aleck Gibson to his father, 17 August 1854; 1 December 1853; Aleck Gibson to Helen Gibson, 1 August 1854; 16 October 1855: NLA, MS 1540.

63 Lucy and John Hart to family, 3 March 1849: MLSA, D 5063 (L).

64 Letters to Purling family dated 30 August 1852; 14 July 1859; 17 July 1864; 19 August 1865: MLSA, D 4468 (L).

65 Kingston, *The Oxford History of Australia*, 181.

66 Russell King, Allan Strachan and Jill Mortimer, 'Return Migration: A Review of the Literature' (Discussion Paper in Geography No. 19 Oxford: Oxford Polytechnic: 1983), 20–1.

67 Peter Wilmot to his mother, 4 May 1839: Mitchell Library, Sydney, MS 26/9.

68 Thomas Hampton to his brother, 20 January 1859: NLA, MS 218.

69 James Little to his mother, 1 December 1853 20 October 1866: NLA, MS671.

70 Archibald Stuart to his cousin, 5 March 1862: NLA, MS 993.

71 John Feazey to his mother, 20 January 1844: Underwood, 'Some Letters from Bedfordshire Pioneers', 231–2.

72 Letters of Thomas Tourle, 27 May and 9 December 1839; 28 July 1843: NLA, MS 18.

73 George R. Johnson to Henry Whittaker, 2 December 1866: NLA, MS 36.

74 Letters of Peter Matthews, 27 February 1853; 15 January 1854; 18 November [1855?]; 19 March 1862: NLA, MS 1367.

75 Letters of George Underwood, 23 May 1879; 27 January, 23 February, 28 June, 6 July, 14 July and 8 August 1880: NLA, MS 673.

76 William White to Anne White, 26 February and 3 May 1874: NLA, MS 676.

77 Frank Bushby to his sister, 16 March, 12 April, 15 July and 11 September 1866; 9 July 1867: NLA, MS 1543.

78 William Campbell, Fragment of Autobiography: ML, A3587.

79 Thurston Correspondence; see above, n. 3.

80 Family letters to England, 1839–77: NLA, MS 7110.

81 Cf. Michael Palairet, 'The "New" Immigration and the Newest: Slavic Migrations from the Balkans to America and Industrial Europe since the Late Nineteenth Century' in T.C. Smout (ed.), *The Search for Wealth and Stability* (London: Macmillan, 1979), 46 f.

CHAPTER SIX

'My wayward heart': homesickness, longing and the return of British post-war immigrants from Australia

Alistair Thomson

In 1962 Mary Holmes emigrated from Newport to Australia with her farmer husband and five children. The Holmes were among more than a million Britons who took an assisted passage to Australia in the quarter-century after the Second World War. Under this migration scheme, British adults paid only £10 to travel to the other side of the world, while their children went free. In Australia these immigrants became known as the '£10 Poms'. In 1963 – and five years before the Holmes family eventually returned to Wales – Mary Holmes wrote a poem, 'The Migrant's Dilemma':

> Oft I toss and turn at night, sleep troubled & uneasy.
> Back and forth my thoughts they dance, in a maddening crazy frenzy.
> The land is good, full of chance, the people kind & friendly.
> So tell me why my wayward heart is always homeward turning.[1]

This chapter explores the experiences and motivations of post-war emigrants to Australia who subsequently returned to live in Britain. It challenges the simplistic and polarized explanations for return offered by contemporary critics in both Britain and Australia, and shows how a life history approach can offer a more complex and nuanced set of explanations of return migration. In particular, the chapter focuses on the nature, meaning and significance of 'homesickness' in the migrant experience.

The argument is informed by analysis of three sets of life history sources. Most important is an archive at the University of Sussex. Funding from the Arts and Humanities Research Board has permitted the collection of over 250 written autobiographical accounts by British migrants who returned from Australia, and these have been supplemented with thirty life history interviews with returnees. The chapter draws upon a second archive at La Trobe University in Melbourne, where Jim Hammerton has a databank of letters from over 1,000 British migrants who settled in Australia, and more than 100 follow-up interviews. The fruits of the project will be disseminated in a book, *Ten Pound Poms: Australia's Invisible Migrants*. A third primary source is a collection of published and unpublished autobiographical accounts by British post-war migrants which are available in Australian archives.[2]

Return migrants: invisible twice over

Return migrants are voices we never hear in Australian history. Migration histories often neglect the experiences of the returnees, focusing instead on the struggles and successes of the migrants who stay on. This type of historical amnesia is especially true of migrant nations – like Australia or the United States – where migration is a central element in the story of the making of a nation, from the federation nation of pioneering settlers and their descendants to the multicultural millennium nation forged by migrants from many lands who have a sought a safe and prosperous home in Australia. In Australia today it could be argued that the post-war British settlers are 'invisible migrants' by comparison with the Italians, Greeks and other non-English-speaking immigrants who transformed an Anglo-Celtic country into that multicultural nation. The British return migrants are invisible twice over.

In fact, return is a common feature of most migration schemes and movements. For example, a surprisingly high proportion of the great wave of migrants who travelled from Europe to North America in the late nineteenth century returned across the Atlantic; it has been estimated that the return rate for British emigrants to all destinations in the period between 1870 and 1914 was a staggering 40 per cent.[3] For the post-war British who journeyed to Australia estimates of return vary but average at around 25 per cent – more than enough to earn nicknames such as 'boomerang migrants' and the 'to and froms' which were ascribed to British return migrants.[4] Reg Appleyard calculated a 29 per cent return rate for his survey of British migrants in the late 1950s, while Alan Richardson concluded that the return rate for these migrants in the period 1959 to 1967 was 24 per cent for married couples and just over 50 per cent for single men and women. More recently, Graeme Hugo has highlighted an increase in the return rate of British immigrants as they reach retirement age.[5] These figures highlight the extent of return migration but also the difficulties of statistical analysis: return rates change over time and they vary for different types of migrants; the statistics struggle to deal with return migrants who came back to Australia (Appleyard estimated that about half his sample of British returnees went back to Australia) and are flummoxed by the serial returnees who go back and forth between the two countries. And of course these statistics do not include the British migrants who were desperate to return but were prevented from doing so by financial or personal circumstances. Sandra O'Neill 'escaped' from Perth back to England after three terrible months in 1972, and recalls that a common saying of the time was 'if they could build a road back to England, it would be full of people walking back, because, so many were trapped . . .'.[6]

So why did so many of the post-war British migrants decide to leave Australia and return 'home'? At the time the tabloid press in both countries had starkly polarized explanations. In Britain the popular press picked up the stories of return migrants like Sandra O'Neill and blamed Australia and its government for misleading advertisements which had attracted the assisted passage migrants to a country which could not deliver on its promises, and for the insecure labour market and the appalling conditions of migrant hostels. For example, in 1962 a Reading man recently returned from Australia wrote to his local newspaper to inform readers that Australian immigration publicity did not mention an acute housing shortage, widespread unemployment caused by an economic slump, and inadequate social service benefits:

> Australia is no longer the land of opportunities and progress for the average working man. Yet Australia House still endeavours to give people the impression that it is. Consequently, when British people arrive here and discover the truth they become frustrated and resent the deception that persuaded them to give up their homes and jobs and come here, in most cases to find that they had jumped out of the frying pan into the fire.[7]

In Australia the popular press – and indeed popular opinion – blamed the 'whingeing Poms' who had enjoyed favoured status by comparison with non-English-speaking immigrants and yet were not able to stick it out through the tough times and make the most of the 'land of opportunity'. For example, in their book promoting emigration to Australia, Elizabeth and Derek Tribe argued that the criticisms of return migrants like the man from Reading were unfair and misleading, and that the 'vast majority' of the post-war British migrants 'have been happy and are now pleased to regard Australia as their home. Unfortunately there will always be some men and women who are misfits. Unfortunately too, these are usually the people who make the most noise.'[8] In a series of *Women's Session* radio programmes broadcast by the ABC in 1964 and 1965, London emigrant and Perth resident Gwen Good spoke to an imaginary friend in Britain about the shock of seeing 'some parts of the Western Australian press counter-attack with sarcastic comment and acrid cartoons, rather like a touchy teenager':

Did I tell you about the group of dissatisfied migrants who returned home last year? There were only about eleven families in all, but how the newspapers jumped on it. Some of the publicity was quite hysterical. In fact some people at Fremantle booed the ship as the migrants left Australia. Thank heavens you didn't treat us that way when we left England.[9]

Not surprisingly, the Australian government was concerned about the high return rate among British immigrants. The emphatic preference of the government's post-war immigration scheme had been for migrants of British stock, and it had been assumed that such migrants would readily settle in a nation of British character, language and institutions. The British immigrants enjoyed comparatively favourable conditions and were heavily subsidized through the assisted passage scheme, but with so many going home they represented a poor return on a substantial investment. In 1957 this prompted the federal government to fund research by Reg Appleyard about the British immigrants and to commission an official inquiry into the problem of return.

Throughout the late 1950s and 1960s a range of explanations for return was advanced. Appleyard's research concluded that while the assisted passage scheme was crucial for the competitiveness of migration to Australia, the high rate of return among the British immigrants was in part due to the relative ease of their selection, passage and return. Though wages and purchasing power were comparatively favourable in Australia, return migrants were also influenced by tax, health, welfare and housing advantages in Britain. Appleyard emphasized the character and sociability of the migrants, and the extent of their cultural assimilation within Australia, as significant factors in the equation of return. Research by the social psychologist Richardson also suggested that a degree of 'acculturation' was an important influence for settlement. The 1967 report of the Immigration Advisory Committee – which focused on Australian return migrants from different countries of origin, including Britain – argued that employment and other economic forces were less significant motivators for return than personal and psychological factors. The report concluded that many migrants returned because they had taken the initial emigration decision too lightly, or because they did not have the necessary character to become successful immigrants.[10]

These conclusions highlight some of the causes of return, but are underpinned by the assimilationist ideals of the period. They tend to accept a rather simplistic model of migrant character – the tough will survive while the weak 'misfits' return with their tail between their legs – and assume that successful settlement is a neat linear process of assimilation through which migrants gradually take on the culture of their adopted home and become contented Australians. There is a fine line between the scholarly and official explanations of return and the complaints of the Australian media of the time. At the opposite extreme are British tabloid explanations that downplayed the ways in which return migrants contributed to their own fate and emphasized the importance of external forces and conditions in Australia.

British migrant life histories offer a rather different perspective on return, and suggest alternatives to these simplistic and polarized explanations.[11] Janet Francis's life story points the way.

Janet Francis: 'I'm not the alien any more'

Janet Francis was born in Bristol in 1938, the first child of Beatrice and Edward Dungey. Janet's mother had a very difficult upbringing, with an alcoholic stepfather and a mother struggling to raise her four children. Beatrice had a limited education and she worked in a shop and as an usherette until she married in 1936 at the age of 19 'for a bit of peace and security'.[12] As a young man Edward Dungey worked in a chemist's shop in the village of Shirehampton just outside Bristol. The chemist took him under his wing and sent him to night school, where he qualified as a dispensing chemist, his profession for twenty-five years before the family emigrated, and then as a chiropodist. In 1939 the young Dungey family bought a house in Shirehampton. Janet recalls that her father's father – a railway engine driver who rented a council house – 'was *absolutely* mortified to think that my mother had put a rope round my father's neck and he thought it was terrible'.

Edward Dungey was called up at the start of the war. For a time he was stationed in Wales and his wife and daughter came to live with him, but when Janet started to speak Welsh they sent her back to Bristol to live with her paternal grandparents, with whom she developed a close relationship. At the end of the war the family home in Shirehampton was occupied by tenants and it was another two years before the house became vacant and Janet went back to live with her parents, and with two new sisters, Maisie and Trish, born in 1944 and 1945 respectively. Growing up in wartime England had a significant effect upon Janet's emerging sense of identity:

> I remember when the war finished *everybody* had parties. We had street parties everywhere and flags came out and I remember all the war songs and that was a great part of my life. I think this is why I hold England so dear now because I know what the boys fought for, you know, to give us the right to live in freedom and in this green and pleasant land and that's why I think I was a bad candidate for Australia because England means *absolutely everything* to me.

Janet has 'lovely memories' of growing up in post-war semi-rural Shirehampton. Though she failed the 11+ exam and spent eighteen months at the local secondary modern school, she took an exam and won a half-scholarship to a private school in Bristol and 'that was the making of me because that gave me the *savoir-faire* and gave me the . . . the grounding that I needed, I think'. Though her father 'was very Victorian' and did not believe in giving girls a private school education, her mother had other ideas and supported Janet and then her sisters in their education. At about this time her parents decided to buy a business and sold the house in Shirehampton. After a couple of false starts they bought an off-licence in the Bristol suburb of St Paul's which Beatrice managed while her husband continued his day job. Janet had failed her end-of-school GCE exams ('I was a *terrible* examination candidate') but a 'terribly boring' job as a laboratory technician persuaded her to go back to school, paying her own fees. This time she passed, got a job with an insurance company and earned a place in a teacher training college in Coventry. 'But then my parents got this *hair-raising* idea about going to Australia and of course that, it was all wiped out.'

Janet struggles to recall and understand her parents' decision to emigrate; even though she was working and contributing to the family income she was not part of the decision making. Beatrice Dungey had met an Australian Battle of Britain pilot, Mr Thorpe, who had an English wife and two adopted children, and she used to help Mrs Thorpe with housework and babysitting.[13] When the Thorpes returned to Australia, where his family had a farm near Victor Harbour in South Australia, they offered to sponsor the Dungey family and provide them with a house on the farm, free produce and £12 a week, in return for which Edward would work on the farm while Beatrice helped to look after the Thorpe children. Janet thinks that they were tempted by this offer 'because Australia was such a young country and because it seemed to have so much to offer and they had three girls, I think they couldn't see any headway'. She recalls too that their inner-city Bristol neighbourhood of St Paul's was beginning to change with the arrival of Caribbean immigrants in the 1950s: 'the dark people were just arriving and one day one came into the shop and came behind the counter and helped himself to the things he needed, you know, like a self-service and that was it. I think that was the time they sort of thought, right, this is it, we're going, and it was all systems on go then.'

Beatrice Dungey was particularly keen to emigrate and Janet is still not quite sure why this was so. Perhaps Beatrice hoped to make the family fortune and return – when things went wrong in Australia she would claim that she had only intended to go for two years. By contrast with Beatrice, Edward Dungey was very close to his family and, according to Janet, 'I don't think he really in his heart wanted to leave his family, but to keep our family together I think he had to go for her sake'. Eleven-year-old Maisie had already moved five times in her short life and this was 'just another one', though she also felt 'quite excited as it was the topic of conversation at school and in the "off licence" we ran'.[14] But Janet was horrified by her mother's plans:

> Well my favourite age was 17 and I had *just* started to live, I had started to make a few friends and go dancing and I had a couple of special friends that I used to go to dances with and . . . (long pause) I think that is one of the reasons I didn't want to go to Australia because I was beginning to live and I just, I couldn't bear the thought of it. . . . I mean, I *hated* Australia with a passion even before I left England. I decided I wasn't going to like it. I did not want to go, so there was, I didn't sort of have any close rapport with my mum over this because she knew I was dead nuts about going and Daddy didn't really want to go so, but we had to go. In those days I was 18, you *had* to go, you didn't have any choice.

At 18 Janet had started to live her own life and had developed relationships – with boys as well as girl friends – outside her immediate family and she did not want to lose them. Most memorably, she wrote to the Minister of Agriculture and Fisheries to see if she could take her pet corgi to Australia, but was told she must leave it behind. Though her father's mother had died in 1948, she was particularly close to her paternal grandfather, who was 'heartbroken, couldn't realise why they wanted to go to the end of the earth'. None of her father's family came to wave them off at Temple Meads station: 'they weren't in agreement with it and I don't think they wanted to see us go'. Two weeks after the Dungeys arrived in Adelaide, and just after he had been notified of their safe arrival, Edward's father died of a heart attack.

Janet has mixed memories of her voyage to Australia on the *Otranto* in April 1956. The old ship was on its second last voyage and 'she creaked and groaned'. 'I remember standing on the deck waving to England thinking oh when will I see it again and feeling absolutely shattered and heartbroken, and realising I *hated* Australia even before I got there.' And yet like many other migrants she enjoyed the entertainments and adventure of an ocean liner. She befriended a girl called Margaret and they each fell in love with a waiter. In retrospect she realizes that she was on the rebound and looking for love, but she imagined travelling back with her Colin to England and even travelled up from Victor to stay with Margaret in Adelaide and meet up with him when the ship stopped off on its way back to England: 'as soon as the ship got back to Tilbury he sent me a "dear John" so that was the end of that romance (laughs).'

Mr Thorpe met the Dungeys at Outer Harbour and drove them through the bush to the farm, which was in a valley twelve miles out of Victor Harbour. Janet sustained her resentment. 'I remember him saying, "See all the sheep in the paddocks", and I sort of, "Don't look like sheep to me, looks like maggots on some green meat", I was trying to be as derogatory as I could about Australia.' Arrival was a terrible shock. There were two houses on the property and it seems that Mr Thorpe had told the immigration authorities that the Dungeys would be living in the comfortable farmhouse he was actually building for his own family, while all along intending to put the Dungeys in a tin shed up the road.

> When eventually we got there it was just heartbreaking. We had no fly screens, we had no screen doors, we had no running water, we had a bucket under the kitchen sink, we had no electricity, we had *nothing*, and I thought is this Australia? I thought it was the end of the earth, never mind Australia. I thought it was dreadful, and I couldn't bear the smell, you know, if it rained a few spots you could smell this dust. It was, outside was all brown. I mean, the grass was that high and it was all brown, it was *horrible*.

The property was not cleared and instead of living off the land as they had imagined they had to buy all their food. At 42 Edward Dungey was totally unsuited to the hard physical labour of grubbing out trees, but when he tried to get a job as a chemist in Adelaide his British qualifications were deemed unacceptable. He started to drink at night and came out in carbuncles on his legs, which Janet thinks was stress-related: 'drinking wouldn't have helped but it was a way of putting yourself into oblivion to forget your troubles'. The domestic conditions were appalling and Beatrice was desperately unhappy from the start. Even young Maisie, who was initially excited by the new life, recalls the primitive housing and terrible problems with mosquitoes and that 'it was hell' for her parents.

Janet's own frustrations continued when she was told that in order to train as a teacher she would have to go back to school for another year. At 18 she had no intention of returning to school and instead started work as a telephonist in Victor Harbour. Through the job she began to make some friends and even attended local dances but she suffered terrible homesickness, and whenever she heard a British accent on the telephone 'I would just home in on them.' The problem was exacerbated by what she perceived to be Australian anti-Englishness and disdain for the complaints of 'whingeing Poms':

> they'd laugh when they said it and that was the thing, you had to laugh ... I stood so much of it and inside I would be crying, I would be laughing outside but crying inside and I got to the stage where I couldn't take it any more, and I think perhaps Mum felt like that too.

Though she had to pay her mother for board and repay her father for the motorbike she rode to work, for eighteen months Janet saved £5 of her £8 weekly salary and schemed about getting back to England.

After eighteen months the Dungeys left the farm and moved into a house just outside Victor Harbour, where Edward started work as a medical orderly in a rehabilitation centre. Soon after the move he came home one day and announced that they had used up their savings and did not have enough funds to return to England. His wife was already in despair and this shocking announcement triggered her nervous breakdown:

> I guess it started with her not wanting to mix and not being involved in anything and then she was trembling, she couldn't put a cup to her mouth without it shaking and she just got herself into such a state and she had to go into hospital and . . . they were going to give her shock treatment but they didn't.

Janet had to take over the mothering alongside her own job, and though Beatrice was hospitalized for only a few weeks Maisie recalls that at this point 'my childhood ended and stark reality took over'.[15] After their mother came out of hospital the Dungeys moved to Adelaide. Beatrice got a job as a cook and Edward started a chiropody practice. Eventually they bought a house in Hazelwood Park and Beatrice began to accept her Australian fate: 'she'd sort of settled down *somewhat* by this time, I think her heart was still in England but her family was there and by this time two of us were married so I think she sort of had to cut her losses and just settle to the best of her ability'. One consequence of the family's migration – and of the loss of their extended family – was that the Dungey family became and remained very close-knit:

> Well, because it was only us, it was just my father, mother and two sisters, so that we always recognised any birthday, we would all go to the house of whose birthday it was and make a big thing of it because there were only the five of us. We had nobody else so we tended to stick very close together.

They were delighted when Beatrice's sister and her husband came out to live near them after retirement in 1967, although paradoxically, Edward Dungey had refused to sponsor his in-laws' migration, perhaps because of his own negative experience of sponsorship, and in a cruel twist of fate the sister died of cancer only two years later.

Before moving to Adelaide Janet had met Alan Francis through a contact at the Victor Harbour telephone exchange. They started to go to dances together and she stopped saving and scheming for return. Alan's family was not entirely happy with the relationship, in part because Janet was three years older than Alan but also because 'I was English. Once Alan and I started going together that was it, we were forbidden to see each other, we used to meet each other in secret . . . They resented English people, they didn't want Alan to marry me 'cause I was a Pom.' Despite these family tensions, Alan and Janet married in 1962, settled in Adelaide and had two sons, Paul and Roger. For Janet the period of her early married life and child raising was a second and very different phase in her life and migration history:

> But when my children were young and I was, I had a job, I went back to being a telephonist and I guess I was very busy educating them and taking them to sports and running a home and doing my job and socialising, I didn't have time to be homesick . . . I loved Alan very dearly and I think our love grew with each day that I was married to him, you know I was accustomed to my lifestyle by then and we had a good lifestyle, we had a good life and we both had a car each and we had lovely holidays together and a lovely family and I settled down, my life, my family was, you know, the most important thing in my life.

And yet though Janet 'didn't have time to be homesick' and assumed that her life would always be in Australia, occasionally her feelings about England would re-emerge:

> If Alan was away . . . he was working for the government, he used to go away for a week in every three or four weeks, and I used to get homesick then, my feelings would sort of come to the fore and I would play 'Land of hope and glory' and I would play it full blast, 'cause it didn't matter, we weren't attached to any house, so I wasn't bothering anybody, but then my neighbour sort of, at the back, he would say the next day, 'Were we feeling a bit nostalgic last night?' (laughs). 'Cause I mean sometimes the windows would be open, so probably he would hear it if he was in the garden, and I would have a couple of drinks and, you know, have a few silent tears I guess, and I guess it's always been there, the homesickness, but I was able to overcome it, I mean it wasn't first and foremost in my mind in that second middle phase. . . . And I used to play Vera Lynn, 'There'll always be an England' and all the war songs. I'm very partial to all her songs 'cause that's my memories, that's what I grew up with. Mmm.

In 1979, four years after the death of their father, Maisie took her mother on a holiday visit to England. This was the first of several trips Beatrice enjoyed before she died: ' she loved them, she always said if she had enough money and her family went, she wouldn't think twice about going home, but I mean it wasn't possible'. As Janet's own sons now grew up and left home the settled pattern of her married life began to feel less complete and her homesickness worsened. She made her first trips 'home' in 1985 with Maisie and then in 1988 with Alan, and she recalls how these trips reinforced a sense of not belonging in Australia and planted the seeds of return:

> I mean, here's me, absolutely homesick, been homesick for the last ten years and what are we doing here, this is ridiculous, and you know I didn't come back for a holiday until I'd been in Australia for twenty-nine years, and people used to say to me out there, 'It's not what you left, it won't be what you think,' and okay, it had changed a little. I mean, when I went out there we didn't have motorways or anything but basically where I went down to Shirehampton where I was bought up the village is still the same, double-decker buses still go down past each other and you sort of step back on the pavement like this, hadn't changed at all. And I knew that, even after twenty-nine years, I knew that this was home and this was where I really wanted to be.

In 1993 Janet's eldest son Paul took a working holiday in England but stayed on after he married an Englishwoman and bought a house. The second son Roger was already married with two young children, but could not find permanent work in recession-hit Australia and he and his family decided to get a one-way ticket to Paul's wedding with the intention of finding work in Britain. Both sons settled in England, where they found work more easily than they had in Australia. Janet's dream of return seemed much closer now, but she did not believe it was possible until she read about a 75-year-old woman who was coming from England to live with her daughter-in-law in Adelaide, and then spoke to the woman on the phone:

> And she said to me, you do it, she said. You're still young, she said. If you want to do it, you do it. And I said, I'm so frightened, I said, I know it's my country and I know they speak English but I said and I understand my parents, what they must have felt when they went out to a strange country *with three kids in tow* not knowing a soul, only the sponsors and not knowing anybody else, to a country they don't know, and I said, I can't believe what they did, and I said here am I so scared about going home, and she said, Well I do miss my friends, she said but I can pick up the phone and I can chat to them, she said, which isn't the same, but, she said, but I've got my son here and my lovely daughter-in-law and, she said, and we are quite settled.

Janet still worried about asking Alan to leave his parents, but he responded that 'my boys are my life' and became 'the main stalwart':

> he was just like the Rock of Gibraltar, he kept saying we can do it and We are going to do it and You've been talking about it for years, we are going to do it. Oh yes, but what if, and maybe, and I don't want to end up destitute and what if we haven't got enough money? and he kept saying, We can do it.

They pulled down their big old rambling house in Adelaide and built two duplexes, planning to use the proceeds of the sale for their retirement in England. When the housing market collapsed in the late 1990s they were forced to delay their departure and the sale produced less capital than they had hoped to take to England. In one final, paradoxical twist Janet took out Australian citizenship shortly before leaving to ensure that if her sons came back to Australia she would not be trapped in England, but on the condition that she would not relinquish her British citizenship and would not have to make a public display of loyalty to Australia:

> I said to the boys, I said well, I'll have to have half my brain removed to become an Australian citizen, no offence [we both laugh]. So of course they laughed and I said, but I'm *not* telling anybody, now this is a big secret, I'm not telling anybody and I said, I'm not going up on the stage, I'm *not* doing it in front of people . . . .

In November 1997 Janet, now aged 59, returned with Alan to live in England after forty-one years in Australia.

Return is never easy and places of the heart rarely stay the same. At first the Francises tried to settle in Bristol, where Alan got a job in a factory and they rented a flat just outside the city and near the kennels where Janet's Australian dog was in quarantine – she had determined not to leave another dog behind. But drugs and crime seemed to be rife and the neighbourhood was *'absolutely the pits, it was dreadful.* And you know, the element that was there was absolutely *disgusting.'* A car accident further rocked Janet's confidence and she began to think about giving up and going back to Australia, but Alan said '"No bloody fear," he says, "we're not, we haven't tried it long enough".' Roger and his wife Karen brought them to live with their family in Surrey and helped them to find a house not far away on the edge of a small town in Sussex. Just as they were about to buy the house Janet suffered one more shocking blow, with a diagnosis of breast cancer. Again her sons rallied around to sort out her health needs and finalize the house purchase.

Nine months after arrival, while in the midst of chemotherapy following a successful mastectomy, Janet and Alan moved into a new home which looks out over a small cottage garden into the green fields of her English dream. The house is not as large as the one they had in Adelaide, but 'for the first time in my life I am happy'.[16]

> I think it's that sense of belonging, when I walk around and I see some sort of layabouts or sheer poverty I think . . . but that is part of England and I don't like some of the things but all the trees and I look at the sky and last night we were having a pot of tea out in the garden – well I was having a pot of tea, Alan was having coffee – at half past nine and it's so quiet around here, and it was so lovely and peaceful and I said to Alan,

this house, I love the house, it's nice and, by English standards it's quite large and I said I just think we were so lucky to have found this place when we did and I think this sense of belonging, that, you know, I'm *one* of them now, I'm not the alien any more, I'm not the foreigner, Alan is now, I've been the foreigner for forty-one years because I *never* felt accepted as a true Australian while I was out there.

Janet has been inducting Alan in British ways of life, including afternoon tea at Buckingham Palace (after their names were drawn out of a barrel at Australia House) and the Millennium Proms in the Royal Albert Hall. 'To see Alan standing there as an Australian waving the union jack, singing "Land of hope and glory", I thought I'd never see that (laughs). It was a sight to behold.' Janet's own migration story has, at last, come full circle.

Explaining return

This kind of in-depth migrant life story highlights the long-term influences which lie behind more superficial explanations of migration and return. For example, family dynamics are part of most return stories, but they are usually deep-rooted and complicated, and we begin to understand their effects only through the long span of a life history. Thus to comprehend the Dungeys' emigration we probably need to know more about how Beatrice Dungey's early life contributed to long-term frustration with England and her idealized hopes of an Australian future, and about her relationship with the Thorpe family. To understand Janet's resistance to emigration and her youthful scheming to return, it helps to know about her close relationship with her grandparents and about the crushing of her teenage aspirations. And her eventual return after forty-one years can be explained only in the light of her sons' decision to live in England as well as Alan's devotion to his sons and to the achievement of Janet's dream.

Similarly, though tangible economic factors are significant within every story of migration and return – for example, the Dungeys' expectation of improved opportunities for their daughters and the brutal reality of their initial years in Australia – these economic forces and their impact upon migrant decision making can be understood only in relation to migrant subjectivity. 'Subjectivity' means the aspirations and emotions which are underpinned by a person's sense of identity: who she is, where she comes from, and what she wants to become. For example, the emotional resonance of Janet's dream of returning to England can be understood when she talks about her wartime childhood in rural Somerset and how it engendered a potent English identity evoked by patriotic songs and symbolized by a pastoral idyll of the English countryside.

The story of Janet Francis and her family spotlights many of the factors which caused migrants to return to Britain, including economic difficulties, homesickness and family reunion. The relative importance of the different factors which influence return can be assessed by quantifying the explanations which members of a panel of over 200 return migrants cite as making a significant contribution to their decision to return from Australia. Of course this provides only a very rough numerical breakdown – it is evident from interviews that the written accounts received from migrants sometimes provide only a partial explanation of return – but the survey does provide an invaluable overview. It confirms some hunches, suggests new directions for analysis and challenges some of the more simplistic contemporary explanations of return.[17]

Firstly, a significant minority (just under a quarter) of respondents cite economic and job-related factors as contributing to their return, though very few returned because of unemployment or desperate financial difficulties. Somewhat surprising, in the light of political controversies in the 1950s and 1960s, is the finding that only a very small minority (twenty) cite housing difficulties as contributing to return, and that conditions in migrant hostels barely rate as a reason for return. Accidents and illness – and resulting concern about long-term security in Australia and the comparative costs of health care – are mentioned slightly more frequently (twenty-eight times) than problems with accommodation. A few returns were influenced by aspects of Australian lifestyle (seven), the character of its people (ten) and the climate (twelve), though very few (only four) reported that negative Australian attitudes to British migrants (the so-called 'whingeing Poms') were influential, and only a handful (six) returned because they 'hated Australia', these being outnumbered by many more return migrants who rather liked – and even 'loved' – Australia, and for whom Australia itself was not a reason for return. Though feelings about Australia and Australians were not particularly significant, homesickness for people and places and ways of life in Britain (fifty-two), or a sense of 'not feeling at home' in Australia (forty), did influence the return of a very significant minority of respondents (well over a third). Most important of all – influencing at least half the return migrants – were the complicated responsibilities, needs, desires and tensions of family relationships, which pulled people back to Britain and then often kept them there despite a personal preference for Australia. Families loom large in the stories of migration and return. The rest of this chapter focuses on homesickness as one significant – and complex – cause of return.

Homesickness

'Homesickness' is a troublesome term. It has often been used – by migration officials and contemporary commentators, by historians and indeed by migrants themselves – as a shorthand explanation which simplifies or even conceals a complex experience. It is frequently dismissed as a feeling which is not particularly important or long-lasting, as something to be grown out of or which eases with time. It carries particular cultural meanings – for example, the British migrant association with 'whingeing Poms' – and is commonly explained away as a female problem, signifying women's particular bonds with place and people or their emotional vulnerability and weakness. Migrant stories confront these assumptions and require homesickness to be considered in both intimate detail and general terms.

It has already been seen, in Janet Francis's account of her mother's breakdown and of her own re-emerging homesickness, that the phenomenon could be a potent aspect of the migrant experience. Two other accounts highlight the diverse ways in which homesickness was experienced as well as its potent effects. Scottish migrants John and Margaret Hardie returned to Scotland with their young daughter Gillian in 1967 after living and working in the LaTrobe Valley in Gippsland for three years. Margaret's homesickness was the root cause of their return. Though John enjoyed the outdoor life and his work as a power station electrician, Margaret was isolated at home with her young, pre-school daughter:

> I was very homesick, very homesick. . . . Not just immediately I would say but I wouldnae like to say how long before it really start to hit home, I really was miserable an awful lot of the time and he said, he'd come in from work and I was preparing the meal, standing at the sink and I've got 'Green Green Grass of Home', Tom Jones, and the tears were flowing, just could not stop them. I was really sometimes very very unhappy. . . . I missed my family, I missed my brother very very much, but then it could go for a while and I was all right again but it never really left me. . . . It was with me *every* day, but some days were worse than others and other times you could forget it. I think maybe if, you know, if Gillian hadnae been so young and I had been out in the workplace that might even have been better but as I wasn't that didn't work so.

The Hardies' decision to return was influenced by concern about John's mother's health, and by a poignant reunion with Margaret's sister, who was herself returning to Scotland from New Zealand. But the 'clincher' was an extraordinary event at a hospital in Traralgon where John used to entertain patients in his spare time. One day he noticed a group of women patients dressed in white but with no obvious injury or illness. A staff member explained:

He says, 'Well, everyone you see dressed in white, they're all Scottish women who are suffering nerves, they've gone into depression, and then it goes into nervous depression', which apparently is frightening. I said, 'Nothing you can do?' He says, 'The only thing we can do is put them on a train, or a plane, or a boat back, that's the only cure', he says, 'Ninety per cent of who you see here won't do it,' because through medical situations, medical bills – touch wood we were never really bothered with that – you know they've got themselves into such a financial hole and owe so much money they would never ever get out of Australia unless someone from the UK could come forward and say, there's your fare.[18]

John concluded that he did not 'want to see Margaret walking around like this' and they agreed to return to Scotland.

John Williams was an electrician who emigrated from Swindon to Queensland in 1965 with his wife Esther and two young children. They built a beautiful house on a block of land outside Brisbane – 'Savernake represented the realisation of all our hopes and dreams' – and two more children were born in Australia. Homesickness set in for John after the house was finished and they were well settled:

We were obviously all very happy with our lot, but something was very wrong. I began to feel vaguely ill from time to time and could discover no reason for it. Then, one day, Esther's mother sent us a calendar showing pictures of England. As soon as I saw it my heart sank and I felt very miserable. Hardly crediting it, I began to consider the possibility that I was homesick, a thing which I had always roundly condemned everyone else for! Little by little, I began to notice other things which caused a similar reaction, such as watching an English comedy on TV.

One late afternoon as the heat of the day began to abate, the time of day I loved on the land, I was outside popping up stumps when I heard a jet high above. I looked up, and what a picture it made! The deep blue sky framed by eucalyptus trees and, far above, the vapour trail and shiny body of a jet, obviously a passenger Boeing 707. Then, as I realised that the aircraft was probably on its way to England (at least, it was heading in the right direction), the now familiar lurch of the stomach hit me, and my eyes welled full of tears. 'How stupid!' I thought, angrily.

As time went by, this feeling became all too familiar and something obviously had to be done about it, but I had no idea what. By now my sleep was regularly disturbed with dreams of England. The things I yearned for most were not, strangely enough, the people, but little peeps of England such as church steeples set in the centre of clustering villages and gently rolling hills. Most powerful of all was the image of myself sitting on an old Cotswold stone wall![19]

Though Esther and the two older children were much opposed to leaving Australia, as John became more dejected and ill they reluctantly agreed to return to England.

These examples highlight a number of points about homesickness. They show how homesickness can be a constant, everyday experience, or how it can be triggered at particular moments through poignant memory association, such as the calendar with pictures of England, or the aeroplane flying overhead. In many migrant stories sound is a potent trigger, and songs – for Margaret Hardie 'The Green Green Grass of Home', for Janet Francis 'Land of Hope and Glory' and 'There'll Always Be an England' – recall another time and place, evoking a sense of loss through their lyrics and emotive music. Events such as Christmas were also poignant reminders of the absence of family and friends, and the stark differences between the two countries were highlighted by rituals which seemed hollow in an upside-down world. Kathleen Upton spent her first Australian Christmas Eve at Fremantle docks farewelling another migrant who was returning to Britain:

> We returned to our house, very subdued. A parcel awaited us from home and there were several cards and letters, but it didn't feel a bit like Christmas. We exchanged small gifts next morning and opened our presents from home; Ron turned the portable radio on and the voice of Bing Crosby filled the room singing 'Silent Night'. I burst into tears. 'Switch it off. I can't stand it,' I cried. The thought of those at home, playing games round the fire, roasting chestnuts, eating turkey and mince pies, the tree with all the lights and small gifts was just too much to bear. We had no special dinner, cold corned beef and tomatoes was all that our budget allowed. I couldn't wait for the day to end.

This emotional association and disturbance also occupied the dream life of many migrants, like John Williams, or Kathleen Upton, who recalls her first night in a bush hut as she and her husband saved to return. 'I fell into a deep sleep, no doubt dreaming my recurring dream, in which I walked down the pavements of my old road, seeing so clearly every crack and kerbstone.'[20]

Alternatively, homesickness might be spoken aloud and reinforced within social settings and relationships. Many return migrants describe the unsettling effects of mixing with other disgruntled British migrants, either in the migrant hostels or at recreational events. Manchester teenager Chris Gray recalls this effect when his family moved to Brisbane in 1956:

> And, all the people we knew, my mum and dad knew, and even the lads I played football with, said, 'Oh, as soon as we save enough money, you know, we're going to go back to England,' and that. And for the first two years I thought, well, I agree with them, I thought, I did miss England a little bit, and Australia wasn't quite as adventurous as I thought it was. And they used to have plenty of parties between all the English people, and they was always saying, 'Oh, wait till we get back to, oh we can't wait to get back to England,' you know.[21]

Homesickness was experienced in terms of the absence or loss of different aspects of 'home'. John Williams longed for rural England; the physical environment had always been important to his sense of identity and belonging, and in Australia he missed an idealized pastoral English landscape – just as he would later miss the Australian bush. Similarly, Janet Francis missed the fields and country buses of her formative West Country childhood, and a pastoral sense of identity and patriotism which had been forged in wartime. Elizabeth and Derek Tribe were a university couple who emigrated to Australia in 1956 and wrote a guidebook for professional migrants based upon their own experiences. They had asked fellow migrants what they most missed of life in Britain and one answer was 'Marks & Spencer's':

> Among the other, and more serious, answers we often get 'English countryside'. It is interesting that although the Australian countryside is often superbly majestic and beautiful, it scarcely ever has the intimate charm of, say, the Cotswolds or Hampshire. . . . if you want to spend your Sunday afternoon pleasantly strolling over downs, along towpaths and through primrose woods, following well worn tracks and climbing well worn stiles, then Australia is a dead loss.[22]

This longing for pastoral England is fascinating in a number of ways. Firstly, the rural England that is missed is usually the very specific landscape of the southern Home Counties. Secondly, most of the post-war immigrants who missed this rural England had come from cities and suburbs. Their Australian longing for pastoral England seems to be an overseas manifestation of the twentieth-century cultural phenomenon by which the English middle and working classes located their national identity within rural England. Apart from Londoners, the urban British were never far from the countryside, and the train, followed by the motor car, had contributed to a rural tourism which was encouraged by advertising and by a prolific cultural industry of ruralist writers and painters. From the vantage point of city slums and smoking factories the English countryside was – after the industrial revolution – perceived as paradise indeed, and working-class emigrants carried this longing in their cultural baggage. The stark and sunburnt Australian countryside may have fuelled a longing for a green pastoral England, but the cultural origins of this particular homesickness were located back home. Significantly, a pastoral idyll does not seem to be a significant factor in the homesickness of immigrants from urban Scotland, whereas both urban and rural Welsh immigrants describe powerful feelings of *hiraeth* (homesickness) for the valleys and hills which are such a resonant part of Welsh identity. Maureen Carter was 19 when she left Neath in south Wales:

There must have been hundreds of people on that railway station, all singing, 'We'll keep a Welcome in the Hillside'! It brings tears to my eyes now! And, one of the lines is, 'We'll kiss away each hour of hiraeth, when you come home again to Wales'! And I – I – I still crack up when I think of it. And I just had that feeling for so long, well it seemed like so long, when I first came[23]

Place was also related to particular ways of life, as the young Worthing mother Anne Cox recalls of her own homesickness in Perth during the early 1970s. 'I missed the public library, the swimming baths, going to the pub with friends, the green of the downs, the public transport system.'[24] Migrants from the north of England, and especially women, often recall that they missed the socializing of men and women in local pubs, and thus invoke one form of urban homesickness as a counterpoint to the more typical ruralism.

But most of all, homesick migrants missed people; a significant number of the sample of return migrants went home so that they could be closer to their family and friends.[25] Dot Hallas had never really wanted to leave her close extended family in Yorkshire but her mother had said that she should follow her husband to Australia, where she 'cried every night for twelve months! . . . I didn't care about England, I wanted me Mum!'[26] In 1960 19-year-old Terry Stephens had been thrilled by the prospect of adventure in Australia with her new husband Ian, but after their first child was born she became lonely and isolated in suburban Melbourne. She missed the cultural life she had previously enjoyed in Brighton, but above all she desperately missed the five brothers and sisters who had been so important in her English life. 'My sister played the piano and every time I heard, I mean we liked a lot of classical music but any time I heard the piano I would just cry.'[27] Anne Barkas recalls her homesickness when she settled in Newcastle, north of Sydney, with her husband and young son in 1960:

Yes, I used to go out and look at the moon at Edgeworth and think: 'Gee, that same moon is shining on England,' you know. I was very, terribly homesick. I think I'd have stowed away to get back to England. Well, when I first came to Australia I would sit watchin' the back door. And when I lived in South Shields, every night me father called in at half past eight. And he was like to go for a pint. And he'd call and see me and go for a pint till half past nine and go home. And I used to think then I'd give *anything* for me father to open the door, you know![28]

Though homesickness involves the migrant articulating a sense of loss or absence from another place and time, it is fundamentally about the here and now. Homesickness grows out of how people feel about where they are and about the life they are leading and the actual or prospective achievement of aspirations. For British migrants homesickness was as much about their lives in Australia as about their 'home' in Britain. Part of the evidence for this argument lies in the stories of migrants who were not homesick, or for whom momentary pangs of longing were offset by the positive challenge and excitement of their Australian lives. These are men and women who had taken a grip on their new lives, who were living the life they had imagined or were actively working – maybe even struggling – towards their migration goals. Though Ray and Irene Spencer's migration came unstuck when they could not buy a house in Perth, neither of them experienced homesickness:

> We only phoned home once didn't we? That's all, to say we were all right and things like that but no never really missed the family. But we were so busy all the time – I mean, I was working, Ray was working, Alan was out all the time with his friends. We didn't really have a lot of time to miss the family. There was so much to do.

Even Janet Francis, who experienced terrible homesickness when she first arrived in Australia and again later in life, recalls that her homesickness subsided when she had a young family of her own. 'But when my children were young and I was, I had a job, I went back to being a telephonist and I guess I was very busy educating them and taking them to sports and running a home and doing my job and socialising, I didn't have time to be homesick.'[29]

By contrast, a closer look at the circumstances of British homesickness in Australia offers an insight into the malady. For example, homesickness was often particularly acute for women who were expecting a baby, especially a first child, or who were at home with young children while the father was working long hours away from home. These women wanted the practical and emotional support of mothers and other members of the extended family back in Britain, and while their husbands made new friends at work they were often lonely and isolated. Contemporary commentators – and many of the migrants themselves – argued that women were more prone to homesickness than men, and it is likely that the significance for women of social and especially family networks is part of the explanation; in the survey women returnees recall significant episodes of homesickness six times more often than do men.

Yet there is also a hidden form of male homesickness. It is rarely labelled as such, partly because of the stereotype of female weakness. In the University of Sussex archive there are several examples of men who were desperate to go home but who blamed their return on the 'homesickness' of their wives, who in turn explain that they felt no such thing and that their husbands were simply unable to admit to their own feelings.[30] There are abundant clues in accounts by wives and children of the physical and emotional breakdown of their menfolk. Elizabeth Gray recalls that after their arrival in 1959 her husband Harry could find little work as a plasterer in Queensland, where most of the houses were timber. He worried about work security and the absence of an Australian equivalent to the British national insurance scheme, he became unwell and developed a facial tick, and he became obsessed with return. Despite the fact that Elizabeth and their three sons were very happy in Australia, the Gray family returned to Essex in 1961. In 1951 Alvyn and Bruce Bates emigrated with their parents and sister to Brisbane, where their father took up a sponsored job as a saw doctor in a timber mill. One of the brothers who owned the mill resented their father and was critical of his work. Alvyn recalls that 'as a consequence he became very unsettled, unhappy and effectively had a nervous breakdown. Towards the end of his time in Australia he began to look very haggard,' and after little more than a year his old employer in England paid for the family's return.[31]

These are tragic stories about the destruction of men's hopes and aspirations. These were proud working-class men whose masculine identity was primarily bound up in their professional craft and an ability to provide for the family, and who found, to their humiliation, that they were unable to sustain this identity in Australia. Barely able to admit failure, their bodies and nerves cracked up, and their only, desperate hope was return. These men might not have labelled themselves as homesick but they had all the symptoms of the malady. Even with men like John Williams, who explains his homesickness in terms of a longing for pastoral England, it is possible to see other explanations within their Australian lives. At about the same time as he began to yearn for the villages and rolling hills of the Cotswolds, John Williams had resigned from a steady electrician's job with Frigidaire and tried to make a living selling his art work; it was a disastrous failure. One dream was deflated, and the other – of building his own home in the Australian bush – had been achieved, and John was thus at a point in his life where homesickness could easily take root.

These case studies also confront simplistic models which explain homesickness as a passing phase, which sufferers get over or grow out of, or alternatively as a constant emotion which festers and deepens over time. Homesickness comes and goes with the phases and events of life. For example, government statistics suggest that in recent years there has been an increase in the return rate of older British migrants. Janet Francis's experiences exemplify this trend of 'retirement migration' by men and women who, in later life, feel a resurgence of homesickness and a growing desire to live out their lives in Britain.[32] At the other extreme are the young men and women who came to Australia as young children with their migrant parents, who enjoyed growing up in Australia, and yet in early adulthood were drawn back to their country of origin. Michael Siberry was 6 when he left Bournemouth in 1963 with his parents and older siblings for Tasmania, where his father worked as a GP. They lived in a lovely house in Hobart alongside a sprawling patch of bush and Michael relished the outdoor lifestyle. After training at drama school in Sydney he had three successful years as an actor with the South Australian State Theatre Company, but something was missing:

> I always remained curious about my dad's brothers, my mum's family, and I just wanted to get back. And all through being in Australia I'd sort of, through watching television and through letters and magazines, built up this image of this place here, and always felt I would go back whether I was an actor or not. I sort of thought, maybe I'll go to college in England because it was part of the outside world, a bigger outside world.
>
> On returning to England in 1979 I actually wrote in a diary 'I feel complete.'
>
> I felt, I felt maybe an outsider as far as Tasmania was concerned and I felt actually, I *belong* where my parents came from, and that was my initial feeling, 'cause I'd wanted to get back. I'd wanted to see England and I wanted to be back and I finally made . . . it had been something I'd been planning for years and I'd done the trip and *was* back and I was terribly excited about being here. And it was the initial sort of feeling that at last I'm back, I've arrived, now I can explore this place. And it was just that feeling that . . . I'd achieved some goal. I'd attained some purpose . . . and then a part of my life which had always been a sort of unexplored territory or was on hold or that I always put over here that was a place I came from as a child, but I'm still curious about it, I want to get back to it, had been resolved because I'd got back. But, that was the initial, that was my, fabulous excitement in the feeling of coming back.[33]

Some British immigrants believed that a short visit back home might cure homesickness. Of course for most migrants a British holiday was not financially possible, though by the 1960s some among the earliest immigrant wave had amassed sufficient savings to afford such a trip, and the reduced cost and comparative ease of jet travel made the return visit a more realistic option. As early as 1963 the university couple Elizabeth and Derek Tribe noted that 'many of our friends, particularly the wives, tell us that, after a trip home, they have returned to settle much more contentedly in Australia'.[34] Ivy Skowronski had emigrated from Bournemouth with her Polish refugee husband and their children in 1959, and settled in the South Australian townships of Whyalla and then Salisbury. For many years Ivy endured 'bouts of homesickness': she missed 'the sweet freshness of the English countryside, or twilight evenings watching the sea', and she 'longed to see

her mother and brother, 'plus umpteen cousins, not to mention friends
. . . on the other side of the world. No longer could I hop on the bus to
visit them for the day.' Ivy explains that in the early 1970s group travel
organizations were arranging cheap rates for British migrants who
wanted to visit the 'old country', and that in 1971 her family
announced that they could manage without her and that she should go
home to see her 90-year-old mother. Ivy enjoyed the reunion with her
mother and other relatives, but England had changed:

> it was all grumble, grumble, about high prices, the government, the
> Common Market, the trouble in Ireland. It was all very depressing. . . .
> Yes, there were marked changes in England and I had not grown with
> these differences, that was why they were so noticeable. I too had
> changed in my ways and outlook on life and because the last twelve years
> had been spent away, I was now able to make a comparison.

Ivy flew back to Australia 'with my homesickness for England cured
for ever'.[35]

Some migrants who returned to live in Britain later wished that they
had come home only for a brief visit to meet relatives and assuage
homesickness. Irene Spencer realized too late that a short visit was all
she had really needed and she deeply regretted selling up in Australia
and resettling in Wales. But for other British migrants a return visit
had the opposite effect on homesickness. For Janet Francis and her
sister Maisie McDonald holiday trips to England only intensified the
dream of a permanent return. Phillip Maile's mother 'had' to travel
back to England on a regular basis to visit her family, but 'even after
thirty-seven years the homesickness ache remains, especially for
Mum'. Phillip married an Englishwoman who herself made several
trips back home:

> Each time she returned to Australia very emotional and homesick for
> a week or two, and tried so hard to explain how and why she missed
> England so much. Her mother was obvious, but also the quiet beauty of
> the place, the genteel way of life, the villages, the history, the culture, her
> roots, her memories. Where had I heard these words before, I wonder?[36]

The contrasting examples of Phillip Maile's family and Ivy Skowronski
confirm that while homesickness is deeply felt in terms of absence and
loss, it is generated by thoughts and feelings about life in the here and
now. Home visits might help the homesick British immigrant to recognize the positive aspects of his or her Australian life, but they are
just as likely to engender a sense of inadequacy and incompleteness,
and a hankering for 'home'.

Janet Francis's story suggests that even when return to England
'cures' homesickness the cure, and return itself, can never be assured.

When Janet describes Alan and herself at the Millenium Proms in the Royal Albert Hall, waving their union jack and singing 'Land of Hope and Glory' at the top of their voices, it seems that Janet's life has come full circle, and that her migration story is over. And yet migration never ends and the future must always be uncertain. At the conclusion of the interview Janet captures this tension when asked if she imagines they will spend the rest of their lives in England:

> Absolutely, wild horses wouldn't get me away now. I went before because I had to, I would never *never*, unless circumstances changed. If say my boys went back and I could see no more future here, well, then I guess I would go back with my tail between my legs but it wouldn't be by choice. I'm home now and this is where I belong and where I want to stay, for ever, for as long as I've got.

Conclusion

It is clear from statistical evidence that a significant proportion of post-war emigrants to Australia returned to live in Britain. This chapter has challenged the simplistic and polarized explanations that were offered by contemporary commentators in both Britain and Australia and which were underpinned by the assimilationist attitudes of the period. Analysis of migrant life histories produces a more complex and nuanced set of understandings of return. Migration and return were profoundly affected by transnational family relations and dynamics. By reviewing the long span of the life course and extended family history it becomes evident how the causes of return were often deeply rooted in pre-migration experiences, and how the prospect of return changes – sometimes in unexpected ways – throughout the life course of the 'settled' migrant.

Focusing on one important cause of return migration, this chapter has explored how migrant life stories also confront simplistic assumptions about 'homesickness'. It has argued that homesickness was about problems with life in Australia as much if not more than about the life missed in Britain; that the nature and extent of homesickness were often related to particular stages in the life course; that feelings about 'home' were informed by unique personal experience and yet were also influenced by powerful cultural representations of place and nationality; and that homesickness could be profoundly affected by the presence or absence of the sustaining social relationships offered by family and friends. Gender analysis offers useful insights into homesickness and helps to explain how and why women migrants in particular often suffered acutely at certain life stages. Yet it has also been demonstrated that there was a distinct and often unrecognized form of male migrant homesickness that was caused by men's failure as worker or family breadwinner and by the collapse of masculine identity. Finally, it has been shown that homesickness is not a passing emotional phase that the migrant overcomes, outgrows or resolves through return, but that it comes and goes with phases and events in life. Even for the most settled of migrants, return is always a possibility.

Notes

1 Written account by Mary Holmes, US H18.
2 The University of Sussex collection will be archived within Special Collections in the university library. These accounts are referred to in the notes with the prefix US (University of Sussex) and the alphanumeric code attributed to each contributor. Accounts from the La Trobe University archive are identified here by the prefix LU. *Ten Pound Poms* will be published by Manchester University Press. For more details about published and unpublished autobiographical accounts by British post-war migrants which are available in Australian archives see Alistair Thomson, 'Recording British Migration: Place, Meaning and Identity in Audio Letters from Australia, 1963–1965' in Wilfred Prest and Graham Tulloch (eds), *Scatterlings of Empire* (St Lucia: University of Queensland Press, 2001), 106–16.
3 Dudley Baines, *Migration in a Mature Economy* (Cambridge: Cambridge University Press, 1985), 279.
4 See the written accounts by John Williams, US W21, and Bruce Bates, US B4.
5 Eric Richards, 'Annals of the Australian Immigrant' in Eric Richards, Richard Reid and David Fitzptrick (eds), *Visible Migrants: Neglected Sources for the History of Australian Immigration* (Canberra: Research School of Social Sciences, Australian National University, 1989), 16; R. Appleyard, A. Ray and A. Segal, *The Ten Pound Immigrants* (London: Boxtree, 1988), 103; Alan Richardson, *British Immigrants and Australia* (Canberra: ANU Press, 1974), 57–61; Graeme Hugo, 'Migration between Australia and Britain: Past and Present' in David Lowe (ed.), *Immigration and Integration: Australia and Britain* (London: Menzies Centre for Australian Studies, 1995), 53.
6 Interview with Sandra O'Neill, 21 September 2000, US O2.
7 Quoted in Elizabeth and Derek Tribe, *Postmark Australia: The Land and its People Through English Eyes* (Melbourne: Cheshire, 1963), 94.
8 Tribe, *Postmark Australia*, 95–6.
9 Gwen Good, 'Strangers on the Shore', and 'Wish You were Here', ABC Radio Perth Women's Session, 1 July 1964 and 16 March 1965, OH 1733ts, Oral History Collection, Battye Library of West Australian History, Perth.
10 See Richardson, *British Immigrants*, 31–73; Appleyard *et al.*, *The Ten Pound Immigrants*, 79–108; Commonwealth Immigration Advisory Council, *The Departure of Settlers from Australia, Final Report of the Committee on Social Patterns* (Canberra Department of Immigration, 1967).
11 For a review of the use of life stories in migration studies see Alistair Thomson, 'Moving Stories: Oral History and Migration Studies', *Oral History* 27:1 (1999), 24–37.
12 Unless otherwise stated, all quotes in this section are from the interview with Janet Francis 8 August 2000, US F4.
13 'Thorpe' is a pseudonym.
14 Written account by Maisie McDonald, 26 June 2000, US M6.
15 *Ibid.*, 2.
16 Written account by Janet Francis, 8 June 2000, US F4.
17 From a panel of 257 respondents the researchers have identified factors contributing to 225 'returns'. Migrants who returned twice (fourteen) and offer two separate explanations have been counted twice (several multiple returnees are counted for

each time they offer separate explanations). Respondents who were members of family groups which returned together have been counted only once, and the survey has excluded respondents for whom it was impossible to identify explanations for return. Of these 225 returns, about half involved families with children; one-third were single migrants; twenty were couples without children (identified separately because their behaviour is often closer to that of the single 'sojourners' than that of families with children); thirteen were people who had emigrated as children of migrant parents and returned by themselves as adults; and five were teenagers who had emigrated by themselves under the Big Bother scheme and then returned as adults. Note that for these 225 returns 440 contributing factors were identified, and that on average each return migrant cites two reasons for return. (Of course, some give only one reason and many outline several contributory factors.)

18 Interview with John and Margaret Hardie, 9 September 2000, US H11.
19 'Ten Pound Boomerang Poms', written account by John Williams, US W21.
20 Kathleen Upton, *To the Undiscovered Ends: An Accurate and Humorous Account of an Australian Sojourn* (Durham: Pentland Press, 1992), 71.
21 Interview with Chris Gray, 20 December 2000, USG4.
22 Elizabeth and Derek Tribe, *Postmark Australia*, 11. On English ruralism see David Matless, *Landscape and Englishness* (London: Reaktion Press, 2002).
23 See the written account by Mary Holmes, US H18; and the interview with Maureen Carter, LU.
24 Written account by Anne Cox, US C8.
25 Twenty-nine returned because they wanted to be with their families; ten because they missed friends; five said they were lonely in Australia (these categories are not mutually exclusive). By comparison, seven said that they missed their British roots and way of life.
26 Interview with Dot Hallas, 22 August 98, LU.
27 Interview with Ian and Terry Stephens, 11 July 2000, US S6.
28 Interview with Anne Barkas, 8 July 98, LU.
29 Interviews with Ray and Irene Spencer, US S7 and S8; Janet Francis, US F4.
30 Both Sandra O'Neill and Dorothy Rooms were furious when their husbands blamed return on their homesick wives – in both cases the real problem was the husband's discontent: interviews with Sandra O'Neill, US O2, and Dorothy Rooms, US R8.
31 Interview with Elizabeth Gray, 5 July 2000, US G1; written account by Alvyn and Bruce Bates, US B7 and B4; see also written accounts by Edward Crooks and Barbara Williams, US C9 and W15.
32 Hugo; 'Migration between Australia and Britain', 53; note that seven of the returnees returned late in life because they wanted to live out their remaining years in Britain: see also accounts by Jean Pritchett, US P7; John Robinson, US R9; and Christine Watkins, US W13.
33 Interview with Michael Siberry, 14 August 2000 and written account, US S9. Note that this feeling of 'completeness' in England was short-lived: 'My return only served to deepen a sense of confusion and isolation. Within six months I felt that I didn't belong anywhere. The England that I kept in my head didn't exist . . .' For a comparable experience (one of four like this in the archive) see the written account by Cliff Pester, US P16.
34 Elizabeth and Derek Tribe, *Postmark Australia*, 11.
35 Ivy Skowronski, *I Can't Think of a Title: An Autobiography* (Adelaide: Skowronski, 1986), 55–65.
36 Written account by Phillip Maile, US M3.

CHAPTER SEVEN

Roots tourism as return movement: semantics and the Scottish diaspora
Paul Basu

> However ambiguous or polysemous our discourse may be, we are still
> able to bring our meanings into the public domain and negotiate them
> there. That is to say, we live publicly by public meanings and by shared
> procedures of interpretation and negotiation. Interpretation, however
> 'thick' it may become, must be publicly accessible or the culture falls
> into disarray and its individual members with it.
> (Jerome Bruner, *Acts of Meaning*[1])

Although the terms 'return migration' and 'return movement' are
sometimes used interchangeably in migration studies literature,
there is actually a significant difference between them. Whilst migration is undoubtedly movement, a movement is, of course, more than
migration: it may be a collective project, a cause or campaign. There
are religious movements, political movements, aesthetic movements. In diasporic contexts there are return movements such as
Zionism and Rastafarianism, movements that are at once religious,
political and aesthetic. With the obvious exception of Zionism, the
role of 'homeland' for most such movements has remained largely
symbolic.

This chapter is concerned with the contemporary phenomenon of
'roots tourism' in the Scottish Highlands and Islands: journeys made
by people of Scottish Highland descent (or part-Highland descent) ordinarily living in the United States, Canada, Australia, New Zealand and
in other regions where Scots have historically settled to places associated with their ancestors in the 'old country'. To borrow a phrase from
the psychologist Jerome Bruner, these journeys are, without doubt,
acts of meaning, but, indeed, what *are* the meanings of these acts?
Might they be understood, for instance, as a form of return movement
in the distinctive sense outlined above? Such a proposition would pre-
suppose the existence of a Scottish diaspora – but on what grounds may
this supposition be made?

Cultural dynamics are affected not only by the spatial migration of people and things, but also by the migration of meanings and discourses across and between groups which may or may not be spatially distinct. Thus, in a context defined by historical migration, indeed, in which migration has become foregrounded (suggesting it had previously formed a background), another kind of migration will be examined – a semantic migration – which makes these propositions tenable. It has been said that 'there is a will to power in nomenclature', and the concern here is with the nomenclature of diaspora and homeland in a Scottish, and particularly Scottish Highland, context.[2]

The following observations are drawn from anthropological field-work conducted between 1999 and 2001. An exercise in 'multi-sited ethnography', the 'field' encompassed both the physical spaces of the Scottish heritage landscape and the discursive spaces of the global 'mediascape'.[3] The research thus involved meeting and making journeys with roots tourists in the Scottish Highlands and Islands, working with genealogists and heritage organizations, participating in heritage events and so forth, but also sustaining a 'conversation' with members of the transnational Scottish heritage community throughout the fieldwork period – maintaining a dialogue, as it were, with the diaspora.[4] The Internet, particularly, has become an important 'contact zone' where members of this dispersed and informal community 'meet' to exchange stories, experiences and opinions, and consequently the Internet formed a key part of the research methodology. The informant comments with which the themes of this chapter are introduced were made in response to an online questionnaire that featured on a dedicated project Web site or in the context of an email discussion list devoted to the research.[5]

Disparate acts and disparate meanings

'Ancestor hunting has been very much a growth industry in recent years,' writes the Scottish historian Gordon Donaldson in the foreword to one family history how-to guide, 'part of the package for visitors from overseas.' [6] Indeed, so popular has roots tourism become that, in 1999, the newly reconstituted Scottish Parliament identified it as one of three key niche markets to be targeted in its *New Strategy for Scottish Tourism* and commissioned the Scottish Tourist Board to research and develop a plan with which to encourage it further.[7] Of course, what the Scottish Tourist Board's visitor profiles and market research statistics fail to answer are those most fundamental questions: Why do people make these journeys? What is it that they find among the ruins and graveyards of their family histories? Perhaps most important, their research fails to ask why it is that these 'tourists' rarely consider themselves to be tourists at all and may even take umbrage at being identified as such. 'My Scotland feelings are very personal to me', writes a Canadian questionnaire respondent.

> Your questionnaire is the very first format that gave me permission to explain such feelings without being labelled 'tourist'. I am not, and never will be, a tourist in Scotland . . . I felt Scotland many years before I was there. I paid tribute to Scotland on purpose and continue through my quest to learn all that I can about it and how Scotland, and especially the Highlander, evolved. It's only through their world, through their eyes, and through their pains and joys that I want to understand Scotland. I owe Scotland that, because I feel that Scotland invites me home, to be me . . . (BV, Ontario, Canada)

Such 'homecomings' take on many forms. They may involve journeys to those sites which recall the grand narratives of Highland history – places like Culloden, Glencoe and Glenfinnan with their 'intentional monuments' – but also to sites which figure in the more intimate narratives of the family history – the graves of relatives never known, the ruins of deserted croft houses and other settlements, places which, in Riegl's terminology, function as 'unintentional monuments'.[8] Some are highly organized, packaged events such as the 'Orkney Homecoming' of 1999 in which over 150 Canadians of Orcadian descent travelled together to their ancestral islands for a week of tours and lectures, concerts, and a special homecoming service at St Magnus's Cathedral.[9] Others are organized by the clan associations and societies which proliferate in the United States and Canada in particular, and which typically involve visits to places associated with clan history and lore, and often culminate in a march through the clan's historical territory behind the clan insignia, saltire, stars and stripes, maple leaf and other flags: a parading of identity which is at once local and transnational.[10] Many are much more personal journeys, undertaken by individuals or small family groups, to ancestral places discovered in the process of family history research or to meet with newly discovered 'cousins', far removed branches of the family tree still rooted in Scotland.[11]

Many issues emerge in these practices – issues that go to the heart of current discussions regarding globalization and localization, mobility and identity, transnationalism and multiculturalism, the perceived loss of continuity with the past. Such themes, and the anxieties they provoke, are often articulated in the comments of questionnaire respondents. Thus an informant from Pennsylvania describes an erosion of traditional values in America, and a consequent sense of disorientation or alienation:

I know that too many people in my country are lost, because they have no set of norms or rules to follow, and they are losing their traditions. I think this is hurting us as a whole, and that people need to take pride in the knowledge of where they come from. You have to know where you come from to know where you are going. (S.S., Pennsylvania, United States)

Interest in family history may be a response to the increasingly multicultural nature of 'New World' societies, the sense of one's particular ethnic identity gradually and inevitably being absorbed into the melting pot. An informant from British Columbia writes:

Canada was built by people from many different nationalities and cultures and I feel it is important to at least attempt to leave some sense of history for my children, grandchildren and generations to come. My personal heritage is Scotch/English, my wife's is English/Polish and now one of our daughters has married a fellow of Dutch origin. As these nationalities meld together as Canadians we must remember our forefathers and their customs and heritage. (D.A., British Columbia, Canada)

Some informants allude to an increasingly problematized sense of belonging in their countries of birth, a post-colonial unsettling of settler society.[12] This from Auckland:

For most of my life [my roots] didn't matter at all, though a vague wonder came to me from time to time. It is now important because, though a fourth-generation New Zealander, there is a feeling of belonging elsewhere. The major importance was in learning about that 'elsewhere' and realising it did have a real connection for me. I dare to say almost a sense of belonging to a place other than the country of my birth. (A.S., Auckland, New Zealand)

To find that 'elsewhere' and to visit it is often an extremely powerful, emotional and even life-changing experience. From New South Wales:

It gives one a sense of belonging and I did not seem to have this before I began the family history research. It is hard to describe but there was no depth to my existence—now I feel there is. (S.J., New South Wales, Australia)

Given the distinctions in the way Scottish heritage is enacted across both geographic and social space, the variety of forms of roots tourism, the different anxieties and desires which motivate an interest in genealogy, and, indeed, the particular contingencies of each individual family history, it is evident that these practices can have no single meaning. It is also evident, however, that in the processes of bringing meaning to these disparate acts, much of this potential for polysemy is lost. As Bruner suggests, the 'symbolic systems' that individuals use in constructing meaning are systems that are 'already in place, already "there", deeply entrenched in culture and language'.[13] The following discussion demonstrates how a dominant cultural narrative of the Scottish Highlands and Islands comes to eclipse the particularities of personal family narratives, and, furthermore, how the meaning of this cultural narrative is determined in relation to other symbolic systems which arguably have little to do with Scottish migration at all. In offering this interpretation, it is not suggested that there are not alternative cultural narratives through which meaning is brought to bear on the practices of genealogy and roots tourism in the Highlands and Islands – there are, for example, explorations of the influence of popular discourses of indigeneity on the desire of people of Scottish descent overseas to identify and visit their own 'aboriginal' landscapes.[14]

A child of the clearances?

The semantic migration with which the chapter is concerned may be introduced by a more detailed examination of the comments of another questionnaire respondent/e-mail correspondent, a 49-year-old businesswoman, born and residing in Vancouver, referred to as Christina. Although also of Irish and Lowland Scots descent, Christina describes her cultural identity as a 'Highlander' of the MacInnes clan. It was her paternal grandparents who emigrated separately from Skye and Sutherland to Canada in the early years of the twentieth century. Christina articulates a sense of problematized belonging in the New World similar to that described above by the informant from Auckland, contrasting the shallowness of her settler roots with the deep-rootedness of native populations.

> I think there is a place on this earth that has the collective history of your people in the very ground you walk upon. If you live in North America you understand that you have only a very tenuous hold on the geography. There has to be a place to which you have a stronger connection, that tells the myths and legends of your ancestors, not someone else's. In this country we will always be immigrants, not really belonging in that very primal way.

In search of such 'primal' connections, Christina has made two visits to Scotland and intends to make another with her daughter. She describes being strongly affected by the Highland landscape, particularly by its emptiness and her encounters with the remains of deserted settlements, which are quite prevalent in certain areas. She attributes this emptiness to that most iconic episode of Highland history, described by Richards as 'one of the sorest, most painful, themes in modern Scottish history': the Highland Clearances.[15] The Clearances, occurring in the period approximately 1790 to 1860, are much mythologized and often evoked as the completion of a process that began in the aftermath of Culloden, involving the eradication of the Highlanders and their culture from their native glens in order to open the land up for intensive sheep farming.[16] The narrative of the Clearances has become well known among Scottish heritage communities throughout the world particularly through the work of popular historians and novelists.[17] John Prebble, in the most popular of the popular Clearance histories, begins:

> This book . . . is the story of how the Highlanders were *deserted* and then *betrayed*. It concerns itself with people, how sheep were preferred to them, and how bayonet, truncheon and fire were used to *drive them from their homes*. It has been said that the Clearances are now far enough away from us to be decently forgotten. But *the hills are still empty* . . . It is worth remembering, too, that while the rest of Scotland was permitting the expulsion of its Highland people it was also forming that romantic attachment to kilt and tartan that scarcely compensates for the *disappearance of a race* to whom such things were once a commonplace reality. The chiefs remain, in Edinburgh and London, but *the people are gone.* (emphases added)[18]

Christina's descriptions of her visits to the Highlands demonstrate how she has internalized this powerful cultural narrative:

> I had been brought up on very positive stories about Scotland and Celticness. When I first went to Scotland I was ready to enjoy the country, and to have some fun looking up all the places that I had heard about. When I got there and as I traveled north my thoughts began to change. *The place was empty, everyone was gone.* There were no places to see that I had heard so much about. No one even knew where they might be. *We weren't missed!* This had been *an ethnic cleansing* . . . If anyone remembered that it had taken place at all, their attitude was that it was really a benefit to the evicted! . . . I also saw the remnants of *broken cottages*, the *remains of runrigs* up the mountains, the *empty glens that used to be full of people* . . . all of this had an impact on me that I truly wasn't expecting . . . *The land is still full of ghosts* . . . and *no one is telling their tale.*

She goes on,

> I find it hard to believe that *my people were so unwanted in their own land*, and especially hard to believe that nothing ever has been done about it.
>
> Maybe it is the fact that we come from Canada where past injustices are expected to be rectified before moving on into the future that we had these views. *We really didn't see that much difference between what happened in the Highlands to the Gaels and what happened in North America to the Native Indian population. Except that the Indians were not actually expelled from the continent.*

Christina was struck by the apparent lack of understanding or care of the Scots she met during her visit.

> It seemed very moving to me and yet oddly surreal, because nobody there seemed to acknowledge or even be aware of the feelings it engendered in someone like myself who is a *child of the outcasts*. I guess I don't understand the *silence* about the whole issue both here and in Scotland. They mostly seem indifferent.

Finally she states,

> I have never understood the way that Scotland ignores its sons and daughters all over the globe. The Irish are not so foolish, neither are the Jews.
> ... I don't think Scotland will ever be completely whole until the question of the clearances is put to rest. Don't forget, *we, on this side of the pond, were not wanted, and made to leave*, so maybe we are starting from a feeling of inferiority that makes us very sensitive. On the other hand, there is, in the *exiles*, a strong feeling of belonging to the land, what is needed maybe is a link to the people. That is really what I think the Irish and the Israelis have done. (emphases added)

Christina's comments reflect convictions that are widespread among people of Highland descent overseas, but a number of important points should be kept in mind. Firstly, knowledge of these 'past injustices' is rarely derived from stories passed down within the family – as Christina explains, she had been brought up hearing 'very positive stories about Scotland'. Such knowledge is instead most often acquired from popular history books (elsewhere in her questionnaire Christina herself recommends the work of Prebble) and historical fiction, as well as at Web sites and heritage centre displays that are often drawn from the same sources and which perpetuate their genocidal rhetoric. Secondly, the equation of Clearance with expulsion overseas is, generally speaking, spurious. The Clearances occurred at a time of huge social and economic transformation throughout the British Isles (and much of Europe), which included the general shift of populations from rural areas to the industrializing urban centres as well as the first waves of mass emigration – migrations driven as much by the so-called 'pull factors' of the New World (land, opportunity, the prospect of wealth, etc.) as by the 'push factors' of rural poverty, famine and, indeed, avaricious landlords.[19] Finally, it should be noted that Christina's grandparents emigrated from Scotland in the early twentieth century, at least fifty and ninety years after the Clearances that occurred in Skye and Sutherland respectively. In others words, Christina's grandparents were not exiles, outcasts or the victims of an ethnic cleansing. It is more likely that they left Scotland voluntarily, hoping, with so many millions of other European migrants, to 'better their fortunes' in America.[20]

[137]

The issue is not, of course, whether the story this and many other informants have constructed around their families' pasts is true or false so much as how and why this particular narrative comes to dominate and shape a new exilic imagination. One explanation may be found in the rubric of 'diaspora' and 'homeland' itself.

The nomenclature of diaspora

In a 1996 article, Khachig Tölölyan, the Armenian-American editor of the journal *Diaspora*, asks: how and why is it that, at the end of the twentieth century, 'a term once saturated with the meanings of exile, loss, dislocation, powerlessness and plain pain' becomes a useful and even desirable way to describe a range of dispersions?[21] He believes 'diaspora' has become a 'promiscuously capacious category that is taken to include all the adjacent phenomena to which it is linked but from which it actually differs in ways that are constitutive' – phenomena such as expatriate communities, immigrant communities, ethnic and racial minorities.[22]

Indeed, within academic discourse there has been much debate regarding the appropriate use of the term. Some believe that if it is to retain any discrete significance, its use ought to be limited to describing the dispersion and exile of the Jews from their historic homeland and that its use in other contexts must remain at the level of metaphor, 'in much the same way', suggests Safran, 'that "ghetto" has come to designate all kinds of crowded, constricted, and disprivileged urban environments, and "holocaust" has come to be applied to all kinds of mass murder'.[23] Whilst many accept that this 'Jewish paradigm' may be applied to the experience of other victimized people – the Armenians, Gypsies and African slaves, for example – there is some consensus that 'Diasporic populations do not come from elsewhere in the same way that "immigrants" do', and that the term, even if it is to be applied broadly, is still a category of subaltern identification.[24]

Others still believe it is necessary to transcend the 'Jewish tradition' and return to the etymological roots of the word, the Greek 'to sow over' or scatter, and its earliest usage in relation to human dispersion, referring to the Greek colonization of Asia Minor and the Mediterranean. Such a tactic permits Robin Cohen, for instance, to recognize the multiple causes of population dispersal and assemble a new ideal typology of diaspora which includes not only victim diasporas, but also trade diasporas, imperial diasporas, labour diasporas, and so forth.[25] Pursuing this project, Cohen has assembled a list of common features of global diasporas, the first two statements of which allude to the causes of population displacement, as follows:

1 Dispersal from an original homeland, often traumatically, to two or more foreign regions.

2 Alternatively, the expansion from a homeland in search of work, in pursuit of trade or to further colonial ambitions.[26]

Within Cohen's inclusive and flexible framework it is certainly possible to posit the existence of a Scottish diaspora and to demonstrate how it displays characteristics of the various types: the Scots as victims of forced emigration, as agents of British imperialism, as colonists appropriating the lands of others.

The contest over the appropriate use of 'diaspora' in academic discourse is made possible because there is a semantic instability around the term. This might be understood as a tension between the denotative meanings and the connotative meanings of the word. At a simplistic level, denotation is the primary, direct or literal meaning of a given text, whereas connotation includes its metaphorical, symbolic or secondary meanings. Roland Barthes explores this distinction in his book *S/Z*. 'Definitionally', he writes, connotation 'is a determination, a relation, an anaphora, a feature which has the power to relate itself to anterior, ulterior, or exterior mentions, to other sites of the text (or of another text).'[27]

If Robin Cohen's argument is accepted, the primary or denotative meaning of diaspora is its original meaning, a neutral term which might be appropriately employed to describe colonization as much as forced exile. It must, however, also be accepted that one cannot divorce the denotative meaning of a term from its connotations. Thus, in referring to a Scottish diaspora, one cannot help but imply an association or relationship with the Jewish diaspora. Thus one might agree with Jonathan Boyarin when he writes, 'It is important to insist, not on the centrality of the Jewish diaspora nor on its logical priority within comparative diaspora studies, yet still on the need to refer to . . . Jewish diaspora history within the contemporary diasporic rubric'.[28]

This, then, is the first semantic migration that affects what may be understood when invoking a Scottish diaspora. But within academic discourse this is somewhat incidental, since the term is rarely used without some qualification as to what exactly is meant. A more serious slippage occurs when the notion of a Scottish diaspora enters popular consciousness, which, without doubt, it has. And here it is necessary to return to Roland Barthes because, in this migration, the hierarchy of denotation and connotation is turned on its head. What is, in academic discourse, the connotative or secondary meaning becomes, in popular discourse, the denotative or primary meaning. Barthes writes that actually: 'denotation is not the first meaning, but pretends to be so; under this illusion, it is ultimately no more than the last of the connotations, . . . the superior myth by which the text pretends to return to the nature of language, to language as nature'.[29] In other words, outside the close readings of academic discourse, it goes without saying that 'diaspora' means victimization, enforced exile and all the other associations of the Jewish paradigm. Thus it is that, in the popular Scottish diasporic imagination, a moral rhetoric of exile comes to dominate a morally ambiguous history of emigration and colonization.

A rhetoric of exile

This rhetoric of exile is particularly conspicuous in that most democratic of media, the Internet. 'We're the children of the clearances . . .' go the lyrics of one song which circulates on Scottish-interest e-mail lists:

> . . . the wanderers old and young
> And a heart and soul in Scotland just like you.
> So when you sing of the great white sheep this you must also know:
> While Scotland mourns her tragedy it was us that had to go.
> In exile now far away from the land of our race's birth
> We're the living flag of Andrew scattered all across the Earth.[30]

And from an Internet essay entitled 'Cries of the never born', written by an American Scot living in Florida:

> In the last 270 years, more than a quarter of a million indigenous people were forced off their ancestral lands, burned out of their homes, sold into slavery, and forcibly assimilated into a foreign culture. But these were not Native Americans, or black Africans, or Jews; these were the white residents of the Scottish Highlands. Their crime: Occupying land that others coveted.[31]

Note how the crimes against the Highlanders have now escalated to include slavery and forced assimilation. At the end of the article, the author encourages readers to contact an Arkansas-based 'Highland Clearances Memorial Fund' for further information. Such are the 'webs of retrospective indignation', Richards describes, through which 'the uninhibited passions and prejudices of a worldwide network of Highland sympathizers' are orchestrated.[32]

The hyperbole is not, however, restricted exclusively to the diaspora. In May 2000, for instance, the letters pages of the Scottish broadsheet *The Herald* were buoyed up with angst for weeks in response to comments made by the historian and columnist Michael Fry, who was accused of issuing 'utterances on the Clearances reminiscent of the Holocaust denial of David Irving'.[33] Thus, one letter writer, Dennis

MacLeod of Easter Ross, leading a campaign to erect a Clearance monument and study centre in Helmsdale, promulgates the popular misconception that to be descended from Highland Scots is necessarily to be descended from the victims of the Clearances when he writes:

> The descendants of the cleared people are measured today in only tens of thousands in the Highlands of Scotland. But throughout the world they comprise tens of millions. The project, therefore, belongs not just to today's Highlanders but as much if not more to all of Highland descent, be they from the Lowlands of Scotland, England, USA, Canada, New Zealand, Australia, Africa, or elsewhere.
>
> It is hoped that such descendants will embrace and support this project as their own. It will be an opportunity for millions of people, scattered to the far reaches of the earth, to focus in one location their long-held quest for the recognition of their unique history, culture, and heritage.[34]

Another letter-writer, again conflating Clearance and emigration, equates the plight of Highland emigrants in Canada with that of the biblical exile of the Jews:

> I remind [Michael Fry] of two exiles who wrote of the agony of being driven from their homeland. The first, the Psalmist, wrote, 'How could we sing the Lord's song in a strange foreign land? If I forget you, O Jerusalem, let my right hand wither away.' The second was written by John Gait [sic] . . . 'From the lone sheiling of the misty island, Mountains divide us and the waste of the seas; Yet still the blood is strong, the heart is Highland, And we in dreams behold the Hebrides.'[35]

Such explicit parallels between Jewish and Highland experiences are not particularly new. Andrew Matheson, a somewhat overlooked land reform agitator, whose father had been evicted from Kildonan and he himself from Dunbeath, published a booklet in 1870 entitled *The British Looking Glass* which is peppered with biblical references, providing precedents for his arguments that his readers would no doubt be familiar with. Thus the 'British landlord' by his practice of rack renting is placed 'in full position parallel with the Egyptian bondage (Exodus 1: 11–14)', while the tenants have become 'white slaves . . . a step lower than the Hebrews were under Pharaoh (Exodus 5: 7–19)'.[36] Even the 'Assyrians, who put the Jews to the sword and took them prisoners of war' were not as evil as the clearing landlords because they 'would not remove them from their places in Samaria till they provided for them in Assyria (2 Kings 17: 6)'.[37] Alas, Matheson was also a man of his time and he apparently did not perceive the inconsistencies in his argument when, with missionary zeal, he justified the forcible appropriation, colonization and exploitation of other people's lands:

Idolatry and abuse of their land talents are the justifiable causes which entitle and warrant Britain to make war upon heathen countries, such as Australia &c., for making their lands, by artificial industries, more fruitful and useful by the yields of both mines and crops to support mankind, and making their inhabitants tributaries (Deut. 20: 11 and 15).[38]

But neither are these parallels limited to the *biblical* history of the Jews: much popular writing on the Clearances today is laced with hyperbolic references to the Holocaust and other modern genocides (see box). Indeed, even the aforementioned proposal for a Clearances monument at Helmsdale arguably draws from the mnemonic architecture of many Holocaust memorials and museums, with its 120 ft high bronze statue, its processional pathway marked with 'standing stones' inscribed with Clearance history, its 'Wall of Descendants', and its anticipated collections of oral testimonies and other records housed in a dedicated 'Clearances Centre'.[39]

The Highland Clearances as Holocaust: excerpts from popular histories, 1962–2000

- the victims of the Clearances [were] objects of intense hatred such as the gypsies and the Jews were to experience under the Nazis and other groups in the Western World (Francis Thompson, *The Highlands and Islands*, 1974)

- like the shipping-off of the Polish and other Jews in cattle trucks (David Craig, *On the Crofters' Trail*, 1990)

- Sellar's crimes against the people of Strathnaver, he said, were to be ranked with those of Heydrich, the man who perpetrated unspeakable acts against the Jews in Prague in the Second World War (Eric Richards, *The Highland Clearances*, 2000, discussing Ian Grimble)

- *Na Hitleran breun Breatannach* — Those stinking British Hitlers
  A mhurt mo thìr mu thuath — Who murdered my northern land
  Gu Lebensraum do chaoraich — To make *Lebensraum* for sheep,
  Is na daoine sgiùrs' thar chuan — Who scourged the people across the ocean
  (Murchadh MacPhàrlain quoted by Michael Newton, *A Handbook of the Scottish Gaelic World*, 2000)

- She had been to Auschwitz concentration camp but there was no statue to Hitler. Back home she felt that the first Duke of Sutherland had dealt in genocide . . . (Rob Gibson, *Toppling the Duke*, 1996, discussing Winnie Ewing MEP)

Furthermore, the influence of a global 'politics of reconciliation' (evinced in the Australian Council for Aboriginal Reconciliation Act of 1991, the South African Truth and Reconciliation Commission of 1995, etc.) is apparent in a motion brought before the Scottish Parliament by Jamie Stone, Liberal Democrat MSP for Caithness, Sutherland and Easter Ross, in September 2000:

> That the Parliament expresses its deepest regret for the occurrence of the Highland Clearances and extends its hand in friendship and welcome to the descendants of the cleared people who reside outwith our shores.[40]

Among many similar contributions to the ensuing 'debate', Fergus Ewing, Scottish National Party MSP for Inverness East, Nairn and Lochaber, supported Stone's motion, reiterated familiar sentiments regarding confronting the past in order to move forward, and again drew parallels between the 'Highland diaspora', Native Americans and Australian Aborigines.

- Highland Holocaust (Gibson, *Toppling the Duke*)

- a planned *blitzkrieg* against the Gaelic civilisation (Craig, *On the Crofters' Trail*)

- Sutherland's managers kept records of their shipments of people with the obsessional thoroughness of an Eichmann (Craig, *On the Crofters' Trail*)

- The policy of genocide could scarcely have been carried out further (Ian Grimble, *The Future of the Highlands*, 1968)

- a diaspora which has many recent counterparts . . . that of the Jews from Germany and Poland (Craig, *On the Crofters' Trail*)

- the first Duke ranked with Hitler and Stalin (Gibson, *Toppling the Duke*, discussing the views of Councillor Sandy Lindsay)

- the cultural genocide of the Highlands (Newton, *A Handbook of the Scottish Gaelic World*)

- the Gaels were, and indeed are today, in no way different from the Red Indians, the Jews, the Eskimoes and the vanishing tribes of the Amazon River (Thompson, *The Highlands and Islands*)

- akin to genocide (Grimble, 'Gael and Saxon Scotland', 1962)

Sources: David Craig, *On the Crofters' Trail* (London: Cape, 190), 3, 72, 79, 129; Rob Gibson, *Toppling the Duke* (Evanton, n.p., 1996), 6, 22, 38, 40; Ian Grimble, 'Gael and Saxon Scotland', *Yale Review* 52 (1962), 3–25; Ian Grimble, 'Introduction' in Ian Grimble and Derick Thomson (eds), *The Future of the Highlands* (London: Routledge, 1968), 23; Michael Newton, *A Handbook of the Scottish Gaelic World* (Dublin: Four Courts, 2000), 73, 281; Richards, *The Highland Clearances*, 142–3; Francis Thompson, *The Highlands and Islands* (London: Hale, 1974), 61–2.

In other countries, the genocide and ethnic cleansing that has taken place, against the Indians in America and the Aborigines in Australia, was acknowledged long ago. Today, the time to acknowledge what happened to those who were cleared from the Highlands has come. We can now acknowledge and regret what happened and perhaps then move on.[41]

Despite the implicit invocation of a 'Truth Commission', Stone and Ewing seem less concerned with interrogating the 'truth' of the Clearance narrative so much as asserting a supposedly self-evident equivalence of this particular cultural trauma with other less equivocal instances of 'genocide'.

As has been suggested, the experience of the majority of my informants is characterized by a sense of discontinuity with the past, particularly the past prior to their ancestors' emigration. Few have grown up knowing just how, when and why their ancestors emigrated, or even necessarily knowing from which country or countries. This lacuna of knowledge partly motivates their current interest in family history research, but it also makes them vulnerable to this vivid cultural narrative that seems to explain their fate. Thus, in popular Scottish diasporan discourse, and according to Robin Cohen's heuristic framework, the Highland Clearances come to constitute the traumatic event which caused the dispersal of their ancestors from an original centre and which provides the diaspora with a 'folk memory' – albeit an 'acquired' one – of the great historic injustice which binds the group together as a diaspora.[42] The strength of this narrative displaces Cohen's second proposition, which, in fact, accounts for the vast majority of emigration from Scotland, i.e. 'the expansion from a homeland in search of work, in pursuit of trade or to further colonial ambitions'.[43]

Homecomings for homeless minds

Before drawing together some conclusions and relating all this back to the phenomenon of roots tourism, it is worth considering another problem that confronts those who seek to imagine a Scottish diaspora. As noted earlier, there is some academic consensus that the category of diaspora remains one of subaltern identification. Using examples as diverse as the Chinese in Malaya, Kurds in Turkey and Sikhs in Britain, Cohen argues that diasporan populations generally experience antagonism and legal or illegal discrimination in the host countries in which they have settled, and may even become the objects of violent hatred.[44] This alienation from the dominant society leads to diasporan communities retaining primary allegiance to their original homeland and thus failing to assimilate as other immigrant groups supposedly do. It would, however, be absurd to refer to people of Scottish descent in the United

States, for instance, either as an ethnic minority or as victims of ethnic discrimination. As is well known, Scottish migrants were influential in shaping those societies in which they settled and thus form part of the dominant culture of the 'host countries', which they are, as a diaspora, supposedly defined against. And yet an implicit assertion of ethnic minority status is also arguably evident in the Scottish diasporic rhetoric of exile.

This claim may be seen in the context of what is sometimes described as the 'new white ethnic movement': the desire of white suburban, middle-class, assimilated citizens to effectively dissimilate themselves and recover a more distinct, particular ethnic identity.[45] Individuals thus turn to their family histories and choose which of their various ancestors' ethnicities to identify with – generally speaking, the more 'ethnic' and the more persecuted the better. This may seem a rather cynical suggestion but the trend is certainly evident in the comments of my informants, and, of course, the phenomenon is not restricted to the descendants of Scottish Highlanders.[46] In a recent book exploring the emergence in the 1960s of a Holocaust-centred Jewish-American identity, Peter Novick identifies the concurrent rise of a more general 'culture of victimization'. He describes a state of 'Holocaust envy' in which different groups, each with its own atrocity to commemorate, compete to be 'America's number one victim community'.[47]

One explanation for this may be found in the desire to maintain a positive or moral self-image in which it is more acceptable to identify with the oppressed than with the oppressors.[48] However, it is also tempting to find some analogy between this social phenomenon and the psychological phenomenon of false memory syndrome, where an identifiable – even though imagined – traumatic episode is believed to account for the symptoms of trauma, the true causes of which remain obscure. Perhaps this sense of exile evinced by many of my informants is less a result of any historical trauma than that consequence of modernity described by Peter Berger et al. as 'a *metaphysical* loss of "home"'.[49] As the familiarly Durkheimian argument goes, with the mobility of modernity comes not only dislocation from a physical home place but also a movement away from the cohesiveness of a 'social' home or milieu represented by 'traditional' society. Whilst this liberates the individual from perceived societal constraints, such mobility has 'correlates on the level of consciousness', resulting in a widespread sense of personal alienation.[50] This, in turn, gives rise to what Berger et al. term a 'demodernizing impulse', which 'seeks a reversal of the modern trends that have left the individual "alienated" and beset with the threats of meaninglessness' and protests 'against the allegedly excessive individualism of modern society'.[51] They go on, 'The individual is to be liberated from this individualism to the solidarity of either old or new collective structures.'[52] Unfashionable though the *Homeless Mind* theory is, there seems to be much to support it in the field of genealogy and roots tourism, practices which may be seen as responses to that demodernizing impulse in which the alienated individual so evidently hungers to belong and seeks to connect itself spatially, temporally and socially with something beyond itself, but authentically of itself. Desiring to relocate the story of the self – the dislocated, ahistorical self – within the history of a people and its place.

Drawing equally from psychoanalytical theories and historiography, a more recent exploration of these themes may be found in the work of Dominick LaCapra. In *Writing History, Writing Trauma*, LaCapra contrasts 'structural trauma' with 'historical trauma'. Structural trauma is described as an 'anxiety-producing condition' to which 'everyone' is subject and is associated with absence (for instance, the 'absence of an absolute').[53] Absence is transhistorical in so far as it 'is not an event and does not imply tenses (past, present or future)', and so the source of anxiety or trauma remains elusive. As part of the cognitive process, however, absence becomes narrativized and is typically misrecognized as loss. 'The conversion of absence into loss,' writes LaCapra, 'gives anxiety an identifiable object – the lost object – and generates the hope that anxiety may be eliminated or overcome' (i.e. through recovering the 'lost object').[54] Structural trauma thus becomes converted into a historical trauma: an identifiable, datable event, 'the scene of losses that may be narrated as well as of specific possibilities that may conceivably be reactivated, reconfigured, and transformed in the present or the future'.[55] Put simply, through this process, the perplexing and irresolvable state of 'paradise absent' is transformed into 'paradise lost', and with this is implied both 'the notion of a fall from a putative state of grace, at-homeness, unity, or community' and the possibility that this Golden Age might be regained. One consequence of this misrecognition of structural trauma as historical trauma is the emergence, as noted by Novick, of a generalized 'wound culture' based on false memory and 'surrogate victimage'.[56] Thus, according to LaCapra, the conflation of absence and loss facilitates 'the appropriation of particular traumas by those who did not experience them, typically in a movement of identity formation which makes invidious and ideological use of traumatic series of events in foundational ways or as symbolic capital'.[57]

In LaCapra's terms, the Highland Clearances emerge as the historical trauma through which the existential anxieties of people of Scottish or part-Scottish descent dispersed throughout the world may be acted out, narrated and brought into the public domain. The Clearances are thus misidentified as the foundational trauma of the Scottish diaspora, a myth in which the Highlanders (who come to stand for all Scots, see note 2) suffered a genocide, were expelled from their ancestral homeland, and forced to live in slavery and exile overseas. According to the mythic structure, prior to this 'Highland Holocaust' was a paradisical Golden Age of 'at-homeness, unity [and] community' – an idealization of all that is perceived to be absent in the postlapsarian modern world of the diaspora.[58] But, as LaCapra argues, 'Paradise absent is different from paradise lost' and, as absence is transformed to loss, there is also created the potential for redemption and return: a (not im)possible homecoming for the homeless mind.[59]

So it is that, at the beginning of the twenty-first century, 'a term once saturated with the meanings of exile, loss, dislocation, powerless and plain pain' comes to be a useful and even desirable form of self-identification by a group for whom such connotations would seem to be largely inappropriate.[60] 'Diaspora', then, provides a language through which such individuals can both articulate generalized senses of personal alienation and recover a sense of belonging to a historical community. The process reaches its zenith in the journey 'home' – to the ancestral homeland where Berger's metaphorical and metaphysical home is made material and where a paradise, of sorts, may at last be regained. Understood in this way, it may indeed be appropriate to describe these two- or three-week return migrations to the Scottish Highlands and Islands as instances of a diasporic return movement.

Notes

1 Jerome Bruner, *Acts of Meaning* (Cambridge MA and London: Harvard University Press, 1990), 13.
2 Ihab Hassan quoted in Khachig Tölölyan, 'Rethinking Diaspora(s): Stateless Power in the Transnational Moment', *Diaspora* 5: 1 (1996), 4. It will be apparent that references to 'Scotland' and the 'Scottish Highlands' (and, consequently, the Scottish and Scottish Highland diaspora) are somewhat imprecise. This imprecision is actually fundamental to Scottish diasporic identity. Generally speaking, when Scotland is imagined outside Scotland, it is Highland Scotland that is imagined. As T.M. Devine points out, 'To the rest of the world in the late twentieth century Scotland seems a Highland country. The "land of mountain and flood" adorns tourist posters and those familiar and distinctive symbols of Scottish identity, the kilt, the tartan and the bagpipes, are all of Highland origin.' This is certainly borne out in Celeste Ray's study of the Scottish heritage revival in North Carolina, where, she reports, 'The identity embraced as "Scottish" by the Scottish-American community is a Highland identity,' though not necessarily one that would be recognizable as such by Highlanders in Scotland. T.M. Devine, *The Scottish Nation, 1700–2000* (London: Allen Lane, 1999), 231; Celeste Ray, *Highland Heritage: Scottish Americans in the American South* (Chapel Hill NC and London: University of North Carolina Press, 2001), 17 and xiii.
3 On multi-sited ethnography see George E. Marcus, 'Ethnography in/of the World System: The Emergence of Multi-sited Ethnography', *Annual Review of Anthropol-*

ogy 24 (1995), 95–117. Concerning global cultural flows, including mediascapes, see Arjun Appadurai, 'Disjuncture and Difference in the Global Cultural Economy', *Theory, Culture and Society* 7 (1990), 295–310.

4 Nikos Papastergiadis, *Dialogues in the Diasporas: Essays and Conversations on Cultural Identity* (London and New York: Rivers Oram, 1998).

5 For a more detailed discussion of the Internet and diasporan consciousness, including the use of online research methodologies see Paul Basu, 'Homecomings: Genealogy, Heritage-tourism and Identity in the Scottish Highland Diaspora', unpublished Phd thesis (University College London, 2002).

6 In Kathleen B. Cory, *Tracing your Scottish Ancestry* (Edinburgh: Polygon, 1996), ix–x.

7 Scottish Executive, *A New Strategy for Scottish Tourism* (Edinburgh: Stationery Office, 2000).

8 Alois Riegl, 'The Modern Cult of Monuments: Its Character and its Origin', *Oppositions* 25 (1982), 21–51. For a discussion of 'intentional' and 'unintentional' monuments in the Scottish Highland landscape see Paul Basu, 'Narratives in a Landscape: Monuments and Memories of the Sutherland Clearances', unpublished MSc dissertation (University College London, 1997) and Paul Basu, 'Sites of Memory – Sources of Identity: Landscape-narratives of the Sutherland Clearances' in John A. Atkinson, Iain Banks and Gavin MacGregor (eds), *Townships to Farmsteads: Rural Settlement Studies in Scotland, England and Wales* (Oxford: Hedges, 2000).

9 See Paul Basu, 'My own Island Home: The Orkney Homecoming', *Journal of Material Culture* 9:1 (2004) 27–42.

10 For a North American perspective on 'heritage pilgrimage' and the Scottish 'clanscape' see Ray, *Highland Heritage*, 127–52.

11 Three such personal journeys are described in Paul Basu, 'Pilgrims to the Far Country: North American Roots-tourists in the Scottish Highlands and Islands' in Celeste Ray (ed.), *Transatlantic Scots* (Tuscaloosa: University of Alabama Press, 2005).

12 D. Stasiulis and N. Yuval-Davis (eds), *Unsettling Settler Societies: Articulations of Gender, Race, Ethnicity and Class* (London: Sage, 1995).

13 Bruner, *Acts of Meaning*, 11.

14 See Basu, 'Homecomings: Genealogy, Heritage-tourism and Identity in the Scottish Highland Diaspora', unpublished PhD thesis (University College London, 2002).

15 Richards, *The Highland Clearances: People, Landlords and Rural Turmoil* (Edinburgh: Birlinn, 2000), 3.

16 The Highland Clearances must, of course, be understood within a much broader political, economic and ideological context which is beyond the scope of this chapter. See, for example, Eric Richards, *A History of the Highland Clearances* (2 vols, London: Croom Helm, 1982, 1985); Charles W.J. Withers, *Gaelic Scotland: The Transformation of a Culture Region* (London and New York: Routledge, 1988); Peter Womack, *Improvement and Romance: Constructing the Myth of the Highlands* (Basingstoke: Macmillan, 1989).

17 See Laurence Gourievidis, 'The Image of the Highland Clearances, c. 1880–1990', unpublished PhD thesis (University of St Andrews, 1993), and Basu, 'Narratives in a Landscape'.

18 John Prebble, *The Highland Clearances* (Harmondsworth: Penguin, 1969), 8.

19 The 1851 Lochboisdale emigration aboard the *Admiral* is a notorious *exception* where there are considerable grounds for associating clearance and forced emigration. Having previously agreed to accept assisted passage to Canada, a number of Colonel Gordon of Cluny's erstwhile tenants absconded from their homes prior to embarkation. With police assistance, the abscondees were pursued and those who were caught were handcuffed and forced on to the waiting ship. See Richards, *The Highland Clearances*, 219–24, for discussion.

20 The phrase appears frequently on emigration certificates.

21 Khachig Tölölyan, 'Rethinking Diaspora(s)', 9.

22 *Ibid.*, 8.

23 William Safran, 'Diasporas in Modern Societies: Myths of Homeland and Return', *Diaspora* 1: 1 (1991), 83.

24 James Clifford, *Routes: Travel and Translation in the Late Twentieth Century* (Cambridge MA: Harvard University Press, 1997), 250.
25 Robin Cohen, *Global Diasporas: An Introduction* (London: UCL Press, 1997).
26 *Ibid.*, 26.
27 Roland Barthes, *S/Z* (Oxford: Blackwell, 1990), 8.
28 Quoted in Cohen, *Global Diasporas*, 3.
29 Barthes, *S/Z*, 8.
30 'Born beyond the Border', lyrics by Maggie Innis, posted to gen-trivia-scotland-l@rootsweb.com, 3 May 1999.
31 Scott Robert Ladd, 'Cries of the Never Born', www.coyotegulch.com/bookart/sym00006.html.
32 Richards, *The Highland Clearances*, 3.
33 Bill Macaskill, Letters to the Editor, *The Herald*, 12 May 2000.
34 Dennis MacLeod, Letters to the Editor, *The Herald*, 19 May 2000.
35 Fred McDermid, Letters to the Editor, *The Herald*, 18 May 2000. See Michael Kennedy, '"Lochaber No More": A Critical Examination of Highland Emigration Mythology' in Marjory Harper and Michael E. Vance (eds), *Myth, Migration and the Making of Memory: Scotia and Nova Scotia c. 1700–1990* (Halifax, Nova Scotia: Fernwood, 1999; Edinburgh: John Donald, 2000) for an examination of nineteenth-century emigrant discourse in Nova Scotia, and Womack, *Improvement and Romance*, 178–80, for analysis of 'The Canadian Boat Song'.
36 Andrew Matheson, *The British Looking Glass* (Wick, 1870; repr. Dunbeath: Laidhay Preservation Trust, 1993), 31, 32.
37 *Ibid.*, 39. I am grateful to Steve Murdoch for drawing my attention to the use of biblical metaphors by Scottish royalists in the mid-seventeenth century to describe the exiled royalist leadership: see Murdoch, 'The Search for Northern Allies: Stuart and Cromwellian Propagandists and Protagonists in Scandinavia, 1649–60' in Bertrand Taithe and Tim Thornton (eds), *Propaganda: Political Rhetoric and Identity, 1300–2000* (Stroud: Sutton, 1999). Regarding the use of biblical precedents in Jacobite rhetoric see Damhnait Nì Suaird, 'Jacobite Rhetoric and Terminology in the Political Poems of the Fernaig MS, 1688–1693', *Scottish Gaelic Studies* 19 (1999), 105–10; also Murray G, H, Pittock, *The Invention of Scotland: The Stuart Myth and the Scottish Identity, 1638 to the Present* (London and New York: Routledge, 1991), 9–10.
38 Matheson, *British Looking Glass*, 46.
39 Clearances Project brief, March 2001. Concerning the mnemonic architecture of the Holocaust see, for example, James E. Young, *The Texture of Memory: Holocaust Memorials and Meaning* (New Haven CT and London: Yale University Press, 1993).
40 Scottish Parliament Official Report, vol. 8, No. 7, col. 700, 27 September 2000.
41 *Ibid.*, col. 703.
42 Cohen, *Global Diasporas*, 23.
43 *Ibid.*, 26. See Devine, *Scottish Nation, 1700–2000*, 468–85, for an overview of Scottish emigration trends; T.M. Devine, 'Landlordism and Highland Emigration' in Devine, *Scottish Emigration and Scottish Society* (Edinburgh: John Donald, 1992), and Eric Richards, *A History of the Highland Clearances II*, 177–283, for discussion of Highland emigration in this wider context.
44 Cohen, *Global Diasporas*, 186.
45 Mary C. Waters, *Ethnic Options: Choosing Identities in America* (Berkeley CA and Oxford: University of California Press, 1990).
46 *Ibid.*, 150–5.
47 Peter Novick, *The Holocaust and Collective Memory: The American Experience* (London: Bloomsbury, 1999), 190.
48 For discussions of 'positive social identity' and 'collective self-esteem' theories in social psychology see Stephen Worchel, J. Francisco Morales, Dario Páez and Jean-Claude Deschamps (eds), *Social Identity: International Perspectives* (London: Sage, 1998).
49 Peter L. Berger, Brigitte Berger and Hansfried Kellner, *The Homeless Mind: Modernization and Consciousness* (New York: Random House, 1973), 82, emphasis added.

50 *Ibid.*, 184.
51 *Ibid.*, 196.
52 *Ibid.*, 196.
53 Dominick LaCapra, *Writing History, Writing Trauma* (Baltimore MD and London: Johns Hopkins University Press, 2001), 82.
54 *Ibid.*, 57.
55 *Ibid.*, 49.
56 *Ibid.*, 40.
57 *Ibid.*, 65. A second consequence is the 'projection of blame for a putative loss on to identifiable others'. In the Highland Clearance narrative this is usually identified as the English or anglicized Lowland Scots.
58 See my analysis of the Highland Clearances as myth in Basu, 'Narratives in a Landscape'.
59 LaCapra, *Writing History, Writing Trauma*, 57.
60 Tölölyan, 'Rethinking Diaspora(s)', 9. This is not to deny the dislocative trauma of even voluntary economic migration, but it is to recognize the qualitative difference between those *forced to choose* emigration owing to the paucity of viable alternatives and those forced to emigrate by the threat of physical violence.

PART III

Mechanisms of return

The following three chapters examine some of the mechanisms through which emigrants to North America in the nineteenth and twentieth centuries maintained links with their home areas in Ireland, Scotland and England, as well as the way in which those who returned continued to nurture their overseas contacts. Letters to and from emigrants offer perhaps the clearest bridge between the old and new land, and in recent years have assumed a higher profile, particularly in Irish migration studies, thanks to the work of Kerby Miller and David Fitzpatrick.[1] Bruce Elliott employs letters to probe the meaning that return held for different members of an extended family, some of whom made a single journey back to Ireland before returning to the new world to marry and 'settle down', others of whom made repeated visits to the homeland and eventually returned for good. In doing so he analyses an extensive set of letters kept by William McLeese, a millwright who left Ireland for Canada 1843.

For some returning emigrants, the maintenance of links with Canada was facilitated or shaped by formal institutions. Kathleen Burke's study of the role that the élite Canada Club played in the lives of those who had sojourned or had commercial or military interests in the Dominion suggests that homesickness was not just the prerogative of those who remained overseas. Equally traumatic, for some, was the process of adjustment to a homeland that had changed during their absence, and to people who did not share a knowledge of their experiences. Through the Canada Club, they could preserve their overseas commitments, enjoy comradeship based on shared experiences and promote a positive image of Canada to government and public alike. They also capitalized on the opportunities offered by Club meetings to make strategic political and commercial connections, since many of Canada's leading politicians and businessmen were dinner guests during visits to Britain.

Transatlantic links continued to be cultivated in the twentieth century. Marilyn Barber's exploration of the Fellowship of the Maple Leaf, a Church of England society formed in 1917, reinforces the argument that emigrants who returned often remained strongly committed to overseas causes and could be active lobbyists for the countries in which they had sojourned. For over forty years the FML promoted imperial unity by sending British teachers, nurses, doctors and church workers – many of them women – to western Canada. As they moved back and forth between Britain and Canada, many of them developed a dual identity and an ambivalent attitude towards the meaning and location of home. It was an ambivalence which finds an echo in the experiences of many of the other return emigrants examined in this book.

Note

1 See, for instance, Kerby Miller, *Emigrants and Exiles: Ireland and the Irish Exodus to North America* (New York and Oxford: Oxford University Press, 1985); David Fitzpatrick (ed.), *Oceans of Consolation: Personal Accounts of Irish Migration to Australia* (Ithaca NY: Cornell University Press, 1994).

CHAPTER EIGHT

'Settling down':
masculinity, class and the rite of return
in a transnational community

Bruce S. Elliott

In his thought-provoking book *Sea Changes* Stephen Fender used emigrant letters and American literature to probe the psychology of emigration and the defining role that separation and differentiation from the Old World assumed for the American nation and the American character.[1] Emigration in Fender's conception becomes the dominant metaphor for the American experience. His assumption was that for the individual, emigration was a decisive psychic break as well as a physical separation: 'Emigrants to the United States had burned their boats: not only left their neighbors and extended families, but also cut the apron strings of imperial hierarchy and the purse strings of government preferment.'[2] This idea was central to his conception of emigration as a rite of passage, as a voyage out to the margins, both actual and metaphorical, and on to a life that was new and fundamentally different from that in the Old World. His central question, however, centres not on the individual but on American exceptionalism and the American nation's founding principles. In what he traces as the dominant discourse of emigration, therefore, return to the Old World is an act of betrayal that demands special pleading. Hopes of inheritance or position at home serve to forestall the 'emotional and conceptual break with the past so crucial to the successful adaptation to new circumstances'.[3]

But did emigrants 'burn their boats'? Mark Wyman estimates that a quarter to a third of all European migrants to the United States in the 1880–1930 period, some four million people, returned to Europe.[4] By that era advancing transport technology, both steamships and railroads, had eased the trouble and cost of ocean travel so much that a transatlantic labour market had been created. Seasonal or short-term migration to work in the factories and on the construction gangs of industrial America became a stage in the life course for millions of Europeans who never intended to become more than sojourners. In the case of some countries back-migration was so extensive that foreign earnings and remittances radically altered the economy and property-owning structure of the sending society.[5]

Can we resolve the question by distinguishing emigration and sojourning? Perhaps the last had only an ephemeral impact upon the American character, or affirmed it by providing, in a later period, an 'other' against which the qualities that had been defined as American in the nation's formative years could continue to be constructed or expressed.[6] Wyman states, more than argues, that before the middle of the nineteenth century (during the period most relevant to Fender's case), the dangers inherent in ocean transport under sail kept the numbers of return migrants low.[7] Back-migration is virtually impossible to quantify in this earlier period because official statistics did not record it. Collections of correspondence[8] nonetheless refer frequently to return and repeat migration in the Age of Sail,[9] and its extent was such that its practitioners articulated an 'alternative voice' to which Fender devoted the third of his book's four parts.

Even if we define sojourning as temporary residence abroad and emigration as a permanent removal from the homeland, it is difficult to distinguish the two, for it was only the final failure to return that converted sojourning into emigration. That certainty of non-return was established only by death, for before that return was always possible, even if increasingly unlikely.[10] Not so for Fender: 'Having been made, the decision to go was conceived and presented as both inevitable and irrevocable, just as though it were a rite of passage. And the choice to leave home, along with its attendant (perhaps necessary) mental adjustment, might be made well in advance of actual emigration.'[11]

David Gerber has pointed out, however, that 'in the age of sail and steam alike, there were significant numbers of European migrants who, no matter how long they stayed in the United States, never had the intention to spend their entire lives here, but rather to go home with their savings'.[12] In doing so they 'live and . . . think in multinational and transnational patterns that are neither here nor there, neither in homelands or hostlands, but in both simultaneously'.[13] In highlighting personal socio-economic aspirations, Gerber espouses the view that migration must be understood in terms of a quest for personal respectability. In the words of James Hammerton, emigration was 'not . . . foreign adventure, but simply another strategy to secure the ideals of domestic partnership'. It offered a means of securing the wherewithal to marry for those lacking sufficient resources to do so in the Old World.[14] For many young men, emigration was a strategy for attaining personal respectability and domesticity rather than the glory of participation in imperial endeavours or a great nation-building experiment.

John Tosh argues that in Britain, domestic respectability assumed hegemonic status over competing, rougher conceptions of masculinity from the 1830s through the 1860s.[15] Thereafter more muscular, bellicose definitions, prevalent in the eighteenth century, resurfaced, partly in reaction against these domesticated middle-class definitions of maleness.[16] Cracks are beginning to appear in this periodization,[17] as in earlier assumptions that transnationalism was characteristic only of the Age of Steam, or even of the late twentieth-century century global village.

For a much longer period, however, 'establishing a household . . . has . . . been a crucial stage in winning social recognition as an adult, fully masculine person'.[18] Respectable definitions of manliness, in the eyes of a man's peers, were tied to his ability to establish and maintain a home, provide for a wife and children, and to give sons a start in life and the desire to aspire to similar values.[19] Most historical studies have focused on the urban middle class whose visions of respectability dominated the early Victorian period. Some studies have explored the hegemony of middle-class conceptions over alternative definitions cast as 'rough' or deviant, and emphasized the capacity of the lower middle class or even the working class to strive for 'decency': respectability on their own terms.[20] Little, however, has been written about the pursuit of these ideals in rural contexts or in Ireland, where Protestants who adhered to larger British cultural norms found in the Roman Catholic population an internal 'other', similar to colonized peoples abroad, against whom to differentiate their own respectability.

A window into the roles played by family, masculinity, marriage, migration, and return in the lives of several related Irish families is provided by the McLeese correspondence, a sequence of over 500 letters received by William McLeese, a Presbyterian millwright from north-western Antrim that begins with his emigration in 1843 aged 27 and ends with his death at nearly 90. Though he emigrated to Canada's Ottawa Valley, many of his nearest relations sojourned in the United States. His most frequent correspondent was his father John, who also lived to be 89 and who wrote him fifty-eight letters spanning twenty-four years. Some old friends wrote only once; a cousin in Philadelphia, William Woodside, wrote twice but was continually reported on via Ireland. McLeese heard more frequently from the brothers who followed him to North America, though Robert went immediately to the United States and Thomas spent only a short time with William in what became Ontario.

For these Irish families assistance to go abroad became a form of inheritance. In the rural townland of Carrowreagh between Ballycastle and Coleraine the McLeeses were able to stave off the impoverishing consequences of subdivision by sending the non-inheriting sons to

America with skills learned through apprenticeship at home. The farm that had been occupied in 1765 by William's great-grandfather had been divided in two by 1804, and that of his grandfather John (c. 1749–1814) was subsequently divided between William's father John (1779–1869) and uncle Daniel (c. 1786–1872).[21] In time John enlarged his holding from twenty-four to forty-six acres and became landlord to a female smallholder with four acres and to five cottiers. John was also a carpenter, and by giving three of his sons a trade to practise in America (training Robert and Thomas as carpenters and apprenticing William as a millwright) John's land would pass to his remaining son, also named Daniel, undivided, though Daniel and his wife in the end had no children to inherit it.[22] Having 'the trade' meant that, just like the weavers for whom Antrim was better known, family members were not dependent solely upon the land for their livelihood. But in Ireland the carpentry trade paid poorly, especially for young men just starting out who worked on short time or by the project. Employment prospects and wages were much better in the lumber woods of Canada

Figure 8.1 By providing his sons with a trade at which to work abroad, John McLeese (1779–1869) was able to pass on his farm undivided to one son. His home at Carrowreagh, Co. Antrim, the survivor of three McLeese houses on an estate plan of 1804, as it appeared in 1992, an outbuilding of current owner Stewart McCormick.

and the thriving commercial cities of America, and it was there that the sons went. As the correspondence reveals, the McLeeses were part of a culture within which emigration and return were already well established,[23] and offered a common and acceptable outlet for supernumerary children. In America these rural tradesmen sought the means of 'settling down' – material success, respectability, and marriage. Emigration could provide the means of achieving this purpose either abroad, or at home.

McLeese's brother-in-law, Robert Woodside Sr of Carnduff, near Ballycastle,[24] had no trade or manual skill to pass on to his four sons, and though he provided them with an education it remained John McLeese's firm conviction that he had done more for his own sons in providing them with a trade than Robert Woodside had for his.[25] The Woodsides obtained employment by tapping into an existing network of friends and relatives working in the Philadelphia area, achieved commercial success and, living in seacoast Philadelphia, came to make frequent visits home. In letters to his son William in Canada, John McLeese constantly constructed the Woodside brothers as ideal sons who worked together rather than scattering across North America, who wrote home monthly even when letters took six weeks to cross the Atlantic, who came home often to visit, and who refurnished their parents' cottage like a mansion. At times the Woodsides seemed everything his own sons were not. This perhaps is why we can construct their story so thoroughly from John's second-hand reporting. The two families' stories of return, too, would prove very different. The Woodsides would return to patriarchal positions as Irish gentry, the McLeeses only to effect a final break with the Old World, to form families in the new.

The rural Irish paterfamilias

Old John McLeese's understanding of respectability, which he impressed upon his children in their youth and revisited repeatedly in his correspondence, centred on a fatherly duty to help his children establish themselves in life, a carrying forward of his name and lineage, a code of creditable male behaviour, and a patriarchal expectation of obedience from the male and female members of the family.[26] If he was successful in the first two of these aims, he came to lament that the latter two were often honoured more in the breach than in the observance.

Having given his children an education and his sons a trade, he urged a similar obligation on his son William when the latter despaired of young cousin Willie McLeese, whom he had agreed to take as an apprentice in Canada: 'you must Doo what you can for him, you cartantly has Dun motch for him and it is your Dutey.'[27] John was especially proud of having a grandson in Canada who was his namesake, William's eldest boy, and he so showered Johnny with keepsakes and special greetings that the boy's sister complained of his favouritism.[28] He bequeathed to him £5 and his fiddle 'because of the name'.[29]

John felt his sons owed him obedience and respect. He did not envision emigration as a severance of contact or obligation, and failure to write home he branded ungratefulness: 'the Should Remember me for I did as mutch for them as anny man in the Cuntrey, acording to my situation I maid them good Scollars and good Treadsmen and that was Quit fitt to mak them Independent whils Health lasted.'[30] And always followed the invidious comparison: 'See what your Cosens the Woodside has Dun for thir father that did not Doo near sow mutch for his soons as I Did . . . . you will be ofinded at me but if you Live to see your famly come forward as I see mine you will think on what I have said.'[31]

Son Thomas exemplified the ingrate. His emigration was an admission of the father's inability to control him. John despaired of Thomas's 'Running at Night' and paying him no heed and persuaded William to invite him to Canada: 'I would Like you to give him ann advise for he Dus not appear to teake mine . . . I have Tried fair means and foul means and all is of now use.'[32] To prepare him John kept him at the carpentry trade 'purty Close', hoping that he 'might pass . . . without sarving a time'. He also sent him to school over the winter 'for to mak him a Little better Scholar'. Though he hoped that 'he may mend his manners if he was from Hom',[33] Thomas's independent streak soon resurfaced. He did not stay long in Canada, striking west on his own. He wrote home seldom and was located in Michigan after a four-year silence by placing advertisements in the press. He reported that he was married, but failed to satisfy his father as to 'what sort of a woman he has gott . . . I would Like to know if he Joined to anny Repectble fanley'. After 1856 he dropped out of correspondence entirely.[34]

Being the head of a household, as for centuries past, also implied dominance over the women of the family,[35] but here, too, John's expectations proved excessively sanguine. When William advanced his Canadian wife's concern over the dangers of a sea voyage to explain his failure to visit, John questioned his manliness: 'you Spake of your Mistres Beeing aganst you, if she has sutch a power over you I Doo not allow you to gow far aganst hir will, I am of opinion that you must be verry far changed from what you formaly was.'[36] John's daughter Jane, a dutiful girl, married neighbour David Hodges, another carpenter, and they lived with McLeese until Hodges obtained land nearby in Croshan, but John's paternal authority was openly defied by his other daughter, Mary. She married a Roman Catholic much against her father's wishes: 'John McDonnal had the asurans to follow me to

Ballycastle to ask my Consent, which I utterly refused and when I Came home I reasoned with hir, and Did my Endever to perswed hir from it, and told hir that she should never be the Better of me to the value of one penny if sutch took plase.' Mary offered to emigrate to her brother if John would pay her passage and fit her out, but in this she 'acted the knave'. Instead she took her clothing and the principal part of the household linens and housed with a Catholic in Ballymoney while arranging to be married by a priest. John instructed Wiliam that 'if Ever you have anny Communications with hir you will disablige me verry mutch'.[37] Within a few months, however, she was creeping back into her father's good graces: 'Mary went a good deal against our minds but I think she will not turn with him, she comes to Mosside Meeting house pretty often.' The Presbyterian minister arranged for the couple to be remarried at the Registry Office in Ballymoney and the generations were reconciled.[38] John was, however, to spend the dependence of his declining years in the shadow of a daughter-in-law, Daniel's wife, who pushed his son to pursue an independent course: 'She would make a verry good Wife if he had kept the athoritee he is intitled to hold.'[39]

Though John encountered his share of disappointments in judging his own manliness by his success in moulding his children's behaviour, he had his successes, too. Son William was more dutiful than John sometimes acknowledged, and Robert, after labouring long and at times in isolation, met paternal expectations of material success and masculine domesticity, though in ways less demonstrative than those of his Woodside cousins.

Striving in and beyond the transnational community

A transnational network provides migrants with many of their opportunities and much of their social life. Transatlantic correspondence exaggerates this, of course, for emigrants are likely to mention every person they meet who has links with home and to omit reference to new friends or acquaintances who are unknown to their correspondents in the Old World. Nonetheless, it is striking what a large role was played by friends from home both in the story of the Woodsides' beginnings in Philadelphia, and in Robert McLeese's epistolary narrative of his economic progress in the New World.

Five weeks after arriving in Philadelphia in 1842 William Woodside secured a position as a warder in the Pennsylvania Hospital for the Insane at Blackley, then a mile outside Philadelphia.[40] Woodside implied that he obtained the job through another employee, Charles Corry, whom he had known in the old country, and who had worked there after coming to America.[41] Woodside hoped to get his friend and travelling companion John McKenzie taken on as well, but another acquaintance, James Wilson, made application at the same time and took the position. His letters attest to numerous friends arriving from Antrim, some seeking work at the asylum. Though in 1844 the institution employed only sixteen male and ten female attendants, remarkably enough two collections of north Antrim letters at the Public Record Office of Northern Ireland mention local people who worked there. Jonathan Smyth from Moycraig, just on the other side of Mosside village from the McLeeses' Carrowreagh, sent word home in 1845 that Archie McKay, brother to D.S. McKay, Esq., the proprietor of Mosside village, was an employee.[42] Archibald Carson from Artiferral near Ballymoney similarly became an attendant at the asylum in 1854. He enjoyed the work less than Woodside, deeming it 'not hard but sometimes unpleasant'.[43] Woodside accounted it easy work. Indeed, there was nothing to do most of the time. He did a lot of reading, and he had two hours free to walk in the evening air after the patients were abed.[44]

By 1845 nonetheless Woodside had worked at the hospital for three years and needed a change. He earned $13 a month with board, washing, and mending, which was three dollars better than McKenzie's earnings as a farm labourer. He could save money out of that, but not enough. His brother John, who had emigrated in 1840, was working for David Rankin, a tea dealer in the city,[45] and William reported that he 'has allways the same situation' in the store, earning $50 a month. Clearly this was a more profitable, if less restful, line of work. Another brother, James, was also in the States working as a farmer and drover.[46]

The Woodside brothers first appear in the Philadelphia directories in 1847, James as a grocer and William as a tea dealer, both at the same address. The letters do not explain how they accomplished this transition, but they quickly became successful. In 1848 John Woodside & Co., tea dealers, were in business on South Front Street, with John, William, and Robert the partners in the business. James ran his grocery on South Second; it was called a tea store only once and he evidently was not in business with his brothers. Robert Woodside is first mentioned in the letters as going to America in October 1850, but because he appears in the Philadelphia directory as having a tea warehouse on West High that year it is probable that he had been there previously.[47]

They succeeded so well that their first visits home convinced their cousin Robert McLeese to ask the assistance of his brother William in Canada to pay his way to Philadelphia in 1851.[48] Once in the United States, he found opportunity mostly through the transnational community of north Antrim people. He was met on the wharf by William and Robert Woodside, who obtained him free lodgings with a son-in-law of John McConaghie of Ballycastle, and the next day he began work in a store. Two weeks later Robert Hodges, an old neighbour, got him a job with a Coleraine man he had worked for during the winter, a speculator building houses, at $4.50 a week. He left that job because the Coleraine man had a nephew wanting it. Robert was compelled to leave 'the trade' for a time and was recommended by William Woodside to an English grocer who was married to a daughter of Dan Lynn of Chatham Hall back in County Antrim. He was put in charge of the store when the Englishman was away, but early the next year, following a quarrel over hauling a barrel of sugar out of the cellar, Robert left and began to find work at his trade but outside the home circle.

He worked for nearly a year for a County Down man building a Presbyterian church for $1.50 a day.[49] He worked steadily at rebuilding another church in Germantown through most of 1854 and his success enabled him to contribute to the economy of his nuclear and extended family. He sent home a $10 gold piece to his father and a $5 piece to his brother Daniel, and loaned $100 to an Irish friend to go out to her cousin in California. By the autumn he was lamenting the cold weather and gave in to a cousin's urgings to join him in Charleston, South Carolina, where he worked the winter building a farm house at $1.75 to $2.25 a day. Despite the increased wages he felt the south to be hot and unhealthy and the manners of its people struck him as too aristocratic. He felt that tradesmen were not respected there as they were in the north.[50] Though he made no commentary on the fact, his letter from Charleston was return-addressed care of John Woodside, 191 East Bay Street. This was John B. Woodside, a cousin to the Philadelphia Woodsides, who operated a bar room at that location.[51] In the spring Robert McLeese returned to carpentering in Philadelphia at his old wage. A year later (1855) he was in charge of a project outside the city and was able to send another $30 home to his father.[52] A dutiful son, he was continuing to contribute to the well-being of the nuclear family at home.

Even when he succumbed to the lure of the California goldfields, Robert did not operate entirely outside the north Antrim network. In the spring of 1856 he put up $110 to take him from New York to San Francisco via Panama.[53] A day before leaving Philadelphia Robert had met a distant relative, Hugh McKinnon, a stockbroker from San Francisco who had returned to New York to see his stepmother. McKinnon was kind to him on the voyage but Robert stayed only a day in San Francisco. He proceeded immediately to the diggings in Nevada County where two acquaintances from Ireland were working. Failing to turn a profit as a prospector, he soon turned his hand to carpentry.[54] By 1857 he had secured steady work with a grandson-in-law of John McConaghie of Ballycastle, making machinery to extract gold ore from rock with two young men from Ballymoney.[55] In spring 1858 he headed once again for the mines with John Woodside, a son of Davey Woodside of Carnduff (another cousin of the Philadelphia Woodsides), who had wintered with McConaghie's daughter and her husband.[56]

After 1857 Robert did not write home and his father learned of his progress on visits to the McConaghies in Ballycastle, who read him extracts from the letters they received from their friends in California. One letter reported that Robert had gone to the Fraser River goldfields in British Columbia in 1859, but that 'it was not Dooing as well as it was Expected'.[57] Nor, presumably, was Robert, for by 1861 he was back in California working at his trade, and making a home with McConaghie's daughter, Mrs Miller, when he was in their part of the country. Following the beginning of the Civil War the Millers ceased writing home to Ballycastle and the McLeeses lost knowledge of Robert's whereabouts. His father thought him dead. In 1863 he had word from San Francisco that Robert was living, but without details.

Sojourners who saw the very purpose of their sojourn eroding, embarrassed that their expectations of progress toward respectability were fading, commonly ceased to write home until their fortunes turned.[58] So it was with Robert. Unknown to his family he had returned to British Columbia as prosperity in California waned. During the period he was incommunicado in that sparsely populated resource colony, Robert found himself isolated for the first time from his transnational network of expatriate Irish friends, but gradually he achieved some measure of economic success. He lived first at New Westminster, the incipient capital of the mainland colony, working as a carpenter, builder, and contractor; among the projects his father did not hear about was the contract for the Survey Office late in 1859. He was also chief engineer of the local Fire Department, and in 1862 became a founding member of the British Columbia Pioneer Association.[59]

The stated purpose of the Pioneer Association was to:

draw together in fraternal unity the pioneers of this country, to aid the sick and destitute, to bury the dead, and to keep a complete record of remarkable events and discoveries from the first discovery of gold, together with important statistical and other information, as well as to collect specimens of geological formations, natural history and botany, &c.'[60]

This curious combination of functions betrays an attempt to overcome the problems of life in a resource colony where women were few and history lacking, and where the wilderness was overpowering. Robert, like many others, was not progressing toward the sojourner's goal of marriage and family. In his location, marriage seemed a dim prospect indeed. Young white men in the colony assumed the embarrassment of

Figure 8.2 *Male culture in interior British Columbia.* Robert McLeese's Colonial Hotel and store served miners and other sojourners at Soda Creek on the Fraser River frontier. He made his fortune, but achieved domesticity only through a return home and visit east. Robert second from left.

domestic duties, lived in a rough homosocial culture of drink and indulgence, or formed liaisons with native women.[61] Little is known of Robert's domestic circumstances during this period, nor during the ensuing years when he operated a stopping place at a steamer landing on the way to the goldfields. Once his correspondence resumed, he was anxious to assert the growing respectability of life in the colony. It is in this light that we can understand his membership in the Pioneer Association and comprehend the congruity of its founding principles. The Association was both a surrogate family in a colony of male sojourners, and an attempt to put down roots, create a history, and subdue through the imposition of scientific categories the wilderness of a distant mining frontier.

In 1863 Robert removed to Soda Creek, a small hamlet in the Cariboo District that marked the point at which navigation on the Upper Fraser began, beyond the violent rapids that made navigation impossible between Soda Creek and Yale. It was at Soda Creek that the wagon road from Yale rejoined the river.[62] Though isolated, eight days' journey from Victoria and receiving only weekly mails, Soda Creek was the distribution point for the Chilcotin country. The rolling grass and farmland around it supplied the beef, bacon, flour and vegetables for the mines. In partnership with another young man Robert McLeese built and owned the Colonial Hotel, one of two hotels and stores at the landing.

Finally in 1866 John McLeese learned from a young man returned to Moycraig from America that Robert was again in British Columbia.[63] Robert had stopped writing while sojourning apart from his home circle, when his prospects seemed dim. Now on the road to economic success, he could at least respond to his distant father's enquiry. But how to respond? Robert was still unmarried. Indeed, he was in a country where marriage was unlikely, but he could present evidence of the respectability of property ownership and argue that he was within reach of taking on the respectability that accrued to public office. Before John died he had the pleasure of hearing once more from Robert:

> Robert appears he has some property gathered value some Thousands of Dollars and has had the honour of serving the peple of the Coleny a publick Sarvant and woold have been Elected to the Legeslative if I had only consented but it is a verrey Expensive and unremunative office at present as ths is a Croun Collany and the people has not a full Repsentitif form of govermint.[64]

Soon afterwards John wrote a very short letter to William in a failing hand – it would be his last communication as his final illness overtook him – urging him to write to Robert, as he was 'verry ancious to hav a Letter from you'. He noted with pride Robert's success ('you Br Robert is a cread to you and all belongin to'), repeating that he was a man of property and 'had it in his power to be a member of the Legsleative'.[65] William did not, however, hear from Robert until the summer following old John's death in 1869. Old John's passing before the marriage of his son left Robert's achievement incomplete. Without a family of his own, Robert would always feel a sojourner in the new land.

A return visit before 'settling down'

In 1873 Robert McLeese, the hotel owner and storekeeper in the wilds of British Columbia's Fraser Valley, made his only visit back to Ireland after an absence of twenty years. He took with him his younger cousin Willie McLeese, who had been sent out twenty years earlier to learn the millwright trade with Robert's brother William in Ontario's Ottawa Valley. On their return to Canada Robert would visit his brother there and both he and Willie would marry. Willie's mother would write of the Irish visit:

I think he did me the gratis feavour he could do me for he came home to let me see him before he settled down So I feel greatfull to him for the same I need not tell you how I feelt you can better imagin than I can describe the state of A mothers mind After 20 3 years sepperation of Mother and son.[66]

Why did the two cousins return home when they did, and what was the purpose of their visit? The marriage of Robert's British Columbia business partner in 1868, the death of his father the following year, and a decline in business with the passing of the Gold Rush first put Robert in a mind to sell out his business at Soda Creek and try somewhere else. As he prepared to sell his share of the business he was feeling acutely his single status and, as he wrote to William, he determined to 'take a trip to the scenes of my childhood and expected to see you and family on the way this summer'. Instead he was compelled to buy out his partner's interest when the latter's wife drowned in the Fraser.[67]

He did not write again for nearly three years, and when he did he structured his letter carefully to present a firmer plan.[68] He attributed his procrastination to unrealized hopes of a new goldfield 300 miles to the north. He was, however, doing well in the wheat trade and enclosed a newspaper announcing that he had been named a justice of the peace. He repeated that he could have been elected to the legislature had he wanted it, and hoped that the promised railroad that would accompany British Columbia's entry into the Canadian confederation would bring greater prosperity. This time declining trade did not picture in his motivation. His intention was to visit William over the winter if business proved good. He ended with a suggestion that his nephews and nieces send their 'Photographs or cartes de visite' and write a letter to 'their Batchelor Uncle'. Then in a postscript he addressed the central purpose of his letter:

I would like to know if you have no objection to let one of the boys come to this country the oldest if the others is not old enough I think that they could do better here than they could do with you I have nobody but Strangers to leave in charge of the Store and Hotel when I leave home So you see I could give one of them a good situation.[69]

A few months later he wrote again and furthered his argument. He thanked his little nieces for their letter, promised to write them by the next mail, and explained how business was improving as the survey for the Canadian Pacific Railway proceeded. He explained how he had made 'very warm friends out of the Surveyors of the Railroad' – friends William might consult in Ottawa about bridge contracts in Ontario. He also emphasized his acquaintance with British Columbia's new senators and members of Parliament, also in Ottawa, two of them Antrim men who could give William reliable first-hand information of his brother. Having learned from William that a relative of his wife had stayed at his hotel the year before, Robert had taken considerable pains to learn his present whereabouts and said that he would 'try to be a friend to him he made a very favourable impression on me for a stranger the first time I saw him'. He also sent a silver watch to William's son Johnny, praised what he had heard of his character and then, finally, returned to the theme of his earlier postscript:

> I would like very much if I had some one of my relations out here with me as I think this is going to be a very prosperous country for some time or during the time of constructing the Railroad
>
> But it is a very rough country and society is not in a verry good state owing to the small number of respectable femails but it is improving materially as there is families settling in various parts of the upper country as we call this part of it.[70]

Thus Robert countered his admission of British Columbia's culture of rough masculinity with his argument that the country was becoming more settled and named a series of respectable individuals from whom William might seek confirmation. All of this built up to a reiteration of his request that one of William's boys be sent out to him.

Perhaps Robert arrived east unheralded in the new year, for we have no more letters from him until he wrote from Ireland, but he achieved his objective. In 1873 young nephew Johnny went west to look after Robert's business, and Robert convinced his cousin Willie to accompany him on a trip to Ireland. Willie's father had died in April 1872[71] and it is probable that news of his death prompted Willie to accompany Robert on what was to be their one journey home.

The Irish kin well knew that the passing of the older generation often resulted in loss of contact with relatives abroad. In reporting the death of old John in 1869 Robert's sisters had written that 'Father used to say when he would be away the Corespond would drop we promised to him otherwise'.[72] But further letters had not come, increasing Robert's sense of isolation and causing him to recognize that he had brought it upon himself through his own failure to write home. He had lamented to William:

> I have not had a letter from home for some time I suppose the have forgotten me the same as what you write they had don to you . . . . When I cam to this country I did not think that I would remain in it any time and I neglected corresponding with nearly every one and I have lost all traces of a number of persons which I would like to hear from now.[73]

His uncle Daniel's wife (Willie's mother) had little expectation that the broader family ties would survive her husband's death, but she hoped that the family remaining in each country would draw closer together, for the sake of respectability. She wrote William:

> it was your uncles diaying requist to your Sister Mary & Jane and my own famlii for friends to draw cloce together for he sayed it was christan loocking And indeed they do live in verry good friendship and I hope my two sons and you will do the same.[74]

After two months in Ireland, a longer stay than they had anticipated, the two cousins embarked at Londonderry on the steamer *Caspian* for Quebec City, and in September arrived at cousin William's in the Ottawa Valley. Robert there married Mary McLaren, a niece of his brother William's Scottish wife – presumably they had met during Robert's visit in the spring – and they proceeded on to British Columbia, arriving there the final day of October.[75] Cousin Willie the following March married an unrelated McLaren, daughter of a man for whom he had built a mill at Osceola two years earlier.[76]

Was the timing of these marriages coincidental? What is the significance of the return journey by Robert and Willie? The deaths of their respective fathers triggered in both a guilty realization that they not lived up to parental expectations. They had let their ties with their families of birth erode, but had not created a domestic circle of their own. It was time to put this right, but before they did each felt a need to make peace with his family of birth.

For this reason, both Robert and Willie McLeese, recognizing that they would not return there a second time, made a symbolic last journey home. Their aim in going abroad had been to make a future for themselves, and Robert at least had only gradually come to accept that his future lay in the New World. Their objectives regardless had been success, respectability, and domesticity. While they worked toward this goal, they had remained emotionally a part of their nuclear family of birth, contributing both to its support and to their own future. Robert had sent substantial amounts of money home from Philadelphia, and even in California had for a time worked and resided with friends he had known in Antrim. But the goal of achieving success and respectability – and with it true adulthood – was so strong that Robert, like many emigrants, had stopped writing when he saw his prospects blasted.[77] It was embarrassment at impending failure rather than the cost of postage that kept him incommunicado, for most letters in this period were sent collect.

Once on the road to economic success, he could at least respond to his distant father's enquiry. But in the predominantly male society of colonial British Columbia Robert was further than ever from marrying and 'settling down'. Though John would not be there to welcome him,

Robert's final ocean journey back to Carrowreagh was itself a rite of passage, a final return to the scenes of his childhood, capped by marriage upon his return to Canada. Willie likewise had missed the opportunity of making a final symbolic break with his father, but after years of peripatetic mill work up and down the Ottawa Valley this sojourner was able to bid farewell to his mother one last time as a single man, and like Robert to marry on his return to the New World.

This final visit as a single member of the parental family of birth differs markedly from contemporary practice among the wealthier classes. For those who could afford it (and this was patently not the McLeeses) the wedding trip was a rite of passage that followed hard upon the wedding itself. Unlike the later honeymoon, which provided the privacy for the young couple's initiation into heterosexual practice in commercialized, non-family surroundings,[78] the function of the wedding trip was the integration of the young people as a couple into the wider family circle through visits to relatives resident at a distance.[79] For most it would be the first visit of many. For the McLeeses, emigrants who recognized that future transatlantic excursions would be beyond their means or forestalled by family responsibilities, the trip to visit kin was undertaken before the marriage, in recognition that this rite of passage would mark a parting and not a reintegration.

Marriage, too, brought them respectability in a society where marriage was the norm. The two travellers, having made their final parting with the Old World, married Ross Township McLarens. Willie's mother wrote to William: 'you say perhaps I will think it strange that you three McLeeses has got Mclarens for Wifes I think it looks the better for the connection they must think highly of the name and as far as I Ever heard it was worth thinking of'.[80] Both men, in other words, had married respectably, even if their circumstances were such – Robert in a womanless country and Willie without the security of property[81] – that they had had to marry within a narrow circle in which William already had established the family's *bona fides*.

Though the 1873 visit had been intended as a parting, in a way that was unanticipated it was to bring Robert into closer continuing contact with his extended kinship circle than he had had any reason to expect during his bachelor days in Soda Creek. Once he had achieved the security of a nuclear family of his own he wrote to brother William seldom, reporting only milestones: his arrival back in Soda Creek in 1873, the birth of little Jennie in 1874, and the devastating news of his wife's death in childbirth in 1876. He claimed that he heard so frequently of William's family via Ireland that he had felt little need to write, but if William was writing often to Ireland in this period he was receiving little response. Robert was flooded with condolences from

Ireland after his wife's death and he continued to receive Irish letters regularly.[82] He was unable to raise his little girl himself and so placed her with a family in Victoria, where he paid her extended visits until she was old enough to join him on the Fraser. He sought to supplement his attenuated domestic circle by offering work to members of his extended transatlantic kin group.

Despite Robert's material success, the isolated British Columbia hamlet proved unattractive to the relatives Robert convinced to join him. His nephew Johnny fled from clerking in Robert's store and worked as a cattle drover and railway employee, ran a stopping place of his own, and rented a farm. He married in the west – to a native woman. Robert at first praised Johnny's morality[83] but within two years he was complaining that Johnny did not confide in him and finally he lamented, echoing his father's lamentations about brother Thomas a generation earlier:

> I did all that laid in my power to make some thing out of him but the more I did for him the more ungreatfull he became and when I found he would not do right either for himself or I I ceased having any further intrest in him . . . . It provokes me to the very quick to see him a hewer of wood and drawer of water when he ought to have been by this time in a more respectable situation.'[84]

None of the nieces and nephews who journeyed from Ireland to join Robert remained with him long. Niece Annie McDonald at least stayed in the province. She had learned the millinery trade in Coleraine and in 1879 Robert persuaded her come to Victoria to run a millinery shop there for a woman he knew. Robert's little Jennie was delighted to have a cousin near by and continued to visit her after Annie married in the city three years later.[85]

Cousin William Woodside's eldest son Willie (William Miller Woodside) left for Soda Creek in November 1882. He had commenced law work in Ireland, but so far we do not know what he did in British Columbia, or how long he remained. He went on to a business career in Philadelphia, and died in 1890 of yellow fever in Rio de Janeiro.[86] His brother Robert started off for British Columbia in October 1883 after spending some time in Philadelphia. He is listed as a clerk in Soda Creek in 1887–89, a fur trader in 1890, and bookkeeper and assistant postmaster in 1891, but disappeared thereafter.[87] It is not surprising that they moved on. Both had tasted life in the wider world, and Willie especially, famous internationally as a champion cyclist,[88] must have been dismayed by life in the rough Fraser Valley.

So, too, with Mary Jane McDonald. She was in regular correspondence with her Canadian cousins by 1883 and had cared for her uncle Daniel McLeese after his wife died, but by 1895 she was tired of the

Figure 8.3 *Domesticity achieved* (I): *lace curtains, trellis, hammock, and garden.* Robert McLeese's home at Soda Creek, 3 August 1897. The male companions in the earlier photograph have been supplanted by the women of his new domestic circle. A family copy identifies, left to right: Robert McLeese, Mary J. McDonald (a niece, visiting from Ireland), Mrs Bevis, daughter Jean McLeese.

hard work and let the farm. Uncle Daniel was in any case spending much of his time in Portrush and Ballycastle. She spent the winter of 1895–96 in Soda Creek. She wrote that it was a quiet place except when the stages and steamships arrived, but she regretted that she had little to do there because Chinese houseboys did most of what, in colonies of settlement, was accounted women's work.[89] Small wonder that she soon returned to Ireland and married an old flame.[90] Though in the end Robert was left alone with his daughter Jennie, through marriage he had achieved the domesticity he craved, and through his visit home closer ties with his extended family.

Return as social mobility

What of the Woodsides, prospering in the tea trade in Philadelphia? They did not break the connection home. They never moved beyond the bounds of their transnational community. They did not go out to the margin but remained in east-coast Philadelphia, where new arrivals from the old country sought them out, and from where return was much easier than from the western littoral of North America, the continent's final frontier. It is significant, too, that the opportunity they found in America was the trade of importing, which tied them economically to the wider world. All this made it more likely that they would, in the end, return to Ireland to stay.

Return visits, when financially possible and sufficiently frequent, increase the likelihood of such a permanent return. As John McLeese was forever pointing out to his sons, their Woodside cousins did far better in writing home, and certainly in the visiting department, though William McLeese was a more faithful correspondent than his father sometimes allowed and Robert's material success was notable, and almost on a par with the Woodsides'.[91] The proliferation of transatlantic steamer traffic late in the 1840s made it possible for the Woodsides, who lived in a major seaport, to visit Ireland without being too long from their tea business. Though at first the fares were steep (£25 in 1849) the brothers could afford to travel cabin class and to come laden with gifts. James made a visit home in 1846, and John spent a month in Ireland in 1849, impressing his two sisters and three cousins with new dresses.[92] William came home via Paris, London, Cork, and the Lakes of Killarney two years later, and brought Glasgow shawls to his McLeese and McArthur cousins. John returned in 1855 and took his sister Ann on a grand tour of the British Isles before going on himself to Paris and Rome. The brothers by this time were improving their parents' house in Carnduff with furniture from Maxwell's in Belfast so that it looked like a gentleman's residence, realizing for their parents the middle-class ideal of comfortable home and dutiful sons.[93] Robert spent two months at home in 1857 and bought an electrotherapy machine to ease his aging father's aches and pains. The following year William took home his wife, a 'bred lady' from near Carrickfergus who had been only a short time in America. After a week at home they spent four months touring France and Italy and made a trip to Edinburgh. At this time old Mrs Woodside died, devastating the eldest daughter Ann, and after William returned to Philadelphia John came to Ireland to obtain medical care for her.[94]

It was at this point (1859) that John Woodside became the first of the brothers to buy a home in Ireland, though he was to live there very little. The house in Ballycastle cost him £575 and he expended another £200 on a thorough renovation. He returned to America later that year and apart from a fortnight's visit in 1861 appears not to have visited Ireland again. By 1863 his father and sister Ann had moved to Ballycastle

Merchants' Hotel.

**NORTH FOURTH STREET,
PHILADELPHIA.
J. M. SANDERSON & SON.**

Figure 8.4 *Male culture in Philadelphia.* The Merchants' Hotel was built exclusively to accommodate young unmarried men of commerce. McLeese's cousin John Woodside, tea dealer, lived there throughout his sojourn in America, even when he accounted himself worth $50,000. Brother Robert Woodside also lived there for a time.

and they probably lived in John's house, since he continued to reside abroad.[95] In Philadelphia he boarded at the Merchants' Hotel, an imposing establishment catering to a clientele of young unmarried men of commerce. He reported himself to be worth $50,000, and he once sent a coach and harness as a present to brother Robert in Ireland. In 1876 he died during a sightseeing tour to Central America, but his body was forwarded to Philadelphia and on to Ireland for burial beside his parents at Ramoan. John's final return to Ireland was achieved only in death, but he was home at last.[96] Brother James died in Philadelphia in the same decade, and was buried at Laurel Hill Cemetery. Why his body was not accorded similar treatment is unclear.

William was the second to buy back home, and he opted for a small country estate. He returned to Ireland for his health in 1862 and two years later purchased Dr Boyd's Dundooan House near Coleraine, with forty acres of land. He paid £3,500 and had it furnished by Maxwell. He was the first of the brothers to retire from business and return to Ireland permanently, though Robert had gone home late in 1859 and seems to have spent much of his time in Ireland thereafter.[97] William returned three or four times to America after resuming residence in Ireland, but embraced his gentlemanly role in Coleraine with enthusiasm, exercising paternalistic direction over a host of public institutions. He was a magistrate for County Derry and a member of the Coleraine Board of Guardians, a director of the Ballycastle Railway Company, a member of the Coleraine Harbour Board, and vice-president and treasurer of

Figure 8.5 *Domesticity achieved* (II). William Woodside's Dundooan House, 35 Dundooan Road, Coleraine, purchased in 1864. The Woodsides returned to Ireland as landed gentry after twenty years in Philadelphia. In 1880 Robert Woodside bought Carnsampson House near Ballycastle; the family appears in *Burke's Landed Gentry of Ireland.*

the Coleraine & Ballymoney Farming Society, as well as a member of the managing committee of the Coleraine Academical Institution, and a member of committee of the First Presbyterian Church, Coleraine. As one might expect, he was politically a Conservative. At his death in 1887 he was memorialized as 'one of the truest and best of gentlemen', and the *Coleraine Chronicle* devoted three entire columns to his obituary.[98]

Robert Woodside married in 1862. In 1867 a child was born to his wife in Ballycastle but he was described in the register as a merchant in Philadelphia and he appears in the directories there for the next two years. He was home in 1869, living in Ballycastle, and thereafter was termed a retired merchant. In 1879 he bought twenty-two-room Carn-sampson House with forty acres of land, very near the old family farm at Carnduff, for £1,406. His sister Ann had suggested to her cousin Robert McLeese that he buy it, but his reply that he could not prof-itably sell out his British Columbia businesses at the time seems an excuse more than an explanation. In the event it was Robert Woodside who bought Carnsampson and became the 'big noise' in Ballycastle. By 1876, before purchasing Carnsampson, he owned 458 acres, and he was accounted 'a most indulgent landlord [who] settled with most of his tenants out of court' on generous terms. He was a director of the Bal-lycastle Gasworks and succeeded his brother as a director of the local railway company. After he died in 1889 the members of Ballycastle Presbyterian Church erected a monument on the church lawn com-memorating 'one of the early teachers of this Sabbath School' and 'an active and devoted member of this Church whose ... liberality increased and helped largely to improve the Church property'. He pro-vided an annual treat to the scholars and donated a house and garden, with the rents appropriated to providing free church accommodation for the poor. He was accounted 'a Conservative of a moderate and pro-gressive type', 'never in the slightest degree an autocrat' but, more retiring than his brother, he declined appointment to the magistracy and 'shrank from an eldership'. His children contributed a commemo-rative window to the church, and the family Bible reposes on its sill.[99]

Despite their material success the Woodsides did not shun their less successful relatives. To be sure, William's much heralded return in 1858 with his wife, the 'bred lady' from Carrickfergus, 'donted the most of the frinds of calling to see them',[100] but the Woodsides visited Uncle John McLeese on their trips home and delighted in news of their McLeese cousins, even at second hand. Of course it would be a mistake to view the McLeeses and McArthurs as 'poor relations', as they were respectable farmers. But they were acutely aware of class differences, John McLeese noting that the Woodsides' houses rivalled that of Mr Miller, the landlord's agent in Ballycastle, and complaining that he could have understood the standoffishness of cousin James Kane's wife had he married into a family that stood higher in society.[101]

Why did the Woodsides elect to go home? We are not privy to their views on the question, but we can advance several explanations that appear likely in the circumstances. William's decision was made for his health and possibly prompted also by economic conditions during the American Civil War, but both surviving brothers continued to have economic interests in Pennsylvania after returning to Ireland. The determining factors probably arose from a series of longer-term and more fundamental considerations. First, the Woodside brothers had acquired no family ties in the United States to non-Antrim families. Only one of the four married there, to a woman from Carrickfergus who was not long in America, who came from a higher social position in the Old World, and whose parents were living not too far from his own Irish home. William McLeese, on the other hand, married a Scottish woman whose family were all in Renfrew County, Canada West, and with whom he enjoyed a close relationship.[102] Secondly, in Philadelphia the Woodsides were at the regional hub of a transnational network and were constantly in touch with new arrivals from home. Philadelphia was the major destination for emigrants from the home area. Thirdly, the brothers took obvious pleasure in their status as sons who had made good and who had become enviable success stories: taking relatives on British or European tours, bringing them presents, and helping out their aged parents constituted a fulfillment of the filial expectations their kin at home had of successful emigrants. They would have been less than human had they not enjoyed the popularity this largesse garnered them, and it encouraged them to return to the heart of their transnational network and leave behind the anonymity of the Merchants' Hotel. Fourthly, by living in a major seaport, having occupations that bound them to the sea rather than to the land the way the demands of agriculture would have done, and enjoying some financial success, they were able to visit home frequently while resident in America, and in the end to decide against establishing families in the new world.

Finally, by moving home the Woodsides were leaving mercantile ranks and becoming landed gentry.[103] Under the old regime, the path to power had long been for successful merchants to earn their fortune in trade, and then to buy their way into the landed classes, adopting the gentry mind set.[104] The path to power and privilege had shifted in England and Canada as the commercial and industrial classes took power, but one could still manage the old transition in the more rural parts of Ireland where the landed ascendancy still dominated and where there was not the same large rising commercial/industrial class coming to political dominance as in England. Early in the nineteenth century many English and Irish merchants had sold out their businesses and emigrated to Canada to become big fish in the colonial gentry pond. But this was not possible for the Woodsides in late nineteenth-century Philadelphia, a large and wealthy commercial city. The Woodsides would never be really big players in the Philadelphia import scene – but they could become prominent back in Ballycastle and Coleraine.

Conclusion

Whether at home in Ireland or sojourning abroad, in Philadelphia or the Ottawa Valley or even distant California, these young men had been part of a face-to-face network of family and community from home. Having been raised to view marriage and family as integral to their achievement of true manhood, material success was not enough. For emigrants the importance of marriage as a rite of passage lay in the recognition that they were planting roots in the New World, and that the youthful stage of sojourning and return or repeat migration was over. Once they established their own families, they became irretrievably a part of the New World. Cost and family responsibilities would make future visits unlikely and, though they would continue to be part of a wider network, their closest emotional ties would now be with their own wives and children. Marriage was the true rite of passage that reconfigured their relationship with the wider community.

Such was the experience of Robert McLeese, sojourner and emigrant, who went out to the frontier, stripped away Old World contacts and culture and moved beyond the reach of the transnational community. In British Columbia Robert found a marginal male culture. Servicing the resource economy there facilitated his transition to economic prosperity, but not his transition to a new domesticity. It was a letter from his distant father, and in the end the jar of his father's death, that made Robert realize his purpose in going abroad would remain unfulfilled so long as he remained single. He was still a part of his family of birth. He needed to reconnect with them to make the final break from his status as sojourner and as son. It was the final parting on his one visit home that made him, at last, an emigrant, and his marriage that crowned his success. Like their cousin Robert McLeese, the Woodsides found economic success as sojourners, and as for him domesticity long eluded them. Their solution, too, was to return, but they had never broken their connection home. They had remained central figures within their transnational community and return permitted them to achieve their greatest success in the land where their network was anchored, exercising paternalism both in the family and in the public sphere. They did not go home to effect a final break, but to 'settle down'.

Stephen Fender saw the assumption of such a break as central to the psychology of emigration and, beyond that, what made the United States different: 'America internalized that ideology and deployed it to invent itself.'[105] In what he terms the dominant discourse of emigration, sojourners were indecisive and therefore perverse; those who returned to the British Isles were traitors to the emigrant vision, and to the new nation: they had nonetheless imbibed the deeper meaning of emigration and reinvented themselves as travellers to disguise their failure.

The men we have explored here did not construct their narratives in these political terms. As sojourners, they were moving less toward independence than toward respectability. It was the psychology of family that dominated their thinking and drew them back. Their aim was to 'settle down', and domesticity could be achieved either side of the Atlantic. Family for them was more important than politics. Robert McLeese applied for naturalization while in Philadelphia. He even wrote to his brother that he could not come to see him in 'Victoria's dominions' because it would 'deprive me of the benefit of becoming a Citizen of the U. S. . . . I will have to defer my visit to next summer as I expect to have all the privelige of being a citizen of the Greatest Republic that ever was in existance by that time.'[106] The Woodsides became naturalized Americans early on.[107] But the personal predominates in both stories. Robert moved to British Columbia and nothing more was heard of becoming American. There he became part of the political power structure – for personal reasons. He told his brother that he did not 'meddle much with politics'[108] but he presented to his father as evidence of his personal respectability the fact that he might have been elected to the legislature, had he consented to take on the bother. To William he emphasized his friendship with politicians and with the surveyors of imperial expansion for exactly the same reason. Domesticity achieved through a journey home, he did go on to become member for Cariboo, as a Conservative, the party that emphasized the British connection. He resigned only to seek a federal nomination. Robert and William Woodside returned home to gentry status and patriarchal oversight of local institutions and were adjudged Conservatives of a progressive stripe; their American citizenship was conveniently forgotten. In both instances the personal overcame the political. Political allegiance to the United States, to Canada, to Ireland was a means to a personal end in which the transnational network of family and community, and the achievement of domesticity within it, of 'settling down', was of greater fundamental importance.

Notes

My thanks to Eric Manchee and Mary Ellen McLeese, the former for the William McLeese correspondence, the latter for sharing additional family papers and photographs and the results of her own research. I am also grateful to David and the late Muriel Honneyman of Belfast for welcoming me to their cottage near Dunluce in the summers of 1992 and 1995, and for acting as my chauffeur and guides around North Antrim. Mr James Leslie, Leslie Hill, Ballymoney, very graciously welcomed me to his home on several occasions to consult his estate records and atlases. My thanks also to Susan E. Hood, Dublin; Ann Creith, Bushmills; Mr and Mrs Stewart McCormick, Carrowreagh; Miss Eva McArthur, Novally; Nevin Taggart, Bushmills; and Lisa Emberson, Ottawa; Marilyn Barber and Maren Wood at Carleton University, Adele Perry in Winnipeg, and Marjory Harper.

1 Stephen Fender, *Sea Changes: British Emigration and American Literature* (Cambridge: Cambridge University Press, 1992), 361.
2 *Ibid.*, 355.
3 *Ibid.*, 222, 209.
4 Mark Wyman, *Round-Trip to America: The Immigrants Return to Europe, 1880–1930* (Ithaca NY and London: Cornell University Press, 1993), 6; and above, 16–17.
5 Bruno Ramirez, *On the Move: French-Canadian and Italian Migrants in the North Atlantic Economy, 1860–1914* (Toronto: McClelland & Stewart, 1991), 59–71, 95–6, 140–1.
6 Fender's chapter 21 sees the American view of later immigrants this way.
7 Wyman, *Round-Trip to America*, 5–6.
8 New ways of looking at letters recently have assumed a new prominence alongside the quantifiable materials that for a time provided the major way forward in Irish emigrant studies. See David Fitzpatrick, '"Oceans of Consolation": Letters and Irish Immigration to Australia' in Eric Richards, Richard Reid and David Fitzpatrick, *Visible Immigrants: Neglected Sources for the History of Australian Immigration* (Canberra: Department of History, Australian National University, 1989): 47–87; Fitzpatrick, *Oceans of Consolation: Personal Accounts of Irish Migration to Australia* (Cork: Cork University Press, 1994), and David A. Gerber, 'Epistolary Ethics: Personal Correspondence and the Culture of Emigration in the Nineteenth Century', *Journal of American Ethnic History* 19: 4 (2000), 3–23.
9 This is one of the most striking features of both the eighteenth- and nineteenth-century correspondence analysed by Trevor Parkhill, 'Philadelphia Here I Come: A Study of the Letters of Ulster Immigrants in Pennsylvania, 1750 to 1875' in H. Tyler Blethen and Curtis W. Wood, Jr (eds), *Ulster and North America: Transnational Perspectives on the Scotch-Irish* (Tuscaloosa AL and London: University of Alabama Press, 1997), 119–20.
10 On occasion even death did not make a sojourner an emigrant: the body of one of the Woodside brothers was returned to Northern Ireland to be interred beside his parents after he died in Central America.
11 Fender, *Sea Changes*, 149.
12 David A. Gerber, 'Theories and Lives: Transnationalism and the Conceptualization of International Migrations to the United States', *IMIS-Beiträge* 15 (2000), 40–1.
13 *Ibid.*, 35.
14 James A. Hammerton, 'Forgotten People? Marriage and Masculine Identities in Britain', *Journal of Family History* 22: 1 (1997), 111.
15 John Tosh, *A Man's Place: Masculinity and the Middle-Class Home in Victorian England* (New Haven CT and London: Yale University Press, 1999), 6–7.
16 Tosh, *A Man's Place*, 176; cf. John Higham, 'The Reorientation of American Culture in the 1890s' in Higham (ed.), *Writing American History: Essays in Modern Scholarship* (Bloomington IN: Indiana University Press, 1970).
17 Hammerton, 'Forgotten People'; Margaret Marsh, 'Suburban Men and Masculine Domesticity, 1870–1915' in Mark C. Carnes and Clyde Griffen (eds), *Meanings for*

Manhood: Constructions of Masculinity in Victorian America (Chicago and London: University of Chicago Press, 1990), 111–32.

18 Tosh, *A Man's Place*, 2–3.

19 *Ibid.*, 6–7.

20 John M. Robson, *Marriage or Celibacy? The* Daily Telegraph *on a Victorian Dilemma* (Toronto: University of Toronto Press, 1995); Hammerton, 'Forgotten People', 111.

21 Rentals and estate atlases of 1765 and 1804, courtesy Mr James Leslie of Leslie Hill near Ballymoney.

22 Estate atlas of 1804, Mr James Leslie, Leslie Hill, Ballymoney; Primary (Griffiths) Valuation, Carrowreagh, Grange of Drumtullagh, 1861. Daniel (c. 1822–1905) did not marry until he was 38 or 39, after all his brothers had emigrated. He lived in later years with his niece Mary Jane Graham, daughter of his sister Mary McDonald. He appears, however, to have had a son John by Ann Hodges, who was raised by the mother. He was not viewed as a potential heir to the farm, but Daniel's father John willed that Daniel 'take care of Joney McLeese and keep him at his tread and when fit send him to America.' Mary McDonald and Jane Hodges to William McLeese, Croshan, 8 February 1869; Public Record Office of Northern Ireland (hereafter PRONI), MIC 15C/2/9, No. 5572, will of John McLeese, 1869.

23 The correspondence mentions 180 Irish acquaintants who went abroad, more following the well worn path, dating back into the eighteenth century, between the port of Londonderry and Philadelphia, than to any other location. Of these, twenty-eight (15 per cent) are mentioned in the context of return.

24 John McLeese and Robert Woodside had married sisters named McArthur. The relationship is revealed by a registered deed of 1830 by which Daniel and Thomas McArthur, John McLeese, and Robert and Mary Woodside sold a house in Ballycastle: Registry of Deeds, Dublin, 868.44.577544. The property was obviously an inheritance. McLeese's wife Jane had died, and the McArthurs, who farmed at Novally near Ballycastle, were brothers of the two women.

25 John McLeese to William McLeese, Carroreagh, 12 November 1852.

26 Tosh, *A Man's Place*, 3–4.

27 John McLeese to William McLeese, Carroreagh, 28 December 1859.

28 John McLeese to William McLeese, Carroreagh, 22 May 1852, 7 May 1853, 23 November 1854, 5 October 1857, 28 December 1859, 18 February, 21 March, 9 May, 24 July, 21 October 1861, 17 March, 12 November 1862; to Johnny McLeese and to Christiana McLeese, 12 November 1862.

29 PRONI, MIC 15C/2/9, No. 5572, will of John McLeese, 1869.

30 John McLeese to William McLeese, Carroreagh, 26 December 1855.

31 John McLeese to William McLeese, Carroreagh, 30 December 1863.

32 John McLeese to William McLeese, Carroreagh, 20 March 1845.

33 John McLeese to William McLeese, Carroreagh, 30 July, 30 October 1845.

34 John McLeese to William McLeese, Carroreagh, 12 November 1852, 7 May 1853.

35 Tosh, *A Man's Place*, 3.

36 John McLeese to William McLeese, Carroreagh, 21 October 1861.

37 John McLeese to William McLeese, Carroreagh, 12 November 1852.

38 John McLeese to William McLeese, Carroreagh, 31 [*sic*] April 1852.

39 John McLeese to William McLeese, Carroreagh, 11 January 1865.

40 The institution had been established the year before under the direction of a Quaker doctor, T.S. Kirkbride. Kirkbride strongly influenced American psychiatry by designing the hospital to facilitate the cure rather than the mere incarceration of the mentally ill. Set in extensive grounds, the Pennsylvania Hospital included 'occupational therapy suites, libraries and swimming pools'. In 1844 Kirkbride hosted the meeting that led to the establishment of the American Psychiatric Association. As the Institute of Pennsylvania Hospital the facility continued to accept patients until merged with another institution in a round of budget cuts in 1997. Howard Sudak, MD, 'A Remarkable Legacy: Pennsylvania Hospital's Influence on the Field of Psychiatry', www.med.upenn.edu/pahosp/about_pahosp/history/stories/psych.html.

41 There were Corrys in Carrowreagh.

42 PRONI, D1828/31, Jonathan Smyth to James Smith, Philadelphia, 24 September 1845. Daniel Henry Stuart McKay, Esq., died at Mosside 6 May 1889 aged 87: *Ballymoney Free Press*, 16 May 1889, p. 3, col. 6. On their proprietorship of the village: John McLeese to William McLeese, Carroreagh, 25 October 1864.

43 PRONI, T2077/4; my thanks to Roger Strong of PRONI for the Carson letters. For both this and the Smith reference I am indebted to the Emigration Database at the Centre for Migration Studies, Omagh.

44 William Woodside to William McLeese, Blackley, near Philadelphia, 2 August 1844.

45 John Woodside worked for seven years with Rankin before establishing his own business, John Woodside & Co. 'The Late John Woodside, Esq.', *Coleraine Chronicle*, 20 January 1877, p. 4, col. 6.

46 William Woodside to William McLeese, Blackley, 18 August 1845; John McLeese to William McLeese, Carroreagh, 14 April 1846; Thomas McLeese to William McLeese, 23 August 1846.

47 McElroy's *Philadelphia Directory*, 1847, p. 383; 1848, p. 394; 1850; 1854, p. 579; 1861, p. 1087; 1862, pp. 734–5; 1867, p. 992; 1867–68; Gopsill's *Philadelphia City and Business Directory* for 1868–69, p. 1657; 1869, p. 1589; 1871; Ann Woodside to William McLeese, Ballycastle, 15 January 1883; John McLeese, Carroreagh, 14 October 1850. Robert Woodside, 25, a farmer from 'Co. Antrim in Ireland', arrived at New York on 11 November 1850 on the *Princeton* out of Liverpool, with his final destination Philadelphia. Family Tree Maker Family Archives, *Ireland to America, 1846–1865* (CD–ROM).

48 Robert McLeese to William McLeese, Carroreagh, 14 March, 25 June, 8 October 1849.

49 Robert McLeese to William McLeese, Philadelphia, May 1851, 14 July 1851; John McLeese, Carroreagh, 12 November 1852; Robert McLeese, Philadelphia, January 1853, 23 January 1854.

50 Robert McLeese, Germantown, 20 September 1854, Philadelphia, 23 October 1854. The cousin was Thomas Kerr, who had accompanied McLeese to America.

51 Robert McLeese, Charlestown SC, 4 December 1854; J.H. Bagget, *Directory of the City of Charleston* 1852, p. 139; *Charleston City and General Business Directory* 1855, p. 115; 1859, p. 228. A William Woodside is listed at the same address as John B. in 1852, as is a Samuel A. Woodside in both 1852 and 1859. William died 29 September 1852 of yellow fever; he was a son of James Woodside of Carnduff: *Belfast Commercial Chronicle*, 30 October 1852, Emigration Database, Centre for Migration Studies, Omagh. William, 19, and Samuel, 17, both labourers, had arrived at New York on 13 November 1850 on the *Henry Clay* out of Liverpool, bound for South Carolina: Family Tree Maker's Family Archives: *Passenger and Immigration Lists: Ireland to America, 1846–1865* (CD–ROM). The registers of Ballycastle Presbyterian Church record the baptism on 9 September 1860 of John James son to John B. Woodside of Carnaff [Carnduff], with the annotation 'belongs to America'. So John B. Woodside of Charleston, too, made a trip home to Ireland. PRONI, MIC 1P/115.

52 John McLeese, Carroreagh, 26 December 1855.

53 This passage proved a memorable one. Robert arrived in Panama half an hour before a fellow passenger's argument with a native over the price of a watermelon erupted into violence and culminated in an attack by 500 or 600 locals on the 1,100 or 1,200 passengers. Forty or fifty Americans were killed and many others were horribly cut and mutilated. The train was looted, and Robert lost all his clothing, baggage, and books, but he escaped unhurt. John McLeese, Carroreagh, 21 October 1856. Robert saw to it that this incident was also mentioned in his short biography in J.B. Kerr, *Biographical Dictionary of Well-known British Columbians* (Vancouver: Kerr & Begg, 1890), 250–1. From the perspective of his narrative this severest of disruptions of social order was a high point in the symbolism of his actual journey to the edge and back again.

54 John McLeese to William McLeese, Carroreagh, 21 October 1856.

55 John McLeese to William McLeese, Carroreagh, 8 March 1858, 28 December 1859.

56 John McLeese to William McLeese, Carroreagh, 29 May 1858. John Hill, son of David Woodside, was baptized at Ballycastle Presbyterian Church on 4 November 1832. PRONI, MIC 1P/115.

57 John McLeese to William McLeese, Carroreagh, 28 December 1859.
58 Fender, *Sea Changes*, 155.
59 *British Columbian*, 5 September 1861, p. 1, col. 3; *British Columbian and Victoria Gazetteer and Directory for 1863* (Victoria: Howard & Barnett, 1863), 151, 168, res. cor. Columbia and Mary Streets. Contract for Survey Office: British Columbia Archives and Records Service (hereafter BCARS), Colonial Correspondence, F 957a, #16, 3 November 1859.
60 *British Columbian*, 31 December 1862, p. 2, col. 1; 7 January 1863, p. 2, col. 2. McLeese later claimed to have lived in British Columbia since 1858. Kerr, *Well-known British Columbians*, 251.
61 Adele Perry, *On the Edge of Empire: Gender, Race, and the Making of British Columbia, 1849–1871* (Toronto: University of Toronto Press, 2001).
62 On 10 July 1863 Sgt J. McMurphy, RE, reporting on the progress of the Lillooet and Alexandria wagon road, found at the Soda Creek steamer landing 'Mr McLeese of New Westminster building a house for himself to start the Whisky Trade'. BCARS, Colonial Correspondence, F 1069, #21, J. McMurphy to Col. R.C. Moody, July 1863. His pre-emption for 160 acres was recorded on 20 July 1863. BCARS: Land and Works, Pre-emption records, GR–1182, file 2, p. 8, No. 16.
63 John McLeese to William McLeese, 20 November 1866.
64 John McLeese to William McLeese, Carroreagh, 31 March 1867. Note how John reverts to the first person in copying the news from Robert's letter.
65 John McLeese to William McLeese, undated.
66 Elizabeth McLeese to William McLeese, Carroreagh, 22 April 1874.
67 Robert McLeese to William McLeese, Soda Creek, 30 August 1869.
68 On the purposive structuring of letters see David Fitzpatrick, 'Oceans of Consolation'.
69 Robert McLeese to William McLeese, Soda Creek, 25 May 1872.
70 Robert McLeese to William McLeese, Soda Creek, 3 December 1872.
71 Gravestone at Mosside Presbyterian, County Antrim.
72 Mary McDonald and Jane Hodges to William McLeese, Croshan, 8 February 1869.
73 Robert McLeese to William McLeese, Soda Creek, 3 December 1872.
74 Elizabeth McLeese to William McLeese, Carroreagh, 22 April 1874.
75 Marriage registration of Robert McLeese and Mary McLaren, 15 September 1873, AO, MS932, reel 12, No. 11242; Robert McLeese to William McLeese, Carroreagh, 21 August 1873; Soda Creek, 3 November 1873.
76 Willie's marriage to Anne, daughter of Alexander McLaren, 11 March 1874, from McLeese genealogy, Upper Ottawa Valley Genealogical Society library; William McLeese to William McLeese, Osceola, 30 November 1872.
77 Fender, *Sea Changes*, p. 155.
78 Karen Dubinsky, *The Second Greatest Disappointment: Honeymooning and Tourism at Niagara Falls* (New Brunswick NJ: Rutgers University Press, 1999), 28.
79 Peter Ward, *Courtship, Love and Marriage in Nineteenth-Century English Canada* (Montreal and Kingston: McGill-Queen's University Press, 1990), 115.
80 Elizabeth McLeese to William McLeese, Carroreagh, 22 April 1874.
81 Since 1871 Willie had had a half interest with his cousin William in an undeveloped farm on the southern edge of Forrester's Falls village. It was let while Willie lived in Hull and worked at Batson & Currier's mills from 1874–1877. Then in 1878 he bought out William's interest, began farming the property, and built saw and grist mills which he ran from about 1880 until he sold them out to Delorma Brown in 1888. William McLeese to William McLeese, various letters, 1871–76; AO, Ross Township Deeds, G.S. 5296, 25 September 1871; D1240, 6 February 1878; F2606, 15 March 1888; Robert McLeese to William McLeese, Soda Creek, 13 February 1880; John McLaren McLeese, *Memoirs of Forrester's Falls* (published privately, 1955), 8, 63.
82 Robert McLeese to William McLeese, Soda Creek, 3 November 1873, 19 July 1874; Victoria BC, 15 April 1876; Soda Creek, 1 July 1876; Victoria, 30 January 1877; John Adams, *Historic Guide to Ross Bay Cemetery, Victoria, B.C., Canada* (Victoria:

Heritage Architectural Guides, 1983), 14; *Daily British Colonist*, 5 April 1876, p. 3, col. 1 (two items re death of Mrs McLeese).

83 'He is a very good young man with none of the vices of such boys of his age as what we have in this country he does not Play cards does not drink and lately he has quite smoking.' Robert McLeese to William McLeese, Soda Creek, 19 July 1874.

84 Robert McLeese to William McLeese, Soda Creek, 11 December 1876, 13 February 1880.

85 Robert McLeese, Soda Creek, 13 February 1880; Mary J. McDonald, Carroreagh, 31 March, 27 August, 2 November 1883. Annie married William Gibson in Victoria 29 January 1883. BC Archives vital event indexes, www2.bcarchives.gov.bc.ca/cgi-bin/www/2vsm, film B11367, LDS [Latter Day Saints] film 1983524, reg. No. 1883–09–002563.

86 Ann Woodside to William McLeese, Ballycastle, 14 November 1882, 19 May 1884; *Coleraine Chronicle*, 28 June 1890, p. 5, col. 4; 5 July 1890, p. 5, col. 4. The year he died he was described in a family deed as a gentleman of Portrush, where his mother and sisters had moved after selling Dundooan House. Registry of Deeds, Dublin, 1890/29/285. His brothers James and John at that time were shipbuilders in Belfast.

87 *British Columbia Directory 1887* (Victoria: Mallandaine & Williams, 1887), 281; Registry of Deeds, Dublin, 1890/29/285, Woodside heirs to Anderson; *Henderson's British Columbia Gazetteer and Directory* (Victoria: Henderson, 1889), 249.

88 On W.M. Woodside's cycling career: Ann Woodside to William McLeese, Ballycastle, 14 November 1882; *The Times*, 23 May 1887, p. 6; 8 August 1887, p. 12; 22 August 1887, p. 12; 9 November 1887, p. 10; 2 July 1888, p. 5; 9 July 1888, p. 5; obituaries *Coleraine Chronicle*, 28 June 1890, p. 5, col. 5; 5 July 1890, p. 5, col. 4.

89 Adele Perry, *On the Edge of Empire*, 141.

90 David Graham. They took up farming in Carrowreagh, and Uncle Daniel McLeese moved in with them in 1904. Mary J. McDonald, Carroreagh, 31 March, 27 August, 2 November 1883; n.d. 1884; Robert McLeese, Soda Creek, 4, 30 March 1895; Mary J. McDonald, Carroreagh, 24 August 1895; Soda Creek, 22 September, 20 October 1895, 19 January 1896; David Hodges to Mrs Wm McLeese, Ancaster, Ontario, 21 March 1898; M.J. Graham, Carroreagh, 29 March 1898, 3 July 1899; LDS reel 0597740, 1901 census, Carnlelis; Margaret Jane Orr, Decatur IL., 30 November 1904. She is recorded as Jane McDonald, 30, spinster, on the passenger list of the *Numidian*, bound for Ashcroft BC, the nearest railway terminus to Soda Creek. National Archives of Canada, reel C-4540, list No. 64, Quebec, 1885.

91 By 1879 he was a part owner of the steamships that plied the upper Fraser.

92 John McLeese to William McLeese, Carroreagh, 14 March 1849.

93 Robert McLeese, Philadelphia, 14 July 1851; John McLeese, Carroreagh, 14 August 1851, 21 September 1855.

94 John McLeese, Carroreagh, 5 October 1857; 29 May, 22 October 1858.

95 John McLeese, Carroreagh, 2 August, 28 December 1859, 21 October 1861. John Woodside returned to Philadelphia in 1859 as a cabin passenger aboard the *City of Manchester* from Liverpool to New York.

96 Philadelphia federal census, 1860, reel M653–1156, Sixth Ward, p. 731; John McLeese, Carroreagh, 24 June 1863; Ann Woodside, Ballycastle, 15 January 1883; *Coleraine Chronicle*, 6 January 1877, p. 4, col. 4; 20 January 1877, p. 4, col. 6; 10 February 1877, p. 8, col. 1.

97 John McLeese, Carroreagh, 22 April 1863, 8 June 1864. John Boyd of Dunduan (sic) House, MP for Coleraine, died 2 January 1865 aged 73: memorial inside Coleraine Church of Ireland, courtesy David Honneyman of Belfast.

98 *Coleraine Chronicle*, 26 November 1887, p. 4, cols 4–6; 3 December 1887, p. 4, cols 4–5; monument, New Cemetery, Coleraine. His widow thereafter sold Dundooan House to Henry McClintock Alexander, Rear Admiral, Royal Navy, and moved to Portrush. Registry of Deeds, Dublin, 1890/9/272.

99 Civil registration of marriage, Ballycastle, 15 July 1862; PRONI, MIC 1P/115, Ballycastle Presbyterian Church, baptismal registers; Robert McLeese, Soda Creek BC, 1 July 1876, 13 February 1880; *Land Owners in Ireland* (Dublin 1876; Baltimore MD:

Genealogical Publishing Co., 1988), 200, 266; *Ballymoney Free Press*, 22 August 1889, p. 3, col. 2; 29 August 1889, p. 4, cols 5 and 6; monument and window, Ballycastle Presbyterian Church; family gravestone, Ramoan Old; PRONI, MIC 15 C/2/31, Belfast District Registry, No. 1146, pp. 273–85, will of Robert Woodside of Carnsampson.

100 John McLeese to William McLeese, Carroreagh, 29 May 1858.

101 John McLeese to William McLeese, Carroreagh, 22 May 1852.

102 The *Bathurst Courier* of Perth, Canada West, on 16 February 1849 reported the marriage at Portage du Fort, Canada East, on the 2nd inst. by the Rev. Mr Melville, of William McLeese, millwright, late from Bushmills, Co. Antrim, to Miss Catherine McLaren, youngest daughter to Lieut. John McLaren, late of Cushervachan, Perth, Scotland. Catherine was born 12 August and baptized 26 August 1824 at Comrie, Perthshire; her mother's name was Christian Ferguson. LDS International Genealogical Index. William and Catherine lived with Catherine's brother James after their marriage until in 1855 McLeese purchased a farm from her brother Dougall, a merchant. Ross Township census, 1852; Archives of Ontario (hereafter AO), reel G.S. 5296, Ross Township deeds, A74, 10 November 1855.

103 Robert's family bears a coat of arms and is listed in *Burke's Landed Gentry of Ireland* (London: Burke's Peerage, 1958), 771, under 'Woodside of Carnsampson'.

104 Harold Perkin, *The Origins of Modern English Society, 1780–1880* (London: Routledge; Toronto: University of Toronto Press, 1969).

105 Fender, *Sea Changes*, 361–2.

106 Robert McLeese to William McLeese, Philadelphia, 2 June 1855.

107 Robert McLeese registered his declaration of intention on 21 October 1854, John Woodside in 1843, William in 1848, and Robert in 1850. At least John and Robert followed through to swear the oath of allegiance. P. William Filby (ed.), *Philadelphia Naturalization Records* (Detroit: Gale Research, 1982), 450, 703.

108 Robert McLeese to William McLeese, Soda Creek, 25 May 1872.

CHAPTER NINE

Canada in Britain:
returned migrants and the Canada Club

Kathleen Burke

Migrants who return to their country of origin undergo two powerful life events. Having adjusted first to a strange land and customs, they return to a homeland which is different from that which they remembered, and to people who do not share a knowledge of the experiences they have undergone. Studies of migrants who return to less developed countries after migration to a metropole indicate that they can, at least, derive some esteem from having lived and worked in a more cosmopolitan and technologically advanced society[1] but, in an age when the majority of people in the homeland had little knowledge of, or interest in, colonial conditions and affairs, migrants who had achieved social status during their stay in less developed colonies faced additional difficulties on their return to the metropole.

Such was the situation that faced Canadians visiting or returning to Britain in the first half of the nineteenth century. Canadians were often dismayed to find that the British knew very little about the colony, nor was there a fitting appreciation of the status of the colonial élite and the trials they had faced in a new and often hostile environment. Attorney General Sir John Beverley Robinson complained of the general ignorance about Canada when he visited Britain in 1815, and was further offended that Londoners asked if his sleigh was pulled by reindeer; former Surveyor General of Upper Canada, Sir David William Smith, found that his Canadian offices and accomplishments meant little in the metropolis, and the merchant and politician Adam Lymburner complained that 'the people here feel little interest in the affairs of distant colonies'.[2] Finding themselves in this situation, some returned migrants from Canada who felt ignored and undervalued in nineteenth-century British society attempted to profit from the migrant experience by maintaining close connections with the land that had been their temporary home. This strategy for profiting from the migrant experience was more easily achieved within a group of like-minded individuals, and the Canada

Club was one institution that offered a small and select number of returned migrants the opportunity to relive their earlier experiences, retain the status they had achieved in Canada and continue to share in colonial affairs.

The Canada Club and its antecedents

The Canada Club is a dining club which is still in existence, and which was established in London in 1810 for 'persons who had resided for some time in Canada' with the 'distinctive character [of being] an assemblage of men knowing and following the interests' of the colony.[3] During the early years of its existence, the club performed a variety of functions. According to the biographer of British merchant and politician Edward Ellice, the primary reason for its formation was 'to pressure the government on behalf of colonial commerce';[4] however, certainly in the early years of its existence, Club dinners also provided a haven for members like fur trader William McGillivray, who, for a few hours, could relive old experiences among men who understood Canadian life.[5] Like McGillivray and others in the fur trade, some members spent much of the year in Canada, others spent protracted periods of time in Britain, and about one-quarter of the members had retired after years spent in the colony.[6] Within this institutional setting, therefore, returned migrants were almost indistinguishable from those members who resided permanently in the colony, although the returners discussed in this chapter can be identified as men who had resided in Canada, who returned permanently to Britain, but who maintained interests in the colony and may even have had some expectations of eventual return. Anthony Richmond has formulated the term 'transilients' to describe migrants with this propensity for geographic mobility. Richmond notes that transilients are usually well educated and occupy high positions in the social structure, and most of the migrants associated with the Canada Club would appear to conform to this pattern.[7]

It was not unusual for displaced colonials to gather in the capital city. Mary Beth Norton has discussed the gatherings of loyalists in certain London coffee houses during the 1770s and 1780s, and she mentions that in 1775 refugees from Massachusetts founded the New England (dining) Club.[8] Although Canada Club members were not victims of war, they seem to have followed in this loyalist tradition; indeed, by the 1820s the New England Coffee House appears to have become an everyday meeting place for Canadians, and Canada Club members occasionally held administrative meetings in the New York Coffee House, which itself had been a meeting place for London merchants involved in the Canada trade since 1765.[9]

There was, however, another, more traditionally 'Canadian' antecedent to London's Canada Club: Montreal's Beaver Club, founded in 1765 by partners in the North West Company with membership restricted to those who had passed a winter in the North West. Regular activities at the Beaver Club meetings included smoking a pipe of peace, voyageurs' songs, and a simulated 'grand voyage', during which members sat on the carpet and 'grasping fire-tongs, poker, sword or walking stick to serve as a paddle', proceeded to make an imaginary journey into fur trading country.[10] Many of the Canada Club's early members had been associated with the Beaver Club, or had engaged in the fur trade. Following in this fur trading tradition, the MacGillivrays, the Mactavishes and the Gillespies were undoubtedly the leaders of early Canada Club festivities, when well liquored members and guests, inspired by the reels and strathspeys played on the 'Northumberland Irish and Scotch Bagpipes', spent evenings of 'dancing, singing, mirth and good humour'.[11] The consumption of five bottles of port, five of sherry, two bottles of Madeira, two of claret, three bottles of champagne, and an unspecified amount of brandy by eleven diners at a January 1836 meeting is reminiscent of early Beaver Club meetings where members drank each other, literally, under the table.[12] When John Beverley Robinson visited the Canada Club in 1816, 'Canadian boat songs and Indian speeches' from merchants Angus Shaw and Robert Dickson were part of the evening's entertainment.[13] In 1825 'visiting "Indians"' were invited to entertain the members with traditional songs and dances,[14] so that, for several years after its inception, British businessmen were presented, not with an image of an urban, modernizing Canada, but with a Canada that many Montrealers or Torontonians had never seen, and which visiting businessmen were unlikely to encounter.

Members

Who were the members of this élite institution? Club records are somewhat confusing; an effort to create a hierarchy of members led to lists of 'original members', 'elected members' and 'honorary members'. The list of 'original members' includes the name of at least one man who was not officially admitted to membership until 1816, and the list of 'elected members' dates back as far as 1810. However, a careful perusal of these lists indicates that fifty-one men were admitted to membership during the first five years of the club's establishment. Similarly, it is not possible to identify every member, but of those who have been identified, approximately half were Scots, or had Scottish ancestry. Many of those men had close connections with Montreal or Quebec commercial interests, set up as a consequence of earlier fur trading activities. Among these, four members of the Gillespie family, two McGillivrays, William and Simon McTavish, and Alexander Mackenzie were most notable.[15] Even the most influential British member, Edward Ellice, claimed Scottish ancestry, and was a member of a merchant company that had been active in the North American fur trade since the mid-1760s.[16]

While the fur trade played an important role in bringing many Club members to prominence, John Forsyth, a partner in the Montreal company of Forsyth & Richardson, is an example of a member who had expanded operations beyond the fur trade. Forsyth and his partner had started operations in the fur trade, but by the early 1800s had begun to make forays into distilling, real estate, property management and importing. Members like Forsyth pursued more diverse commercial interests in the colony, but again, were likely to be of Scots origin, and because of this connection the early meetings had a decidedly Scottish tone.[17]

However, membership extended to a number of 'returned migrants' of English origin, including military officers who had contributed to the growth and defence of Canada. Members of the Royal Engineers were among their number, including Colonel Robert Pilkington, who claimed to be a founding member of the club, Colonel John By, supervisor of the Rideau Canal project, who was introduced to Club members in 1811, and John Simcoe Macaulay, who had become a member by the 1820s. Ex-colonial officials like Sir George Pownall, Lower Canada's Secretary, Registrar and Legislative Councillor, joined their ranks. After protracted discussions about admitting as honorary members 'gentlemen connected with Canada, though not having resided in that country', the rules were changed in 1811 to allow 'gentlemen connected with Canada by official situations or extensive mercantile transactions, but who have never resided in that country . . . to become Honorary Members of the Club'.[18] One of the obstacles to reaching a decision on the question was, apparently, difficulties connected with the 'vague and indefinite' use of the term 'gentleman' in Canada. As the club's historian, J.G. Colmer, notes, once this semantic difficulty had been overcome 'business associates of the North-West Company in London, . . . representatives of London commercial houses trading with Eastern Canada, and Canadian importing houses with Agents in London' gained entrée to the Club.[19] Within a couple of years of its inception, then, despite the persistence of old fur-trading traditions, and the preponderance of Scots associated with the trade, the club's membership had grown and diversified.

The Scots/Quebec connection remained strong, but increasingly varied associations emerged over time; as the years passed, membership was extended to more and more men whose primary place of residence was still Canada, and from the 1830s, names strongly associated with the Atlantic provinces began to appear on the membership lists.[20] Nevertheless, membership remained limited, and perhaps because of the relatively small number of members, the club soon acquired, among expatriate Canadians at least, an exclusive reputation, especially because every visiting politician or businessman of note attended Club dinners when visiting London, these visitors including such diverse figures as Sir John A. Macdonald and the venerable Archbishop John Strachan.

Returned migrants

Given the increasing cachet of Club membership, it is easy to understand why some returned migrants would await an invitation to Club dinners as a sign that their status in Canada had been recognized by their peers. But returned migrants had additional reasons for seeking admittance to an establishment which afforded an opportunity to retain ties to Canada. Some colonial officials were loathe to relinquish connections and influential posts in Canada until they had made a full commitment to a permanent home in Britain. Sir George Pownall, for example, returned permanently to England in 1805, but waited until 1807 before officially seeking permission for retirement, and his colonial status continued to be recognized among club members.[21] Old fur traders looked for companions who had shared lives to which most Englishmen could not relate. Others still fostered the hope of making financial gains in Canada. Whatever their reasons for retaining ties with the adopted country, these men were able to keep their interests in Canada alive at Club meetings where members and their guests reminisced about their experiences in a masculine atmosphere of joviality, good food and plentiful drink.

While nostalgic tales and entertainment may have evoked fond memories as the evening's festivities progressed, Club meetings were also occasions for conversation with many of the colony's most active businessmen and politicians. Most members of the Montreal merchant class were represented by one or more of their partners and social intercourse at dinner provided returned migrants with more practical opportunities to retain commercial interests in Canada, remain up to date with Canadian affairs and act as advisers to British businessman who were able to capitalize on first-hand knowledge of local conditions. An evening at the club, then, promised returned migrants acknowledgement of their old status and allowed them to reinforce their own activities with respect to Canada while continuing to prove their usefulness as conduits between Britain and the colony.

[188]

Commercial interests

Few of these men devoted their entire capital to one branch of trade, indicating the multiplicity of commercial ventures in which most early Canadians invested. We can, somewhat artificially, categorize interests and investments, but returned migrants, like others interested in Canadian opportunities, tended to be involved in a variety of ventures. For the purposes of this chapter, however, commercial investments will be divided into land speculation and resettlement schemes, and various forms of trade and commerce, including the timber trade, banking and, as the century progressed, railways.

Many of the club members were involved in trade and commerce, for they were part of a broad commercial and family network whose business interests and affiliations were closely tied. For example, William Parker, a founding member of the Canada Club, had been in a trading and shipping partnership with Club members Thomas Yeoward, John Mure, John Ogilvy and two of the Gillespie family. Mure later formed a partnership with Alexander Mackenzie and others within the New North West Company. Mackenzie employed Club member Thomas Thain as an agent; this brought Thain to the attention of William and Simon McGillivray, who left Thain in charge of their operations when they left for England in 1821.[22]

Clearly, these close familial and business connections served to broaden members' ventures in Canada. The varied interests of George Garden, who spent extended periods in England between 1809 and 1827, are typical of many Canada Club members. He was a partner in Auldjo and Maitland's Montreal wholesaling firm, an agent for a fire insurance company, a member of the Lower Canada House of Assembly, and director and vice-president of the Bank of Montreal.[23] Samuel Gerrard, a Club member normally resident in Canada, was the president of that bank. Banking was also favoured by at least two other Club members who sat on the board of directors of the Bank of British North America.[24]

In general, however, merchants seem to have been most successful in continuing to profit from Canadian ventures. John Mure's career was typical of a returned migrant's successful continuing connection with Canada. Mure, who became a Club member on his return from Canada in 1816, was a former Lower Canada assembly member, timber and lumber exporter and shipping agent. After his retirement to Glasgow, he continued to communicate with other expatriate Canadian merchants in Britain, and was active in land sales in Quebec.[25] Mure's former partner, timber merchant Henry Usborne, retired to Britain in 1809, but continued to direct his Canadian business from London, as well as acquiring a seigneury in the Gaspé and speculating in land settlement schemes.[26] Another returned migrant who kept an interest in his Canadian commercial holdings was John Forsyth, a partner in a Montreal trading company, who became a member of the Canada Club in 1812, twenty years before his final retirement to England.[27]

Fellow Club members also provided a useful pool of potential subscribers to or promoters of other commercial schemes. When John By was introduced to the club in 1811 he distributed complimentary tickets to view his model of Quebec, constructed in 1810 and then on display in London.[28] In 1850 Samuel Cunard, who was a migrant rather than a returned migrant to Britain, was facing competition for the cargo and passenger traffic his ships carried across the Atlantic; that year, he offered Club members free rail travel to Liverpool and dinner on board his new steamer, the *Asia* – 'the finest yet built for the line'.[29] Transatlantic mercantile partnerships were formed between Montreal merchants and London investors, and Club members Edward Ellice and Alexander Gillespie were part of a 'London Committee' formed to sell shares in the proposed St Lawrence & Atlantic Railway.[30]

Land speculation

Most Club members had acquired land in Canada, and several returned migrants became involved with their associates in promoting some ambitious land settlement schemes in the 1820s and 1830s. Indeed, Peter McGill may well have been describing fellow members when he assured the Colonial Office that most of 'the originators and promoters of the [British American Land] company' were 'intimately connected with, and deeply interested in the prosperity' of British North America; rather than being 'greedy speculators' they were 'gentlemen well known . . . for their talents, wealth, honour and general respectability'.[31]

The land and settlement schemes with which Club members were involved varied widely. Montreal and Quebec merchants sent Club member and land company sponsor W.B. Felton to Britain in 1825 to solicit subscribers to the proposed Lower Canada Land Company. Edward Ellice and Henry Usborne as well as Nathan Gould and George Gillespie were among Club members who invested in that short-lived scheme.[32] John Galt was a guest at Club dinners during the 1820s and when he was appointed secretary of the Canada Company in 1824 he became subject to the instructions of Club members Henry Usborne, Simon McGillivray and Hart Logan, who joined Edward Ellice as directors of the company. In 1825 the firm of Hart, Logan was appointed the Montreal agent for the company, with the task of directing immigrants to Canada Company lands.[33] Although Galt's career with the company was over by 1829, he was listed as a member of the Canada Club in 1831 and continued his association with former directors in the early 1830s when he became secretary of the British American Land Company. That company, established to sell and settle land in the Atlantic provinces and, more important, the Eastern Townships of Lower Canada, also drew investors from the Canada Club.[34] Company investors were knowledgeable about fears of American movement into the Eastern Townships of Lower Canada, and used this knowledge to their advantage to persuade the lieutenant-governor that the settlement of British migrants in the area would be of benefit to the colonial powers. Alexander Gillespie, junior, and Russell Ellice sat on the company's board of directors, while George Moffatt and Peter McGill, a club member normally resident in Canada, were appointed commissioners in the colony. With involvement, too, in the settlement scheme of the North American Colonial Association of Ireland and the New Brunswick Land Company,[35] it is clear that several Club members were investors in or aware of opportunities for land speculation.

Despite the flurry of land speculation, however, not all investors were successful in their transatlantic endeavours. The New Brunswick Land Company was not profitable for Samuel Cunard and his fellow investors; Edward Ellice sold his Beauharnois seigneury to the North American Colonial Association of Ireland, but when the proposed settlement scheme proved unsuccessful he was obliged to buy the land back.[36]

Some individual speculators, too, had little success in returning a profit on their Canadian holdings. Like other returned migrants, Robert Pilkington had invested in land in Canada, hoping to realize a future profit on it. His largest purchase was 29,000 acres in Wellington County, Ontario. Pilkington's individual attempts to encourage settlement in the township met with little success and his suggestion for a government-sponsored Highland settlement programme was not received with enthusiasm by the British authorities. Further efforts to draw attention to the desirability of his land holdings may also have prompted him to draw up and submit an unsolicited 'Plan of the Principal Settlements of Upper Canada' to Colonial Under-Secretary Henry Goulburn in 1817. However, although Goulburn sent a polite note thanking Pilkington for the submission, there is no evidence that he acted on the information that, according to the map, Pilkington township was one of those 'principal settlements'.[37]

Colonel John By was another Club member who invested in land in Canada. In 1832 he purchased a large tract of land in present-day Ottawa. According to one history of the construction of the Rideau Canal, John By's purchase was an 'almost certain' indication that he expected to return to the colony.[38] However, By did not return to Canada, although he did retain ownership of the land until his death, and the property became the centre of a protracted transatlantic court case in the latter part of the century, with London solicitors acting on behalf of By's descendant and claimant to the land.[39]

Like most Canada Club members, then, returned migrants speculated in land in the colony, but several faced a common difficulty when attempting to realize on their investments: distance from Canada prevented them from having the up-to-date information that would help them decide the most profitable time to sell; nor were they able to oversee necessary improvements to the land before settlement could begin. Nevertheless, this very distance served to perpetuate ties with Canada, for most expatriates employed agents there to manage their real estate holdings and finances. James Crooks and his brothers were particularly active in this regard, acting along with Christopher Hagerman as agents for sales of Robert Pilkington's land in Ontario. Crooks and his brothers also 'employed . . . immigrants in their stores and mills', relying, in part, on the assistance of Club member George Auldjo who acted as a hiring agent for several Upper Canadian businessmen.[40] Banker William Allan of Toronto handled the sale of property or business matters for several former Upper Canadians, including members of the Simcoe family, and William Warren Baldwin was effective in managing Club member Laurent Quetton St George's estate.[41]

Politics

As men who retained nostalgic memories of Canada, who had sometimes fought in its defence, and who were still in constant contact with former colleagues, members participated in group solidarity actions in support of their temporary homeland. In 1812 Club members voted to contribute £62 5s 6d of surplus funds 'towards the relief of those inhabitants of Upper and Lower Canada who have suffered or may hereafter suffer in their defence'.[42] And, deeply regretting 'that ever their Club . . . should have ranked or fostered so unworthy a member', members unanimously agreed to expel their former associate and now traitor, John Henry, testifying to their 'detestation and abhorrence of principles which could, under any circumstances, have actuated an individual to so disgraceful and criminal a proceeding as that of betraying to a foreign country the best interests of his own'.[43] Their knowledge of wartime events came from first-hand reports: Governor Gore and Major Halton were among the 'graceful figures . . . tripping along . . . on the light fantastic toe' at a club dinner in 1812.[44]

Club members continued to be informed about every notable Canadian development, and with limited effect attempted to influence Canadian affairs. Edward Ellice successfully petitioned the British government to bring an end to the detrimental dispute between the Hudson's Bay Company and the North West Company, lobbied fellow politicians in the House of Commons to accept the Webster–Ashburton Treaty, and was instrumental in interceding with the Colonial Office for compensation for the Hudson Bay Company's surrender of claims in the North West in the 1860s.[45] Adam Lymburner, another merchant and former Executive Councillor, had worked closely with emigrants from the Edinburgh area while in Lower Canada and retained a 'continuing, almost nostalgic interest in the colony'. For sixteen years after Lymburner's return to Britain, he kept up a correspondence with the Roman Catholic Bishop of Lower Canada, Joseph Plessis, attempting to advise him on Church–state relations.[46] However, despite their efforts to influence British politicians or the Colonial Office, most members of the club were not particularly successful in their lobbying endeavours. Sir Alexander Mackenzie spent his first protracted return to Britain writing an account of his voyages in the northwest, but was unsuccessful in gaining approval for plans for a merger between the North West Company, the Hudson's Bay Company and the East India Company that he presented to the Colonial Secretary. His second sojourn in Canada lasted for about a year, and thereafter he lived in London and Scotland, buying up HBC stock in 1808 and hoping thereby to influence the company to open up its supply route in Red River to Montreal traders – once again an unsuccessful venture. Though these activities took place before the formal institution of the Canada Club, Mackenzie played an active role in Club activities until his death in 1820.[47]

Nevertheless, Club dinners certainly became a venue for political discussion, especially in later years when Canadian politicians visited London in greater numbers. As the Canada Club established its reputation as an elite meeting place for those with an interest in Canada, visiting politicians from Canada made a dinner at the club an integral part of their London activities. Discussions regarding responsible government in the late 1830s, preliminary talks on confederation, internecine strife in the provinces – every significant Canadian political event requiring consultation with London brought members into contact with guests who were at the centre of colonial activities. Returned migrants who were members of the Canada Club were, therefore, able to hear first-hand accounts of colonial affairs, and could continue to participate in Canadian concerns after their retirement to another country. Their status confirmed by nomination to Club membership, they could relive past experiences in a convivial atmosphere, remain current with Canadian affairs, champion their old comrades in the colony, and take advantage of opportunities for continuing investment in a country which had been the scene of early adventures.

Conclusion

In his study of the Scots in Canada, David Macmillan has emphasized the ties that continued to bind them to their temporary home even after their return to Scotland.[48] His comment, however, could be applied to all the returned migrants discussed here, who tried to ease their return to the homeland and profit from the migrant experience by attempting to perpetuate their influence on Canadian affairs. These men belonged to a small and select group whose experiences in Canada had been generally positive, and it is clear that their return 'home' did not mean complete divorce from their adopted country. Rather than influencing affairs in their homeland, the migrant experience for these men led to persistent investment in Canada and Canadian affairs, even though those efforts were not always successful. An investigation of the activities of returned migrants like them – especially those who joined with others in an institutional setting – suggests that a focus on the long-term impact of returned migrants on the temporary homeland might offer a broader perspective on transatlantic ties.

Notes

1 George Gmelch, *Double Passage: The Lives of Caribbean Migrants Abroad and Back Home* (Ann Arbor MI: University of Michigan Press, 1992), 290–4.

2 Patrick Brode, *Sir John Beverley Robinson: Bone and Sinew of the Compact* (Toronto: University of Toronto Press, 1984), 33; Kathleen Burke, '"I was everything when with you, but here nobody . . .": Upper Canada's First Surveyor General returns to Britain', *Ontario History* 41, 1 (1999), 1–18; David Roberts, 'Lymburner, Adam', *Dictionary of Canadian Biography* (hereafter *DCB*) VII (Toronto: University of Toronto Press, 1988), 525.

3 J.G. Colmer, *The Canada Club (London): Some Notes on its Origin, Constitution and Activities* (London: Committee of the Club, 1934), 14.

4 James M. Colthart, 'Ellice, Edward', *DCB* IX (Toronto: University of Toronto Press, 1976), 234.

5 Marjorie Wilkins Campbell, *McGillivray, Lord of the Northwest* (Toronto and Vancouver: Clarke Irwin), 3, 175.

6 It is difficult to give an exact figure for the number of 'returned migrants'; some names cannot be identified, some men returned to Britain and died very shortly thereafter, and some members were admitted to the club several years before they returned permanently to the mother country.

7 Anthony H. Richmond, 'Explaining Return Migration', Rosemarie Rogers, 'Return Migration in Comparative Perspective', in Daniel Kubát (ed.), *The Politics of Return: International Return Migration in Europe. Proceedings of the First European Conference on International Return Migration* (Rome and New York: Center for Migration Studies, 1984), 274.

8 Mary Beth Norton, *The British-Americans: The Loyalist Exiles in England 1774–1789* (Boston MA: Little Brown, 1972), 76.

9 Brode, *Sir John Beverley Robinson*, 95; National Archives of Canada (hereafter NAC), MG 28, 151, vol. 1, reel A–521, Canada Club – Minutes, passim. Donald Creighton, *The Empire of the St Lawrence* (Toronto: n.p., 1956), 43.
10 'Hardy Pioneers Spent Gay Nights in the Famous Old Beaver Club', *Montreal Daily Star*, 12 November 1932.
11 NAC, MG 28, 151, vol. 1, reel A-521, Canada Club – Minutes, 4 April 1812.
12 *Ibid.*, vol. 6, reel A-1508, Canada Club – Receipts and Vouchers, 9 January 1836. For an amusing description of a bibulous Beaver Club evening see Michael Bliss, *Northern Enterprise: Five Centuries of Canadian Business* (Toronto: McClelland & Stewart, 1987), 98.
13 C.W. Robinson, *Life of Sir John Beverley Robinson* (Edinburgh: Blackwood, 1904), 94.
14 NAC, MG 28, 151, vol. 1, reel A-521, Canada Club – Minutes, 12 March 1825.
15 *Ibid.*, 1 December 1810.
16 'Phyn, Ellice & Co. of Schenectady' in *Contributions to Canadian Economics* IV (Toronto: n.p., 1932), 7–41.
17 A number of authors have commented on the high representation of Scots among both the original shareholders and later employees of the North West Company, as well as the commercial companies with which they traded. See Elaine Allan Mitchell, 'The Scot in the Fur Trade' in W. Stanford Reid (ed.), *The Scottish Tradition in Canada* (Toronto: McClelland & Stewart, 1976), 34–6; David S. Macmillan, 'The "New Men" in Action: Scottish Mercantile and Shipping Operations in the North American Colonies, 1760–1825' in David Macmillan (ed.), *Canadian Business History: Selected Studies, 1497–1971* (Toronto: McClelland & Stewart, 1872); Bliss, *Northern Enterprise*, 92–106.
18 Colmer, *Canada Club*, 15.
19 *Ibid.*
20 Samuel Cunard became a member in 1831, Michael Tobin 'of Halifax' in 1837.
21 Christine Veilleux, 'Pownall, Sir George', *DCB* VI (Toronto: University of Toronto Press, 1987), 615.
22 Gratien Allaire, 'Thain, Thomas', *DCB* VI, 764.
23 Gerald Tulchinsky, 'Garden, George', *DCB* VI, 271–3.
24 John Forsyth was a founder, director and vice-president of the Bank of Montreal; Samuel Gerrard, a Canadian member of the Canada Club, was the bank's president. Tulchinsky, 'Forsyth', *DCB* VII, 310. Alexander Gillespie, Jr, and William Pemberton are both shown as directors of the Bank of British North America in the *Post Office London Directory for 1840* (London: n.p., 1840), 826.
25 David Roberts, 'Mure, John', *DCB* VI, 531–4.
26 Christine Veilleux, 'Usborne, Henry', *DCB* VII, 873–4.
27 Macmillan, 'The "New Men" in Action', 102; Gerald Tulchinsky, 'Forsyth, John', *DCB* VII, 309–11.
28 NAC, MG 28, 151, vol. 1, reel 521, Canada Club – Minutes, January 1811.
29 Colmer, *Canada Club*, 58.
30 Gerald Tulchinsky, *The River Barons: Montreal Businessmen and the Growth of Industry and Transportation, 1837–53* (Toronto: University of Toronto Press, 1977), 139.
31 Norman Macdonald, *Canada, 1763–1841: Immigration and Settlement* (London: Longman, 1939), 293.
32 J.H. Little, 'Imperialism and Colonization in Lower Canada: The Role of William Bowman Felton', *Canadian Historical Review* 66:4 (1985), 517.
33 Clarence Karr, *The Canada Land Company: The Early Years* (Ottawa: Love Printing Service, 1974), 34.
34 Roger Hall and Nick Whistler, 'Galt, John', *DCB* VI, 338; NAC Canada Club – Minutes, 12 February 1831. For the British American Land Company see B. Critchett, *The Post Office London Directory for 1836*, 37th edn, London: n.p., 1836), 720.
35 *Montreal Gazette*, 15 August 1840; Macdonald, *Canada, 1764–1841*, 305.
36 *Montreal Gazette*, 15 August 1840; 'Ellice', *DCB* IX, 236.

37 Public Record Office, CO42/144, 31 July 1811, Pilkington to Percival; CO42/360, 16 May 1817, Royal Arsenal, Pilkington to Goulburn.
38 Robert Leggett, *Rideau Waterway* (Toronto: University of Toronto Press, 1955, repr. 1964), 207.
39 NAC, MG 24 A66, By, John and Estate, 'Documents concerning the John By estate', vols 1 and 2.
40 Gerald Tulchinsky, 'Auldjo, George', *DCB* VII, 28.
41 'Allan, William', *DCB* VIII (Toronto: University of Toronto Press, 1985), 10; Robert L. Fraser, 'Baldwin, William Warren', *DCB* VII, 36–7.
42 NAC, MG 28, 151, reel 521, Canada Club – Minutes, 6 November 1812.
43 *Ibid.*, Saturday [n.d.] June 1812.
44 *Ibid.*, 4 April 1812.
45 'Ellice, Edward', *DCB* IX, 237.
46 Roberts, 'Lymburner', *DCB* VII, 524.
47 Roy Daniels, *Alexander Mackenzie and the North West* (Toronto: Oxford University Press, 1971), 171–9.
48 Macmillan, ' The "New Men" in Action', 103.

CHAPTER TEN

'Two homes now': the return migration of the Fellowship of the Maple Leaf

Marilyn J. Barber

And so I came Home.
But I've got two Homes now
Which is very puzzling[1]

These words concluded the December 1938 diary entry of Monica Storrs, a mission worker aided by the Anglican Fellowship of the Maple Leaf. On this occasion, Storrs was writing not from her English home of Rochester where her father had been dean of the cathedral but from her Canadian home, the Abbey that she had built near Fort St John, British Columbia, on the north-western frontier of settlement. While Storrs was referring most immediately to her personal dwelling, the sense of belonging to two homes had wider national reference to Canada and Britain. The dual commitment that Storrs expressed not only influenced her work in Canada but also travelled with her when she returned to England on furlough and in retirement. The puzzlement is equally significant. Storrs did not perceive any conflict in her loyalty to two homes within the British Empire, but only gradually came to identify with her new home in Canada as well as her continuing home in England. The Fellowship of the Maple Leaf, a Church of England missionary society, relied on workers like Monica Storrs to link Britain and Canada. Founded and led in England by Anglican clergymen who returned from Canada, the Fellowship sought to rouse the British public to its Christian responsibility for empire mission and empire settlement. In the process, the Fellowship called upon return migrants to stimulate recruitment and sustain its work.

Recent studies of British imperialism have emphasized the influence of empire on domestic British history. For example, the Manchester University Press series on 'Studies in Imperialism' was founded in 1985 in part because 'it became apparent that the effects of Empire upon the United Kingdom had been too little studied'.[2] It is now recognized that movement back and forth across the web of empire contributed to the formation of 'imperial culture' and British identity in the United Kingdom as well as in the wider empire.[3] Because of interest in the post-colonial era in unmasking relations of race and power, most attention has been focused on the impact on Britain of imperial administrators and explorers returned from Asian, African or Caribbean colonies. Yet, as Phillip Buckner noted in his 1993 presidential address to the Canadian Historical Association, white settlement Dominions, such as Canada, also helped to shape the sense of identity held by the British at home.[4] More attention is now beginning to be given to the varied understandings of Britishness in the settlement dominions and the United Kingdom. A study of return migration from the dominions makes an essential contribution to that larger field of investigation.

The institutional role of the Church of England in return migration

Missionary activity that accompanied imperial expansion was one important influence on domestic British culture. Missionaries regularly returned every three to five years on furlough and often retired to the homeland at the end of their service overseas. Missionary workers on return to the United Kingdom became some of the most active and effective proponents of imperial commitment. Missionary speakers and missionary literature reached beyond an élite to a wider public. As John M. MacKenzie notes in *Propaganda and Empire*, missionaries were adept at using the materials of imperial propaganda, such as lantern slides and patriotic songs, and attracted audiences that filled the largest halls.[5] Moreover, women participated actively in mission work. By 1900 roughly two-thirds of Protestant missionaries were women, and women formed a majority of church congregations and home mission supporters.[6] Nor was Canada excluded from British missionary endeavour, even in the inter-war years when both religious and imperial commitments were declining. At the same time as Canadian Protestant churches participated in the Anglo-American missionary effort by sending missionaries to Asia, British missionaries of the Church of England were moving back and forth between the United Kingdom and western Canada.[7] These Church of England workers should be considered not as exceptional cases whose vocation set them apart from secular affairs but as travellers on the two-way transatlantic migration route that linked Britain and Canada.

The Church of England missionary circuit that took workers to western Canada and back to Britain remained essential in the twentieth century because rapid immigration overwhelmed Canadian Anglican resources. Until World War II, the western Canadian missionary dioceses of the Church of England in Canada relied on the United Kingdom more than eastern Canada for personnel and financial aid. The Missionary Society of the Church of England in Canada (MSACC), formed in 1902 with headquarters in Toronto, showed greater interest in foreign missions than in home missions. By contrast, the large long-established voluntary missionary societies of the Church of England with headquarters in London devoted considerable effort to western Canadian missions. In addition, the Archbishops of Canterbury and York responded to Canadian needs through a special appeal known as the Archbishops' Western Canada Fund that included support for a railway mission from 1910 to 1920.[8] After the First World War the Church Missionary Society (CMS) withdrew its support of native missions, but western dioceses continued to depend upon the Society for the Propagation of the Gospel (SPG) and the Colonial and Continental Church Society (CCCS). This established Church of England missionary circuit provides the framework for the formation in 1917 of the Fellowship of the Maple Leaf (FML), a small society, but one dedicated exclusively to keeping Canada British and Christian by supplying British Anglican teachers and, later, church workers.

Interpreting Canadian needs in Britain: returned missionaries develop the FML

One English migrant, the Reverend George Exton Lloyd, organized the FML when he returned to London during the First World War, and another returned migrant, the Reverend Philip Andrews, sustained the Fellowship until the 1960s. As English migrants and Anglican clergymen who travelled the missionary route between England and Canada, Lloyd and Andrews brought both their English heritage and their Canadian experience to the direction of the FML. The aims of the Fellowship reflect their dual interest in Britain and Canada, a duality that was united in their aspirations for a strong Christian British Empire. For both Lloyd and Andrews, time in Canada reinforced rather than challenged a belief in British cultural superiority and the need to preserve the British race. They returned to Britain with a strong commitment to Canada, but as a Dominion that would reflect the British image. Although there was debate within mission circles concerning the relation of Christianity to British culture,[9] that debate did not seem to include mission work among white settlers in Canada. Lloyd personally had no doubt that the furtherance of Christianity was inextricably intertwined with the progress of the British race. As he later wrote, 'I am a firm believer in God's call to the British race . . . . Not because we are White or Black but because, as far as I can see, we are the most

Christian nation.'[10] Similarly, Andrews in the FML magazine called upon the English people to maintain the Christian values of their race.

Here in this great Empire we have an immense persuasive agency. Try to imagine the effect if only lofty souls could be sent wherever British people settle to maintain the noblest traditions of our race with the spirit of adventure . . . The FML seeks the extension of the imagination of the English people, and also asks support for principles which, if only partially operating, would shake the world.[11]

Christianity for Lloyd and Andrews was generally synonymous with the Church of England, which, as the established Church in England, although not in Canada, was associated most closely with loyalty to empire. Similarly, as migrant Englishmen, Lloyd and Andrews perceived little need to differentiate between English and British. The FML did not confine its propaganda and recruitment entirely to the English, but as a small society appealing principally to British Anglicans, it concentrated its effort on the geographical territory of England. In recruiting British Anglican teachers, nurses, doctors and church workers to be community leaders in western Canada, the FML tried to instil in its home audience a sense of British identity that spread beyond the bounds of Great Britain to encompass 'our own kith and kin' in Canada. The Fellowship concurred with Kipling's advice, 'Bring in people of your own race; let them possess the land and your immigration problem is solved.'[12] Although a missionary rather than an emigration society, the FML hoped to stimulate British emigration to Canada by providing better institutional support for the settlers. At the same time, the FML affirmed in England the superiority of the British race, not in relation to the indigenous peoples of Canada but in contrast to continental European immigrants who were presented as threatening the British Christian character of western Canada.

The Reverend Lloyd: a transatlantic traveller for Church and empire

The Reverend George Exton Lloyd, founder of the FML, frequently returned to England during his long ministry with the Church of England in Canada. In part, Church of England institutional ties drew Lloyd back to England. Often, though, he chose to return to seek more resources for the Anglican work in western Canada to which he devoted most of his life. After emigrating to Canada in 1881 as a young man of 20 in charge of a party of 140 Scottish boys destined for farms in Ontario, Lloyd increasingly identified with Canada as a vital part of a Christian British Empire.[13] While completing his theological training at Wycliffe College, the evangelical college of the Church of England at the University of Toronto, Lloyd first travelled to western Canada with the University Company of the Queen's Own Rifles, sent to subdue the Métis and Indian challenge to Canadian authority known as the North West Rebellion.[14] Wounded in May 1885 while rescuing comrades at Cut Knife Creek, he received recognition for his courage. When ordained shortly thereafter, Lloyd insisted on wearing his military uniform, visibly proclaiming the clergyman's willingness to fight for the nation. In August 1885, Lloyd married Marion Tuppen of Brighton, England, with whom he would have five children, but he seems to have kept his family quite separate from his public crusade for Church and empire.[15] After serving in Ontario and New Brunswick, Lloyd returned to England in 1900 to act as deputation secretary for the CCCS. He achieved wide publicity and a place on the map in 1903 when he travelled back to Canada as chaplain and eventually leader of the all-British colony that settled on the Saskatchewan/Alberta border around a new townsite named Lloydminster.[16] Remaining in Saskatchewan as agent of the CCCS and principal of Emmanuel College, the Anglican theological college supported by the CCCS, Lloyd developed innovative schemes to reinforce the quite inadequate resources of the Church of England in Saskatchewan. He spent the winters of 1906–07 and 1909–10 in England recruiting itinerant lay readers or catechists who would minister to the settlers at the same time as they received their theological training. A charismatic speaker, Lloyd made Saskatchewan a very important mission field for the CCCS.

Lloyd's determination to fight for British Christian values in Saskatchewan led him to return to England in the midst of the First World War, for a few years rather than a few months. Breaking with the CCCS that refused to implement his plans in wartime, Lloyd organized the Fellowship of the Maple Leaf to supply British Anglican teachers for western Canada. From Lloyd's Canadian perspective, the need was urgent. War service had drawn Anglican clergy from western Canada and wartime tensions had focused on unassimilated foreign immigrants. Anglican teachers in state schools could hold the ground for the Church and reach into districts of non-British settlement where Anglican clergy were less welcome. By naming the new society the Fellowship of the Maple Leaf Lloyd conveyed the Canadian focus of the mission and also sought to create a 'fellowship' uniting British supporters with Canadian interests. A Canadian emblem, the maple leaf identified Canadians abroad, including those Canadian soldiers who were fighting and dying on the European battlefields. Writing in March 1917, Lloyd drew a close connection between 'such work as ours, of the Maple Leaves, and that of the army of the Maple Leaf in France.' He acknowledged to a British audience that he felt 'Canadian enough' to be very proud of the accomplishments of Canadian troops.[17] The outstanding Canadian victory at Vimy Ridge a month later has been mythologized in some versions of Canadian history as marking the beginning of Canadian recognition as an independent nation. Lloyd attached a quite different meaning to Canadian participation in the Great War. Although he made no reference to his family in surviving FML records, Lloyd had a very personal bond with the Canadian forces. His youngest son, Lieutenant Arthur Lloyd, was killed fighting in France with the army of the Maple Leaf in 1917 at the age of 18. Captain Exton Lloyd, his eldest son, was wounded three times, gassed twice, contracted pneumonia and died after the war of tuberculosis resulting from his war injuries. For Lloyd, the war, and the sacrifice of his sons, symbolized the unity of Canadian and British interests forged in the battle for a common cause. Sons of the empire literally had joined their blood together in defence of country and home. Lloyd attributed the spirit of loyalty that put the army of the Maple Leaf into France in large measure to the work of the Church of England in Canada.[18] Therefore, he had been drawn to England in the midst of the war crisis because he believed more had to be done to reinforce the greatly depleted resources of the Church of England in western Canada. Lloyd had become 'Canadian enough' to give priority to Canadian needs within the empire.

As a return migrant, Lloyd drew both upon the authority of his Canadian experience and upon his continuing British connections to recruit support and workers for Canada. He considered 'Propaganda' to be the most important part of FML work in Britain. He always valued education and recruitment over finance. The Fellowship pledged first 'to educate the British public at home' and second 'to issue the call for fit candidates to undertake this work and to advise and direct those who offer to serve'. Raising money for the work and especially for loan bursaries for the teachers followed in third place.[19] Hence Lloyd stressed the vital necessity of addresses and lantern lectures to schools, colleges, and organizations such as QMAAC, even though no revenue could be collected from such work. Lloyd, who excelled at public speaking, devoted much of his energy as director of the FML to the work of propaganda. He reported that in an eighteen-month period he had visited seventy-four cities and towns, many of them several times for different parishes. His activities included 132 Sunday sermons, eleven children's addresses, eight weekday sermons, seventy-seven lantern lectures, eighteen drawing room meetings, twenty lectures in colleges or schools, nineteen addresses to various meetings, eight lectures to QMAAC, eleven special meetings to GFS – university – civil service and such like, making a total of 302 sermons, addresses, or lectures on the work of the Fellowship.[20]

Lloyd travelled to wherever an opening for presenting the work could be obtained, but the reliance on local support for providing an opportunity to speak meant that his activities tended to be more concentrated in certain regions of England. Lloyd built in part on connections that he had already established through his work for the CCCS. Tunbridge Wells, the home of Lloyd's sister, was an early centre of FML support, as were the parishes of Brompton and Campden Hill in London. The Bishops of Norwich, Colchester, Ipswich and Bury St Edmonds participated actively on the FML General Committee and encouraged FML work in their dioceses. The Bishop of Lincoln welcomed Lloyd to Lincoln Cathedral and Lloyd also spoke in Doncaster, Sheffield, Rugby, and Nottingham.[21] The Vicar of All Saints' Church, Nottingham, who was the son of the Archbishop of Melbourne, Australia, extended a particularly warm welcome because of his interest in empire missions.[22] Much FML activity took place in south-western and southern England. The centres visited by Lloyd that supported the FML included Plymouth, Bude, Exeter, Weston-super-Mare, Bristol, Salisbury, Winchester, Portsmouth, Chichester, Brighton, and Hastings.[23] While Lloyd appealed to committed church congregations through Sunday sermons, he reached a wider audience with other addresses. For example, in the Plymouth area he preached in various churches but also addressed a drawing-room meeting in the ballroom of Admiralty House and presented a lantern lecture in the Guild Hall with the mayor of Plymouth presiding. Similarly at Rugby, he preached in parish churches and Rugby School chapel, but also gave an evening lecture in the main hall of Rugby School by invitation of the headmaster.[24] In Lincoln, he preached at the cathedral and gave a lantern lecture at the municipal technical school. One Salisbury visit included sermons in the cathedral and two parish churches and lantern lectures in the training college, at Godolphin Ladies' College and at the town hall.[25] Lloyd also addressed several Rotary Clubs such as those in Portsmouth, Southampton, and Manchester.[26] Through all these promotional efforts, he made western Canada better known to British audiences and publicized the opportunities for British teachers to make a real contribution to empire settlement.

Individuals who became members of the Fellowship continued to be informed of the work on a regular basis and, in return, were expected to contribute to FML activities. An executive committee of twelve, composed initially of supportive clergy, administered the ongoing work of the Fellowship, but the organization was governed by a much larger General Committee which met annually and was intended to represent the whole British Isles.[27] While the overwhelming majority of the General Committee always came from England, representatives from Swansea and Llandudno, Wales, and from Belfast, also participated in the early years. At the local level, Lloyd encouraged the formation of branches that met mainly in private homes to discuss the work and organize fund-raising events. Women's voluntarism had become vital to the success of most missionary societies and the FML was no exception.[28] The FML relied heavily on women's commitment to sustain local branches and in recognition of women's role formed a Ladies' Committee and elected women to the Executive Committee beginning in 1921. A monthly magazine circulated to members became the main channel of communication between the central office and supporters around the country. Appropriate symbolism reminded members of the British responsibility to maintain Canada's imperial Christian connection. The letters KCBC in the four corners of the magazine stood for 'Keep Canada British and Christian' and the magazine also was illustrated by the FML badge, three intertwined flags, the union jack on the left, the Canadian flag on the right, and the Church flag in the centre. At the same time, Lloyd always ensured that British supporters were made aware of Canadian identity as a Dominion within the empire. Under Lloyd's direction, the FML annual general meeting took place on 1 July, Dominion Day, and the Canadian version of the Church of England Prayer Book was made available for FML meetings.

In addition to educating the British public and especially British members of the FML, Lloyd succeeded in recruiting teacher candidates for Canada. Applications were obtained through advertisements and articles in Church papers and teacher periodicals, but many candidates also responded to Lloyd's sermons and lectures. The Maple Leaf teacher scheme enabled educated British women to participate as equals with men in empire migration and empire development. Among FML teacher candidates, women outnumbered men by a ratio of six to one. They were motivated by a call to service, enthusiasm for travel, or simply the desire for better employment. Dorothy Watkins, a teacher on the staff of Portsmouth secondary school, heard the call during Lloyd's visit to Southsea.[29] Marion Green wrote to Lloyd that 'I shall always be thankful that you came to Ilford on March 19th, 1918, for then through you I heard my call'.[30] A candidate of 17 years of age who attended a lantern lecture that Lloyd gave in one of the southern England county schools five years previously stated, 'I made up my mind then that I wanted to be a teacher in Western Canada and I am of the same mind now.'[31] These testimonials appeared in the *FML Magazine* to encourage supporters, but teachers interviewed decades later similarly recalled being inspired by Lloyd. While teaching in London, Doris Black happened to go with a friend to one of Lloyd's lantern lectures and seized the opportunity to travel.[32] Another candidate, a typist in a London income tax office, responded to the appeal Lloyd made at St Paul's Cathedral.[33] A third, who had an excellent position at the Imperial Institute in South Kensington when she heard Lloyd's call for teachers, thought 'it would be nice to go where you are needed'.[34] Lloyd's stirring oratory also attracted an extremely important anonymous donor who through the FML gave impressive sums of money to support the Church of England in western Canada. After her death, the anonymous donor was revealed to be Mrs Marion Beatrice Smith, who chose the FML to be the recipient of her benefactions in memory of her son, who had been killed in the war. Lloyd had influenced her son when he addressed the Oxford undergraduates and Mrs Smith too had been impressed when she accompanied her son to another of Lloyd's lectures. Coming into a bequest after the war, Marion Smith gave approximately £150,000 over the years to the FML, including the entire cost of building a hostel for FML teachers in Regina.

After spending almost six years in England promoting the Fellowship of the Maple Leaf, Lloyd returned to Canada to become Bishop of Saskatchewan at the age of 61 and passed leadership of the FML to another returned migrant, the Reverend P.J. Andrews. While Lloyd crossed the Atlantic many times as a function of his Church of England ministry, his decision to return to Saskatchewan in 1922 reflected the strength of the Canadian bonds he had developed. Clergy whom Lloyd had recruited for Saskatchewan helped elect him to the prestigious position of bishop. In addition, Lloyd had surviving children in Canada. As an indication of the British Canadian identity he had acquired, Lloyd on retirement in 1931 did not return to England but instead moved to Victoria, B.C. When he died on 8 December 1940, he was buried in Royal Oak Cemetery, Victoria. Several years after Lloyd's death, P.J. Andrews also suggested that Lloyd returned to Canada to escape responsibility for the FML. In Andrews' words, 'When Lloyd resigned from FML as he couldn't carry on, I found a frightful financial shambles . . . Lloyd, though it is unknown to others, threw in his hand and luckily for him he was made a Bishop.'[35] Lloyd was impulsive, a man of action who excelled at initiating projects but lacked perseverance for the essential routine administration to maintain them. Fortunately for Lloyd, linking his two homes in Britain and Canada gave him ample scope for new endeavours. Fortunately for the FML, Andrews had more sustaining power.

The Reverend P.J. and Alice Mary Andrews: back in England thinking of Canada

The Reverend Philip John Andrews and his wife Alice Mary Andrews, like Lloyd, followed the Church of England missionary circuit to western Canada and back to England. Unlike Lloyd, having assumed responsibility for the FML, they remained in England for the rest of their lives with only occasional visits to Canada on behalf of the FML. P.J. Andrews, a native of Devon, was one of the ordinands whom Lloyd recruited for Saskatchewan in 1910. Aged 26 when he responded to Lloyd's appeal, Andrews preferred scholarship to prairie ministry. After ordination in 1916, he combined work as rector of the Saskatchewan parish of Humboldt with academic studies that led to first place in Canada in the 1918 Church of England bachelor of divinity examination and two years later an MA from the University of Saskatchewan with first-class honours in history and philosophy. While lecturing part-time at Emmanuel College, Andrews married Alice Mary Lile, an Englishwoman whom Lloyd had enticed to Saskatchewan to 'mother' his ordinands.[36] As a young woman in England, Alice Mary Lile had devoted herself to the work of Catherine Gurney's police orphanages. At the University of Saskatchewan she not only cared for the ordinands, but also helped with social functions for the 2,000 university students and established a Sunday school for the children of university staff. After marriage in the chapel given by Rugby School to Saskatoon, Alice Mary Andrews adapted to life as a rector's wife in a struggling rural community with few amenities. If necessary, she camped parishioners on the floor of her home at night, and when the 1918 influenza epidemic struck fear into the district, Mrs Andrews took charge of a hospital she and her husband set up in the local school.[37] The interests of her husband took Alice Mary Andrews back to England, but when P.J. Andrews accepted leadership of the FML, she became a full voluntary partner in the work.

Scholarly links between Canada and Britain, as well as the religious ties of the Church of England, drew P.J. Andrews back to England. In 1920 few opportunities for advanced study existed in Canada, so aspiring scholars in Canada often turned to the richer academic resources in Britain. Andrews followed this path in seeking to obtain a doctor of divinity degree and an academic career through research at the British Museum. He may not have had any intention of returning permanently to England, but, as he later explained, Lloyd 'hauled' him into the FML.[38] Like so many other migrants, Philip and Alice Mary Andrews thus found that unforeseen circumstances changed the course of their lives. P.J. Andrews acknowledged that he was 'very much adverse [sic] to the rough and tumble of sustaining voluntarily the financial burden of work like the FML' and that he had difficulty following a 'spell-binder' like Lloyd as a speaker.[39] Nonetheless, Andrews attracted influential people. L.S. Amery, Colonial Secretary and a strong imperialist, became a staunch advocate of the FML, speaking at its annual meetings, after his wife heard a 'very moving' sermon by Andrews.[40] Andrews brought other essential qualities to the FML. While Lloyd paid no attention to finances, Andrews called in an auditor, stabilized the almost bankrupt society, and worked closely with the Governing Board of the FML to enlist increasing support. Alice Mary Andrews' contributions were as important as her husband's. She served as secretary of the Ladies' Committee and encouraged women in local branches to hold drawing-room meetings and sales for the FML. All who knew her agreed that Alice Mary Andrews' unfailing hospitality and love for others made the FML a true fellowship. She took a deep personal interest in overseas workers and friends in Britain alike. As her husband stated, 'If indeed religion is a link that binds, then Alice Mary Andrews had it in full measure.'[41]

Personal knowledge of western Canadian conditions gave the Andrews credibility in dealing with FML candidates. By 1930, the FML had sent approximately 500 British Anglican teachers to western Canada. Those who already had teacher training proceeded directly to prairie schools, while candidates without professional qualifications first attended Saskatchewan normal school. When the economic depression of the 1930s ended the acceptance of British teachers for western Canadian schools, the FML transferred its sponsorship to medical and Church workers for pioneer districts of the western Canadian dioceses. The FML assisted only a few female doctors and nurses, but from 1933 until the 1960s, the Fellowship aided over seventy-five women church workers who served districts lacking clergy, as well as a few men from Balliol College, Oxford, who ministered to the Makwa district of northwestern Saskatchewan.

FML workers: employment, family ties and return migration

The FML believed its workers served the cause of Church and empire equally well whether they remained in Canada or returned to the United Kingdom. FML teachers entered Canada as permanent immigrants, but many were uncertain of their future intentions. When asked if she planned to stay in Canada, a 1922 migrant replied, 'I don't know. You don't think much ahead when you're young, do you. Oh no, I was going back again. I told my mother I'd be back in two years and

[207]

she said maybe.'[42] Another teacher on receiving her papers for Canada was very surprised to discover that she was being admitted as an immigrant. Her parents assumed that she would go for two years and then return home.[43] Like the majority of FML teachers who have been traced, these two young women eventually married and settled in Canada. FML teachers were mobile, moving from school to school in western Canada and sometimes back to the UK. For example, Doris Black taught in three schools during her first two years in Saskatchewan and then returned to teaching in London as she had planned. Still restless several months later, while walking on the Strand, Black accidentally met Andrews, who immediately recruited her to accompany a party of FML teachers to western Canada. Black missed her dog which she had left behind in Canada and she certainly had not exhausted her enthusiasm for travel. She returned to Canada, with her dog moved to northern Alberta and was considering Australia when she agreed to marry a handsome young farmer and fur trapper.[44] In a number of instances, the return of FML teachers to England similarly seems to have produced a wish to leave again, or to have been a necessary preparation for a longer commitment to Canada. The FML sailing list indicates repeat sailings of twenty teachers, and these are only the teachers who officially returned to Canada with a FML party.

Some FML teachers did make England their permanent home after several years in Canada. Hilda Simpson and Donald Banks were the first pair of FML teachers to marry in Canada. Hilda Simpson, a teacher in Lincoln and the daughter of a master craftsman at Lincoln Cathedral, answered Lloyd's call when he preached in Lincoln in 1919. Donald Banks, the son of the former headmaster of Rugby School and a war veteran, continued his courtship of Hilda by correspondence during the two years she taught in Canada and proposed to her when she returned to England. Hilda and Donald travelled together to Canada as part of a 1922 FML party, taught in separate communities and married six months later. Donald Banks had decided that after what he went through in the war he wanted to give his life to the Lord, so he had taken some theological as well as teacher training in England. Therefore, he answered the call of the Church to serve in quite isolated communities where he ministered to Cree and the few other Europeans as teacher, preacher, and even doctor, calling upon his army medical training. He taught English to the Cree children and they taught him Cree, which he used in church services. After several years, continually moving as requested by the Church, from Cedar Lake to Duck Lake to Onion Lake and onwards again became wearing. By 1931 Donald and Hilda Banks had not only themselves to consider but also two children born in northern Canada. Their folks in England wanted to see the grandchildren. Donald Banks answered an advertisement in a Church of England newspaper and returned to England, where he became headmaster of Dunmow Church of England School until his retirement in 1959 at the age of 60. Donald and Hilda Banks kept in contact with Canadian friends, so after retiring in England they spent three years at the Devon Mission at The Pas in northern Manitoba. When interviewed at Dunmow at the age of 93, Donald Banks was most eager to convey the wealth of experience he had acquired overseas and his appreciation of the people he had known and the natural world he had inhabited. While not necessarily promoting imperialism, he must have brought to his Dunmow pupils a better knowledge of Canada than they would have otherwise acquired.[45]

Unlike the teachers, FML church workers went overseas on a short service system, usually committed to remaining three years in western Canada. As Andrews later explained, in addition to promoting the spiritual well-being of Canadian settlements, the idea was to widen the viewpoint of the workers who would then return to the UK and stimulate the home parishes. Instead the FML found that many women were 'so bitten with the job' they refused to leave it.[46] Nonetheless, most church workers did make the UK their final home after serving from one to more than twenty years in western Canada. The Church workers, ideally between age 25 and 35 when recruited, were considerably older on average than FML teachers. Because of both age and vocation, they were less likely to acquire Canadian roots through marriage. Some like Monica Storrs returned to the UK on retirement, while others continued to work, usually within the Church of England.

The responsibility and initiative required by women Church workers in western Canadian missions generally far surpassed the opportunities available to women within the institutional structure of the Church in England.[47] Nonetheless, some women were able to build upon their Canadian leadership experience after their return. Cecilia Goodenough, a bright Oxford graduate and a co-worker with Monica Storrs in the Peace River district from 1931 to 1936, became head of a women's settlement in East London (the Talbot Settlement) and a lecturer within the diocese of Southwark.[48] Dorothy Bee, who had served in Canada from 1938 to 1946, worked in London with a religious agency for young *au pair* women from the Continent, and organized an ecumenical Travellers' Aid Association to meet new arrivals.[49] Marion Kettlewell, on furlough in England at the outbreak of the Second World War, joined the WRNS, advancing to be an officer and eventually director. On leaving the WRNS, Dame Marion Kettlewell became head of the Anglican Girls' Friendly Society before retiring in London.[50]

Concerns for aging parents or sometimes for their own health often brought women Church workers back to the UK. Caring for elderly family was a female more than a male responsibility, and religious women who were not married were expected to have the time and skills for this service. In addition, mission work in the pioneer districts of western Canada taxed the endurance of both men and women. The women workers travelled many miles on foot, by horse, or sometimes by car over cold, treacherous winter trails and through summer mud and mosquitoes. In contrast to missionaries in Asia, who had servants, the Church workers in western Canada attended to household chores themselves, hauling water or melting snow for cooking and cleaning. They worked extremely long hours and, especially in winter, ate a severely restricted diet. Not surprisingly, accidents, back problems, illness or exhaustion forced some missionaries to seek respite in the UK or alternative service in less strenuous conditions. The FML publicized the isolation, hardships, and commitment of the missionaries and the settlers among whom they worked in its magazine which during the later 1930s included a photographic supplement. Such publicity was well designed to enlist support for Canadian missions suffering depression conditions, but less suited to encourage future British emigration.

Living links of empire

The Church workers did fulfil FML expectations that they would widen their horizons and, in turn, extend the 'imagined community' of others in England. They served as living links of empire in England as much as in Canada, connecting their two homes across the Atlantic. Returned workers actively helped to stimulate interest in Canada by speaking at FML local branches, at FML annual general meetings, and on other occasions. A number also became members of the FML executive, bringing their Canadian knowledge to the direction of the Fellowship. For example, Dr Mary Johnstone, participating on the executive on her return from Canada in the early 1930s and again during the Second World War, helped to initiate support of women Church workers and also, less effectively, drew FML attention to missed opportunities for recruiting in Scotland, where many people had Canadian ties.[51] It is less clear to what extent returned workers challenged the intertwining of Christianity with the mission of the British race so strongly advocated by Lloyd and Andrews. Their voice has been filtered through the official records of the FML. Moreover, in reports at the time and in interviews decades later, workers found talking about activities much easier than explaining values. They definitely returned with a deeper appreciation of different cultures and a more informal way of life. As Marion Kettlewell reflected: 'All of us who did this work realized in the end that we learned much more than we ever gave to anybody else.' She found her three years in Canada 'action packed' for someone from England who had led a fairly conventional life.[52] Similarly, Dorothy Bee wrote, 'My years in Canada were so happy, colourful and enlightening – with deep admiration for the homesteaders from England and other European countries.'[53] Such appreciation, however, did not necessarily lead to a reconsideration of British identity or an analysis of racial assumptions.

The passage of time did change the Church of England missionary circuit between Britain and western Canada. The UK emerged from the Second World War burdened by debt and destruction while Canada prospered. The western Canadian dioceses of the Church of England assumed self-support or turned primarily to the central Canadian Church for assistance. In 1955, the Church of England in Canada became the Anglican Church of Canada. P.J. Andrews, entering final retirement at age 80, grew very disillusioned when Canada adopted a new national flag in 1964.[54] The new Canadian flag proudly featured a red maple leaf, seemingly the perfect emblem for the Fellowship of the Maple Leaf, but the symbolism of a united empire carried by the Union Jack was missing. A younger generation led by Canon Stephen Burnett, one of the Balliol men who had served in Saskatchewan, guided the FML from missionary outreach to a reciprocal relationship with Canada. The FML ceased raising money and sending British missionaries to Canada, but used endowment funds to promote transatlantic sharing of experience within the Church.[55] Thus the FML continued to assist the movement of Anglicans back and forth between the United Kingdom and Canada, but ended the implications of Canadian dependence and severed the link between Christianity and the mission of the British race.

The FML existed because two Church of England clergymen who had returned to England from service in Canada devoted their energy to publicizing the missionary needs of western Canada. While Lloyd and Andrews drew upon ideas of Christian mission and the responsibility of the British race common to the thought of social imperialists in the early twentieth century,[56] their passion for a particular cause and place derived from their personal migration experience. Although Lloyd resided in England only at intervals after his emigration to Canada, whereas Andrews resumed permanent residence to direct the FML, both men dedicated their lives to uniting Britain and Canada. The FML, like other Church of England missionary societies, integrated return migration into the structure of its activities. Institutional provisions, however, only partly explain why FML workers returned to England either temporarily or permanently. FML teachers and Church workers moved back and forth between the United Kingdom and Canada, influenced by work and service opportunities, personal health, a desire for continuing travel and adventure, and especially by family ties. FML teachers who married in Canada usually became permanent settlers whereas unmarried Church workers were more often drawn back to Britain by responsibilities for their family of birth. Many FML participants, like Monica Storrs or Lloyd himself, developed an identity that encompassed their two homes. Certainly, the FML regarded its workers who returned to Britain, whether temporarily or permanently, as essential living links of empire.

Notes

1 British Columbia Archives, Add. Mss 482, Monica Storrs Diary, September 1938–March 1939, 15. See also W.L. Morton (ed.), *God's Galloping Girl: The Peace River Diaries of Monica Storrs, 1929–1931* (Vancouver: University of British Columbia Press, 1979); Vera Fast (ed.), *Companions of the Peace: Diaries and Letters of Monica Storrs, 1931–1939* (Toronto: University of Toronto Press, 1999), 197.

2 John M. MacKenzie, 'General Introduction', *Emigrants and Empire: British Settlement in the Dominions between the Wars* (Manchester: Manchester University Press, 1990), vii.

3 Antoinette Burton, 'Rules of Thumb: British History and "Imperial Culture" in Nineteenth- and Twentieth-century Britain', *Women's History Review* 3: 4 (1994), 483–500; Ian Christopher Fletcher and Fanny Elisabeth Garvey, 'What Goes Around Comes Around: British Imperial History', *Radical History Review* 67 (1997), 165–74; Mrinalini Sinha, 'Teaching Imperialism as a Social Formation', *Radical History Review* 67 (1997), 175–86.

4 Phillip Buckner, 'Whatever happened to the British Empire?' *Journal of the Canadian Historical Association*, new series, 4 (1993), 3–32. *Emigrants and Empire*, a book that focuses specifically on migration to the white settlement Dominions, deals with government policy more than issues of culture and identity.

5 John M. MacKenzie, *Propaganda and Empire: The Manipulation of British Public Opinion, 1880–1960* (Manchester: Manchester University Press, 1984), 33.

6 Jeffrey Cox, 'Audience and Exclusion at the Margins of Imperial History', *Women's History Review* 3: 4 (1994), 507; Patricia Grimshaw, 'In Pursuit of True Anglican Womanhood in Victoria, 1880–1914', *Women's History Review* 2: 3 (1993), 331–47, deals with gender relations and the predominance of women within the Church of England in Australia.

7 Ruth Compton Brouwer, *New Women for God: Canadian Presbyterian Women and India Missions, 1876–1914* (Toronto: University of Toronto Press, 1990), and Rosemary R. Gagan, *A Sensitive Independence: Canadian Methodist Women Missionaries in Canada and the Orient, 1881–1925* (Montreal and Kingston: McGill-Queen's University Press, 1992), deal with Canadian women missionaries in Asia. Less attention has been given to the missionary efforts of the Church of England in Canada.

8 David J. Carter, 'The Archbishops' Western Canada Fund and the Railway Mission', *Saskatchewan History* 22: 1 (1969), 13–27; L.G. Thomas, 'The Church of England and the Canadian West' in Barry Ferguson (ed.), *The Anglican Church and the World of Western Canada, 1820–1970* (Regina: Canadian Plains Research Centre, University of Regina, 1991), 16–28.

9 Andrew Porter, 'Empires in the Mind' in P.J. Marshall (ed.), *The Cambridge Illustrated History of the British Empire* (Cambridge: Cambridge University Press, 1996), 204–5; Cox, 'Audience and Exclusion', 508.

10 Anglican Church General Synod Archives, Toronto (hereafter ACGSA), Lloyd Papers I A2, H.B. Hall Correspondence 1938–39 re chapter 3 'On Migration'.

11 ACGSA, Fellowship of the Maple Leaf Papers (hereafter FML) III A *Magazine of the Fellowship of the Maple Leaf* (hereafter *Magazine*) No. 130, March/April 1934, 4. Italics in original.

12 William Blakemore, *Westward Ho!* (1907), quoted in Peter Jackson and Audrey Kobayashi, 'Narratives of Empire: British and Canadian Readings of Kipling's Colonial Fiction', *British Journal of Canadian Studies* 2: 2 (1996), 301.

13 ACGSA, FML, *Magazine*, April 1917, 10. The son of a London schoolmaster, William Jones Lloyd and his wife Anne Brown, Lloyd was born on 6 January 1861 at the School House, Suffolk Street, Bethnal Green. F.A. Peake, 'Anglican Theological Education in Saskatchewan', *Saskatchewan History*, 25: 1 (1982), 30. Peake refers to Lloyd's birth certificate, General Register Office, London.

14 The Northwest Rebellion was viewed as a threat to the imperial expansionist aims of western Canadian colonization. In the imperialist imagination, the pastoral myth of the 'last best west' offered redemption from the urban decay of Britain. Doug Owram, *Promise of Eden: The Canadian Expansionist Movement and the Idea of the West, 1856–1900* (Toronto: University of Toronto Press, 1980); Cecily Devereux, '"And let them wash me from this clanging world"', Hugh and Ion, '"The Last Best West" and Purity Discourse in 1885', *Journal of Canadian Studies* 32: 2 (1997), 106–7.

15 H.J. Morgan, *The Canadian Men and Women of the Time* (Toronto: Briggs, 1912), 660; ACGSA, Lloyd Papers, I A2 HB Hall Correspondence 1938–39, Lloyd to Hall, 19 July 1938; P7508 Photos.

16 Lynne Bowen, *Muddling Through: The Remarkable Story of the Barr Colonists* (Vancouver and Toronto: Douglas & McIntyre, 1992) is the most recent history of the All-British or Barr Colony. The Reverend Isaac Barr, another Church of England clergyman, organized and conducted the all-British colony to the prairies. When Barr left the colony amid controversy and dissension, Lloyd replaced him as leader and assumed credit for rescuing the colony.

17 ACGSA, FML, *Magazine*, March 1917, 5.

18 *Ibid.*

19 ACGSA, FML, Minutes, 31 May 1917, 162.

20 *Ibid., Magazine*, No. 24, July/August 1918, 9–10.

21 *Ibid.*, Minutes, July 1917, April 1918, March 1920.

22 *Ibid., Magazine*, No. 21, April 1918, 5–6.

23 *Ibid.*, Minutes, January 1921.

24 *Ibid., Magazine*, No. 14, July 1917, 25–6.

25 *Ibid.*, Minutes, December 1917.

26 *Ibid.*, May 1918.

27 *Ibid.*, 31 May 1917, 162.

28 Brian Heeney, *The Women's Movement in the Church of England, 1850–1930* (Oxford: Oxford University Press, 1988). Part I deals with volunteers and 'the context of subordination' of women within the Church of England in Britain. Elizabeth Gillan Muir and Marilyn Fardig Whiteley, 'Introduction' in *Changing Roles of Women within the Christian Church in Canada* (Toronto: University of Toronto Press, 1995), consider the constraints and opportunities within the institutional structures of Canadian churches.

29 ACGSA, FML, *Magazine*, No. 29, February 1919, 1.

30 *Ibid.*, No. 29, February 1919, 6–7.

31 *Ibid.*, No. 50, January 1921, 6.

32 Interview with Doris (Black) Lizotte, Edson, Alberta, 26 and 27 May 1994.

33 Letter from Wilhemina E. Ware to M. Barber, 27 August 1978.

34 Interview with Grace (Warwick) Christie, Saskatoon, Saskatchewan, 24 May 1979.

35 *FML Records*, Church Office, Lichfield, Andrews Retirement file, Andrews to S. Burnett, 18 October 1966.
36 ACGSA, FML, *Magazine*, No. 229, January 1958.
37 *Ibid.*, January 1958, 2–3.
38 *Ibid.*, No. 222 June 1954, 9.
39 *Ibid.*, No. 222 June 1954, and No. 229 January 1958.
40 *Ibid.*, No. 223, January 1955, 11.
41 *Ibid.*, No. 229, January 1958, 1–7.
42 Interview with Grace (Warwick) Christie, Saskatoon, Saskatchewan, 24 May 1979.
43 Interview with Doris (England) Perry, Saskatoon, Saskatchewan, 11 November 1983.
44 Interview with Doris (Black) Lizotte, Edson, Alberta, 26 and 27 May 1994.
45 Interview with Donald Banks, Dunmow, Essex, England, 20 May 1992. Letters from Donald Banks to Marilyn Barber, 3 April and 17 June 1992.
46 ACGSA, FML, Minutes, July 1943, 498.
47 Marilyn Barber, 'The Motor Caravan Mission: Anglican Women Workers on the Canadian Frontier in the New Era' in Muir and Whiteley (eds), *Changing Roles of Women within the Christian Church in Canada*, 219–37; Vera Fast and Mary Kinnear, 'Introduction' in Fast (ed.), *Companions of the Peace*, 10.
48 Interview with Cecilia Goodenough, London, England, 25 April 1995. See also 'Introduction', *Companions of the Peace*.
49 Interview with Dorothy Bee, St Anne's Court, West Wickham, Kent, England, 27 June 1994. I also had interviews with Dorothy Bee in Llandrindod Wells, Wales, 3 May 1991, and in West Wickham, Kent, 15 May 1992 and 15 May 1995. At present these tapes are in my possession.
50 Interview with Dame Marion Kettlewell, London, England, 23 April 1991 and 14 May 1995.
51 ACGSA, FML, Minutes, especially October 1932. *Edmonton Journal*, 9 March 1974, 'Faith gave courage to pioneer doctor', by Shirley Hunter. Dr Johnstone, living in Edmonton at the age of 95 at the time of the article, stated, 'The happiest years of my life have been here, as a doctor, in Canada.'
52 Interview with Dame Marion Kettlewell, London, England, 14 May 1995.
53 Dorothy Bee to Canon Burnett, Llandrindod Wells, Wales, 14 January 1988.
54 *Canada One Hundred, 1867–1967* (Ottawa: Queen's Printer, 1967), 50, states, 'The most recent indication of Canada's attainment of complete national sovereignty has been the proclamation by Her Majesty the Queen on February 15, 1965 of the National Flag of Canada as adopted by the Canadian Parliament on the preceding December 15, after prolonged debate.'
55 FML Annual Report 1993, FML Records, Lichfield.
56 Bernard Semmel, *Imperialism and Social Reform: English Social-Imperial Thought, 1895–1914* (London: Allen & Unwin, 1960; repr. New York: Anchor Books, 1968); Pau B. Rich, *Race and Empire in British Politics* (2nd edn, Cambridge: Cambridge University Press, 1990).

PART IV

The impact of return

The final part of the book, which investigates the impact of returners on their homelands, is concerned with the return of emigrants to Scotland from Europe and the East Indies in the seventeenth and eighteenth centuries. Alexia Grosjean turns the spotlight on the Aberdeenshire parish of Belhelvie, in order to demonstrate the ways in which, during three centuries, resources brought back by successful emigrants were used to buy land, titles and status, as well as to enrich the home community by endowing schools and churches, and funding road building and poor relief. Belhelvie's story was not unique; few parishes in Scotland did not experience the effects of money and ideas repatriated by returning emigrants, some of whom, like the Northern Islesmen who worked for the Hudson's Bay Company, decisively shaped the economy and society of the localities to which they returned.[1] Emigrants came home from the east as well as the west, and Andrew Mackillop raises the profile of the underdeveloped debate about the effects on Scotland of return movement from the Indian empire in the eighteenth century. By tracking the career of Sir Hector Munro, an Easter Ross laird who returned home in the 1760s, and again in the 1780s, he demonstrates that imperial profits from India percolated through Scotland to a much wider extent than was the case with transatlantic tobacco revenues. He considers how Munro deployed his wealth, looking at his political aspirations, his charity work and his estate improvements, as well as at the way he deliberately used these strategies to generate a potent and acceptable domestic image of the successful nabob.

Note

1 Marjory Harper, *Adventurers and Exiles: The Great Scottish Exodus* (London: Profile, 2003), 300–8.

[215]

CHAPTER ELEVEN

Returning to Belhelvie, 1593–1875: the impact of return migration on an Aberdeenshire parish

Alexia Grosjean

As Mark Wyman has demonstrated, the subject of return migration is a vital component in the story of human mobility, but one which has begun to attract the serious attention of scholars only in recent years. The focus of these studies has included topics as varied as emigrant return to Finland between 1860 and 1930, the return of Jews to Austria after the Second World War and the homeward migration of the Surinamese labour force from The Netherlands.[1] Other studies include return migration to Finland from Sweden in the period since 1945 and general studies on the sociology of return migration.[2] Aina Tollefsen Altamirano's work takes a comparative approach and contrasts the US–Mexican and Swedish–Chilean return movements.[3] It is surprising, given the scale of the exodus from Scotland over the centuries, that the subject of return migration has not generated similar studies. Perhaps it is because returnees have been viewed as 'failures' in some way, not having adapted to their host country or culture. As will become apparent in this chapter, however, and as Mark Wyman has discussed in the context of return migration from the United States to continental Europe, the impetus for return was often the result of success abroad or a call to return home from family who remained behind.[4] In addition to a biographical approach to the subject, investigating the economic impact of return migrants on the land as well as the people of one Scottish parish yielded some interesting results.

The parish of Belhelvie is approximately six miles long and five miles wide and lies eight miles north of Aberdeen. It rarely appears in historical studies of migration, or of any other topic for that matter. Largely due to its proximity to the city, Belhelvie has often served as a suburb of Aberdeen, and land transactions and development in the parish have therefore tended to involve Aberdonian merchants, burgesses and provosts as well as people from Aberdeenshire. With an historical emphasis on this particular rural–urban dynamic, Belhelvie might not seem an obvious candidate for involvement in international migration studies. Yet from an early period the parish maintained, or was forced into, international relations. During the Middle Ages much of the parish comprised the barony of Belhelvie and at one time belonged to King Eric II Magnusson of Norway, at least in terms of revenue from parish rents. Later Belhelvie was held by Alexander Stewart, Earl of Buchan, and was eventually granted to the lords of Glammis by the early modern period. In the mid-seventeenth century the recently created Earl of Panmure was given the land and barony of Belhelvie as part of his reward for loyal service to the Stuart monarchy.[5] The barony of Belhelvie was broken up in the following century, when the Panmures were forfeited for their tenacity in the Jacobite cause, and parts of the parish were bought by an English buildings company, eventually being sold off to private buyers. It was the break-up of the Panmure estate that particularly facilitated the purchase of smaller plots by returning emigrants.

Looking at a map of Belhelvie parish today, it is difficult to determine a corner of the parish which has not been affected by the influence of return migrants, whether those returning from the Baltic mercantile migrations of the sixteenth century or those who had participated in the British Empire in India in the eighteenth and nineteenth centuries. These influences occurred over three centuries and ranged from simply acquiring and developing land in the area to building stately homes and providing employment for the local population, to actively injecting cash into projects related to the broader community, such as the kirk, education, poor relief and road building. Four of the most impressive buildings in the parish were built on estates owned by individuals who were themselves return migrants – Menie House (Forbes), Orrok House (Orrok), Belhelvie Lodge (Lumsden) and Balmedie House (Lumsden). Not all these buildings were maintained or developed to the same high standard, and their condition depended largely on the fortunes of their occupants. In 1875 the mansions of Balmedie and Menie were described as elegant and modern.[6] Orrok House may have been in a period of decline, as it was observed that it was inhabited by the tenants of the home farm.[7] Belhelvie Lodge also received a less than glorious review, being described as 'an old square building, which probably has more pretensions to comfort within, than to appearance from without'.[8] Ten years later all but Orrok House were still noted as 'chief mansions' of the parish in the *Ordnance Gazetteer of Scotland.*[9]

The monuments to the return migrants of Belhelvie described above are only one aspect of the impact they had on the parish. Many of them had left Scotland and earned money abroad, before returning to

Scotland with their accumulated wealth with which they purchased estates and property. Whether return to their homeland had always been the prime intention of the emigrants cannot be ascertained definitively, but the fact remains that some migrants did come back to Scotland after many years abroad, albeit for a variety of reasons – including family obligations, ill health or simply retirement – and with varying degrees of impact.

Early examples of migration to the Baltic region

Often migration studies, including case studies of returning emigrants, focus on the period from the late eighteenth century through to the twentieth century. However, Scottish examples of both types of migration have their roots far beyond the familiar phenomenon of the transatlantic journeys of the nineteenth and twentieth centuries. Long before the large numbers of Scots headed west to the New World, a well used route had been established to the east, across the water toward Scandinavia, the Baltic region and the Netherlands. Even by the late sixteenth century migration in this direction had become quite large-scale and the sheer quantity of immigrants to his kingdom led Sigismund III of Poland–Lithuania to design laws in 1594 in the hope of curbing the influx.[10] The motivation for this movement was mostly economic, as the significant number of Scottish burgesses and merchants in northern Europe reveals, particularly in Poland-Lithuania.[11] Scots formed a privileged community in Warsaw, where they gained royal protection and even obtained special appointments as servitors to the Crown. Indeed, contemporary sources note the presence of 30,000 Scottish families in Poland in 1620 alone, albeit this statistic is difficult to verify.[12] It is not surprising that emigrants from Belhelvie should figure amongst them, particularly given the parish's proximity to such a major port as Aberdeen, although it is impossible to determine what percentage of the total they formed. The earliest return migrants of the parish whom we can actually name are typical examples of this 'Belhelvie to the Baltic and back' syndrome.

Robert Skene, a burgess of Aberdeen, settled in Belhelvie parish in 1572. His third son, David, went to Poland as a young man and after several years there he became a burgess of the city of Posen in 1586.[13] The exact length of David Skene's sojourn in Poland remains unclear, as his arrival there does not appear to be documented. What is known is that he returned to his native parish in Scotland by 1593, and that in the same year his elder brother, Robert Skene junior, emigrated to Poland at the age of 43, perhaps to continue the family connection there. However, it is probable that Robert junior died in Posen within a short time of arriving, as very soon after David's return to Belhelvie he was registered as 'of the Mylne of Potterton', the same title which had previously been accorded to Robert, as the eldest son.[14] In 1597 a 'horning' (a proclamation as an outlaw, rebel or bankrupt) was served against David Skene of the Mylne of Potterton, which originally dated from 7 June 1593. Again, it is undetermined whether David was already back from Poland in June, or whether he returned to Scotland to face the charges of the horning. However, he remained in the parish and was still living in Potterton in 1606. Seemingly the Skene family's ventures to Poland inspired the next generation, as David's second son, also called David, retraced his father's footsteps and settled in Zamoski, where he married the daughter of another Scottish merchant, Robert Chalmers, of Danzig.[15] Presumably David Skene's eldest son remained in Potterton to inherit the mill, whilst the second son went abroad to make a living, typical of the 'second son' syndrome which has already been documented for early modern England.[16]

The example provided by the Skene family affords us a view of not only the kinship networks at play in migration, but also the strength of Scottish communities maintained abroad. Three members of one family had migrated to the same country, and the last one settled there, marrying not a local girl, but another Scottish emigrant. This pattern of intermarriage within the Scottish community was common among the Scottish diaspora elsewhere and even extended into the second and third-generation Scots. For example, in Sweden during the seventeenth century it was found that of eighty-seven Scottish officers serving in the Swedish army, 59 per cent of them married women of British (mostly Scottish) origin, and in the Netherlands at this time 34 per cent of the Scottish soldiers serving in the Dutch army married Scottish women.[17] These relationships were integral to the maintenance of a sense of Scottish identity and played a significant role in the return migration of foreign-born Scots as discussed elsewhere in this volume.

The Skene family shows the multi-layered nature of Belhelvie's link with the Baltic, but there is another individual with a link to the parish who is better known for his Polish connections. William Forbes, commonly referred to as 'Danzig Willie', was the second son of William Forbes, fourth Laird of Corse, and the brother of Patrick Forbes, Bishop of Aberdeen.[18] Bishop Forbes had his seat at St Machar Cathedral in Old Aberdeen, which still uses a communion chalice made in Danzig c. 1621.[19] As William Forbes gained much of his wealth through his evident mercantile success in Danzig, there is probably a link between the two Forbes brothers and the communion chalice, although this supposition remains to be proven. Forbes's mercantile success was not limited to foreign shores, and in addition to his status as a burgess of

Danzig he became a merchant burgess of Edinburgh. It was through the wealth he gained in his Baltic trade that William Forbes could acquire several properties in Aberdeenshire. He bought land in both Craigievar and Fintray, and indeed he is often referred to as Forbes of Craigievar.[20] However, his first purchase was of the lands of Menie in Belhelvie parish. A charter, dated 11 February 1607, confirms that Forbes bought the property from David Carnegie of Kinnaird.[21] Although he was still known as Forbes 'of Menie' in 1617, his right to the barony of Craigievar had already been formalized as early as February 1610, and he obtained further land in Fife and Aberdeenshire that year.[22] Forbes's connection with Belhelvie ceased in July 1618 when he resigned his lands of Menie to George Gordon of Gight,[23] but he maintained his ties with Aberdeen, as in March 1619 he was made a royal commissioner of the old and new academies of the burgh.[24] Forbes did not relinquish his ties with the Scottish-Baltic world after he settled at home in Scotland. In fact he had connections to James Spens of Wormeston – who became the fulcrum of the Stuart network in Sweden between 1610 and 1632 – through his brother Patrick's marriage to James's sister, Lucrecia.[25] This is intriguing, given that Sweden's arch-enemy at the time was Poland, and it reveals that the Scottish network abroad did not allow the politics of their host nations to break personal connections.[26]

Scottish migration to Poland continued into the eighteenth century, and in 1705 two Belhelvie parishioners wrote from Danzig to the Aberdeen town council. James Stewart, described as a merchant in Poland, and his sister Margaret were seeking proof of their Scottish origins in the form of official birth brieves from the burgh.[27] Indeed, on 8 November 1705 Charles Earl of Errol and Lord High Constable of Scotland, William Earl Marischal and others all swore and testified that James was the lawful son of Alexander Stewart of North Colpnay. Although there is no evidence as to whether either James or Margaret ever returned to Scotland at any point, connections were clearly maintained with home and could even prove vital to success abroad. Margaret, like many women of her time, had a role beyond that of wife or sister, as other examples of Scottish women in positions of economic importance come to light.[28]

Poland and the surrounding area were not the only destinations of interest to the inhabitants of Belhelvie parish. This eastward flow of migrants appears to have peaked by the early eighteenth century, but well established Scottish communities in these and other countries continued to receive new waves of migrants.[29] However, it must not be forgotten that Scottish emigration was not limited to the easterly direction and by the late seventeenth century Scots were already crossing the Atlantic to the Scottish and English colonies, as well as travelling to Africa, the Dutch East Indies and Cambodia.[30] After the Treaty of Union in 1707 overseas mercantile, and particularly military, opportunities increased in the service of the expanding British Empire as access to areas formerly belonging to England officially opened up to Scotland. Of course this in itself was nothing new, as Scots had been part of the expansion from the start.[31] It was in such overseas service that Belhelvie migrants came to the fore as the histories of three parish families – the Orroks, the Turners and the Lumsdens – reveals.

Belhelvie and the Indian subcontinent

The Orrok family originated from Fife, but moved into Belhelvie when Captain John Orrok bought land at Colpnay for the sum of £4,630 sterling from an Aberdeen provost some time after 1750. The estate was subsequently renamed Orrok and the area is still known as such today, although some house names have reverted to the historical use of Colpnay. Captain Orrok was the only landowner to rename his property, as the others retained the traditional names. John Orrok was the nephew of Robert, laird of Orrok, who had sold his land in Fife, leaving his nephews to seek their own fortunes elsewhere. Wemyss Orrok was captain of a ship that traded with the East Indies and William Orrok served in the East India Company army.[32] William earned a degree of notoriety for being in charge of the 64th Highlanders when the regiment was devastated at the battle of Assaye in 1803 during the First Maratha War.[33] Although he survived the incident, William died a few years later at Seringapatam in June 1810. Another family member, Lieutenant William Innes Orrok, of the Royal Scots, also died in service, but at Trichinopoly in July 1821. Not much appears to be known about John Orrok's pre-Belhelvie life, apart from his description as 'late Captain of ships trading to the East and West Indies'.[34] He was probably engaged by the East India Company in July 1758 when he and his ship, noted as an English vessel, were captured and brought into Gothenburg harbour.[35]

It is uncertain when Orrok House was actually built, although it was completed by 1781, and just seven years later, in 1788, Orrok was noted as 'not rich' in a list of Scotland's voters. This could relate to the expense of building a large mansion on his estate – although the more cynical observer would believe that any plea of poverty was simply a handy method to avoid heavy taxation.[36] Thirty years later, in 1812, the Orrok estate was worth £541 Scots in valued rent alone, placing it among the most lucrative of the parish.[37]

The influence of Captain Orrok and his family went beyond just buying and developing an estate in Belhelvie. In 1790 the Sheriffs of

Aberdeen divided the Belhelvie kirk seats amongst the heritors of the parish, at a cost of 1–2s each, and in July 1796 Captain Orrok decided to donate two seats, Nos 56 and 57, for the use of the poor.[38] The kirk officially seated 519 persons, and contemporary records note that it was often filled with 600–700 people, so seats 56 and 57 would conceivably have been sought-after locations close to the pulpit.[39] It was in any case his last donation to the parish, as John Orrok died shortly thereafter in November that year. The Orrok family continued to make an impact on the parish, however, and the captain's son and successor, Walter Orrok, made a contribution of rather greater significance to the wider north-east community.[40] In 1799, along with Turner of Menie (of whom more below), he was among the first subscribers to fund the building of a turnpike road from Aberdeen to Belhelvie parish, replacing stretches of track which had gone along the shoreline with permanent road surfacing. This road was not only eventually extended to Ellon, but in 1802 the extra stretch to Peterhead and Fraserburgh was added at a cost of £350 sterling per mile, which gives an indication of the kind of cost shouldered by local landowners for these kinds of projects.[41]

The money used to develop the parish in the nineteenth century came from a variety of foreign ventures, usually trade, but increasingly from the military income as the century wore on. The economic exploitation of the Indies, both East and West, proved to be a vital source of income for the empire and the Honourable East India Company (EIC) was the main instrument of this exploitation. EIC merchants needed military support to enable them to ply their trade and this came in the form of the EIC army, protecting both the merchants and their goods. Not only did John Orrok lose his brother William and his nephew William Innes to this service, but also his son Walter. Walter Orrok, who, like his father, ventured out to the subcontinent for economic reasons, was lost aboard the *Calcutta* on his return from India in 1810. Not only did he perish, but all the money he had earned specifically with the intention of reacquiring the original family estate in Fife was lost.[42]

These men were survived by John's other son and namesake, Captain John Orrok, who served in the 17th regiment of the EIC army and inherited the estate in Belhelvie after Walter.[43] The younger John Orrok returned to Belhelvie in August 1823, invalided home from India on half pay after some twenty-four years of service.[44] That same year he married Mary Cockburn at Cheltenham, but died shortly thereafter in October from a burst blood vessel in his head sustained through falling from a second-floor window in Orrok House.[45] Even at the time there was speculation as to whether Orrok was pushed, jumped or fell accidentally, and ever since there has been the obligatory rumour of a ghost in Orrok House. Orrok's funeral memorial still hangs on a ruined wall of the old Belhelvie Kirk and is inscribed as follows: 'Sacred to the memory of John Orrok of Orrok, captain in the Hon. East India Company, 17th Regt. No. 1, second son of John Orrok Esq., of Orrok and Sarah Dingwall of Rainiston his wife' and describes both his marriage and death.[46] Although the estate remained in the Orrok family a little while after John's death, by 1827 it was for sale, implying that the family could no longer afford to keep the house.

The small estate of Menie, mentioned above in relation to 'Danzig Willie' in the seventeenth century, also figured prominently in relation to return migration again in the nineteenth century. Robert Turner inherited Menie from his father George, who was a sheriff-clerk of Aberdeenshire and a son of Turner of Turnerhall. In 1812 Turner's valued rent for Menie was £500, placing him alongside the Orroks as amongst the wealthiest of Belhelvie.[47] The Turner family of Menie provided several officers in the EIC army in India. In conditions not too dissimilar to the Orrok family, four of the Turner family – John, Robert, William and Alexander – died working for the company. However, one brother, George, survived his service to become not only a colonel-commandant of the 12th Brigade of the Royal Artillery but, by 1862, a Knight Commander of the Order of the Bath. George Turner returned to Belhelvie to inherit the ancestral home and eventually it passed into the hands of his daughters before it too was sold.

Another family with India connections in the parish were the Lumsdens. This family obtained its land in Belhelvie after the Panmures had been forfeited for their support of the Stewarts during the Jacobite rebellions. When much of the parish was put up for sale, an English entity, called the York Buildings Company, acquired the land at a very reasonable price of £60,400 despite its stated value of £316,896.[48] However, the company very quickly began leasing and selling some of its holdings. Harry Lumsden, an advocate in Aberdeen, acquired what would later become Belhelvie Lodge from the company in 1780. In 1812 his valued rent in Scottish pounds totalled £575 for lots 9 and 13 of Belhelvie estate, thereby ranking him with the Orroks and the Turners as one of the wealthier parishioners.[49] Indeed, in a manner similar to the Orroks and the Turners, several of the Lumsden boys entered military service in India, but this family had a greater share of luck, and more of them survived to retire to their native parish.

The wealth that the Lumsdens of Belhelvie earned in India certainly provided a large economic boost to the parish. Colonel Thomas Lumsden, a son of Harry, returned home on leave from India in 1819 to marry Hay Burnett of Elrick after serving with distinction during the Pindari campaign of 1818–19. It is not known if he visited Belhelvie during this vacation, but it would have been surprising if he had not. In any case, after another twenty-three years of service, and perhaps other unrecorded journeys home, he eventually retired with his wife to Belhelvie Lodge in 1842. The fact that he had made his fortune abroad clearly had an effect on his family. Indeed, of Colonel Thomas Lumsden's six sons, three emigrated to Canada and two entered the military, serving in India.[50]

During his retirement Thomas Lumsden had a direct impact on education in the parish at a time when schoolmasters were suffering from meagre salaries. In 1848, he made a personal contribution of £3 to the parish minister, the Reverend William Thomson, as part of his salary in his the capacity as the schoolmaster of Belhelvie.[51] A few years later, in 1854, Reverend Thomson summoned Colonel Lumsden and General George Turner of Menie as the senior heritors in the parish to agree to a specific salary for the schoolmaster. It was decided that, until the other heritors could be asked, the salary being paid should be maintained at the £27 per annum already provided for the job.[52] The schoolmasters of Belhelvie had other benefits, including the use of a house and garden. Importantly, some of their funds were provided through the Dick Bequest, amounting to approximately £25 per annum, although the distribution of the money is difficult to ascertain. Nonetheless, this source of funding is particularly interesting as it highlights that a return migrant to Scotland could make a direct impact on the parish of Belhelvie without settling in it, or even visiting it. The establishment of the Dick Bequest came after the death of James Dick of Forres in 1828. Through his various dealings and ventures in Jamaica, Dick had amassed enough wealth to leave £4,000 in a fund he wished to be used toward the salaries of north-east schoolmasters, which included those in Belhelvie.[53] As parish education had been funded largely by heritors up to that point, teachers were always keen to obtain extra income and the Dick bequest was particularly useful.[54] It is not known if Dick ever even saw Belhelvie, and his bequest highlights just one way in which return migrants could have an effect on Scottish society in general. What can be said for certain is that both Indian and Jamaican money was used to fund education in Belhelvie parish through the Dick, Lumsden and Turner families.

On the death of Thomas Lumsden, Belhelvie Lodge was inherited by his son Harry, who himself had a direct relationship with India, having been born aboard the EIC ship the *Rose* in 1821.[55] Harry made the return journey to Belhelvie several times throughout his life, if indeed 'return' is the correct word, given the context of his birth. As a boy, Harry Lumsden was initially sent 'back' to the parish aged 6 and was thereafter schooled in Aberdeen before being sent south to Kent to complete his education. He entered the military in 1838 and served with distinction in India for fifteen years before he obtained leave for a year in November 1852, apparently in order to recuperate from some problems with his health.[56] Lumsden had already written several times to his father in the previous year expressing his desire to return home to Belhelvie.[57] On a subsequent trip to Britain, Harry travelled to England, where he married Fanny Myers of Cumberland in 1866, but he appears to have travelled back to India almost immediately. He eventually retired with the rank of lieutenant-general and a Knight Commander of the Star of India. He inherited the family lodge in Belhelvie on the death of his father in 1875 and it was there that he ended his days.

Harry Lumsden's uncle, William – a younger brother of Colonel Thomas Lumsden – also earned his wealth in India, but in the civil service in Bombay rather than the EIC or regular army. With the money he gained abroad he bought Balmedie in 1834, along with some other Aberdeenshire land in Monquhitter and Leslie. William Lumsden had a new manor house built, Balmedie House, the same building that now serves as the Church of Scotland Eventide Home in Balmedie village. However, William's impact on Belhelvie parish continued after his construction work, and indeed his death. In his will he left £500 to the Scottish Episcopal Church, in a trust known as the Lumsden Fund, which he intended should be used for the 'poor clergy' of Aberdeenshire.[58] However, Lumsden's legacy appears to have provided a source of charity beyond the hard-up clerics of the north-east despite his original intentions. Not long after it was established, the fund became known as the 'Balmedie legacy', valued at £300 and set aside in 1875 for the use of the poor who lived on William Lumsden's estate, whether they were clergymen or not.[59]

Beyond the aforementioned money from the Dick Bequest, there is also at least one other example of a return migrant's money impacting on Belhelvie, and on this occasion, occurring a generation after it was brought back from India. The parish village of Whitecairns came into the hands of Sir Charles Stewart Forbes, fourth baronet of Newe and Edinglassie. Sir Charles's father's career had included being head of Forbes & Co. in Bombay, the first mercantile house to have been established there. Upon his return to Great Britain Forbes became a generous contributor to public charities in Scotland, funding the building of schools, kirks, houses, bridges and roads on his estates.[60] When his son bought land at Whitecairns it was through the wealth initially gained by his father in India.

Conclusion

There are numerous themes that emerge from this limited investigation into the settlement in Belhelvie of former overseas emigrants. It is also important to note that emigration and return from abroad were often conducted by those who were mobile within Britain anyway. Throughout the period studied, the search for work drove people to migrate regularly across parish, national and international borders. Captain Orrok not only undertook trade in the Indies; he also migrated from Fife to Aberdeenshire on his return. In search of work or education, Harry Lumsden migrated from India to Scotland and back to India, but had also moved from Belhelvie to Kent as a child, before his eventual retirement to Belhelvie parish. The records of the various churches in the parish reveal that the parishioners, whether migrants or not, had an understanding of the wider world they lived in, informed by the numerous migrants who settled in the parish. The church bell of the old kirk, for example, had been obtained from the Netherlands in the seventeenth century, and undoubtedly represents the endeavours of return migrants who have left no written record yet discovered. During the nineteenth century collections were regularly made in the various churches for overseas missions: in 1850 for the Americas, in 1853 for India, and again in 1860, 1877 and 1896.[61] Indeed, Reverend William Gillespie, who ministered to Shiels Kirk (one of the three kirks in the parish) in 1852, was himself a return migrant from an earlier mission to China.[62] Whether they had migrated themselves or not, all Belhelvians were affected by return migrants. Their attendance at school or church, their use of the public highway, their employment in construction or simply their work improving the various Belhelvie estates bought and run on money made abroad are all testament to that fact. Apart from William Forbes and David Skene, there is no direct evidence of other early return migrants' impact on the parish, but those of the eighteenth and nineteenth centuries certainly ploughed their wealth back into Belhelvie.

The availability of land in Belhelvie, either through personal or public sales, royal donations or forfeitures, meant that the parish was open to people from outwith the community to move in. The popularity of this corner of Aberdeenshire as a destination for return migrants must have been echoed by other parishes elsewhere in Scotland, and a comparative survey would undoubtedly prove interesting. Yet it cannot be overlooked that the majority of the return migrants studied here were the sons of landowners or tenants in Belhelvie – the Skenes, John Orrok junior, the Turners or the Lumsdens. Indeed, many had inherited land from their fathers and so had a reason and a place to return to in the parish, despite having the wealth to move elsewhere had they wished, and only William Forbes of Menie appears to have done so. These men were from landed and reasonably wealthy families, and their reasons for choosing Belhelvie undoubtedly had something to do with inheriting ancestral homes, but more probably had something to do with a sense of place. Whether retiring through ill-health, such as John Orrok junior or Harry Lumsden, or simply retiring home, as David Skene, George Turner and Thomas Lumsden did, Belhelvie was viewed by its globally experienced parishioners as a suitable final destination. As Colonel Thomas Lumsden is alleged to have told his colleagues in India, Belhelvie Lodge was 'just a suitable chateau for a worn-out old ramrod to wind up his days in'.[63] More telling, perhaps, of the attraction that Belhelvie offered some return migrants is Lord Tweedsmuir's explanation for giving up Braemar Castle for Potterton House: not only was he making a home in Scotland after a generation's absence in Canada with the Hudson's Bay Company, it was 'where my wife, and her forebears, had always lived'.[64] Attraction to a location could come through marital connections as well as direct personal experience.

Another theme apparent from these case studies is that the migrants formed part of the general commercial and military migrations from Scotland so common from the late sixteenth century onwards. The majority of the individuals for whom we have information did not settle in their host countries, although it is likely that many others for whom we do not have information did, and their papers remain undiscovered in foreign archives. However, for those that we have been able to study, their migration appears to have been undertaken for a specific reason and was intended largely as a means to generate income. The fact that many became stranded abroad, were killed abroad, or went native in their host country, makes it difficult to establish how many of them actually intended to return to Belhelvie when they left Scotland. Such intent was often noted in correspondence, but not always put into practice.[65] With regard to the Turner, Orrok and Lumsden families there was a high rate of non-return, but usually always caused by the death of a family member while still in service, rather than of an individual who had settled abroad in retirement.

It appears that it was not uncommon for emigrants to travel abroad with their families, or for several members of the same family to undertake the same routes of migration. Women can also be counted among the emigrants, be it Margaret Stewart in Poland or the mother of Harry Lumsden who gave birth to him aboard the *Rose*. Wives accompanied their men to the Indies, as in the cases of Captain John Orrok (the nephew of the first Belhelvie Orrok) and Lieutenant General

Lumsden, who returned to Britain at one point to marry, then took his wife back out to India. The detail of advice published in the numerous volumes of *The East India Directory* for those making the journey to India included specifics of individual items of clothing.[66]

Another point raised relates to the social level of these migrants. Many came from a financially comfortable background and this would also have meant that they were educated beyond the parish school level, although that education itself perhaps gave them an advantage over people from other parts of Britain. The parish school was the institution of choice for Harry Lumsden's primary education, particularly as his family had invested in the parochial school system. It certainly appears that from the eighteenth century onwards the migrants from Belhelvie were university-educated. One of Robert Turner's sons, John, was enrolled at Marischal College for two years between 1793 and 1797.[67] Attendance at university was carried over into the subsequent generations, and during the 1828–34 period three Turner boys, John, Robert and Alexander, listed India or Madras as their home when they enrolled at Aberdeen's King's College in the early nineteenth century.[68] Similarly with the Orrok boys: Walter and John, sons of Captain Orrok, were enrolled at Marischal College in Aberdeen between 1794 and 1798.[69] In the nineteenth century several of the Lumsden boys also matriculated at the same college: Walter of Balmedie from 1808 to 1812 and Harry, John and John McVeigh were all registered there between 1835 and 1842.[70] However, we also know that, apart from these educated migrants, ordinary Belhelvians also made the trip to India, and Harry Lumsden once remarked that any of them who could not face military service there should be thrown out of the parish.[71]

Migration patterns are most commonly studied in an outward approach from a given country of origin. However, this study of a small north-eastern parish in coastal Aberdeenshire can show the value of studying the return migrant and investigating the impact such an individual had on his/her final destination. Every estate and mansion in Belhelvie parish was built or subsequently expanded by return migrants, some like Menie House several times. They appear not to have been acquired in order to gain a title, as several of the migrants already had titles or gained them through other pursuits. Scots with Belhelvie connections could be found from Baltic trading ports to the more distant shores of the East and West Indies, and from the Caribbean to India. Poland and India in particular proved popular and frequent destinations for Belhelvie migrants who left economic, educational, architectural and topographical imprints on the parish.

Many questions still remain regarding return migrants and the pattern of their migration. Can one overarching 'model' of return migration be found? Belhelvie parish revealed personal pull factors to be the most compelling, be it the death of a family member or simply the desire to retire at 'home'. Indeed, these factors appear to have remained similar across three centuries, and are still relevant today. Emigration and return migration from and to Belhelvie are a process that continues, with many parishioners working abroad in Scandinavia, Indonesia and Malaysia in the oil industry, or serving abroad in the armed forces. The ideal of retiring to their home parish is undoubtedly one retained by many of these migrants, as indeed it has been by parishioners since they were first noted down in historical records.

Notes

1 K. Virtanen, *Settlement or Return: Finnish Emigrants (1860–1930) in the International Overseas Return Migration Movement* (Turku: Migration Institute, 1979); F. Wilder-Okladek, *The Return Movement of Jews to Austria after the Second World War, with Special Consideration on the Return from Israel* (The Hague: Nijhoff, 1969); F. Bovenkerk, *Terug naar Suriname. Opnamecapaciteit van der Surinaamse arbeidsmarkt voor Surinaamse retourmigratie uit Nederland* (Amsterdam: University of Amsterdam, 1973).

2 L. Borgegård, *Return Migration from Sweden to Finland after the Second World War: A Methodological Study* (Umeå: Nordiska Muséet, 1976); F. Bovenkerk, *The Sociology of Return Migration: A Bibliographic Essay* (The Hague: Nijhoff, 1974).

3 A. Tollefsen Altamirano, *Seasons of Migrations to the North: A Study of Biographies and Narrative Identities in US–Mexican and Swedish–Chilean Return Movements* (Umeå: University of Umeå, 2000).

4 See Wyman, 'Emigrants Returning, Chapter Two.

5 George, the second Earl of Panmure, obtained the land in February 1667. See J.H. Stevenson (ed.), *The Register of the Great Seal of Scotland, AD 1660–1668* (Edinburgh, repr. Scottish Record Society, 1984), 508. Some sources list his father as the first holder of Belhelvie.

6 Alexander Smith, *A New History of Aberdeenshire* I (Aberdeen: Smith, 1875), 258.

7 *Ibid.*

8 *Ibid.*

9 F.H. Groome (ed.), *The Ordnance Gazetteer of Scotland* I (Edinburgh: Jack, 1884), 139.

10 'Edict against the Scots issued by Sigismund III', 12 September 1594, trans. and repr. in Th.A. Fischer, *The Scots in East and West Prussia* (Edinburgh: Schulze, 1903), 158.

11 See for example A. Biegańska, 'Scottish Traders and Merchants in Seventeenth and Eighteenth Century Warsaw', *Scottish-Slavonic Review* 5 (1985), 19–34; M. Bogucka, 'Scots in Gdansk (Danzig) in the Seventeenth Century' in A.I. Macinnes, T. Riis and F. Pedersen (eds), *Ships, Guns and Bibles in the North Sea and the Baltic States, c. 1350–c. 1700* (Phantassie, East Linton: Tuckwell Press, 2000); S. Murdoch, *Britain, Denmark-Norway and the House of Stuart, 1603–1660* (Phantassie, East Linton: Tuckwell Press, 2003); A. Grosjean, *An Unofficial Alliance: Scotland and Sweden, 1569–1654* (Leiden: Brill, 2003). For previous studies of Scottish migration see also Th. Fischer, *The Scots in Sweden* (Edinburgh: Schulze, 1907) and *The Scots in Germany* (Edinburgh: Schulze, 1902).

12 W. Lithgow, *The Totall Discourse of the Rare Adventures and Painefull Peregrinations of long Nineteene Yeares of Travalyes from Scotland to the most famous Kingdomes in Europe, Asia and Affrica* (Glasgow: Maclehose, 1906); Chamberlain to Carlton, 24 March 1621, *Calendar of State Papers, Venetian, 1619–23*, 237.

13 Th. Fischer, *The Scots in Eastern and Western Prussia* (Edinburgh: Schulze, 1903), 184–5, and W.F. Skene, *Memorials of the Family of Skene of Skene* (Edinburgh: New Spalding Club, 1887), 124; A. Grosjean and S. Murdoch, *Belhelvie: a Millennium of History* (Belhelvie: Belhelvie Community Council, 2001), 22.

14 Skene, *Memorials of the Family of Skene of Skene*, 127.

15 Skee, *Memorials of the Family of Skene of Skene*, 125; Grosjean and Murdoch, *Belhelvie: a Millennium of History*, 22.

16 See J. Thirsk, 'Younger Sons in the Seventeenth Century', *History* 54 (1969), 182.

17 M. Ailes, 'From British Mercenaries to Swedish Nobles: The Immigration of British Soldiers to Sweden during the Seventeenth Century', unpublished thesis (University of Minnesota, 1997), 81–2; M. Glozier, 'Scots in the French and Dutch Armies during the Thirty Years' War' in S. Murdoch (ed.), *Scotland and the Thirty Years' War, 1618–1648* (Leiden: Brill, 2001), 135. The reason for this discrepancy between the percentages of marriages in Sweden and the Netherlands has not yet been identified.

18 A. and H. Tayler (eds), *The House of Forbes* (Bruceton Mills WV: Scotpress, 1987), 316, 318.

19 Rev. Dr A.S. Todd, *St Machar's Cathedral* (Derby: Pilgrim Press, 1988), 13.

20 Rev. R. Lippe (ed.), *Selections from Wodrow's Biographical Collections* (Aberdeen: New Spalding Club, 1890), 81; Grosjean and Murdoch, *Belhelvie: a Millennium of History*, 22, 32.

21 J.M. Thomson (ed.), *The Register of the Great Seal of Scotland, A.D. 1593–1608* (repr. Scottish Record Society, 1984), 674.

22 J.M. Thomson (ed.), *The Register of the Great Seal of Scotland, A.D. 1609–1620* (repr. Scottish Record Society, 1984), 90, 571, 623.

23 *The Register of the Great Seal of Scotland, A.D. 1609–1620*, 685.

24 *Ibid.*, 726.

25 For Spens-Forbes contacts see *The Register of the Great Seal of Scotland, A.D. 1593–1608*, 772, and *The Register of the Great Seal of Scotland, A.D. 1609–1620*, 127. For the Spens-Forbes marriage see A. and H. Tayler, *The House of Forbes*, 317, and Lippe (ed.), *Selections from Wodrow's Biographical Collections*, 83. Thanks to Alex Forbes for highlighting this.

26 In 1587 the son of King Johan III of Sweden was elected King of Poland, and the Polish monarchs continued to claim a hereditary right to the Swedish throne during the seventeenth century. See R.I. Frost, *The Northern Wars, 1558–1721* (Harlow: Longman, 2000), 45, 148, 157, 167.

27 *The Miscellany of the Spalding Club* V (Aberdeen: Spaling Club, 1852), 368; A. and H. Tayler (eds), *The Valuation of the County of Aberdeen for the Year 1667* (Aberdeen: Third Spalding Club, 1933), 333; Grosjean and Murdoch, *Belhelvie: a Millennium of History*, 22.

28 See A. Grosjean and S. Murdoch database *Scotland, Scandinavia and Northern Europe, 1580–1707* for further examples such as Anna Cummings, a burgess of Gothenburg from 1625 (SSNE 4687) and Sophia Forbes, a businesswoman and shareholder in a Stockholm-based shipping company from the 1660s (SSNE 6318).

29 See the work of Dr D. Catterall on the seventeenth-century Scottish community in Rotterdam in Douglas Catterall, *Communities without Borders: Scots Migrants and the Changing Face of Power in the Dutch republic, c. 1600–1700* (Leiden: Brill, 2002). See also David Worthington, *Scots in Habsburg Service, 1614–1648* (Leiden: Brill, 2003).

30 James Couper, for instance, served as governor of parts of Java and Sumatra for the Dutch in the later part of the century. See W.Ph. Coolhaas (ed.), *Generale missiven van gouverneurs-generaal en raden aan Heren XVII der Verenigde Oostindische Compagnie* (11 vols, 's-Gravenhage, 1960–97) IV, *1675–1685*, 473, n. 1; R. Law, 'The First Scottish Guinea Company, 1634–1639', *Scottish Historical Review*, 76: 2, (1997), 185–202; and S. Murdoch, 'The Good, the Bad and the Anonymous: A Preliminary Survey of Scots in the Dutch East Indies, 1612–1702', *Northern Scotland* 22 (2002), 1–13.

31 Particularly those in EIC service when it was an English company, who had long been sending money back to Scotland. For example in 1625 Harry Schenks [Shanks] sent funds for Trinity hospital in Leith; National Archives of Scotland (hereafter NAS), GD 226/18/21. Thanks to Professor A.I. Macinnes for this reference.

32 Lady Helen Forbes, *Letters of John Orrok*, ed. A. and H. Tayler (Aberdeen: Milne & Hutchison, 1927), 1.

33 Orrok's men had broken ranks and charged straight into the Maratha cannon. Sir Arthur Wellesley, Orrok's commanding officer, certainly did not blame or reprove the colonel for this incident, remarking that 'it was not possible for a man to lead a body into a hotter fire than he did'. P. Mason, *A Matter of Honour: An Account of the Indian Army, its Officers and Men* (London: Cape, 1974), 161.

34 This is intriguing, as it was strictly illegal to undertake simultaneous trade with the East and West Indies at this time. See the Walker Family Papers held in Special Collections, University of Aberdeen, MS 2769/I/35/1. Undated although 1781 written in the corner.

35 Riksarkivet, Stockholm: Förteckning over landshövdingens i Göteborg och Bohus-län skrivelser till Kungl. Maj:t 1657–1840, 77–8. That a director of the Swedish East India Company, Abraham Grill, was brought in to deal with Orrok's case also implies a connection with Indies trade.

36 C.E. Elphinstone (ed.), *View of the Political State of Scotland* (Edinburgh: Douglas, 1883), 16. Thanks to Dr Andrew Mackillop for this reference.

37 NAS, CH2/32/9.

38 NAS, CH2/32/8, 1791–1826, Minutes of Session, Belhelvie; Grosjean and Murdoch, *Belhelvie: a Millennium of History*, 21.

39 *The New Statistical Account of Scotland*, 12 (Aberdeen, Edinburgh and London, 1845), 246–7.

40 J.A. Henderson (ed.), *Index and Notes to Aberdeen Journal, 1747–1847* III.

41 J. Patrick, *The Coming of Turnpikes to Aberdeenshire* (Aberdeen: Centre for Scottish Studies, 1982), 51; Grosjean and Murdoch, *Belhelvie: a Millennium of History*, 3; A. Dean and J. Gardner, *The History of Menie* (n.p., 1994), 5.

42 Lady Helen Forbes, *Letters of John Orrok*, 212.

43 He is noted as a lieutenant-captain of the 17th Regiment of the Bengal Native Infantry from October 1799. See J. Mathison and A.W. Mason, *The East India Directory for 1806* (London: n.p., 1807), 70.

44 Captain John Orrok had been listed as 'on furlough' from 1818, and in January 1820 he retired to Britain. See A.W. Mason and G. Owen, *The East India Directory for 1821* (London: n.p., 1822), 444.

45 Henderson, *Index and Notes to Aberdeen Journal* III.

46 S.M. Spiers, *The Kirkyard of Belhelvie* (Aberdeen: n.p., 1992), 6. Orrok's will can be found in the Aberdeen Sheriff Court records.

47 NAS, CH2/32/9.

48 A. and H. Tayler, *The Jacobite Cess Roll for the County of Aberdeen in 1715* (Aberdeen: Third Spalding Club, 1932), 233.

49 NAS, CH2/32/9.

50 University of Aberdeen Special Collections, MS 875/1, Genealogical records of the family of Lumsden, compiled by Arthur Lumsden-Bedingfield, 1928, unfoliated.

51 N. Leslie (ed.), *Index and Notes to Aberdeen Journal, 1848*, IV, 25.

52 NAS, CH2/32/10 1850–1878, Belhelvie Session Records.

53 J. Scotland, *The History of Scottish Education* I (London: University of London Press, 1969), 296; Grosjean and Murdoch, *Belhelvie: a Millennium of History*, 39. It has even been claimed that this money produced the 'highest standard of intellectual instruction in any parish schools in Scotland', Scotland.. *The History of Scottish Education*, 1, 297.

54 The term 'heritor' is a fifteenth to seventeenth-century Scottish term for a proprietor of heritable land whose duties included financial responsibility toward the parish.

55 For a biography of Harry Lumsden see. P.S. Lumsden and G.R. Elsmie, *Lumsden of the Guides* (2nd edn, London: John Murray, 1900). The *Rose* was quite a large ship,

of 801 tons, carrying a cargo worth £40,535 in 1799. See J.H. Thomas, *The East India Company and the Provinces in the Eighteenth Century* I (Lampeter: Edwin Mellen Press, 1999), 135, 271.

56 Lumsden and Elsmie, *Lumsden of the Guides*, 121.
57 *Ibid.*, 99–100.
58 University of Aberdeen Special Collections, MS 875/1, Genealogical records of the family of Lumsden, compiled by Arthur Lumsden-Bedingfield, 1928, f. 224.
59 *Aberdeen County Council Local Government (Scotland) Acts, 1894 to 1929* (Aberdeen: n.p., 1946), 18; Grosjean and Murdoch, *Belhelvie: a Millennium of History*, 22.
60 *Dictionary of National Biography* VII (Oxford: Oxford University Press), 380–1.
61 NAS, CH2/32/10, Belhelvie Kirk Session Records, and CH3/41/4, Belhelvie Free Church Deacons' Court Minutes, 1857–1906.
62 W. Mackelvie, *Annals and Statistics of the United Presbyterian Church* (Edinburgh: Oliphant, 1873), 62.
63 Lumsden and Elsmie, *Lumsden of the Guides*, 279–80.
64 Lord Tweedsmuir, *One Man's Happiness* (London: Hale, repr. 1970), foreword.
65 For example, the letters of Captain John Orrok, son of Colonel William Orrok (who died in India in 1810), survive in Lady Helen Forbes, *The Letters of John Orrok*. These provide great detail on the tactics used by young unemployed men to obtain well paid work in order to gain personal security.
66 See for example *The East India Directory for 1827* (London: n.p., 1827), where three separate lists of 'necessaries for ladies travelling to India' were printed, 580, 583 and 585.
67 P.J. Anderson (ed.), *Fasti academiae mariscallanae Aberdonensis* II (Aberdeen: New Spalding Club, 1898), 376.
68 Alexander, Robert and John appear as students at Aberdeen's King's College between 1828 and 1834, their provenances being listed as Madras and India. See P.J. Anderson (ed.), *Roll of Alumni in Arts of the University and King's College of Aberdeen, 1596–1860* (Aberdeen: n.p., 1900), 146, 147, 152, 154.
69 Anderson, *Roll of Alumni*, 377, 378.
70 *Ibid.*, 403, 496, 502, 506.
71 Lumsden and Elsmie, *Lumsden of the Guides*, 86; Tweedsmuir, *One Man's Happiness*, 276.

CHAPTER TWELVE

The Highlands and the returning nabob: Sir Hector Munro of Novar, 1760–1807

Andrew Mackillop

Although the Scottish Highlands are synonymous with emigration, it is of a particular kind and to a particular place.[1] In geographic terms, this involves an almost exclusively Atlantic focus for the eighteenth and early nineteenth centuries. The origins of this transatlantic emigration lay in the dislocation of large numbers of estate tenantry through the process of agrarian and tenurial 'improvement'. Another key element in the traditional explanation of Highland depopulation is poverty or, more accurately perhaps, the realization among tenants that land-lordism represented an unstoppable threat to their material security.[2] And finally there is the assumption that emigration from the region was an irreversible phenomenon in which returnees were not an important element. All these aspects have been woven together into a widespread perception of poverty-stricken Highlanders being coerced to overseas destinations that were then colonized permanently by extended family and even community groups.[3]

Emigrant homecomings, therefore, are not readily associated with the region. Yet this partial understanding of Highland emigration reflects a failure to explore eighteenth-century sojourning in a fully systematic way.[4] Otherwise known as a 'career' or 'episodic' emigrant, the sojourner differed in almost all respects from the better known agrarian type just outlined. Predominantly but not exclusively male, the sojourner was usually single and unencumbered with family members.[5] Another vital distinction that assisted mobility was that many were often trained in an artisan skill such as carpenter, smith or mason, or, alternatively, were professionals like soldiers, doctors, schoolmasters, engineers or bookkeepers. One consequence of this greater socio-economic leverage was that such emigrants never matched the numerically greater diaspora of estate tenantry. Higher social status aside, sojourners differed in two other crucial ways. Whilst lack of domestic opportunity undoubtedly narrowed their options, coercion was far less apparent when contrasted with the pressure applied by Highland landlords to their estate populations. Secondly, far from viewing their destination as final, many intended to return home with enough capital to remedy the lack of material or social status that had prompted their emigration in the first place.[6] This determination to repair home was doubly significant. While it obviously had repercussions for the emigrant's own home community, it also influenced where sojourners were prepared to contemplate as a possible destination overseas. Areas that could never hope to attract permanent settlers appealed to sojourners because they knew (or hoped) their stay would be relatively short. Arctic North America, the West Indies, West Africa and India would never attract colonists for obvious climatic reasons. As a result, labour, especially skilled labour, was scarce and often well rewarded in these areas. Mortality and personnel turnover were also so high that promotion prospects were significantly enhanced. Sojourners thus took a calculated risk on rapid profits and a quick return home before death made their stay unintentionally permanent.[7]

Few studies have been made of Scottish sojourning and, of those that have, most are limited to the Atlantic. However, while Jamaica and the Chesapeake have received scholarly attention, this has concentrated upon activities and networks in the colonies themselves rather than the impact of such individuals back in Scotland.[8] The influence of the tobacco lords upon the Clyde basin remains the most systematic examination of returnees and their profits to date.[9] Recent evidence, however, has demonstrated that West Indian fortunes were deployed in Stirlingshire, the north-east, Inverness-shire and Argyll. By means of estate purchase and improvements, industrial investment and promotion of educational facilities, Atlantic returnees played a crucial and not yet fully explored role in the modernization of Scottish society from *c.* 1740 to *c.* 1800.[10] It is thus surprising that India, which also attracted episodic Scots emigrants, has received almost no attention whatsoever. British returnees from India were known as nabobs, from the Mughal word *nawab*, meaning provincial governor or prince.[11] One such individual was an Easter-Ross laird from the parish of Alness, Sir Hector Munro of Novar. His nabob reputation and substantial Eastern fortune ensured that he faced particular problems when reintegrating into a Scotland ill at ease with the material and moral effect of Indian profits upon its society. Munro sought to complete the process of homecoming by means of a paradox. He set about confirming his family's traditional status through the conspicuous and multifaceted deployment of his recently acquired, morally questionable fortune. His credentials as both a Highland laird and improving North British landlord were to rely upon income acquired in the utterly alien environment of India. Ultimately, that he was able to achieve his goal of reintegration reveals the remarkable level of political, economic and social power wielded by Scottish nabobs upon their homecoming.

Sojourning Scots in Asia

In order to understand the importance of Scottish nabobs, as well as the peculiar problems and advantages they faced upon arrival back in Britain, the context of their emigration must be understood. Similarly, their actions once at home were dictated to a considerable extent by their social background and their reasons for sojourning in the first place, as well as their political, economic and cultural experiences in India. In many ways South Asia exhibited all the classic characteristics of a transient destination. To defend its monopoly the East India Company sought to regulate the presence of Britons in India. Those seeking official employment in the Company's administration needed anything from £500 to £10,000 to act as caution for their adherence to orders. The Company also demanded high educational standards in writing, arithmetic and bookkeeping. Even the far less prestigious military cadetships still required their recipients to be well educated in order that commissioned rank could follow at a later date.[12]

While permanent British settlement in India was not actually forbidden in theory, it was actively discouraged in practice. Alongside severe climatic and cultural differences, this ensured that permanent residence was highly unusual.[13] More important, few had any wish to stay. As in the West Indies and Africa, death was omnipresent. Roughly 57 per cent of all writers appointed in the eighteenth century died before they could return to Britain.[14] Scots described India as 'vile' and akin to living 'in hell', while James Campbell of Succoth made it clear in 1793 that acquiring sufficient wealth to live comfortably at home was the only reason for his stay in South Asia.[15] These factors combined to shape the size and composition of the Scottish presence in India, making it one of the most distinctive sojourning communities within the British Empire. In stark contrast to the tens of thousands involved in transatlantic departures, emigration eastward was on a far smaller scale.[16] The two exceptions to its relatively elite nature were the rank-and-file Scottish soldiers and ordinary seamen of the Company's merchant marine.[17]

Three broad characteristics thus defined the Scottish sojourner in India. Beyond the small numbers involved, financial and educational requirements ensured they came from affluent, even relatively elite backgrounds. Thirdly, they had a determined, almost obsessive desire to return home. This last characteristic was common to all Britons in

India and its importance cannot be overestimated. It ensured that the means of acquiring wealth tended to stress speed and efficacy, not morality. Scots were in fact part of a small but remarkably aggressive cadre of political, commercial and military elites that wielded inordinate authority within India in order to accrue profits by any legal and, if necessary, dubious means. From Calcutta in 1770 George Bogle told his father in Lanarkshire:

> One of the greatest checks on a man who wants to increase his fortune by unfair means in Europe is the odium that he is liable to draw upon himself, and be despised by all his acquaintances, but that is not the case here, and several people keep the best company and are extremely well regarded who are great rogues not only from suspicion but even by their own confession.[18]

It is not necessary to detail here the methods used to generate wealth in the British East. Suffice to say that tax supervisors practised malfeasance on a large scale. In alliance with Scottish free traders like Hugh Baillie, others monopolized commodities like Bengal salt and opium to corner supplies, inflate prices and generate huge profits, particularly prior to the 1780s.[19] Likewise, as the Company acquired military influence in Bengal and Madras from the 1750s, senior military officers accepted financial inducements or 'presents' to act as effective kingmakers. Alternatively, they embarked on what amounted to freebooting expeditions in areas like Tanjore in 1773 and on the Malabar coast and western Mysore in the early 1780s.[20]

Hostile homecomings: the nabob controversy and criticisms of Eastern sojourning

These developments ensured that the nabobs and their profits came in for particular attack back in Britain. The first criticism related to the morality and legitimacy of the Company's regime. The annexation of Bengal in 1765 had secured a province that was seen in Britain as extremely populous and wealthy. With revenue equivalent to approximately 25 per cent of Britain's total tax base, it was felt by domestic opinion that the East India Company now had sufficient capital to conduct an extremely competitive trade. By 1772, however, it was clear from plummeting share prices and defaults on official payments to the Crown that the Company and its servants had botched a situation that should have confirmed the benefits and equity of British imperialism.[21] Substantial withdrawals of specie back to Europe had induced a severe liquidity crisis that crippled Bengal's markets and textile production. This near bankruptcy of Britain's official economy in the East only served to cast into starker contrast the private, unofficial fortunes of the sojourners. Nabob wealth, in popular perception, rested upon 'the spoils of ruined provinces'.[22] Yet hostility in Britain towards nabobs had little to do with any widespread sympathy with Indians. Their real crime was that their regime undermined the domestic conceit that stressed the unique ability of Britain's constitutional rule to guarantee liberty and prosperity to all its subjects.[23]

Besmirching Britain's idealized image of its own imperialism was only one negative consequence of sojourning in India, however. The second undesirable connotation related to the various ways in which nabobs acquired their wealth. Generating profits was a respectable, even patriotic endeavour in eighteenth-century Britain.[24] However, certain forms of wealth were more acceptable than others. Land represented the ideal source of income. Land served the laudable function of providing necessary physical sustenance and steady, beneficial employment. Land was productive and profits from it were justified because they were based on something tangible, like a crop of grain or sugar. Despite its reliance on slave labour, West Indian planter wealth was acceptable for precisely this reason.[25] Ultimately, those who owned and managed land ensured social stability and thus political order. Fortunes made from trading and commodity exchange, meanwhile, became ever more acceptable as the century progressed. In the decades after 1688 an ideology evolved that emphasized how trade and commerce inevitably enhanced concepts of property which, in turn, preserved political and legal liberties.[26] To contemporary British opinion, wealth made in India had none of these virtues – in fact the opposite was the case. Commercial nabobs made money from what seemed to be murky sources, such as speculation in shares and contracts that were highly unstable, transient and prone to corrupt abuse.[27] Where they did deal in commodities these tended to be frivolous luxuries like tea, silks and brightly painted cotton calicos. Whereas agricultural produce supported the basics of life, Eastern commodities were unnecessary items that the lower orders could ill afford. Moreover, it encouraged among them dangerous pretensions to the social tastes and etiquette of their betters.[28]

This potential for domestic social instability and its negative political ramifications was projected directly on to the nabobs themselves. The Company's original commercial character meant that its servants were believed to have originated from rather vulgar, artisan or trading social backgrounds. Although this had ceased to be the case by the later 1700s, it had been true to some extent at the beginning of the century. In 1700, 42 per cent of writers came from artisan or trading families, while 39 per cent had gentry antecedents.[29] Eastern sojourners thus remained associated with social classes that lacked the education,

tradition of duty, or intellect to rule effectively. This political imma-
turity meant Company servants would, it was feared, end up infected
with Asian concepts of government and authority. This applied not
least to the new generation of generals that exemplified the territorial
direction in which the Company seemed to be moving after the annexation of Bengal. These men were conquerors, not traders, and could
carry home with them very 'un-British' notions of militaristic government and absolute sovereignty. As the number of such men entering
Parliament went from twelve in 1761 to twenty-seven by 1780, public
debates thrust the returning nabobs into the limelight. Their political
influence was routinely condemned as malignant, with many fearing
they would corrupt the Commons and slavishly reinforce the Crown.[30]

No matter which way nabobs made money, be it from commerce,
administration or war, the political, economic and social impact of
their actions seemed detrimental to the overseas empire and positively
poisonous for the metropole itself. Even their supposedly effeminized
physical form, colour and distasteful over-reliance on numerous syco-
phantic servants was seen as evidence that India had literally soaked
into their very character.[31] Upon their arrival home no other type of
eighteenth-century sojourner met such a welter of class prejudice, con-
tempt, fear and outright hostility.[32] Set against these debates it is clear
that Scottish nabobs faced real problems coming home. Arrival back
necessitated a deliberate attempt to ensure their peers recognized them
and their wealth as innately virtuous, patriotic and conducive to the
public good. It was the attempted completion of this process of rehabilitation, reassimilation and social acceptance that dictated the activities of men like Sir Hector Munro when they returned from India.

Preparing for return: Novar in India

Nothing better illustrates the mobility of elite sojourners like Munro
than the fact that his Indian career had two quite separate phases. He
first arrived with his regiment in the autumn of 1761 and left for
Britain in February 1765. This short period was to prove remarkably
successful and graphically illustrates the scale of profits to be made in
the East. In August 1764, at Chapra, he ordered eight mutineers to be
executed by means of the old Mughal method of blowing them away
from the mouth of a cannon.[33] Clive himself recommended him to the
directors in London for his willingness to exercise the utmost disci-
pline even over white European troops.[34] The real breakthrough, however, came on 23 October 1764 at the battle of Baksar. There he
commanded the Company army that heavily defeated the combined
forces of the emperor Shah Alam II and the Nawabs of Bengal and

Oudh. Although the action guaranteed British supremacy in Bengal, Munro did not receive the dividends of his military efforts from the East India Company. It was the new client Nawab of Bengal and land-holders, such as Bulwant Singh of Benares, whose status was entrenched in the aftermath of Baksar who distributed at least £13,000 in presents to the victorious general.[35] The full extent of Munro's profits is unclear. In 1772 he informed a committee of the Commons that he had declined £300,000 in 'presents', including a Jagir of £12,500 per annum for life which the Company authorities in Calcutta had ordered him to refuse. Although Munro was probably exaggerating these figures in order to demonstrate his commendable restraint and avoidance of Eastern corruption, he did admit to receiving at least £19,250 while defending Bengal in 1764.[36]

The magnitude of this wealth becomes apparent only when con-trasted with income from the Novar estate. In 1747, whilst still held by his uncle, George, the property yielded a money rent of £72 and a total rental of approximately £100. Even by 1803, after decades of improvement and consolidation, the rental of the Novar and Culrain estate in Alness parish was still only £502.[37] One year of military entre-preneurship in India, in other words, produced the equivalent of approximately thirty-eight years of income from a modernized High-land estate. Baksar was the high point of Hector's career and provided him with the wealth and reputation that would secure his material and social position for the rest of his life. Nonetheless, his eagerness to return home is evident from the fact that within four months of the battle he was prepared to quit India.[38]

Substantial expenditure on property, improvements and politics, as well as heavy losses in the Ayr Bank debacle left Munro financially straitened by the mid-1770s. The willingness of Scotland's landed gentry to contemplate even the most extreme long-distance sojourning is reflected in the fact that his immediate solution was to return again to the East. This suggests a remarkable inclination for mobility, and that even high-risk sojourning was a readily accepted tactic for address-ing a host of mundane domestic difficulties. It also implies that distant geographic destinations may in fact have loomed surprisingly close on the mental horizons of certain Scottish élites. Munro's post-Baksar reputation gave him automatic leverage with the Company's directors who, in the spring of 1777, appointed him commander-in-chief of the Madras army.[39]

The second phase of his career in India could not have been more of a contrast, however. Initially things went well. One of his immediate concerns was securing presents and 'obligations' still due to him from Zamindari, who had gained land under the client regime established in

Bengal after Baskar. So clearly did finance dominate his motives for this second stay in India that Munro used Sir Eyre Coote, commander-in-chief of the Bengal army, to force Rajah Cheyte Singh, the heir of Bulwant Singh, to finally pay his father's debt of £12,500.[40] In September 1778 Munro successfully completed the siege of Pondicherry, the main French base in the south, a victory that gained him a public note of thanks from King George III and a Knighthood of the Bath.[41] Thereafter, although still remunerative, his military operations were characterized by bad luck and poor judgement. This culminated in the battle of Polillur on 10 September 1780 during which one of his Madras detachments of nearly 4,000 men, led by Lieutenant Colonel William Baillie of Dunain from near Inverness, was captured and around 1,900 men were killed. Munro's reputation never really recovered from what amounted to the worst defeat inflicted on British arms in India during the entire century.[42] He did, however, rehabilitate himself to a degree through his actions as a divisional commander at the battle of Porto Novo in July 1781, as well as his successful prosecution of the siege of Negapatnam on 12 November the same year. The city yielded between five and six lakhs in prize money (c. £50,000–60,000). His entitlement as commander meant Munro received around £5,000.[43] Having salvaged something of his reputation he retired quickly from India for the last time and returned to Britain in 1782.[44]

Certain aspects of Munro's career both assisted and hindered his preparations for resettlement and reassimilation at home. His clearly corrupt acceptance of gifts from the Nawab and his disastrous role in the Pollilur defeat fall into the latter category.[45] However, other elements worked in his favour. While clearly an integrated part of a wider British presence in India, Scottish sojourners exhibited some relatively, if never absolutely, distinct characteristics. One was social background. The extent to which East India Company personnel came from lower-class origins was prone to undoubted exaggeration by those hostile to homecoming nabobs. Yet is it also clear that, in contrast to this widespread domestic perception, India attracted a surprisingly high ratio of Scots from landed and even aristocratic families. Exactly 50 per cent of all Scottish writers between 1750 and 1813 were from such backgrounds. In the case of military cadets appointed between 1790 and 1813 the incidence was less impressive – only one-third – but still higher than those from the mercantile and artisan classes, who made up 28 per cent of all applicants.[46]

Hector's own background in this respect was ambiguous. His father, Hugh Munro of Clayside near Golpsie in Sutherland, was a merchant and shopkeeper. Yet Hector did not fit the nabob stereotype of the artisan's son made good. His father was the second son of Hector, laird of

Novar, a cadet branch of the leading Munro family of Foulis. Young Hector thus had impeccable landed credentials, which were further reinforced by the fact his mother was Isabel Gordon, daughter of Sir Robert Gordon of Embo. This kinship link with the Gordons proved particularly helpful in assisting Hector's initial involvement in India and his later domestic reintegration. The Dowager Duchess of Gordon, for instance, secured him a major's commission in the family regiment, the 89th Highland Regiment, raised in 1759.[47]

Rank in a regular line regiment was another common characteristic of Scottish military sojourners in the East. Half of the royal regiments sent to India from 1754 to 1784 were Scottish in origin.[48] A large proportion of Scots officers thus held the King's commission, a fact that gave them two distinct advantages. In India it gave them technical seniority over those holding an equivalent East India Company commission. Regular rank also bestowed status, a sense of moral and professional superiority, and above all an association among peer opinion back in Britain with a service ethos of honour and virtue.[49] As such, it was ideal: in India it enhanced promotion prospects whilst for those returning home it provided a shield or antidote to some of the negative characteristics of nabobs. Munro certainly differentiated between royal and Company service. In April 1764 all royal troops and officers were informed that they should either accept Company service or return to Britain for demobilization. Munro had not yet made a substantial fortune and might thus have been expected to stay in India. Yet he refused to consider a Company commission and was at Bombay preparing to return home when the Nawab of Oudh's invasion saw him recalled to Bengal.[50] Although financial losses in the early 1770s later forced him to accept a commission from the Company, it is clear that Novar put greater store by his royal rank. More generally, Munro's military standing was to prove a central element in his homecoming. Pollilur aside, he was genuinely respected amongst his peers as one of a handful of men directly responsible for carving out Britain's increasingly important territorial empire in India.[51]

Another crucial dimension of a nabob's homecoming was that preparations were made for return while he was still in the East. In India Munro nurtured political networks that stretched back to his home community and which sustained his reputation and profile there. The benefits of such links were twofold. By assisting the relations or clients of his own social equals, Munro created a sense of obligation and indebtedness among those with whom he wished to reintegrate at a later date. By accepting and helping newly arrived Scots in India, he in turn ought to be accepted once back in Scotland. This helps to explain why Munro protected Charles Munro, who was related to Lady Stuart of Castlemilk. Similarly, he appointed Basil Cochrane, brother of the ninth Earl of Dundonald, and James Brodie joint agents of a lucrative Madras army contract. He could thus reasonably expect a sympathetic homecoming reception from Basil's uncle, Andrew Stuart of Torrance, the MP for Lanarkshire, and a figure closely connected with Henry Dundas. The second benefit related to political credit with gentry and burgesses in Munro's own immediate locality. Highland politics and kinship were central to Munro's favourable treatment of Brodie. Novar's own grandmother was a Brodie, while his standing was enhanced with the Laird of Brodie Castle, who wielded strong electoral influence in Moray and the burgh of Forres.[52] The same concern for his interest in and around Inverness explains why he sought to advance Lieutenant John Baillie of Dunain, brother to the lieutenant-colonel captured at Polillur.[53]

The importance of these connections extends well beyond whether they succeeded in easing the passage of nabobs back into their own society. The existence of such a close, ongoing relationship between the temporary emigrant and his original community reveals how sojourner homecomings became self-perpetuating, mutually reinforcing and ultimately the basis of a multiplier effect. The very desire to return home prompted the initial individual to encourage and assist others from his region to follow him. This dynamic between homecoming and further departures remains one of the most neglected aspects of Scottish emigration history. Its role in shaping patterns of episodic emigration within the Eastern empire was crucial, and explains the tendency, usually ascribed to traditional clannishness, for Scots to appear in relative concentrations in particular areas.[54] In performing these vital functions the returnee not only ensured acceptance back at home but also that his authority would be enhanced considerably there.

Homecoming strategies: politics

Upon arrival back from India it was not unusual for particularly wealthy nabobs to enter politics. Most were aware that such a decision had both benefits and drawbacks. By committing themselves in the public arena there was a risk of confirming the stereotype of the ambitious sojourner displacing traditional leaders and corrupting the body politic. Yet there were also clear advantages, both practical and social, in becoming an MP. It provided useful influence at the political centre should an individual's reputation need defending, while also allowing nabobs to confirm their civic worth. Munro's actions demonstrate a remarkably astute approach to his political homecoming. His choice of constituency and opponent is telling. He sat as MP for the Inverness

Burghs (Inverness, Fortrose, Nairn and Forres) from 1768 until 1802.[55] His landed background was crucial in this respect, not least because his estates lay in close proximity to Inverness, Fortrose and Forres. This enabled him to appear as the resident local patriarch, rather than a 'carpetbagger' candidate on the make. The incumbent was Sir Alexander Grant of Dalvey, a West Indian planter and merchant who, it was perceived locally, had relied on political leverage in London to bypass constituency opinion.[56] By choosing to stand against this particular candidate Munro was distancing himself from the very attributes that as a nabob could easily have been used against him.

All his subsequent actions were designed to project the image of a responsible, traditional leader whose loyalty to the established political order and British state could not be disputed. He confirmed his patriotism and sense of civic responsibility by calling on Forres in 1775 to support the war in America. Likewise, he took shares in the British Fisheries Society and the Forth & Clyde Canal, and invested £5,000 in Pitt's loyalty loan of 1797.[57] Given that the central objective in his homecoming was acceptance amongst his elite peers, it is almost inevitable that Munro was a ministerial supporter. He certainly deferred consistently to the management of Henry Dundas. In Ross-shire he was a sympathiser with David Ross, Lord Ankerville, who by 1784 opposed the incumbent MP, Francis Humbertson Mackenzie, Earl of Seaforth.[58]

It is a measure of how far he was accepted by his peers during his first homecoming from 1766 to 1777 that Novar was considered as a candidate for Ross in 1780. Shires were the most prestigious constituency seats, reflecting the superior status accorded to landholding within contemporary views of political power. Munro eventually refused the candidature in favour of Dundas's preferred choice, his own kinsman, Colonel John Mackenzie, Lord Macleod, heir to the forfeited earldom of Cromartie. Nothing better illustrates the underestimated political influence of nabobs planning their return home than the fact that the three main Ross-shire candidates in 1780 – Lord Macleod, Seaforth and Munro – were all serving in India at the time.[59]

One reason why Munro proved so accommodating towards Dundas was in order to secure command of the 42nd Black Watch, which he finally did in 1787. Preserving his status as a military officer once back in Scotland served, as it had done in India, to lessen any taint of colonial adventurer in his reputation. Through his association with such a high-profile unit he was able to benefit from a wider process of cultural rehabilitation which stressed the military valour, virtue and steadiness of the Highland soldier.[60] All were clearly attributes that contrasted absolutely with the perceived vices of the quasi-orientalized nabob. Commanding such a prominent regiment enabled

Munro to take centre stage in public displays of loyalty and commit-ment to Britain's establishment. At Edinburgh in 1794 he reviewed and passed as fit for duty the newly raised Fencible Regiment of Sir John Sinclair of Ulbster.[61] The explicit political message was that, far from causing the social and political instability linked with irresponsible Eastern sojourners, Munro's return from India actually strengthened the *status quo*.

Just how important this political dimension was to Munro's self image can be sensed from the level of expenditure involved. In order to acquire leverage over Forres he purchased the estate of Muirtown in Kinloss parish, Morayshire, from Rose of Kilraick for £14,000 in April 1767.[62] In Ross-shire he embarked upon a policy of land acquisition including parts of Culcairn and Wester Teaninich in Kiltearn in 1774 and Culrain in Kincardine parish by 1787.[63] At a conservative estimate, Munro spent at least £22,750 on acquiring these and other properties.[64] Although this enlargement of his property was one facet in a wider agenda of agricultural improvement, it also had important political con-sequences. In 1777 Captain James Munro of Teaninich, Hugh Munro of Achany and Novar's own nephew, George Munro of Rives, were given life rents in Muirtown to qualify as freehold voters.[65] Not only did this give Hector a presence in county as well as burgh politics in Moray, it also reveals how he avoided the appearance of exploiting the financial woes of his neighbours. In assisting the traditional families he had to some extent superseded, he prevented the appearance of overly disturb-ing the county's established social order. He might well have bought Munro of Teaninich out of his estate in Kiltearn, but he conspicuously preserved his local prestige. Novar's determination that his homecom-ing would not overly disrupt the social hierarchy also explains why a large component of his expenditure took the form of loans to heavily indebted neighbours, such as Ross of Ankerville (see Table 12.1).

One final dimension to Munro's successful political homecoming was his willingness to expedite the flow of local landed gentry and their sons to India or imperial service in general. Returned sojourners did not, therefore, abandon the connections they had built up between their own locality and their overseas destination. Instead, their practi-cal knowledge of those areas and of potential problems and solutions were used to assist successive emigrants. This underscores how the temporary nature of sojourning can be deceptive and was in fact responsible for creating permanent, long-term connections between areas like Ross-shire and India. In January 1789 Munro lobbied for a Company post on behalf of the son of Baillie of Knockbrich. Unsur-prisingly, his used his interest in April 1791 to obtain an East India Company cadetship for the 16-year-old Hugh Munro, son of Munro of

Table 12.1 Sir Hector Munro's expenditure, 1786–97

Activity	Total (£)
Novar estate improvements	10,236
Novar House	1,569
Mains of Novar and new home farm	1,429
Stables	564
Seed nursery and garden	320
Lands of Drummond	844
Masons and carpenters, etc.	915
Loans to other landlords	30,000
Total	45,877

Source: This information is drawn from estate accounts. See HCA, Munro Mss, Box 1, 'Accompt betwixt General Munro and George Munro, his factor for rents 1785–6'; Box 2, 'Accompt and Victual Rent, 1792'; 'Accompt and Victual Rent, 1789', 1–13; 'Accompt of George Munro's intromissions, crop 1788 and money rent 1789'; Box 6, 'Victual Rent of Novar and Culrain, crop 1787 and money rent, 1788, 1–14; Accompt victual rent for Novar, crop 1791 and Money rent, 1792', 1–10; 'Accounts, 1795, 1–12; Box 8, 'Novar Accounts, Victual rent, crop 1794, money rent, 1795', 1–9.

Teaninich. This would have eased any residual alienation caused by Novar's enhanced material superiority over his kinsman, while adding to the sense that his homecoming was generally beneficial for other local elites.[66] Given their influence in Ross-shire, he lobbied for the scions of Mackenzie gentry. Having helped acquire a Bengal cadetship in 1768 for one such individual, he immediately assisted in obtaining another for Kenneth Mackenzie, the second son of his neighbour in the Black Isle, William Mackenzie of Belmaduthie.[67]

The converse, albeit complementary, of this assistance to those heading eastwards was his offer of guidance to colleagues returning home. This often took the form of using his renewed contacts and social position in Britain to benefit later returnees. In 1797 Novar arranged to introduce the recently arrived James Campbell of Succoth to Dundas. Through such actions Novar was continuing at home the type of protection he had earlier provided to James at Madras in 1778. Nor was his motivation purely altruistic. Succoth's brother was Ilay Campbell, Lord President of the Court of Session and a central figure in Dundas's political interest north of the border.[68] Helping James would clearly win friends in high places and consolidate Novar's already successful return to the Scottish political arena. This relationship of mutual assistance between those at different stages of arrival back from India shows how central homecoming was to Scotland's links with India.

Ultimately, the wish for acceptance back at home explains why sojourners encouraged successive waves of migration to the East while also assisting the return of their peers. Yet homecoming must not be understood just in the physical sense. Money, and the status it secured, constituted a fundamentally important element in a successful homecoming from India. In the case of Alexander Mackenzie, younger of Coul, who was attempting to remit cash home, Munro provided financial advice on currency rates and obtaining bills of exchange.[69] He performed a similar service for his two deceased nephews, Captain Alexander Munro and Ensign Robert Munro. By conveying their Indian profits to their families in Sutherland and Ross-shire, he ensured that at least in one sense the boys did return home.[70]

Homecoming strategies: improvement

The economic and social dimensions underpinning the hostile critique of nabobs ensured that Novar spent the bulk of his fortune and efforts on agricultural and estate improvements. In all, he reputedly spent £120,000 on land purchases and estate development. As late as 1803 routine expenditure was still running at £500 per annum.[71] The scale of Novar's activities is remarkable, and entailed a massive injection of imperial profits into the Alness locale. Table 12.1 demonstrates that his homecoming impacted across a wide range of activities, including land acquisition, the promotion of advanced agricultural techniques on his home farms, and large-scale estate change more generally. Given his spending in just one decade, the alleged total of £120,000 is certainly realistic.

Through such conspicuous activity Munro demonstrated that his Eastern fortune assisted economic development, provided employment, reduced local poverty, and stimulated civic progress. Estate improvement overlapped with his strategy of political reintegration, one reinforcing the other. In 1769, for instance, he paid for a new steeple clock for the burgh of Nairn: similarly, in 1791, he subscribed £200 for an equivalent in Inverness.[72] Munro supported Inverness's subscription for a new academy that would inculcate the latest practical and enlightened forms of education. In January 1789 he subscribed £105, enabling him to sit for life on the board of what became Inverness Royal Academy.[73] Through such actions Munro demonstrated his commitment not just to the development of his own property but to local urban renewal more generally. Moreover, this largesse had the clear political benefit of swaying voters towards his candidature as their MP. Such thinking also determined his actions on the recently acquired estate of Muirtown. Situated on the coastline immediately north of Forres, his management of the estate was visible to the burgh electors and county gentlemen he was trying to impress as part of his homecoming. With this agenda in mind, and to facilitate the marketing of Muirtown's arable crop, Novar invested £584 in building a larger and deeper pier at Findhorn. In 1778 he obtained an Act of Parliament enabling him to levy tolls on the increased traffic generated by the new facility.[74] Clearly, the investment of his Indian profits was fundamental in securing the high-profile public approval that Munro sought.

Although it encompassed urban areas, the main thrust of activity was in estate development. Enclosure and liming on the Novar property was well under way by 1777, with a typical grid pattern of drainage and dyking imposed over the open run-rig field systems of farms like Loanbain (see Figure 12.1). Activity was concentrated around the Mains of Novar in particular. In 1747 this farm was occupied by seven tenants and pendiclers for just under £4: by 1803, however, the much enlarged and improved Mains was held by the proprietor himself and had a value of £130.[75] An estate map drawn in 1777, the year Munro departed to India for a second time, reveals that the process of improvement was still ongoing. Within the enclosed fields the old rig arrangement was still evident. The incomplete nature of improvement, allied to his financial losses, explains why he chose to return to India.[76] Tree plantation was another highly visible indicator of modernization. The *Statistical Account* for the parish of Kiltearn, where he had acquired property, noted that the new woods planted by the various proprietors would total £30,000 when they reached maturity.[77] The main effort, however, was concentrated at Fyrish to the north of Novar House. By 1775, twenty locals, mostly boys and girls on lower wages, were employed solely for the purpose of planting.[78] By the time a second plantation at Blackstobb was established, Novar's tree planting activities had reached remarkable proportions. Between 1788 and 1792 around 778,000 firs and Scots pine had been ordered and planted.[79]

This particular aspect of Novar's homecoming had a substantial material and psychological impact on ordinary tenantry. While they undoubtedly gained from the regular wages involved, planting absorbed part of the farm of Loanbain and much-needed hill grazing elsewhere. Trees were also a tangible and dramatic expression of the enhanced power Munro wielded over his locality. In demonstrating his new-found ability to transform Alness's physical landscape and appearance, Novar was at once proclaiming and celebrating the significance of his homecoming. A crucial part of this agenda entailed beautifying Novar House and its immediate environs. Large regular avenues were formed to the east of the family seat in order to emphasize its appearance while also serving the far more practical purpose of giving shelter to crops growing in the new enclosed fields.

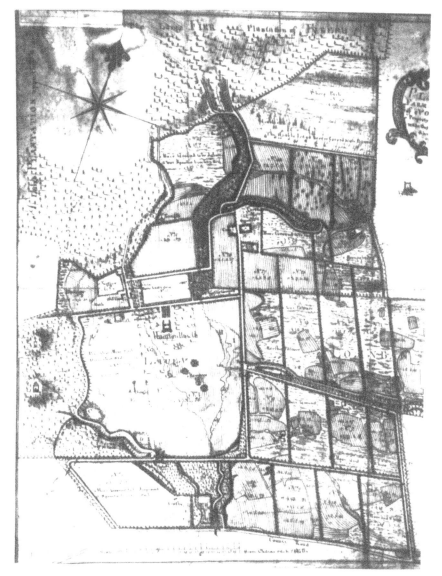

Figure 12.1   Plan of the improvements made by Sir Hector Munro, 1777

Furthermore, a series of monuments was commissioned which in their differing ways represented the idealized self-image that Munro wished to portray at home. Some were designed to project his local power as a traditional gentleman and military victor, rather than as a nabob. Situated in the parkland directly in front of Novar House itself, and immediately obvious to any visitor, was a column topped with an eagle, the Munro symbol.[80] This stressed Novar's prescriptive right to hold the estate and that he could not be treated as a vulgar social upstart and *arriviste*. This was complemented by the idea that his wealth was conducive to the public as well as private good. Standing opposite the eagle was its symbolic counterpart, a column topped with a statue of the Roman god, Mercury. Associated with commercial exchange and, intriguingly, with the movement of people, goods and ideas, this figure clearly proclaimed the positive properties of mobility.[81] Mercury was thus an apt emblem for a sojourner anxious to demonstrate that the cycle of departure into imperial service and return benefited the development of a commercialized, progressive society.

By far and away the most dramatic monument, however, was that built on the top of Cnoc Fyrish, just above the tree plantation. Constructed in 1792 to provide work for his underemployed tenantry, the structure was a highly symbolic gesture that typified the apprehensions of, and solutions adopted by, homecoming Scottish nabobs. Dominating the skyline of Alness parish and covered in white paint in order to attract attention, the monument was a mock Asiatic-style representation of the gates of the city of Negapatnam (Figure 12.2). As such, it was designed to send out multiple messages. It proclaimed that defeat at Pollilur had not been the summation of Munro's Eastern sojourn. Instead, it asserted that his last days in India, and thus the beginning of his homecoming, had been marked with triumph.

Figure 12.2 Fyrish monument

Secondly, the monument was the most visible expression of Munro's consistent attempt to portray his arrival back as that of a British and imperial soldier.

Simultaneously, however, Fyrish reveals how sojourning inevitably and irrevocably differentiated the returnee from his own community. Negapatnam had been a Dutch city, albeit situated in southern India, yet Munro's monument endowed it with symbolic eastern characteristics. While distancing himself from certain attributes of the nabob, the 'oriental' aspect of Fyrish shows that Munro was prepared to be associated with India, albeit in a very specific, positive way. This seems at odds with the whole tenor of Novar's homecoming, which was designed to downplay publicly his association with the East. The mixed message projected by the Fyrish folly reveals how complicated and riddled with internal tensions sojourner homecomings could be. As the statue of Mercury hinted on a smaller scale, Munro celebrated the augmented material and ideological resources which his departure and return ensured. Fyrish was a grander acknowledgement that his enhanced power and prestige sprang from the East and that his homecoming entailed bringing aspects of India back with him. This is even more evident in the names that Munro gave to the new improved and enclosed fields surrounding Novar House, such as Madras, Calcutta, Bombay and, of course, Baksar field.[82]

The relationship between the returned sojourner and his temporary destination was thus a profoundly ambiguous one. Dissociation on the one hand was tempered on the other by recognition of the overseas territory and its importance to the standing of the returnee in his home community. The key lay in celebrating the link with India in a way that was acceptable to Scottish and British prejudices. The commissioning of a temple folly in the Chinese style within the enclosed woodland immediately behind Novar House is another example of this cultural process of domesticating and Scotticizing the East in order to facilitate return.

Ultimately, however, Munro's improvements went far beyond aesthetically pleasing plantations, avenues and follies. Indian profits enabled him to fundamentally reappraise the basis of his estate economy and so alter the day-to-day lives of his tenantry. The later eighteenth century witnessed a dramatic increase in rentals across the entire region, often in the range of 300–400 per cent, between 1750 and 1800.[83] This suggests that Novar's wealth was not in any way singular or even unusual. However, such upward movement in income did not produce sufficient surpluses for sustained reinvestment in estate modernization. Indeed, the traditional indebtedness that had characterized Highland landlords since the seventeenth century remained and even intensified. Servicing these debts left little scope for large-scale, capital-intensive estate reorganizations of the type witnessed in Sutherland after 1807. It ensured that many lairds retained some tried and tested methods rather than risking all-out experimentation and the possible loss of ancestral holdings. It has been suggested that these conditions changed only with the emergence of rich Lowland and English industrialists as Highland landlords after the 1810s. This revolution in land ownership ensured sufficient capital from non-agrarian sources to reconstruct estates and resettle or evict populations in a systematic way.[84]

Although he sprang from the region's own indigenous elite, Munro's return from India was in fact an earlier 'imperial' variant of this crucial development in Highland emigration history. He had none of the worries over income that induced caution or limited ability to improve among other landed families. This left him free to test new methods of production without fearing that a temporarily reduced or severely disrupted rental would result in bankruptcy. The practical consequences of this strong financial position found their most dramatic expression in tenurial consolidation and the introduction of sheep farming. At a time when landlords to the south of the Great Glen had not yet established specialized sheep ventures on their Lochaber land, Munro had created a holding park for sheep by the mid-1770s.[85] Although it increased the estate's pastoral export capacity, it entailed the removal of outfield arable land and an initial but ominous reduction in the resources available to the multiple tenants. This strain was compounded by Novar's increases in rent. Keen to promote a paternalistic image of his patron, Alness's minister denied that any increase had occurred since Hector acquired the property from his uncle, George, on 16 August 1766.[86] While it was true that rentals did not rise steeply, Table 12.2 shows that moderate increases did occur, largely by charging a higher conversion rate on victual due to the landlord.

Clearly, Novar's homecoming and his determination to improve had a differing impact across his various estates. Situated in Moray's highly commercialized grain economy, Muirtown experienced a more draconian rental regime than either Novar or Culrain. With few financial worries, Munro did not rack-rent his Highland properties to the extent evident on many other estates. Yet this does not mean that a returning nabob ensured beneficial conditions for his tenantry. The loss of landed resources through the expansion of Novar's home farms, when coupled with the amount of hill acreage given over to planting, impacted hard upon the old multiple tenancies. In 1747 the three farms of Kinlochglas, Balnacoul and Achnagaul, which made up the core of the Alness estate, were let between ten tenants for £10 10s 0d. In 1804, by contrast, they

Table 12.2   Rentals of Novar, Culrain and Muirtown estates, 1761–99

Estate	Year	Total rent (£)
Novar	1761	£113
	1786	£176
	1793	£191
	1799	£201
Culrain (purchased 1787)	1788	£201
	1793	£279
	1799	£298
Muirtown (purchased 1766)	1766	£327
	1771	£556
	1794	£724

Source: HCA, Munro Mss, Box 1, 'Accompt Charge and Discharge betwixt General Hector Munro and George Munro, 1786'; Box 6 'Accounts, 1795'; Box 7 'Accompt of the Factor of Novar, 21 December 1799'; Box 8; Box 10, 'Miscellaneous Bundle of Accounts, 1770s–1790s'; Box 18, 'Judicial Rental of the lands and estates of Novar, 16–17 June 1761'.

were leased to twenty-one tenants for £34 19s 11d. Another crucial factor behind this severe overcrowding was the consolidation of multiple tenancies into single tenancies specializing in sheep farming. Held by two tenants and let at just over £3 10s 0d in 1747, the farm of Refarquhar had been substantially extended by 1803 and leased to Alexander Cameron, a Lochaber sheep farmer, for £44 10s 0d.[87]

Novar was certainly not alone in pioneering this form of production, with all the demographic consequences for Ross-shire that came with it. Prior to the outbreak of the American revolutionary war, Sir John Lockhart-Ross of Balnagown began developing land in Kincardine parish along similar lines. It is telling that, like Munro, Ross was a sojourner. The latter's efforts, however, withered on the vine after being disrupted by his recall to active service in 1778.[88] By contrast, Novar's second sojourn and return from the East enabled him to intensify his policies and pursue the new economy in a far less incremental manner. In this way, a homecoming nabob could influence the process of Highland depopulation and emigration. The scale and intensity of Munro's sheep farming are evident from the fact that his estate was among the first to witness large-scale opposition to sheep north of the Great Glen. The events of late June to August 1792 mark a major staging post in the history of the Highland Clearances and became known as 'The Year of the Great Sheep'.[89] By 1791 most of Strathrusdale's grazing, including that of the Novar farms of Kenlochglas and Refarquhar, was leased to the Lochaber sheep farmers Captain Allan Cameron and Alexander Cameron.

Faced with reduced grazing and overcrowding in their increasingly non-viable *bailtean*, the population refused to pay for the release of cattle seized by the Camerons in June. Munro's property thus lay at the heart of a violent confrontation between competing single and multiple tenant interests.[90] On 27 July 1792 tenants from Novar's farm of Boath and other Strathrusdale small tenancies marched to the sheep farm of Kildermorie on Munro of Culcairn's estate. There they assaulted Allan Cameron and forcibly released their own cattle stock. What happened next serves as a stark indication of how a returning nabob could dramatically affect social conditions in the north of Scotland. Four days after the events at Kildermorie, over 200 tenantry from Alness and the surrounding parishes demanded a reduction in rents, the return of arable resources and an end to the enclosure of common grazing.[91] While tenantry besides his own were certainly involved, Novar's property remained at the centre of a popular reaction which now disturbed and angered the political authorities. Judicial process against those who had assaulted Cameron met a wall of organized silence. The population upped the ante still further when 400 people began herding over 6,000 sheep from Novar and surrounding estates towards Boath with the intention of driving them physically from the shire.[92]

Only a non-fatal confrontation on 5 August between the army and forty local men guarding the sheep on Novar's own property at Boath ended the considerable disquiet among Scotland's propertied establishment. The incident could easily have proved extremely damaging to Munro's reputation. His estate had been the epicentre of events and his policies had seemed to generate the social disorder and instability associated with the returned nabob. The Edinburgh *Evening Courant* and other newspapers never named any specific landlords, but noted that estate regimes in the area must have been 'more than commonly oppressive'.[93] While trying to portray himself as an enlightened returnee, devoid of the nabob's arbitrary love of wealth, Munro came close to confirming these characteristics to the detriment of his own and his neighbours' reputations.

The events of 1792 confirm how delicate a process homecoming could be. In the end Munro weathered the incident with little problem. By 1792 reaction to events in France created an elite political climate supportive of anyone who held property, regardless of their emigration history. Yet Novar still needed to act sensitively. It was hardly coincidence that the three companies of regular troops sent into Easter Ross to deal with the rioters at Boath were from the Black Watch, Munro's own regiment.[94] Any negative impressions of his activities as a nabob landlord were thus safely neutralized by his standing as a King's officer and an agent of order and legitimate authority. This underscores the sophistication of Munro's decision to concentrate on his military status. Moreover, he deflected some criticism by fashioning a paternalistic relationship with his tenantry. Indeed, as early as 1774 he initiated an annual distribution of twelve bolls of oatmeal to the poor of Alness.[95]

Yet however easily he negated hostility to his estate activities, there is little doubt that Munro's improvements had a substantial impact on local demography. No direct examples of emigration from the estate are evident; but what figures are available clearly point to the conclusion that his policies had a detrimental effect on population levels. Whilst mainland Ross-shire and Easter Ross in particular did not exhibit the steep increases of population evident in western kelping districts, the trend was still generally upward. However, as Table 12.3 illustrates, all three of the parishes that encompassed the bulk of Munro's estate showed near zero population growth during his first return home from 1765 to 1777. This was followed by absolute decline after his second homecoming in 1782. Over the last half of the eighteenth century only seven out of a total of twenty-nine mainland Ross-shire parishes experienced a real fall in population. It is telling testimony to the effect of a returning nabob that the core of Novar's estate in Alness and Kiltearn encompassed two of these seven parishes.

Table 12.3 Parish populations of Alness, Kiltearn and Kincardine, 1755–1801

Parish	1755	1790–91	1801
Alness	1,090	1,121	1,072
Kiltearn	1,570	1,616	1,525
Kincardine	1,743	2,361	1,865

Source: Withrington and Grant, *The Statistical Account of Scotland* XVII, liii.

Conclusion

Episodic emigration to India by men like Munro of Novar and their subsequent homecomings constitute the flip side of the better known mass transatlantic departures. Whereas the movement eastward consisted of middle-class professionals and elements of the landed gentry, the western emigrations were overwhelmingly non-elite in character. Arguably one of the reasons for the emotive and high-profile status of the exodus to North America is the fact that for the majority it was permanent. In this it could not have differed more from the transient, highly fluid context of the East, where the ultimate aim was to return home. Novar was in India for less than eleven years, broken by an interlude of nearly twelve years back in Britain. Nor was his movement back and forth between Europe and India by any means unusual. Sir Archibald Campbell of Inverneil in Argyll served in Bengal during the mid to late 1760s before returning to Britain in 1772: however, he sojourned again to the East from 1786 to 1789. Alexander Mackenzie of Coul arrived home in Ross-shire in 1777 after sixteen years' military service, before setting out a second time in 1784.[96] India was seen therefore as a practical, accessible solution to problems of elite employment, increased indebtedness or, in Novar's case, sudden and unexpected financial loss. Far from being some exotic and marginal destination, India was in fact far more central to Scotland's economic and social development than hitherto suspected. Indeed, while stress has been placed on 'provincial' interconnections with North America, the pattern of repeated departure and return to the East in response to domestic conditions shows that the same held true for India also.[97]

However apposite the subcontinent was for acquiring substantial income, it did constitute a particular problem in terms of homecoming. For much of the later eighteenth century India was universally perceived as the least acceptable and morally desirable component part of the British Empire. Those associated with India thus had unique political, social and cultural prejudices to surmount upon arrival home. Munro's actions in this respect are revealing. During both his preparations for and eventual completion of his homecoming he sought to de-orientalize his fortune and status. This was achieved though certain techniques such as stressing his role as a soldier of His Majesty and his credentials as a scion of an established Scottish landed family. His purchase of Muirtown, less than a year after his return, demonstrates how crucial was this gentrification element in homecoming. Deploying a range of political, civic and improvement activities that illustrated his non-nabob virtues, his final aim was to traditionalize his recently acquired imperial position and fortune. That Novar sat as an MP for thirty-five years reveals how comprehensively he had won the acceptance of his peers in this particular regard. His experience shows that returning Scottish nabobs were at the forefront of a much wider and crucial process of legitimizing and normalizing domestic perceptions of Britain's new and hitherto controversial empire in South Asia.

Yet it would be wrong to assume that sojourners returning from India merely constitute a case of a narrow *arriviste* elite making themselves acceptable to other elites. Nabob homecomings entailed far more than the fate of one or two rich individuals because they ultimately impacted on the issue of Atlantic emigration. One obvious reason for the severe imbalance in knowledge between Scottish emigration across the Atlantic and to India relates to numbers. The former may be seen as worthy of more attention simply because of the sheer volume of people involved. Likewise, the mass of Highlanders who ended up in North America did so with little or no meaningful choice. By contrast, sojourners could and did make relatively free decisions with respect to the timing, duration and termination of their time in India.

However insignificant they appear numerically, Scottish sojourners to India require to be acknowledged as a central element in the country's overall emigration experience. In fact their small numbers totally belie their importance. Men like Novar already wielded considerable social power and authority in the Highlands because of their family backgrounds. Migrating to and returning from India gave them the resources to increase that power many times over. India supplied the financial wherewithal to reconstruct estates fundamentally, the material security to experiment with new forms of agrarian production and, above all, a negative cultural imperative to do so on a demonstrable and systematic scale. The result was eviction, dislocation and subsequent depopulation. For many, including the tenants of Novar's estate, the return of their nabob landlords from India denoted the start of their own emigration experience to North America. From this, however, there was rarely a similar process of homecoming.

Notes

I wish to thank Mr Bob Steward Archivist and Ms Fiona Macleod, Assistant Archivist, at Highland Council Archive in Inverness for their extremely helpful approach in facilitating access to the Novar collection. Similarly, the assistance and patient co-operation of Mr Munro-Ferguson of Novar in making available his family records is gratefully acknowledged.

1 E. Richards, *A History of the Highland Clearances II, Emigration, Protest, Reasons* (London: Croom Helm, 1985); T.M. Devine, *Clanship to Crofters' War: The Social Transformation of the Scottish Highlands* (Manchester: Manchester University Press, 1993); I. Adams and M. Somerville, *Cargoes of Despair and Hope: Scottish Emigration to North America, 1603–1803* (Edinburgh: John Donald, 1993); M. McLean, *The People of Glengarry: Highlanders in Transition, 1745–1820* (Montreal: McGill-Queen's University Press, 1991).

2 M.I. Adam, 'The Highland Emigration of 1770', *Scottish Historical Review* 16 (1919), 283–6; J.M. Bumsted, *The People's Clearance: Highland Emigration to British North America, 1770–1815* (Edinburgh: Edinburgh University Press, 1982).

3 For reassertions of the evicting role of landlords see T.M. Devine, 'Landlordism and Highland Emigration' in T.M. Devine (ed.), *Scottish Emigration and Scottish Society* (Edinburgh: John Donald, 1992), 85; J. Hunter, *The Making of the Crofting Community* (Edinburgh: John Donald, 1976), 5; B. Bailyn, *Voyagers to the West: Emigration from Britain to America on the Eve of the Revolution* (London: Tauris, 1987), 201–3.

4 T.C. Smout, N.C. Landsman and T.M. Devine, 'Scottish Emigration in the Seventeenth and Eighteenth Centuries' in N. Canny (ed.), *Europeans on the Move: Studies in European Migration, 1500–1800* (Oxford: Clarendon Press, 1994), 84–91, 99.

5 For career emigrants see M. Harper, *Emigration from North East Scotland I, Willing Exiles* (Aberdeen: Aberdeen University Press, 1988), 319–39. In a peculiarly drastic form of marriage counselling, an exception to this rule was the incidence of married Orcadians serving the Hudson's Bay Company thousands of miles from their spouses. See D.J. Withrington and I.R. Grant (eds), *The Statistical Account of Scotland* XIX (Wakefield: EP Publishing, 1978), 81.

6 D. Hancock, *Citizens of the World: London Merchants and the Integration of the British Atlantic Community, 1735–1785* (Cambridge: Cambridge University Press, 1995), 196; Withrington and Grant, *The Statistical Account of Scotland* XIX, 135.

7 R.B. Sheridan, 'The Role of the Scots in the Economy and Society of the West Indies' in V. Rubin and A. Tuden (eds), *Comparative Perspectives on Slavery in New World Plantation Societies* (New York: New York Academy of Sciences, 1977), 97; Hancock, *Citizens of the World*, 196–8 n. 68. Alienation, isolation and lack of social amenities produced life-threatening levels of alcoholism in all these destinations. E.E. Rich (ed.), *The History of the Hudson's Bay Company* (London: Hudson's Bay Record Society, 1958), 295, 497–9; National Archives of Scotland (hereafter NAS), Abercairney Muniments, GD 24/3/313: Madras, 17 September 1727: John MacRae-John Drummond.

8 A.L. Karras, *Sojourners in the Sun: Scottish Migrants in Jamaica and the Chesapeake, 1740–1800* (Ithaca NY: Cornell University Press, 192), 4–5, 19–22.

9 T.M. Devine, *The Tobacco Lords: A Study of the Tobacco Merchants of Glasgow and their Trading Activities, c. 1740–1790* (Edinburgh: John Donald, 1975), 20, 34–48.

10 A.I. Macinnes, 'Landownership, Land Use and Elite Enterprise in Scottish Gaeldom: from Clanship to Clearance in Argyllshire, 1688–1858' in T.M. Devine (ed.), *Scottish Elites* (Edinburgh: John Donald, 1994), 24–5; D.J. Hamilton, 'Patronage and Profit: Scottish Networks in the British West Indies, c. 1763–1807' PhD thesis (University of Aberdeen, 1999), 290–313.

11 M. Edwardes, *The Nabobs at Home* (London: Constable, 1991), 13.

12 P. Lawson, *The East India Company: A History* (London: Routledge, 1993), 71–2; India Office Records (hereafter IOR), B/110: Court Minutes, September 1789–April 1790, 842. Writers' applications had to include certificates of education. See IOR, J/1/1–19, 21–8. For cadets see Huntington Library, Pasadena CA (hereafter HL), Pulteney Papers, Box 19, Broomholm, 2 September 1780: John Maxwell-William Pulteney.

13 In practice many Britons, particularly those from lower social backgrounds, became *de facto* permanent residents. P.J. Marshall, 'British Society in India under the East India Company', *Modern Asian Studies* 31: 1 (1997), 90, 101; NAS, Melville Castle Papers, GD 51/3/3/58.

14 P.J. Marshall, *East Indian Fortunes: The British in Bengal in the Eighteenth Century* (Oxford: Clarendon Press, 1976), 214–18.

15 G.J. Bryant, 'Scots in India in the Eighteenth Century', *Scottish Historical Review* 64 (1985), 23–4, 27; Glasgow City Archive (hereafter GCA), Campbell of Succoth Papers, TD 219/10/133 (1–2).

16 At any one time the number of Scots in India, aside from rank and file, probably never numbered more than 1,000. See IOR, L/F/10/1 and 2; L/F/10/111 and 113; O/5/26: European Inhabitants, Bengal, 1793–1807, 'List of Europeans resident Calcutta and in the several Districts, 13 November 1804'; HL, Stowe-Grenville Collection, STG Box 198 (14): 'General State of the Company's Army in India', 1 January 1805.

17 Bryant, 'Scots in India', 23–4. For details on seamen and marine officers see A. Farrington, *A Biographical Index of East India Company Maritime Service Officers, 1600–1834* (London: British Library, 1999).

18 GCA, Bogle Papers, Letter Book of George Bogle of Calcutta, 1770–71, 55–7, 62.

19 P.J. Marshall, *Bengal: The British Bridgehead, 1740–1828* (Cambridge: Cambridge University Press, 1990), 93–103; W. Bolts, *Considerations on India Affairs* (London: Almon, 1772), vii, 180–4, in P. Tuck (ed.), *The East India Company, 1600–1858* I II (London: Routledge, 1998); IOR, Papers of Sir Henry Strachey, Mss Eur F128/104, f. 332.

20 J. Phillips, 'A Successor to the Moguls: The Nawab of the Carnatic and the East India Company, 1763–1785' in P. Tuck (ed.), *The East India Company, 1600–1858* IV (London: Routledge, 1998), 168–82; B. Lenman, *Britain's Colonial Wars, 1688–1783* (London: Longman, 2001), 255–6; National Library of Scotland (hereafter NLS), Stuart Stevenson Papers, Ms 8252, ff. 1–4; Anon., *A Vindication of the Conduct of the English Forces, Employed in the Late War, under the Command of Brigadier General Mathews against Nabob Tippoo Sultaun* (London: n.p., 1787), 8–29.

21 P. J. Marshall, 'Britain and the World in the Eighteenth-Century' I, 'Reshaping the Empire', *Transactions of the Royal Historical Society*, sixth series, VIII (Cambridge: Cambridge University Press, 1998), 17.

22 W.J. Barber, *British Economic Thought and India, 1600–1858* (Oxford: Clarendon Press, 1975), 73–5; G. Taylor (ed.), *Plays by Samuel Foote and Arthur Murphy* (Cambridge: Cambridge University Press, 1984), 84. Quote from Foote's play, *The Nabob*.

23 G. Carnall and C. Nicholson (eds), *The Impeachment of Warren Hastings* (Edinburgh: Edinburgh University Press, 1989); P.J. Marshall, 'Burke and Empire' in S. Taylor, R. Connors and C. Jones (eds), *Hanoverian Britain and Empire: Essays in Memory of Philip Lawson* (Woodbridge: Boydell, 1998), 296–8.

24 L. Colley, *Britons: Forging the Nation, 1707–1837* (London: Pimlico, 1994), 55–100.

25 Hamilton, 'Patronage and Profit', 293–6.

26 D. Armitage, *The Ideological Origins of the British Empire* (Cambridge: Cambridge University Press, 2000), 143–5.

27 For contemporary critiques of government contracting see Hancock, *Citizens of the World*, 228, 237–8; W.D. Rubinstein, 'The End of "Old Corruption" in Britain, 1780–1860', *Past and Present* 101 (1983), 63–4.

28 J. Walvin, *Fruits of Empire: Exotic Produce and British Taste, 1660–1800* (New York: New York University Press, 1997), 21–3, 194–7.

29 IOR, B/43, Minutes of the Court of Directors, Old Company, 27 April 1699–27 April 1702, 1–375.

30 P. Lawson and J. Phillips, '"Our Excretable Banditti": Perceptions of Nabobs in Mideighteenth-century Britain', *Albion* 16: 3 (1984), 226–34. See also J.M. Holzman, *The Nabobs in England: A Study of the Returned Anglo-Indian, 1760–1785* (New York: Holzman, 1926), 15–20, 50; NLS, Minto Papers, Ms 11020, ff. 2–5.

31 For a fine summary of cultural perceptions of the nabob as an individual see E.M. Collingham, *Imperial Bodies: The Physical Experience of the Raj, c. 1800–1947* (Cambridge: Polity Press, 2001), 13–36.

32 For a classic contemporary summary of the nabob written within a year of Munro's return see J. Price, *The Saddle put on the Right Horse: or, An Enquiry into the Reason why certain Persons have been denominated Nabobs, with Arrangement of those Gentlemen into their proper Classes or Real, Spurious, Reputed, or Mushroom Nabobs* (London: n.p., 1783), 1, 16–17.

33 Public Record Office (hereafter PRO), WO 1/614, f. 259; WO 4/59, 204, 555; W.C. Macpherson (ed.), *Soldiering in India, 1764–1787: Extracts of Journals and Letters left by Lieutenant-Colonel Allan Macpherson and Lieutenant-Colonel John Macpherson of the East India Company Service* (Edinburgh, n.p. 1928), 13; NLS, Mackenzie of Delvine Papers, Ms 1337, f. 32.

34 HL, Stowe-Grenville Collection, STG Box 20 (17): 30 September 1765: Robert Clive to Court of Directors.

35 Holzman, *The Nabobs in England*, 10.

36 *Reports of the Committees of the House of Commons* III (London: n.p., 1803), 170–1. I am grateful to Professor P.J. Marshall for drawing my attention to Munro's evidence to Parliament.

37 Brodie Castle, Forres (hereafter BC), Brodie of Brodie Papers, Box 10/4: Novar, 28 November 1752: George Munro to Alexander Brodie of Brodie, H.C.A., Novar Papers, D/538/39, 'Valuation of the Teinds of the Lands belonging to Hector Munro Esq. of Novar', 8 June 1803.

38 NLS, Mackenzie of Delvine Papers, Ms 1337, f. 38; Ms 1367, f. 100.

39 GCA, Campbell of Succoth Papers, TD 219/10/54: London, 3 May 1777: Archibald Edmonstone to Archibald Campbell of Succoth; NAS, Fraser–Mackintosh Collection, GD 128/1/3: Madras, 14 September 1777: Major William Baillie to Lieutenant Godsman.
40 NAS, Kinross House Papers, GD 29/2137, 111–12, 188, 195–6, 256–7.
41 NAS, Kinross House Papers, GD 29/2137, 223.
42 GCA, Campbell of Succoth Papers, TD 219/10/54 TD 219/10/70(1–2); NAS, Fraser–Mackintosh Collection, GD 128/1/1/18: Letter, Madras, 1 July 1784: Captain John Baillie to Captain David Baird.
43 H.D. Love (ed.), *Vestiges of Old Madras, 1640–1800, traced from the East India Company's Records* III (London: John Murray, 1913), 239; NLS, Stuart Stevenson Papers, Ms 8326, ff. 154–6.
44 HCA, Munro Mss, Box 5: Letter, Dingwall, 15 January 1782: Andrew Robertson–Baillie Alexander Shaw.
45 NAS, Kinross House Papers, GD 29/2061/18: Calcutta, 10 October 1780: David Killican to George Graham.
46 For social backgrounds see IOR, J/1/-19, 21–6; L/MIL/9/107/1–3; L/MIL/9/108/1–3; L/MIL/9/109/1–3.
47 A. Mackenzie, *History of the Munros of Fowlis with Genealogies of the Principle Families of the Name* (Inverness: Mackenzie, 1908), 510–16; BC, Brodie of Brodie Papers, Box 10/5, '13 November 1725, Marriage account of Hugh Munro of Clyderhall and Isabel Gordon'.
48 Bryant, 'Scots in India', 23–4.
49 Colley, *Britons*, 180–7.
50 *Reports of the Committees of the House of Commons* III (London: n.p., 1803), 167.
51 HCA, Munro Mss, Box 10: Letter, Furrakhabad, 22 November 1778: Lieutenant Robert Stuart to Hector Munro; Letter, Calcutta, 27 November 1778: Claud Alexander to Hector Munro.
52 BC, Brodie of Brodie Papers, Box 10/4, 'Payments by the Family of Brodie to Mrs Anne Brodie, Lady Novar, Wife of John Munro of Novar and their son George, now of Novar'; NLS, Stuart Stevenson Papers, Ms 8326, ff. 148–8; Ms 8250, f. 63.
53 NAS, Fraser–Mackintosh Collection, GD 128/1/2/4: 27 March 1781: Sir Hector Munro to Lieutenant John Baillie.
54 For the classic contemporary account of the clannishness of Scottish sojourners in India, precisely in order to facilitate wealth and thus the ability to return home, see J. Price, *Some Observations and Remarks on a late Publication entitled Travels in Europe, Asia and Africa* (London: n.p., 1783), 113–17.
55 L. Namier and J. Brooke (eds), *The History of Parliament: The House of Commons, 1754–1790*, III (London: HMSO, 1964), 180–1; R.G. Thorne (ed.), *The House of Commons, 1790–1820*, IV (London: HMSO, 1986), 643–4.
56 Hancock, *Citizens of the World*, 50–9.
57 NAS, Seafield Muniments, GD 248/52/2/68; NAS, British Fisheries Society, GD 9/3/123–8.
58 C.E. Adam (ed.), *View of the Political State of Scotland in the Last Century* (Edinburgh: Douglas, 1887), 294–7.
59 Namier and Brooke, *The History of Parliament* I, 494; British Library, Liverpool Papers, Add. Ms 38192, f. 15; NLS, Stuart Stevenson Papers, Ms 8326, f. 105; Ms 8330, ff. 58–61; PRO, SP/41/27: Letters from Secretary of War, 1778, St James 24 September 1778.
60 J.E. Cookson, *The British Armed Nation, 1793–1815* (Oxford: Oxford University Press, 1997), 149.
61 R. Clyde, *From Rebel to Hero: The Image of the Highlander, 1745–1830* (East Linton: Tuckwell, 1995), 154–9; NLS, Melville Papers, Ms 641, ff. 186–7.
62 Mackenzie, *History of the Munros of Fowlis*, 534.
63 HCA, Novar Papers, D538/Box 39, 3–8, 29.
64 Muirtown was purchased at the vastly inflated rate of forty-three years of its annual rental. Highland estates went at around twenty-five times their annual rental. For

other purchases see HCA, Munro Mss, Box 6, 'Abstract of the Lands of Shandwick and Ankerville, 17 April 1786'; Box 18: Dingwall, 8 September 1795: George Munro to Hector Munro.

65 NAS, Seafield Muniments, GD 248/462/4/49x; HCA, Novar Papers, D538/Box 39, 33–4; Munro Mss, Box 6: Bundle, 'Papers concerning the Estate of Muirtown to Colonel Hector Munro'. Letter, Edinburgh, 9 January 1786: John Fraser to Hector Munro.
66 IOR, Cadet Papers, L/MIL/9/107/3/No. 194.
67 NLS, Mackenzie of Delvine Papers, Ms 1328, f. 208.
68 GCA, Campbell of Succoth Papers, TD 219/10/139: London, February 1797: James Campbell to Ilay Campbell; TD 219/10/60(1–2): Madras, 15 March 1778; Namier and Brooke, *The History of Parliament*, II, 184.
69 NLS, Mackenzie of Delvine Papers, Ms 1328, f. 208; Ms 1336, f. 264.
70 V.C.P. Hodson, *List of the Officers of the Bengal Army, 1758–1834* III (London: n.p., 1927), 352, 54; HCA, Munro Mss, Box 10, 'Remittances from Bengal and Madras on Account of the Estate of Captain Alexander and Ensign Robert Munro'.
71 Mackenzie, *History of the Munros of Fowlis*, 534; HCA, Novar Papers, D/538/39, 'Valuation of the Teinds and Lands belonging to H.A.J. Munro Esq. of Novar, parish of Alness, 8 June 1803'.
72 Mackenzie, *History of the Munros of Fowlis*, 535.
73 HCA, Munro Mss, Box 10: Inverness, 3 January 1789: Alexander Shaw-Hector Munro.
74 HCA, Munro Mss, Box 1, Cash Account betwixt General Sir Hector Munro and Provost Andrew Robertson, 1784, 3; Novar Papers, D/538/39, 'Declaration of Sir Hector Munro re Robert Davidson, 12 February 1791', 2. The Act was entitled 'An Act to enable Sir Hector Munro Esq. to build and maintain a harbour and pier at the Town of Findhorn in the County of Elgin and Forres'.
75 BC, Brodie of Brodie Papers, Box 10/5, 'Judicial Rental of the Lands and Estates of George Munro of Novar, 9 January 1747'; HCA, Novar Papers, D/538/39, 'Valuation of the Teinds and Lands belonging to H.A.J. Munro Esq. of Novar, parish of Alness, 8 June 1803'.
76 M. Ash with J. MacAulay and M.M. Mackay (eds), *This Noble Harbour: A History of the Cromarty Firth* (Edinburgh: John Donald, 1991), 94–8.
77 Withrington and Grant, *The Statistical Account of Scotland* XVII, 479.
78 HCA, Munro Mss, Box 19, 'Day Labourer Accompts, 1 October 1771–1 June 1776'.
79 HCA, Munro Mss, Box 8, 'Novar Accompts, Victual Rent crop 1796 and Money Rent, 1797, 1–9; Box 2, 'Novar Accompts and Victual Rent, 1792'; Box, 14, 'George Munro's Factory Accompts, October 1788, 5; Box 6, Letter, Inverness, 14 December 1791: Alexander Watson to Hector Munro.
80 Ash, *This Noble Harbour*, 96; For the central place of the eagle in Munro heraldry see J.S. Keltie (ed.), *A History of the Scottish Highlands, Highland Clans and Highland Regiments* II (Edinburgh: Fullerton, 1875), 231.
81 For a summary of Mercury's properties see S. Hornblower and A. Spawforth (eds), *The Oxford Classical Dictionary* (3rd edn, Oxford: Oxford University Press, 1996), 962.
82 NAS, RHP 42696: Map of Novar Estate, 1788.
83 A. Mackillop, 'Highland Estate Change and Tenant Emigration' in T.M. Devine and J.R. Young (eds), *Eighteenth-Century Scotland: New Perspectives* (East Linton: Tuckwell, 1999), 239.
84 Devine, *Clanship to Crofters' War*, 58–9; 'The Emergence of the New Elite in the Western Highlands and Islands, 1800–60' in T.M. Devine (ed.), *Improvement and Enlightenment* (Edinburgh: John Donald, 1989), 114–30.
85 NAS, Gordon Castle Muniments, GD 44/27/11/114; GD 44/43/193/20.
86 Withrington and Grant, *The Statistical Account of Scotland* XVII, 280; HCA, Munro Mss, Box 18, 'Inventory of Writs belonging to Colonel Hector Munro of Novar, 14 December 1769'.
87 BC, Brodie of Brodie Papers, Box 10/5, 'Judicial Rental of the Lands and Estates of George Munro of Novar, 9 January 1747; HCA, Novar Papers, D/538/39, 'Valuation

of the Teinds and Lands belonging to H.A.J. Munro Esq. of Novar, parish of Alness, 8 June 1803'.

88 A.M. Ross, *History of the Clan Ross* (Dingwall: North Star, 1932), 39–41; Withrington and Grant, *The Statistical Account of Scotland* XVII, 513.

89 For a detailed analysis of events in Easter Ross during the summer of 1792 see K.J. Logue, *Popular Disturbances in Scotland, 1780–1815* (Edinburgh: John Donald, 1979), 58–62.

90 Confusion seems to have emerged over the ownership of the property on which opposition began. See Ash, *This Noble Harbour*, 100 n. 105. Boath, Kenlochglass and Refarquhar were indisputably part of Novar and confirm the central role of Munro's estate tenantry in the move against sheep farming. Kildermorie, admittedly, was part of the estate belonging to Munro of Culcairn.

91 The popular reaction against sheep is also dealt with by Eric Richards. See E Richards, *A History of the Highland Clearances* I, *Agrarian Transformation and the Evictions, 1746–1886* (London: Croom Helm, 1982), 255–7.

92 HCA, Munro Mss, Box 6: 6 August, 1792: Donald Macleod of Geanies – Meeting of Inverness Heritors.

93 Richards, *A History of the Highland Clearances* I, 269.

94 NAS, Home Office Domestic Entry Books, RH 2/4/218, 99.

95 Withrington & Grant, *The Statistical Account of Scotland*, XVII, 281.

96 NAS, Campbell of Inverneil Muniments, RH 4/121/6, 48–9; RH 4/121/7, Ft William, 3 December 1772; NLS, Mackenzie of Delvine Papers, Ms 1336, ff. 230, 269; Ms 1337, f. 56; NAS, Mackenzie of Coul Papers, GD 1/1149/30/3.

97 N.C. Landsman, 'The Provinces and the Empire: Scotland, the American Colonies and the Development of British Provincial Identity' in L. Stone (ed.), *An Imperial State at War: Britain from 1689 to 1815* (London: Routledge, 1994), 260–1.

INDEX

Note: numbers in bold refer to main entries.

Karlskrona 62
Linköping 64
Parliament 61
Privy Council 61
Queen Christina 63
Stockholm 63
Uppland 68
Uppsala 56, 62, 63, 64, 68
Vannersborg, 61
Switzerland 18

Taagepera, Rein 28
teachers 200, 201, 202, 204, 207, 208–9, 212, 224, 233
technology 3–5, 47, 153
telegraph 4
telephone 5
tenants 27, 217, 233, 247–55 *passim*
ten pound tourists 5, 105
Thain, Thomas 189
Thirty Years' War 55, 59, 66, 69
Thompson, Christopher 38
Thomson, Alistair 9, 10, 15, 53
Thomson, Tobias 57
Thomson, Reverend William 224
Thorpe, Mr and Mrs 110, 112
Thurston, Albert 99–100
Thurston, Annie 99–100
Thurston, Ettie 78
timber trade 189
tobacco lords 234
Tokoi, Oskari 26
Tölölyan, Khachig 138
Tonkin family 93
Tosh, John 155
Tourle, Thomas 98
tourism 5, 53, 132–3
  see also 'roots tourism'
tourists 77
'transilients' 185
transport 38, 81, 153
Travellers' Aid Association 209
Treaty of Limerick 34
Treaty of Paris 39, 41
Treaty of Westphalia 58
Tribe, Elizabeth and Derek 107, 122, 126
Trollope, Anthony 86
Trollope, Tom 86

Tuppen, Marion 201
Turner, Alexander 223, 228
Turner, George 223, 224, 227
Turner, Colonel James 58
Turner, John 223, 228
Turner, Robert 222, 223, 228
Turner, William 223
Tuttle, John 35

Ukraine 18
Ulmanis, Kārlis 26
Ulster-American Folk Park 45
  Centre for Migration Studies 40
  Irish Emigration Database 15, 35–6, 46
Underwood, George 99
unemployment 87, 107, 118
United Kingdom *see* Britain
United States 2, 5, 6, 11, 15, **16–31**, 40–1, 42, 100, 131, 141, 177, 216
  1812–14 war 40, 42
  California 19, 20, 90, 95, 161–2, 167, 176
    San Francisco 19, 20, 99, 161, 162
  Chesapeake 234
  Chicago 21, 24
  Civil War 19, 90, 162, 175
  Georgia 45
  Harvard 18
  Knights of Labor 20
  Maryland 38
    Baltimore 37
  Massachusetts 17, 20, 185
    Boston 23
  Michigan 158
  National Public Radio 28
  New England 3, 17, 35
  New York 41, 44, 46, 47, 161
    Brooklyn 26–7
    New York City 37, 42
  Pennsylvania 7, 18, 133–4, 175
    Oxford township 36
    Philadelphia 12, 37, 41, 43, 45, 151, 155, 157, 159–61, 167, 169, 170–6, 177
    Pittsburgh 24
    Pennsylvania Hospital for the Insane 159, 179n.40
  railway construction 19, 23

Lightning Source UK Ltd.
Milton Keynes UK
UKOW06f1703200416

272651UK00003B/199/P